Facts & Memories

A Family Genealogical Collection

By Watson C. Smith

Facts
&
Memories

A Family Genealogical Collection

Facts & Memories: A Family Genealogical Collection
By Watson C. Smith
© Copyright Watson C. Smith, 2021

No parts of this book may be reproduced, stored in a retrieval system, or transmitted by any means without written permission from the publisher except in the case of brief quotations for the purpose of critical articles or reviews. For information or permission, contact:

Mission Point Press
2554 Chandler Road
Traverse City, Michigan 49696

www.MissionPointPress.com

231-421-9513

Cover design by Nancy Brooke Smith

Printed in the United States of America

ISBN: 978-1-954786-66-0

Library of Congress Control Number: 2021924489

Facts
&
Memories

A Family Genealogical Collection

By Watson C. Smith

MISSION POINT PRESS

Table of Contents

Introduction 1
Part 1: Those Europeans — Our European History. 5
    Chapter 1: The Gewisse and Wessex in Early Britain (410–1042) 9
    Chapter 2: The Welsh (950–2021) 16
    Chapter 3: The Danes and Vikings (782–1031) 23
    Chapter 4: The Vikings and Normans (845–1146) 26
    Chapter 5: The Franks (580–1087). 35
    Chapter 6: The Plantagenet to Smith (1027–2021). 41
    Chapter 7: Edward I to Spencer to Smith (1239–2021) 49
    Chapter 8: Wars of the Roses (1339–1509). .54
    Chapter 9: Edward I to Linda Knoop (Smith) (1239–2021) 61
Part 2: On to America — Jamestown and Plymouth 65
    Chapter 10: Newport — The Founding of Jamestown 68
    Chapter 11: Hopkins — An Extraordinary Life 71
    Chapter 12: Brewster — Steady Faith and Leadership 74
    Chapter 13: Gookin — A Servant to Mankind. 78
Part 3: My Smith Side of Our Family — In America. 83
    Chapter 14: Smith — The Most Common of Names. 84
    Chapter 15: Kaddeland — A 20th Century Viking Connection 114
    Chapter 16: Blake — A Very American Family 125
    Chapter 17: Shelton — Early Strong Roots in England,
        Virginia & Connecticut 132
    Chapter 18: Miller — Early Rowley, Middletown and Middlefield 150
    Chapter 19: Cornwall — Early Middletown and
        a Native American Connection 160
    Chapter 20: Christopher — Early in Florida 165
    Chapter 21: Prout — A Long Line from England to America 168
    Chapter 22: Ritter and Post — In New York City 171
    Chapter 23: Nicholson — Col. John at Quebec and in the Revolution. . . . 176
    Chapter 24: Moffat — From Scotland to Orange County, New York. 180

Chapter 25: Spencer — Another Long Family Line and Founders
in Hartford and Haddam, Connecticut 184
Chapter 26: Roberts — Very Involved in Early Connecticut 188
Chapter 27: Gale & Denton — England to Boston
to Orange County, New York 192
Chapter 28: Clark — So Many Branches 196
Chapter 29: Selkregg — A Branch Connection to John Adams
and also the *Mayflower*. 201
Chapter 30: Strong — A Very Involved Family 203
Part 4: My Wife Linda Knoop's Side of the Family — In America 206
Chapter 31: Knoop — A Louisville Family 207
Chapter 32: Hund — Another Louisville Family 216
Chapter 33: Reukauf — A Typical Immigrant Family 224
Chapter 34: Sheets — Early Kentuckians. 226
Chapter 35: Litton — Early Virginians. 232
Chapter 36: Tracy — Early Maryland and then Moving West 236
Chapter 37: Tanner — Switzerland, Virginia, North Carolina
& on to Kentucky 240
Chapter 38: Wooten — The Line that Connects Us 245
Part 5: My Story 247
Part 6: The Last Word 293
Appendix A: Charles Rosfjord Smith 311
Appendix B: Col. Paul Robert Knoop 314
Appendix C: Spahr 325
Appendix D: Dreisbach. 328
General References 331
Acknowledgements 333
Index 335

Introduction

I think all amateur genealogists are curious and inquisitive. Those traits led me to become an engineer in my younger days and motivated my endeavors in family history in these closing days of my existence. So, while assembling our family tree, I developed what seemed to be an ever-growing volume of names and information. This material needed to be organized and disseminated, which became the embryo for this book.

My intention here is to tell what is known in FACTS and to add MEMORIES, from research and recollections, before they are lost. I have also tried to connect the genealogical material to the history of the time so that it may help readers get a truer feeling for our ancestors' lives, experiences and values.

I admire the dedicated research of true fact-finding genealogists. The volume of their factually sourced data grows exponentially. As the volume of available data expands, it becomes almost impossible for laymen interested in their family tree to follow up, sort out and properly document all of the facts. Not only is more data available for our recent ancestors, connections are being made to generations much further back than we would ever have thought possible.

My genealogical associates tell me that I must document all my facts with at least two firm sources. But in this day and age of thirty-second sound bites, "crisis" news flashes and questionable internet postings, it becomes harder to differentiate fact from fiction and gossip. This is particularly true in the arena of politics and ideological views, but I think it is also true in the area of genealogy and family history. While we sincerely struggle to find solid information to document facts about our ancestors, much of what we find is conflicting and therefore set aside. As any good detective knows, there is much good evidence to be found by pursuing a hunch. So, we need to follow all our leads of known FACTS and vague MEMORIES.

As I faced the challenge of deciding which ancestors to include in this volume, my feelings changed somewhat as I learned more about certain lines or branches of our tree. The tree has considerably grown, or let's say become more visible, as this writing has gone

Introduction

along. The tree was always there, I just didn't see all those other branches. If I have slighted anyone, it has not been intentional. In documenting the fog of history, sometimes we make a leap of faith, occasionally assuming "facts" that may or may not be certain, but in our mind just must be so. I humbly accept any proven corrections, which are surely forthcoming. God has given me only so many hours in the day and a limited number of years. So, it is all His fault, certainly not mine.

Our tree has grown to include more than 9,800 individuals that we know of, not including most of their children. As my research has progressed, I found that there seemed to be a threshold at about 2,000 names beyond which just more and more information became available, thanks to multiple genealogical websites on line. These sources of data have provided alleged connections back 50 generations to the 5th century AD. This changed my view of things. While I offer the whole tree open for reference on the ancestry.com website, my writing initially concentrated on our family in the United States, going back twelve generations, with only minor mention of European ancestors.

Tracing ancestry back through America has been challenging, but very rewarding, in that we have successfully found a large percentage of our ancestors with reasonably accurate data. Extensions of these branches back across the ocean to their origin in Europe has been successful far beyond my expectations. This is of course due to the diligence of so many people over the centuries keeping records and passing on legends.

Almost all of our ancestry can be traced through Europe. I find only a very few known ancestors included in our present tree that were not European and there is uncertainty on the accuracy of information about those possible Native American ancestors. However, even among all of the Europeans, their basic roots must have originally been from elsewhere as archeologists certainly have discovered. So, the real search could go back further. But we will begin in Europe.

Our European ancestors comprise over 75 percent of our tree as it is known at this time. So, concentrating roughly on the years from 1600 to the present day in the United States leaves many people out. The settlement of America from Jamestown in 1607 and Plymouth in 1620 is such a distinct point in time, that I had initially chosen that as the dividing point on which I could properly concentrate in order to manage this writing project. To leave out such a large group, the Europeans, seemed to be only telling a small part of our story, so I decided to expand the project and begin in Europe. "Part 1 — The Europeans — Our European History" has been added. This gives a much fuller picture of our heritage.

It seemed incomplete to leave Europe and America entirely separated, so "Part 2 — On to America — Jamestown and Plymouth" was added to provide some insight into the adventurous individuals who left Europe to settle in America. Parts 3 & 4 are my original

Introduction

endeavor to bring out the ancestors and information of our families in America. Parts 5 & 6 are my recollections and those of my wife, Linda, which are added to give family and friends more insight into our lives than they already know.

It is a thrill to find our heroes and villains of yesteryear who may be well known, but let's also remember and document the ordinary citizen ancestors in our trees. Perhaps we have startling facts and surprising memories to discover and also some kind, beautiful people to get to know.

I've always thought of our family as English in origin, but as I progressed, I soon realized our Smith line of ancestors were Scots. This also became meaningless when looking at the branches of the spouses. In our family we have English, Scots, Welsh, Irish, Germans, Flemish, Dutch, French, Spanish, Italians, Danes, Swedish and Norwegians that we know of.

Over 90 percent of my ancestor families emigrated from Great Britain to America. However, when I received my DNA results, it showed I was 47% Southern Norwegian, 23% Northern European and only 12% from Great Britain. I was quite surprised to say the least. Especially since the only known Norwegian was my Grandfather Kaddeland, which would make it 25%. So somehow those Saxons, Vikings and later the Normans were quite active in settling among what, I thought, were very Anglo populations and territories within Great Britain. What more don't we know? I'm sure there is much. It seems that the "Great Migration" has been in motion for a very long time. I had to realize that all the world is a melting pot with people moving and mingling continuously.

That's when my wife, Linda, explained the six degrees of separation idea, which says that if we go back six generations, we can connect to everyone in the world. So, it seems we are all in this together. We are all searching for our roots and all looking for connections to others and therefore we want to help each other in this endeavor and succeed as best we can. There are interesting FACTS and MEMORIES to be shared.

I've tried to stick to our direct lineage, only including aunts, uncles and other related parties when their lives directly intersected with people in our line in a significant or interesting way.

With each generation we go back, more branches are recognized to be initially or further explored. It becomes an ever-expanding effort to explore the endlessly growing number of branches. Of course, this is part of the fun and satisfaction, especially when one connects their tree with someone they know, but to whom they previously had no idea they were related. This brings out new FACTS, closer friendships and fond MEMORIES.

In order to orient and locate our various generations as they connect between families, I have numbered the generations and placed the generation number before the person's name. Table 1 is intended to assist in this also. I hope these help guide the reader to follow

Introduction

the convolutions of our history. I certainly have referred many times to these assists to keep everyone straight.

Some surnames have been more active in the history of our ancestors. Therefore, more is known of them and they have stories that have been passed down. It is interesting to me to find the origin of various names, as far as they are known, and I have dug a little to try to find more, hoping it would lead to some good information. Our Smiths came from Scotland, but almost every clan had a Smith to work metal for tools and armor. Miller is another name widely used by many in their very own specific occupation. Fitz, I learned, was used for the son of a king. The word "of" or "de" only means that the person was from that place. And everyone from a town or place may or may not be the "Lord" of that place and may or may not be bloodline connected at all. Our ancestors might have been part of the common herd of population who served the local lords and barons of that time and place.

Some names changed spelling due to language translations and other unknown reasons. It took me a while to understand the Scandinavian use of "sen" for "son of" and "dtr" for "daughter of." In the Germanic heraldry Ritter means a knight or baron and "Von" means a step higher. And those dear Sheltons have a name that means shelter or place so they as many others could come from anywhere.

The convention of using maiden names is applied throughout this writing with married surnames added in parenthesis where useful or needed for clarity. If a person has legally changed their name, I have used their latest name.

The pictures throughout this book are mainly from our family collection of photos, files and records in our possession. All others are noted with the source of the photo acknowledged and are greatly appreciated to help tell our story.

Histories of early times are sometimes very uncertain with many contradictory writings, but it is amazing how much is really known and basically agreed upon. The ancestors listed in these chapters are direct bloodline ancestors as I know of them and understand them. Any others discussed are noted otherwise.

The book generally progresses by chapter in the same way the Pedigree Chart does as far as family names go, but under each family name we progress from the earliest forward. For many ancestors we have only names and a few facts. It makes one wonder why other ancestors around them took the limelight and they didn't. I suspect their lives were also very interesting. And of course, the famous have volumes written about them, but I have tried to keep my discussions limited to not overwhelm the lesser folks. So, many very interesting people have been included and others set aside for future family genealogists to work on.

Part 1

Those Europeans — Our European History

We begin in Europe. I have connected us to so many European continuations of American branches that it almost overwhelmed me. The short European ancestral branches have been included with their American descendants in Parts 3 and 4. The longer and more famous branches are discussed in the following chapters of this Part 1. While I really want to include all ancestors from all walks of life and levels of society, not much information is known of ordinary people, only prominent people. So we go with information that is readily available.

Being ancestrally connected to a king or royalty at first excited and amazed me. But then, I researched, studied and realized everyone could be related and connected by the 'degrees of separation" rule. So, I have calmed down and gotten more realistic.

Then I read an old newspaper article that my father had saved, and left in his family genealogy files, from the *New York Sun* on Wednesday, December 11, 1929. The article, with the headline "Family Tree Hunting Popular," states that tracing one's family 22 generations and allowing 25 years per generation back to the time of Henry III in the year 1358, you have over 2 million related people in Great Britain at that time. This was at a time when the total population of Great Britain was only about 2-½ million people. That indicates that in 1929, 80% of people with English heritage were related. Now we are 3 or 4 more generations removed from that time of the article in 1929. And we are now actually looking back 50 generations. So, there is a very high mathematical probability of factual bloodline connections.[1]

Our English heritage is defined in many ways through these multiple tree branches. It is beyond the scope of this book to cover all of our thousands of ancestors in Great Britain during these hundreds of years between the early Roman occupation or the Norman invasion of 1066 and the *Mayflower* voyage of 1620. This of course means we only cover the special people about which so much is known and written. We wish we had some tales to relate about our ordinary ancestors who lived in these times. Suffice it to say we wish we had known them and hope for the most part they lived happy, productive and generally successful lives.

---

1 *New York Sun*, "Family Tree Hunting Popular," 12/11/1929," Publisher *New York Sun* — William Dewart, Owner

TABLE 1 — THOSE EUROPEANS AND ON TO AMERICA

CHAPTERS		1	2	3	4	5	6	7	8	9
YEAR APPROX	GEN	GEWISSE	WELSH	DANES & VIKINGS	NORMANS	FRANKS	PLANTAGENET	EDWARD I TO SMITH	WARS OF ROSES	EDWARD I TO LINDA
500	50	CERDIC								
500	49	CYNRIC								
	48	CAEWLIN								
	47	CUTHWINE								
600	46	CUTHWOLF								
	45	CEOWALD				ST ARNULF & PEPIN				
	44	COENRED				ANSEGISEL				
700	43	INGILD				PEPIN II				
	42	EOPPA				CHARLES M				
	41	EAFA				PEPIN				
	40	EALHMUND				CHARLEMAGNE				
800	39	ECGBERHT		RAGNARSSON		LOUIS				
	38	AETHELWULF		HARDACANUTE		CHARLES-BALD				
	37	AETHELRED I / ALFRED		GORM ENSKE		BALDWIN I				
900	36	AELFTHRYTH		HAROLD		BALDWIN II				
	35			G HAROLDSSON	ROLLO	ARNULF I				
	34			HARALD	WILLIAM LS	BALDWIN III				
1000	33		LEOFWINE	GUNNORA	RICHARD I	ARNULF II				
	32		LEOFRIC		RICHARD II	BALDWIN IV				
	31		AELFGAR III		ROBERT I	BALDWIN V				
	30		EALDGYTH		WILLIAM I	MATILDA				
	30				ADELAIDE		WILLIAM i & MATILDA			
1100	29		NEST VERCH GRUFFYDD		JUDITH OF LENS		HENRY I			
	28		NEST VERCH OSBERN		MAUD/ MATILDA		MATILDA - GEOFFREY			

						Gen	Year
	IVO DE NEWMARCHE	HUGH DE ST LIZ	HENRY II			27	1200
	AWBRERIA NEWMARCHE	EMMA DE ST LIZ	JOHN PLANTAGENET			26	
	BRAYBROOKE		HENRY III		EDWARD I	25	
	BRAYBROOKE		EDWARD I		EDWARD I	24	
	BRAYBROOKE		EDWARD II		JOAN OF ENGLAND	23	
	BRAYBROOKE		EDWARD III	EDWARD I	M DE CLARE	22	
	BRAYBROOKE		LIONEL PLANTAGENT	ELIZABETH	M DE AUDLEY	21	1300
	BRAYBROOKE		PHILLIPA PLANTAGENET	M BOHUN	H STAFFORD	20	
	BRAYBROOKE		MORTIMER	E COURTENAY	M STAFFORD	19	
	BRAYBROOK		H PERCY	H LUTTRELL	R NEVILLE	18	1400
	CHAWORTH		H PERCY	E LUTTRELL	J NEVILLE	17	
	E SCROPE		M PERCY	E STRATTON	J NEVILLE	16	
	W DARCY		GASCOIGNE	M ANDREWS	GASCOIGNE	15	1500
	T DARCY		TAILBOYS	J MERRILL	A C VAUX	14	
	A DARCY		F DYMOKE	A MERRILL	N THROCKMORTON	13	
	E DARCY		WINDEBANK	M SPENCER	A THROCKMORTON	12	1600
	I DARCY		DENTON	G SPENCER I	M THROCKMORTON	11	
	M LAUNCE		DENTON	G SPENCER	T WOOTEN	10	
	G SHERMAN		DENTON	N SPENCER	R WOOTEN	9	1700
	W PROUT		GALE / D SMITH	D SPENCER	R WOOTEN	8	
	H PROUT		D SMITH	E SPENCER	S WOOTEN	7	
	W PROUT		F SMITH	S SPENCER	M WOOTEN	6	1800
	R PROUT		F SMITH	R L PROUT	E TANNER	5	
	V MILLER		W C SMITH	V R MILLER	G TRACY	4	
	G BLAKE		C H SMITH	G BLAKE	E F TRACY	3	1900
	CC SMITH		CC SMITH	CC SMITH	M F SHEETS	2	
	W C SMITH		W C SMITH	W C SMITH	R HUND	1	2000
					L KNOOP		
							2100

7

Chapter 1

The Gewisse and Wessex in Early Britain (410–1042)

As Christians we are taught and believe everything began with Adam and Eve. The monks who wrote *The Anglo-Saxon Chronicles*, some of the earliest writings of British history, even give a listing of chaps from Adam and Eve all the way down to our Cedric, but I'm starting with the Romans in England.[2]

The Roman occupation of England began with their initial invasion about 43 AD and lasted until their final withdrawal in 410. The indigenous population of Great Britain at that time was already a melting pot of peoples. They are called the Britons or the Britonic tribes and were a mixture of peoples including Scots, Picts, Gauls, Celts and others. The main population of Celtic Britons (or Ancient Britons) was in place long before the Roman occupation. The Ancient Britons were said to have originally come from Armorica, an area of northwestern France that was settled even earlier.

The Britons both accepted and resisted Roman control. By the 5th century the Romans were increasingly attacked by local Celtic Britons, the Picts, the Hibernian Scots and other northern Europeans. With the gradual collapse of the Roman Empire these attacks became more successful. After the Romans left, the country became controlled mainly by local Celtic Briton tribes or clans, but also by northern European forces of Angles, Saxons, Jutes, various Scandinavians, and maybe others who attacked and settled in parts of the British Isles.

One particular group of Anglo-Saxon peoples was called the Gewisse who settled on the Thames near Dorchester. They flourished and became predominant in the area and

---

2 Savage, Anne, *The Anglo-Saxon Chronicles* translation, William Heinemann Ltd., London, 1983

Chapter 1: The Gewisse and Wessex in Early Britain (410–1042)

gradually merged with the Celtic Britons in the area of West Saxon or Wessex. In later centuries they were dominant in all of what we know as Great Britain.

Wessex is the southern coastal area of England, generally west of London. As the Gewisse population and control grew, at times it extended east into Kent and London and west to the Irish sea. Later their control included much of Wales and extended to the north. In any event, after the Romans left, the population of Wessex began to organize from tribal villages into a kingdom. Acknowledging that the historical record is rife with variations, theories and conflicts, we will begin here.

I initially thought our longest documented ancestral branch extended straight back to Cerdic, a fifth century Anglo-Saxon leader in Wessex. But further research revealed a possible break in that line. I found that there were many women with the name Aelfgifu. And that Aelfgifu of Mercia (c997–c1097) was not Aelfgifu of Northumbria (997–1042). So, I had to separate the two women which split this incorrect connection into two lines. Thus, we have Chapter 1 about Wessex and Chapter 2 introducing the Welsh.

Intending to include here the Gewisse people and Wessex as early history and fodder for perhaps future family genealogy researchers, I moved on to other early lines among the Danes, Vikings, Normans and Franks. While sorting out all of their roots, I came upon generation 36 Aelfthryth of Wessex (877–929), a daughter of Alfred the Great who married Baldwin II, Margave of Flanders (c865–918). Thus, a bloodline connection exists after all and is further explained in Chapter 5: The Franks. Cerdic is our oldest bloodline connection–50 Generations.

I am indebted here to a reference which gave me considerable understanding of these early ancestors, their lives and their families — *The Saxon Kings* by Richard Humble.[3]

50. Cerdic (??–534)

In *The Anglo-Saxon Chronicles*, Cerdic is listed as the leader of the Anglo-Saxon settlement of Britain.

It is written that he landed in Hampshire in about 495 with five ships and fought the local Britons to establish his settlement. Other accounts indicate he may have been invited in to help the Britons hold off the Picts and the Scots. Or, he might have been a leftover Roman officer, a local Celtic Briton or even a mythical legendary character. In any event, it is noted that under his leadership began the Cerdicing Dynasty of the Kingdom of the Gewisse, which lasted 400 years, from 519 to 927 AD. His reign ran from 519 until his death in 534 AD.

---

3 Humble, Richard, *The Saxon Kings*, George Weidenfeld & Nicolson Ltd., London, 1980

Chapter 1: The Gewisse and Wessex in Early Britain (410–1042)

49. Cynric (495–560)
Cynric was the son (or Grandson) of Cerdic. According to *The Anglo-Saxon Chronicles*, he arrived in Britain aboard the ship with Cerdic. He ruled from his father's death in 534 until his death in 560 during which time they fought many battles with the Britons.

48. Caewlin (c535–c592)
Caewlin was the son of Cynric and became ruler upon the death of his father. He won many battles and under his leadership much of the territory in Wessex was consolidated. He ruled from 560 to 592 when he was deposed and exiled. He died a year later.

Here we lose information on the next few generations, since other family relations ruled and only they are recorded in *The Anglo-Saxon Chronicles* and the *West Saxon Genealogical Regnal List and the Chronology of Early Wessex*. These resources provide a significant amount of available recorded history on early Britain.[4][5]

47. Cuthwine (c565–592)

46 Citha Cuthwolf (592–??)

45 Ceowald (??)

44 Cenred/Coenred (640–??)

43 Ingild of Wessex (672–718)
Ingild was a brother of Ine. Ine was born about 670 and ruled from 688 to 726 when he abdicated. Ine is listed as a descendant of Caewlin so it should follow that Ine's brother, Ingild, is also a descendant of Caewlin.

42 Eoppa (706–??)

41 Eafa of Wessex (c732–772)
Eafa supposedly married a Kentish princess and they had Ealhmund.

40 Ealhmund of Kent (c750–784)
The father of Ecgberht (c775–839). There are several legends of Ealhmund, including

---

4 Savage, Anne, *The Anglo-Saxon Chronicles* translation, William Heinemann Ltd., London, 1983
5 Dumville, D. N., *The West Saxon Genealogical Regnal List and the Chronology of Early Wessex* 1985

Chapter 1: The Gewisse and Wessex in Early Britain (410–1042)

questionable certainty of his being King of Kent or even "of Kent" which some mention. If his father did marry a Kentish princess then he could very well be "of Kent."

39 Ecgberht/Ecgbryth/Egbert, King of West Saxons (c775–839) m Redburga
Ecgberht was the son of Ealhmund, and, therefore, a descendent of Ine's brother. He came to the throne as King of West Saxons after their confederate, the King of Mercia, died and they, the West Saxons, had also lost power over the area. He took several areas by force or as a protectorate including Kent, Sussex, East Anglica and, for a time after 829, Mercia. He consolidated what was called Wessex and sent his sons as sub-kings out to control outlying areas. He reigned from 802 to the time of his death in 839. I say "King" as they were called, but at that time they were more large tribal leaders. So, England had several simultaneous "Kings." And the area of their respective "Kingdoms" continually changed and shifted depending upon local and regional alliances as well as the belligerent action of open warfare.

38 Aethelwulf, King of Wessex (c795–c858) m Osburg/Osburth of Wessex (810–876)
We don't know his exact birth year, but Aethelwulf was probably born around 795. He married Osburg/Osburth for his first wife, who was said to be the daughter of his butler. They had six children together, five boys and one girl. Aethelred was their fourth son. Alfred the Great was their fifth son.

There were several battles with the Vikings during Aethelwulf's reign from 839 to 858, but they were not consequential. He was successful in unifying many areas. He divided his holdings into separate sub-kingdoms and deployed his sons as sub-kings to manage these outlying areas. This proved effective.

Aethelwulf made a one-year pilgrimage to Rome. During his return trip in 858, he visited Charles, the Bald, King of West Francia, which is essentially modern-day France. During his month-long visit, he married Charles's eldest daughter, 37 Judith of Flanders (c843–870), who was 12 or 14 years old at the time. It is surmised that Charles was under pressure from the attacking Danes and was looking to make alliances by condoning the marriage. Charles insisted that his daughter be given the title of Queen, which went against the custom of the time. Rather than being known simply as "the wife of the King" Judith was given the title of Queen. This was a major concession.

Aethelwulf's first wife, Osburg/Osburth may have previously died or was set aside when he took the second wife, Judith. With Judith, he had no children and Aethelwulf died in the same year they were married.

After Aethelwulf's death, Judith remarried his eldest son, Aethelbald, who was now the king. This apparently caused a major uproar as it was against conventional Christian dignity and considered incest.

Chapter 1: The Gewisse and Wessex in Early Britain (410–1042)

Some say Aethelbald set her aside in 859. Anyhow, Aethelbald died in 860 and Judith returned to her father, Charles, in Flanders. There is no record of any children by this marriage. Judith of Flanders comes back into our family in Chapter 5: The Franks.

37 Aethelred I, King of Wessex (c837–871) m Wulfthyrth of Wessex (825–870)
Aethelred, born about 837, was the fourth son of Aethelwulf by his first wife Osburh. Various historical notes exist to name Aethelred's wife. I believe that he married Wulfthyrth of Wessex. She is referred to as "Queen" by some.

Their daughter Elgiva/Elgira of Wessex, or Alfgifu Aethelreding (870–964) married Harold Parcus, King of Sjaelland in Denmark (c858–899). It is ironic that Aethelred and Wulfthyrth's daughter married a Dane. This marriage again was made to create an alliance between the more friendly Danish and the English rulers. We have an alternate or parallel line beginning from here with Harald II Parcus and his Danish line in Chapter 3.

Aethelred became King of Wessex upon the deaths of his older brothers and served for a short period from 865 to 871. During this time the Danish Vikings were getting much more serious in their incursions and attacks into England. He and his younger brother, Alfred, led troops against these attacks with some successes and some failures. His reign is mainly noted as a period of setbacks against the Danish "Great Army." Aethelred died in 871 at around the young age of 24 years.

37 Alfred, the Great, King of England (849–899) m Ealhswith (852–905)
Alfred was the fifth and youngest son of Aethelwulf and his wife Osburg. He was a bright child and his mother made a special effort to see that he learned to read and write. She challenged her children with the gift of an illuminated book to the first who could read it. Alfred was fascinated by the beautiful illumination and took the book to his tutor to teach him how to read it. He was able to win the challenge by reciting the entire book from memory. At age 5 his father sent him with a contingent to Pope Leo in Rome. At about age 9, Alfred again traveled to Rome with his father. On their way back, his father married Judith of Flanders who was only 3-5 years older than Alfred and was now to be his stepmother.

Alfred fought alongside his brothers. Alfred bonded with his brother King Aethelred in a coordinated effort to resist the Danish Great Army. After Aethelred's death, Alfred became king and continued the fight. The Danish Great Army continued to gain ground and Alfred was forced to retreat to a small island in the swamps of Wales until he could regroup and gain forces to begin recovery. Danish attacks lasted until Alfred the Great could unify the English and gather sufficient force to repel the invaders from his area of Wessex and western Mercia. The Danes finally retreated to the north.

Alfred was much more than a great leader. One of Alfred's greatest and unnoticed

Chapter 1: The Gewisse and Wessex in Early Britain (410–1042)

accomplishments was his new Code of English Law which combined laws from the multiple English Kingdoms and the Danish laws from areas formerly controlled by the Danes. This went a long way toward unifying the various territories with laws fair to both English and Danish communities. During his later years he translated five books from Latin into English.

Alfred and Ealhswith's youngest daughter, 36 Aelfthryth of Wessex, married 36 Baldwin II, Count of Flanders. This is the connecting link from Wessex to the Franks, then Normans, Plantagenets and down to the Smiths.

Edward, the Elder, King of England (c871–924) m Eadgifu (??)
Edward was the elder son of Alfred, the Great, and inherited the throne. He fended off a claim for power from his cousin, Aethelfaed, a son of Alfred's elder brother. Along with keeping the throne, Edward inherited Alfred's unification of the people and forces. He continued to recover areas from Viking rule. He joined forces with his oldest sister, Aethelflaed, who was Lady of the Mercians after her husband, Aethelred, Lord of the Mercian's death. Together they recovered all areas of England except Northumbria. Edward has not received the historical acclaim of his Father, but was admired in his day for the effectiveness of his rule.

Edward had three wives and nine children. Eadgifu was his third wife.

Edmund I, the Magnificent, King of England (921–946) m Aelfgifu of Shaftesbury (??)
Edmund was very young when his father died, and he inherited the throne later when his much older half-brother, King Aethelstan, died. Edmund had grown up under Aethelstan and fought in the Battle of Brunanbufh as an adolescent and became king while still a teenager. His reign was noted by almost constant warfare and conflicts within Great Britain and with the French.

Edmund had two wives and two children, both sons by his first wife Aelfgifu. While attending a dinner associated with a church mass, he noticed an intruder and attacked the man. In the fight Edmund was killed. It is said that Edmund was assassinated.

Edgar, the Peaceful, King of England (943/4–975) m Aelfthryth, wife of Edgar (??)
Edgar was the younger son of King Edmund I and came to power as a teenager after his uncle Eadred and then his brother Eadwig both died. The period of his reign was peaceful and with the Kingdom of England now established it allowed him to build institutions of government. A standard of measurement was established. His coronation set the standard for current coronations and included crowning of the queen. Its effect was to bring

Chapter 1: The Gewisse and Wessex in Early Britain (410–1042)

the various kings from around Britain such as the King of Scots to pledge allegiance and support.

Edgar had three wives. Edgar's wife Aelfthryth bore him a son, Aethelred II. He also had a son, Edward, by Aethelflaed and probably a daughter by Wulfthryth. Edward became king upon Edgar's death.

Aethelred II, the Unready, King of England (968–1016) m Aelfgifu (968–1002)
The unready in old English means ill advised. This is a joke about his name which actually means well advised. Aethelred became king as a young child in 978 after his half-brother Edward's assassination. He had a continuing struggle with the Danish invaders who forced Aethelred to flee to Normandy in 1013. He remained in Normandy for about two years until Sweyn Forkbeard's death in 1014. Upon his return he regained his crown which he kept until his death in 1016.

Aethelred married twice. His first wife was Aelfgifu who bore him ten children. His second wife was Emma of Normandy, a sister of Richard II, Duke of Normandy. They had three children including Edward (the Confessor), Aelfred Aetheling and Edred. Emma provides us another bloodline connection with the Normans should we wish to explore it. I'm not going to do so because we are complicated enough as it is.

Aelfgifu of Northumbria (997–1042) m Uchtred/Uhtred, the Bold, of Northumbria (??–1016)
Uhtred, the Bold came from a long line of Northumbrians who ruled from the castle of Bamburgh. He was a leader and led a victorious force against Malcolm II of Scotland who was invading Northumbria. Because of this effort he was appointed Ealdorman of Bamburgh and later Ealdorman of York. He married for political gain. First, he married Ecgfrida, the daughter of Bishop Aldun, from whom he received some church lands. After dismissing her, he married Sige, the daughter of a rich Yorkist. He was trying to make political allies in York. They had three children together. Lastly he married Aelfgifu with whom they had a daughter, Ealdgyth, who married Maldred, Brother of Duncan I of Scotland.

We know little of Aelfgifu of Northumbria, but reviewing what we do know she is not Aelfgifu of Mercia.

Chapter 2

The Welsh (950–2021)

After finding my disconnect in Chapter 1 concerning Aelgifu, I started exploring the Welsh in more detail. While the Anglo-Saxons of Chapter 1 did settle into Britain and establish an identity to the island of Great Britain, the Welsh were there before them. They were the Celtic tribes of early Britons who came from Europe centuries before. Wales as a unified area came into being in the 6th or 7th century and continues to be identified as such even today as a part of Great Britain. Welsh is still a predominant language spoken in certain parts of Wales.

Our line of English ancestors begins in Wales, but it is then quickly connected to Anglo-Saxons and definitely taken over by the Norman invader influence as you can readily see by the names.

33 Leofwine, Ealdorman of the Hwicce (c950–c1023) m Alwara (c955–c1055)

Leofwine was appointed Ealdorman of Hwicce by King Aethelred II in 994. Ealdorman is a Danish word meaning Earl. Hwicce was an area of the western midlands later named Mercia on the eastern edge of Wales. Not much else is known except it is believed his family was from there. After the Danes took control under Cnut/Canute, he still kept his position.

32 Leofric, Earl of Mercia (968–1057) m Godgifu (Lady Godiva) (c1010–c1086)

Leofwine's wife Godgifu (Lady Godiva) is known for her action to protest her husband's excessive taxation on his tenants by riding a horse through the streets of Coventry while naked, "covered only by her long hair." In spite of this they had nine children and worked together to establish churches and monasteries. It is believed Godgifu might have been Leofric's second wife which accounts for his son's earlier birthdate.

Chapter 2: The Welsh (950–2021)

Continuing from his father, Leofwine, Leofric also was appointed Earl of Mercia in the favor of King Cnut/Canute and also King Harold (Harefoot), King Harthacnut and then King Edward (the Confessor). As Earl he was quite powerful, but still subject to the King's orders. He was ordered to destroy the city of Worcester, a city of his people, after two of his tax collectors were killed. A bittersweet position.

31 Aelfgar III, Earl of Mercia (c1002–c1062) m Aelfgifu of Mercia (c997–c1097)

Aelfgar succeeded to become Earl of Mercia when his father died in 1057. And for a short time, he was also Earl of East Anglia until Earl Harold Godwin returned to the graces of King Edward. Then Aelfgar fell out with the king and was exiled. This prompted him to raise an army in Ireland and Wales and to march against the King. They clashed at Hereford causing the King's forces to flee with many killed. Another battle loomed but both sides came to their senses and Aelfgar was restored as Earl of Mercia.

According to *The Anglo-Saxon Chronicles*, Aelfgifu of Mercia was the "daughter of Sigeferth (Thegn of the Seven Boroughs) and Ealdgyth (of Mercia)" which is the fact that broke my line in Chapter 1. The use of the mother's name for their daughter is some reinforcement here also. They had three sons and one daughter.

30 Ealdgyth of Mercia (c1034–c1086) m Gruffydd Ap Llewelyn, King of Wales (c1011–1063)

Gruffydd's father, Llywelyn Ap Seisyll, had ruled the northern half of Wales until his death, at which time others quickly grabbed control of the two sub-kingdom areas, Powys and Gwynedd. Gruffydd responded by attacking and mostly defeating them, with some losses but many wins. Over a period of fifteen years, he gradually became recognized as King of all Wales in 1056 and this included areas of Mercia.

In an early battle of 1041 to reclaim his father's rule he carried off his opponent, Hywel's, wife and took her for his own wife. Her name is unknown.

Later he married a second time to Eadgyth of Mercia. After Gruffydd died, Ealdgyth married a second time to Harold II Godwinson who in 1066 became King of England and then was killed at the Battle of Hastings. Ealdgyth and her children fled the country. Their son Harold laid claim to the throne but to no avail as William I (the Conqueror) was in control.

29 Nest Verch Gruffydd (1059–1152) m Osbern, Fitz Richard (1055–c1100)

Osbern's father, Richard, Fitz Scrob, a Norman knight, was granted an area of land in Hereford and Shropshire near the border of Wales and built a castle there. Osbern inherited the castle and lands and became the Lord of Richard's Castle, Sheriff of Hereford and 2nd Barron of Burforf.

Chapter 2: The Welsh (950–2021)

28 Nest Verch Osbern (1082–1163) m Bernard de Newmarche (1075–1133)
Nest was also known as Nesta of Hereford. Bernard was the son of Geoffery Neufmarche and Ada de Hugleville, born near Normandy. His mother's family descends from Richard II Duke of Normandy which gives us another connection.

Bernard came to England as a warrior and was given Nest as a wife by her father, Osbern, who saw Bernard's potential. Through his continued efforts to gain power and territory, Bernard is recognized as the first conqueror of Wales. As a pacification effort he allowed the Welsh nobles to retain their high hill land positions while granting the low agricultural lands to the invader Normans.

Bernard's ancestors connect us back to Richard I in Chapter 4.

27 Ivo de Newmarche (1096–1146) m Emma de Saint Liz/Elizabeth (1110–1146)
Ivo was born in the town of Braybrooke and is therefore named Ivo de Neufmarche of Braybrooke leading some to name him Ivo de Braybrooke. Very confusing. Braybrooke is a small town in Northamptonshire in central England which in 2011 had a population of only 378 people. It makes one wonder what size it was in 1096. The name Braybrooke in early times meant "the broad brook."

Emma's ancestors connect us back to William, the Conqueror, and Richard I in Chapter 4.

26 Awbreria de Newmarche (1120–1146) m Ingebaldus Braybrooke (1118–1167)
Little is known of Awbreria and Ingebaldus.

25 Ingebald Braybrooke (1146–1167) m Albreda de Newmarche (1146–1168)
Ingebald was born and died in Braybrooke, Northamptonshire. It is mentioned that he married his aunt, but little detail supports this.

Ingebald was a justiciar, a position as an administer of justice who presided over a Norman court, maybe even a Chief Justice.

24 Robert de Braybrooke (1168–1210) m Henrietta (1172–1210)
Robert was also known as Robert Le May. He was a landowner and High Sheriff which meant he was the Justice also. Robert accumulated land by paying off debtors' mortgages to receive ownership. As a member of King John's council he is listed as one of the king's "evil" counsellors. He built the Braybrooke Castle.

23 Sir Henry de Braybrooke (1188–1234) m Christina Ledet (1190–1271)
Henry married Christina as part of a settlement with her father, Wischard Ledet, who was

losing his lands to Henry's father, Robert. Henry succeeded his father as landowner and High Sheriff under King John, but later lost his position. He ultimately lost his lands and was ordered by King Henry III to destroy Braybrooke Castle.

Henry and Christina had three children.

22 John de Braybrooke (1220–1293) m Joan De Weldebof (1227–1302)

21 Gerard de Braybrooke Sr. (1264–1325) m Lora Piccott (c1273–??)

20 Sir Gerard Braybrooke II (1307–1359) m 2) Elizabeth Dakeney (1311–1388)

19 Sir Gerard Braybrooke III (c1332–1403) m 2) Isabel Maynell (after1337–1393)

This was a 2nd marriage for Gerard and a 3rd marriage for Isabel.

Gerard had a brother Reynold/Reginald (1396–1426), who is covered in Chapter 7 and gives us another cross connection to the Plantagenet line, which is covered in Chapter 6.

18 Nicola Braybrook (c1386–1411) m Sir Thomas Chaworth (1385–1459)

Sir Thomas was the heir to a fortune through his mother, Alice Caltoft, who had inherited her family's vast estate. Sir Thomas succeeded his own father in a government position. He held many positions, including being called to Parliament, several shire Sheriff assignments and Justice of the Peace for Nottinghamshire.

Nicola and Thomas were married by their parents at about the age of eight. They had one child, Elizabeth, when Nicola was about thirteen. After Nicola died at around age twenty-five, Thomas remarried and had several more children.

17 Elizabeth Chaworth (1391–1467) m John Scrope (c1388–1455)

John was the 4th Baron Scrope of Masham. Masham is in north central England. John became Baron after his elder brother, Henry, was executed for a part in the Southampton Plot to kill King Henry V in 1415.

John was knighted in 1424, became a Privy Councilor and held many positions including on the Council of Regency for Henry VI and Treasurer of England from 1432–1433. He bought back lands which had been taken away after his brother's demise.

Elizabeth was John's second wife. They had eight children together, three sons and five daughters.

16 Eleanor Scrope (1424–1471) m Richard Darcy, Lord de Knayth (1424–1458)

The name Darcy has several potential sources. It is written that it's from Ireland and means dark, but it is unclear if this refers to skin or hair color or even a mood. Then there is the theory that the family came from Arci, a part of Normandy, and therefore were known as D'Arcy. But I find Arci/Arcis east of Paris and not in Normandy. I favor the theory that a likely ancestor is Richard II D'Arcy, who came with William in 1066. The D'Arcys were given considerable lands in Yorkshire and Lincolnshire. Anyway, our Richard here (several generations later) was the 7th Baron Darcy of Knayth/Knaith. Knaith is in Lincolnshire.

They had three sons and one daughter. Eleanor married a second time after Richard died.

This was the time of the Wars of the Roses. The Darcy families were located in Yorkshire. I assume they supported the York side, but see no record of their participation. Many families split up as members supported opposing sides. Some even changed allegiance depending upon the actions of the kings or of family members. See Chapter 8: Wars of the Roses.

15 Sir William Darcy (1443–1488) m Eupherne/Euphemia Langton (1443–1471)

Sir William was the 8th Baron Darcy of Templehurst (Temple Hirst). Templehurst is located in northern Yorkshire. The name comes from the Knights Templar being granted a manor there in 1152. Hirst means hill or knoll.

14 Sir Thomas Darcy (1467–1537) m Dousabella Tempest (c1475–c1500)

As the only son and heir, Thomas inherited the family lands and became the 1st Baron Darcy of Darcy. Dousabella/Dowsabel was Thomas's first wife and they had four children. After her death he remarried to Edith Sandys.

Sir Thomas served King Henry VII, leading 1,000 men on an expedition to France. He served in many capacities and on many commissions. However, he was unhappy with the separation of England from the Papacy and participated in rebelling against it. For this he was charged and convicted of high treason. He was beheaded on Tower Hill.

13 Sir Arthur Darcy (1505–1561) m Mary Carew (1530–1568)

Sir Arthur was a Lieutenant of the Tower of London, which is ironic since his father was beheaded there. A Lieutenant of the Tower of London is a position just under the Constable of the Tower of London. The Constable is in charge of the Tower when the King is not there. These positions have been in place since the 14th century and are usually lifetime appointments.

Mary and Arthur had fifteen children, ten sons and five daughters.

12 Sir Edward Darcy, Knight (1543–1612) m Elizabeth Astley (1526–1600)

Sir Edward was educated at Trinity College of Cambridge University and was admitted to the Inner Temple, a legal society. In 1584–1585 he was member of Parliament and groom of the Privy Council under Queen Elizabeth. She granted him recovery of two manors and some lands which had been taken away from the family previously.

Sir Edward was granted an exclusive patent on playing cards in 1598, but it was invalidated by the court four years later.

Edward and Elizabeth had fourteen children, five sons and nine daughters.

11 Isabella Darcy (c1600–c1669) m John Launce (1597–1639)
John was from Penneare in St. Clement's, Cornwall, and was a Parliamentarian. They had seven children. Mary was their third child.

John died of wounds received during an altercation. After John died, Isabella married a second time to Reverend Sydrach Simpson, Master of Pembroke Hall at Cambridge University.

10 Mary Launce (1625–1710) m Rev. John Sherman (1613–1685)
Mary Launce was John's 2nd wife. Mary and Reverend John came to America in the Great Migration. He came in 1635 on the ship *Elizabeth* from Ipswich to Boston, Massachusetts. See Part 3, Chapter 21: Prout.

9 Grace Sherman (1659–1712) m Dr. Ebenezer Prout (1656–1735)
Grace and Ebenezer are the first generation of this line born in America. See Part 3, Chapter 21: Prout.

8 William Prout (1699–1789) m Rachel Harris (1707–1799)
See Part 3, Chapter 21: Prout and Chapter 26: Roberts.

7 Harris Prout (1732–1822) m Pricilla Roberts (1736–1810)
See Part 3, Chapter 21: Prout and Chapter 26: Roberts.

6 William Prout (1779–1822 m Sally Spencer (1783–1852)
See Part 3, Chapter 21: Prout and Chapter 25: Spencer.

5 Ruth Lucrecia Prout (1821–1898) m Watrous Ives Miller (1822–1885)
See Part 3, Chapter 21: Prout and Chapter 18: Miller.

4 Virginia Ruth Miller (1848–1939) m Halsey Horatio Blake (1843–1930)
See Part 3, Chapter 18: Miller and Chapter 16: Blake.

Chapter 2: The Welsh (950–2021)

3 Genevieve Blake (1879–1933) m Charles Herbert Smith (1878–1967)
See Part 3, Chapter 16: Blake and Chapter 14: Smith.

2 Charles Clement Smith (1904–1980) m Carolyn Clark Kaddeland (1907–1966)
See Part 3, Chapter 14: Smith and Chapter 15: Kaddeland.

1 Watson Christen Smith (1936–) m Linda Knoop (1939–)
See Parts 5 and 6.

This establishes a 33-generation bloodline from Leofwine and Alwara to myself within which there is much more to explore and so much we don't know.

In the following chapters we will cover several connecting, alternate and parallel bloodlines which proved very interesting to me. The following chapters also provide the connections for the extension to the full 50 generations.

Chapter 3

The Danes and Vikings (782–1031)

The Danes and other Vikings had been trading, attacking and settling for years but became seriously active attacking and colonizing in England in the late 9th century. Scandinavia in the 9th century was a collection of clans and minor fiefdoms or kingdoms where people survived by farming and fishing along the coastal lands and waters of the Baltic Sea. As these groups grew, formed alliances and became more dominant, they concentrated large forces to be reckoned with. I have great difficulty trying to follow and understand who controlled what and when among the Danes, Swedes and Norwegians. I won't even try to enter the exact history of the time since power seems to have shifted continually. Norway did not become a united kingdom until around 900. But the Danes did become the prominent group about this time. Their location between the Baltic and North Sea gave them a strategic position to carry on trade and to control the activities in the region.[6,7,8]

How these kings managed control of the various areas of their kingdom in Scandinavia, Flanders, Normandy and Britain is beyond me, but they did with varying degrees of success. They must have traveled the region extensively in their conquests and defense of territory, alliances and power.

The validity of the references and sources I have studied here leaves me wondering what really is factual and what is historical fantasy. I proceed with the statement that Harold

---

6 Hall, Richard, *Exploring the World of the Vikings*, Publisher Thames and Hudson Ltd., London, Copyright 2007
7 Pringle, Heather, "The Vikings–Lords of Sea and Sword," Produced by National Geographic Partners LLC, Published by Meredith Corp., New York, Copyright 2018
8 History, "Vikings–The Rulers of Sea and Sword," Meredith Premium Publishing, Meredith National Media Group, Meredith Corp., Waterbury Publications Inc., Copyright 2020

Parcus's wife may be a direct blood connection between Wessex and the Danish. I'll let future family history genealogists verify that.

But, 33 Gunnora here was definitely Richard I's wife and is our ancestral bloodline connection of Danes, Vikings and Normans in Chapter 4. See 33 Gunnora below.

39? Ragnarsson, King of Denmark (782–803) m Heluna Bledja (784–814)

We don't know much about them, except he is referred to as King even though there was a questionable kingdom. "Kings" of this era ruled as chieftains over certain areas with varying power and influence. The fact that he and his wife died in York, England, indicates to me that they traveled, conquered and settled many areas.

38? Hardacanute Sigurdsson, King of Denmark (814–850/84) m Althilda Gandolfsdotter (??-??)

We know almost nothing firm and factual of this couple. He is referred to as a king but their rule and control was very fractional and fluid at best.

37 Gorm Enske Frothoson, King of Sjaelland in Denmark (c820–c875) m Sida, Queen of Denmark (c830–860)

Sjaelland (or Zealand in English) is the largest and most populated island in Denmark and located on the Eastern side of the country. From that location, Gorm Frothoson ruled and controlled areas of Denmark and Scandinavia. Gorm obviously did travel, since he married Sida who was the daughter of Frionnlaith, King of Ireland. Sida died in Denmark.

36 Harold, Parcus, King of Sjaelland in Denmark (c846–899) m Elgiva/Elgira (Elfgifu) of England (870–964)

Harald (Parcus) is a possible connection between Wessex and the Danish. He also must have traveled a bit to marry a lady from Britain.

35 Gorm, the Old, Haroldsson Gammel, King of Denmark and East Anglia (890–c958) m Thyra Klacksdatter /Dannesbod (844–935)

Gorm was the "first historically recognized ruler or King of Denmark, reigning from c.936 to his death c.958."[9] His predecessors had been regional rulers, though they also ruled parts of Britain. Gorm probably only controlled an area called Jutland from a seat in Jelling. He is also noted for his erection of the first of the Jelling runestones, which are stone markers with runic inscriptions to commemorate certain events. Gorm erected this stone in

---

9   Wikipedia, the free encyclopedia 2018

memory of his wife, Thyra.

34 Harald Blaatland (Bluetooth) Gormson, King of Denmark (910–986) m Gyrithe Olafsdotr, Queen of Denmark (905–??)
Harald is credited with uniting Denmark into a solid country. He erected the largest of the Jelling stones in memory of his parents. And, he is noted for officially converting Denmark to Christianity.

33 Gunnora of Denmark/Gonnor De Crepon, Duchess of Normandy (936–1031) m Richard I, the Fearless, First Duke of Normandy (933–996)
Gunnora/Gonnor was born, lived and died in Normandy, France. After a several year relationship with Richard I, which included children, they married and she formally became the Duchess of Normandy.

From here we pick up our line in Chapter 4 with 33 Richard I, the Fearless, and discuss the Vikings settling into the Normandy area of France.

Chapter 4

The Vikings and Normans (845–1146)

The word "Vikings" means many different things depending upon the usage. We most frequently use it as a noun, meaning a group of people. The word "viking" really is a verb, which means the undertaking of the adventure of going forth to explore and conquer. And that is what these people did for a few hundred years. About the year 900, Norway became united as a kingdom, under Harald (Fairhair) and, as a result, became a larger and stronger force. Most people think of Vikings as Norwegians, and some sources state that they were the first on record to "viking," but Vikings came from all over Scandinavia. The Danes probably did more "viking" than others, simply because they had a larger population. And they could easily follow the coast down to more temperate locations to raid and settle. The Vikings traveled much farther than most people realize. They traveled west to settle in Iceland, Greenland and Eastern Canada with possible evidence of a trading post inland on the Great Lakes. Definitely, they went east into Russia and down their rivers to the Black Sea to Constantinople and even the Caspian Sea. And they went south through the North Sea and Atlantic Ocean into the Mediterranean Sea and on to the Middle East. Ireland, Britain and the Normandy area of France were prime locations to trade, plunder and settle into. The name "Normans" evolved naturally because they were men from the North or Northmen.[10][11][12][13]

---

10 Hall, Richard, *Exploring the World of the Vikings*, Publisher Thames and Hudson Ltd., London, Copyright 2007
11 Pringle, Heather, "The Vikings–Lords of Sea and Sword," Produced by National Geographic Partners LLC, Published by Meredith Corp., New York, Copywrite 2018
12 H History, "Vikings–The Rulers of Sea and Sword," Meredith Premium Publishing, Meredith National Media Group, Meredith Corp., Waterbury Publications Inc., Copyright 2020
13 Depping, M., "Viking Expeditions to France in the 9th to 11th Century", Orig Edition–Didier Paris 1843, Translation by Dr. George F. Nafziger, The Nafziger Collection, West Chester, Ohio 2020

Chapter 4: The Vikings and Normans (845–1146)

Photos taken at Viking Ship Museum, Oslo, Norway

The Normans, of course, were the peoples who lived in the Normandy area of France and conquered England by invasion in 1066 under William I the Conqueror. They were a mixture of ethnicities, including early French (originally Franks from Germany) and remnants from the Roman occupation, but strongly Viking settlers and all living in that northwestern area of France.

The settlement of the Norsemen in Normandy obviously caused problems. There was resistance from the local population and the rulers of that area of France. Differences of culture and religion were major problems also. It seems remarkable that the Norsemen leaders from Rollo down to William I worked hard and made tremendous progress in assimilating with the local population and local leaders. They did this sometimes condescendingly, sometimes amicably, and sometimes by force. They wanted to stay.

36 Rognvald Eysteinsson (825–894) m Ragnhild

35 Rollo/Rolf Rognvaldsson, the Viking King (845–931) m Poppa, De Renness (872–??)

Rollo's ancestors were Danish or Norwegian, but it seems most researchers think he was born in More, Norway. He made himself independent from the Norwegian King, Harald, and took up the Viking spirit. With his Viking group he traveled all over the Baltic and the North Sea. Essentially, he was a pirate rover whose army raided Scotland, Ireland, England, Flanders and France. They did not plunder and ravage like many Vikings. Rollo spared and made friends in the areas he conquered. He finally settled on the coast of France, along the Seine River in the area of Rheims, where he and his followers established themselves, first in wintering quarters and later in settlement. Rollo was an aggressive rogue as he attacked the French to acquire more territory. The French government under Charles III (the Simple) gave him land for peace under the Treaty of Saint-Clair-sur-Epte.

Over a period of time Rollo and his people converted from Norse Paganism to Christianity and married into the local population. Rollo married Poppa, the daughter of Berenger, Count of Rennes. It has been called a "more danico" marriage in that it was not a church wedding. We would call it a secular or common-law marriage or even a forced relationship. Such marriages were not always consensual as some spouses were the prizes of war. It was not uncommon for men to have several such wives, since they were not Christian and saw no need for Christian wedding traditions and the related rules of marriage.

34 William I, Long Sword, Duke of Normandy (893–942) m Sprota De Bretagne (911–940)
Not much is known about William I in his younger years. William succeeded his father as Duke of Normandy in about 928. William's wife, Sprota, was a Breton concubine who was captured in war and so his was also a "more danico" marriage. They had a son, Richard. Announcement of Richard's birth was kept from his father, William, for several years. When William finally met his son, he readily accepted him and declared him his heir.

William faced rebellion from some of his people who thought his reign had become too closely identified with the Frankish population. He later fought with Flanders and he was assassinated by the Count of Flanders during a meeting to resolve their conflicts.

33 Richard I, the Fearless, Duke of Normandy (933–996) m 33 Gunnora of Denmark/Gonnor De Crepon, Duchess of Normandy (936–1031).
Richard I was raised in Bayeux and was about 10 years old when his father was killed. King Louis IV of France took control of him. Louis at first gave Richard his position as Duke but later reneged on it. He split the Duchy up, giving control to others and kept Richard in confinement. When he was 14 Richard escaped and joined with Norman leaders. King Harald (Bluetooth) of Denmark sent men to assist Richard. They defeated Louis's forces and captured Louis. Louis was held until he agreed to return Norman control rightfully to Richard as Duke of Normandy.

Richard's first wife, Emma, was the daughter of Hugh, Count of Paris. Richard used this relationship to form and build alliances. Emma died having no children.

Louis continued to foment trouble and several battles were fought, but Richard's leadership prevailed and he received "the Fearless" nickname. Through his leadership and diplomacy, the last 30 years of his reign in Normandy were peaceful. Richard concentrated his efforts on stabilizing control in Normandy rather than territorial expansion. During this time, he established certain relationships with England which later gave his grandson, William, the Conquerer, cause for invasion of England in 1066.

Richard's second wife, Gunnora, is our specific blood connection with the Danes. After many years into their common-law relationship and grown children, they married around 990. Their formal marriage was precipitated by their son, Robert, being proposed as a Bishop, but the church resisted. Without a church marriage, their children were considered illegitimate in the eyes of the church. Therefore, Richard and Gunnora married to legitimize their children which allowed their son to become a bishop. They both were born in Faecamp, Normandy, and also died there.

Richard was known to have many affairs and relationships; one involved a woman named Papia with whom he had a daughter named Papia II Moriton de Normandy (980–1075). Papia II is part of what I call a branch loop. This is where a descendant branch of the family after a few descending generations marries with another descending branch of the family. This loop connects the Dane, Viking, and Norman line with the Welsh line of Chapter 2.

- 33 Richard I (the Fearless) Duke of Normandy (933–996) and Papia I de Crepon (c936–c1031)
- 32 Papia II Moriton de Normandy (c980–c1075) m Gilbert (Gautier) de St. Valery (c977–c1077)
- 31 Richard Fitzgilbert De St. Valery (1002–after1053) m Ada De Hughleville (c1005–c1039)
- 30 Ada De Hughleville (c1039–1114) m Geoffery de Newmarche (1025–1100)
- 29/28 Bernard Newmarche (1075–1133) m 28 Nest Verch Osbern (1082–1163)

This connects the Danes to the Normans, to the Welsh, to the Smiths and myself.

32 Richard II, the Good, Duke of Normandy (963–1027) m Lady Judith of Brittany (982–1017)

As the eldest son, Richard II succeeded his father as Duke of Normandy in 996. In about 1000, Richard II of Normandy and Judith of Brittany were married in a dual wedding exchange alliance in which Judith's brother, Geoffery I of Brittany, married Richard II's sister, Hawise. These were church-sanctioned marriages and held at Mont Saint-Michel.

Geoffrey was 16 years of age at the time. However, he had assumed the title of Duke at about age 8. This was a double marriage alliance between Normandy and Brittany and necessary due to opposing forces pressing on both areas.

Viking attacks, English attacks and also attacks from Burgundy pressed Richard II but he persevered. He attempted to appease the English by giving his sister Emma in marriage to the English King Aethelred. In 1013, when Sweyn Forkedbeard, King of Denmark, invaded England, Aethelred, Emma and their two sons fled to Normandy where Richard II gave them protection. This was a major factor later in his grandson William's claim to the throne of England in 1066.

Richard II, of course, had descended from Vikings generations before. He kept good relations with the Scandinavians and hired them at times as mercenary troops when necessary. He also honored gift commitments made by his great grandfather Rollo, the Viking King, to various Catholic monasteries in France.

Richard II and Judith had six children together. After Lady Judith's death in 1017, Richard II remarried to Poppa of Envermeu with whom he had two children.

31 Robert I, the Magnificent, Duke of Normandy (1000–1035) m Unknown
Before Richard II died he had announced that his oldest son, Richard III, would succeed him. As brothers, Richard III and Robert I had continuously been at odds with each other. When Richard II died and Richard III was anointed, Robert I rebelled with armed force. Richard III laid siege to Falaise, Robert I was defeated and forced to swear allegiance to his brother. Richard's victory was quite short lived, however, since he died within a year and Robert I assumed the position as Duke of Normandy. Robert I reigned for eight years until his death in 1035, while he was on a pilgrimage to Jerusalem.

30 William I, the Conqueror, Duke of Normandy (1027/8–1087) m Matilda of Flanders (1031–1083)
Robert I, the Magnificent, had an illegitimate son, William, born in 1027/8 in Falaise, Normandy, by a mistress named Herleva of Falaise. William, as Robert's only son, was to become Duke upon Robert's death. This occurred only after much disagreement and argument within the nobles. At times he was slanderously called "William, the Bastard" but in spite of the opposition he gradually overcame all to be renamed William, the Conqueror.

He became Duke at eight years of age upon his father's death and faced many challenges to his early reign. His uncle Robert, Archbishop of Rouen, was key to guiding and protecting him as he grew and became more able and powerful. His marriage to Matilda of Flanders greatly assisted William by giving him connections to obtain help and backing from surrounding nobles. By 1060 William had succeeded in subduing or forming alliances with most of his neighbors.

Matilda was the niece and granddaughter of a king of France, as well as a descendant of Charlemagne, which gave William improved stature, compared to his illegitimate beginning. Matilda's ancestry is fully covered in Chapter 5. Their proposed marriage was initially opposed because they were cousins, but that was negotiated aside as they promised to build two churches. Their marriage was very successful with nine or ten children and apparently a good relationship throughout their time together.

William had befriended the childless Edward, the Confessor, King of England and had received a promise of being his successor upon his death. Upon the King's death that didn't happen, and the new Saxon King Harold denied William the throne, which caused William to decide to invade. He built a large naval force and army, invaded and defeated Harold at Hastings in 1066.

Matilda supported William's reign and paid for outfitting his flagship to invade England. During the invasion and the subsequent year which William spent in England getting things under control, Matilda was entrusted to run things in Normandy, which she did very effectively. She also was very interested in the education of their children and employed an Italian educator to teach them.

William spent considerable time in England and had good success in bringing his rule in England solidly under control by 1075. He had difficulty in his later years with some of his continental holdings and also with those troublesome Danes trying to invade England. Upon his death their eldest son, Robert, became Duke of Normandy and their second surviving son, William II Rufus, became King of England.

William I is in our direct line which descends through the line in Chapter 6 — The Plantagenet. But, here our direct line continues through his half-sister, Adelaide.

30 Adelaide of Normandy, of Aumale (c1030–before 1090) m Lambert II, Count of Lens (??–1054)

Robert I, the Magnificent, also had an illegitimate daughter, Adelaide, by an unknown woman. Adelaide was a half-sister of William I the Conquerer. She married three times or I should say was married off three times. When William assumed control and became Duke of Normandy, he sought to build relationships and pledges of fidelity after years of fighting with surrounding dukes and opponents. Marrying his sister off to obtain loyalties was what William did. It was not at all uncommon at that time. Her first marriage was with Enguerrand II, Count of Ponthieu, which gave William an ally to the North, but that marriage was annulled by the Church. A second marriage was arranged with Lambert II, Count of Lens, forming an alliance between Normandy and Boulogne. This second marriage was also short-lived when Lambert was killed in battle at Lille. With a dowery from her marriages, Adelaide settled into a semi-religious retirement. But again, her brother, William, arranged a third marriage with Odo, Count of Champagne.

As a sort of compensation for all this William and his wife Matilda arranged a life tenancy for Adelaide at the abbey of the Holy Trinity in Caen, France. In addition, she accumulated large land holdings and the title of Countess of Aumale.

Adelaide had one child with each of her husbands. By her second husband, Lambert II, she had a daughter, Judith of Lens.

29 Judith of Lens (c1054–c1086) m Waltheof, Earl of Huntington and Northumbria (c1054–1076)

Adelaide's daughter, Judith of Lens, was born in Lens, France, about the same year that her father died, 1054. She was married at age sixteen to Waltheof, a man of means in England. I can only conjecture that her uncle, William I, had a hand in this, giving his niece away in marriage to secure the northern areas of a country he had just conquered.

Waltheof was the last of the important Anglo-Saxon earls in England to remain in power after the invasion of 1066. William I gave Waltheof his niece to marry to keep his loyalty. Judith and Waltheof had three children including a daughter, Maud/Matilda.

However, in 1075 Waltheof was involved in the Revolt of Earls. Judith informed William of her husband's activities and William ordered Waltheof beheaded for his treason.

After Waltheof's death, William tried to marry Judith off again, but she refused and left the country.

28 Maud/Matilda, Countess of Huntington (c1074–c1130) m Simon I, the Crusader, de Saint Liz/Elizabeth (??–c1111)

Maud married Simon I in about 1090. This is the same man whom her mother, Judith, had refused to marry. Maud marrying Simon I somewhat reconciled her mother, Judith, with William. Simon I had come with William on the invasion in 1066. It is interesting to see the numbers of people who came to England and stayed. Of course, they received the bounty of being conquerors and opportunities which that presented. Due to Maud's vast holdings, Simon I was made Earl of Huntington-Northampton and received the "Honour of Huntington." Their lands covered most of eastern England. William at this time traveled extensively throughout England and worked hard to solidify his conquest. To protect themselves from revolt, his supporters built castles throughout the land and Simon built one too.

Chapter 4: The Vikings and Normans (845–1146)

Both Maud and Simon I were descended from Richard II and his wife Judith of Brittany. They were cousins and this is a good example of the family intermarriage prevalent at that time. Simon I also descended from Richard II and Judith through their son, Richard III, and a concubine who had a daughter, Alice/Alix. Alice/Alix married Ranulph (the Rich), Viscount of Bayeau. Their son was Simon I.

Richard II, the Good, Duke of Normandy (963–1027) m Lady Judith of Brittany (982–1017)
Richard III (1001–1027) m Concubine
Alice/Alix (??) m Ranulph de Saint Liz (c1030–1047)
Simon I de Saint Liz (??–c1111) m Maud, Countess of Huntington (c1074–c1130)

After Simon I died, Maud remarried in about 1113 to David, the brother-in-law of King Henry I of England. Through this marriage David gained control of his wife Maud's large estate in addition to his own lands. David became King of Scots in 1124 and ruled until his death in 1153. He was called "the Saint" for his efforts to bring the Catholic church to Scotland to replace the Celtic religions. Maud was the 2nd Countess of Huntington mainly due to her own holdings and later also the Queen of Scots due to her marriage to David.

27 Hugh de Saint Liz/Elizabeth (c1079–c1110) m Hawisia de Ridel (c1083–??)

Not much is known about Hugh and Hawisia, except that he died very young.

26 Emma de Saint Liz/Elizabeth (1110–1146) m Ivo de Newmarche (1096–1146)

See Chapter 2.

This line first connects the Danes, Vikings and Normans through Richard 1 and Gunnora. Then it connects the Vikings, Normans, Franks and Plantagenets through William the Conqueror and Matilda. And lastly it connects the Vikings, Normans, and Welsh through Emma de St. Liz and Ivo de Newmarche. This connection to the Welsh in Chapter 2 is the key link to continue down that line to the Smiths and myself.

Chapter 4: The Vikings and Normans (845–1146)

Photos taken at Viking Ship Museum, Oslo, Norway

Chapter 5

The Franks (580–1087)

The Franks were a group of people who established themselves in the area of western Germany and spread to control the areas west and south to include all of present-day Netherlands, Belgium, Luxembourg, France and parts of Switzerland and northern Italy. The people were a mix of early Middle Easterners, Romans and Balkans who migrated north and west to the area. Frankfort, Germany, still retains its name from those early times of the Franks.

The first organized control of the many kingdoms called Francia or the Kingdom of the Franks began in the 5th century. When Arnulf of Metz and Pepin of Landen merged their families and their forces, they began the Carolingian Empire or dynasty. The name comes from the Latin name for 42 Charles Martel (see 42 below) which is Carolus and was added to name the dynasty at a later date.

45 Saint Arnulf of Metz (582–640) m Doda
As Bishop of Metz, Arnulf had a long family history. Some say it goes back to Flavius Afranius Syagrius in 4th century Rome. Arnulf was made a saint by the Church. Their son, 44 Ansegisel, married Pepin's daughter–see 44 below.

45 Pepin I, the Elder/the Old, of Landen (c580–640) m Itta
Born in Landen of modern-day Belgium, Pepin was the Mayor of the Palace of Austrasia. He was known for wise counsel and good government. Their family was called the Pepinids after him. Through the marriage of their daughter, Begga, the clans of the Pepinids and the Arnulfings were united.

Chapter 5: The Franks (580–1087)

44 Ansegisel of Metz (602/12–before 662/79) m Begga

Their marriage united the two families or clans. Ansegisel served as a Duke and military leader for the King Sigebert. They had three children. Ansegisel was killed by an enemy.

43 Pepin II of Herstal (c635–714) m Alpaida

Pepin II became a military leader and the Mayor of the Palace of Austrasia just as his grandfather, Pepin I, had been. He kept gathering power and control until he was the unofficial ruler of three Frankish kingdoms: Austrasia, Neustria and Burgundy.

Alpaida was his second wife or mistress with whom he had two sons. The older son, Charles, inherited the Mayor title but was opposed by Pepin's first wife's petition for her son and line to become the next Mayor. Charles was able to find favor with the Austrasians and overcame Pepin's first wife's petition.

42 Charles Martel (688–741) m Rotrude of Trier

Charles is recognized as a military leader and statesman who was effective in battle and enabled the Franks to become rulers of all of Gaul. He is criticized for taking Church lands, but did so to fund his armies to repeal Islamic invaders for which he is praised. He arranged that, after his death, his lands be divided into three parts, one for each adult son Carloman, Pepin and Grifo.

41 Pepin, the Short, King of the Franks (714–768) m Bertrada of Laon (??)

Pepin succeeded his father as Mayor of the Palace and reigned over Francia with his older brother, Carloman. Pepin ruled Neustria, Burgundy and Provence while his brother ruled the other areas. In 747 Pepin became sole ruler of the Franks, but had to fight off revolts by other family members. He became King of the Franks in 751 when his brother entered the monastery, but still had to fight off rebellion by his half-brother Grifo.

Pepin had five children by his first wife before she was repudiated. She and the children were sent to a convent.

For his second wife, Pepin married Bertrada and they had eight children. He divided the Kingdom in two for each of his sons Carloman I and Charlemagne.

40 Charlemagne (742–814) m Hildegard of the Vinzgau (757/8–783)

Charlemagne, Charles the Great, Charles I, King of the Franks, Father of Europe, Holy Roman Emperor are among the many names and titles given to him. He was to be co-ruler with his brother, Carloman I, but that changed when Carloman died and Charlemagne became sole king. Charlemagne was very effective in uniting Western Europe for the first time since Roman governance.

Chapter 5: The Franks (580–1087)

Charlemagne had four wives and six concubines and sired eighteen children. Hildegard was his second wife and mother of nine of the eighteen children.

Charlemagne raised his only surviving eldest son Louis to the position of King of the Franks and also co-emperor during his last year/s.

39 Louis, the Pious, (778–840) m Judith of Bavaria (797–843)

Louis, being Charlemagne's son, had big shoes to fill. As King of the Franks and also King of Aquitaine, he had to defend against Muslim invaders on the southern border and he did by driving them well back to Barcelona in Spain. Also, as Emperor of the Carolingians, he sought to reform much of the old pagan habits and associated corruption. And he did so by replacing many people. This of course caused much ill will, which he did manage. Louis, the Pious, was also called Louis, the Fair.

Louis had three sons by his first wife, Ermendgarde, and had announced how he would divide the rule and titles upon his death. Then Ermendgarde died and he was encouraged to remarry. Judith was Louis's second wife, with whom he had two children, one daughter and one son, Charles. All had been fine until Judith bore their son, Charles. When Louis saw fit to announce a redistribution of titles and territory, civil war broke out among the heirs. And not just one but three civil wars. This did not get resolved until after Louis died and the Treaty of Verdun was signed in 843. Even then the family feuding continued for several more years.

38 Charles, the Bald, (823–877) m Ermentrude (823–869)

Charles was not bald; he was actually very hairy. The name refers to him being without land. Being the only son of his father's second wife gave him a limited start, since his three older half-brothers had already been given all the spoils. But before his father died a small territory was carved out for Charles. After one half-brother died, Charles gained more territory until he ruled all of former Roman Gaul. But he endured constant Viking incursions from the north, Muslims from the south and the Bretons on the west. He also was obligated to support Rome and died in the Alps while returning from an expedition to Italy.

Charles and Ermentrude had ten children. Judith of Flanders was their oldest child. Charles gave Judith away in marriage at 12 or 14 years of age to the Wessex King, Aethelwulf, who was visiting. See Chapter 1. The marriage was made to secure an alliance since both kings were under attack by Vikings.

37 Judith of Flanders (c843–870) m Baldwin I, Margrave of Flanders (c830–879)

Being given away in marriage at age twelve or fourteen shocks us, but at the time it seems to have been common. Her father insisted that she be crowned Queen when it was the

Wessex policy for kings not to crown their wives. They were only the wife of the king. Despite this, Judith was crowned Queen. Aethelwulf, King of Wessex, carried his bride off home to Wessex, England, where he died within a year. Judith then married Aethelwulf's son, Aethelbald, which caused a major scandal. Aethelbald also died within two years. She then, as Queen, sold her royal inheritance in England and returned to her father in France. Charles then put her in a monastery with firm instructions as to how she should behave until he decided her future. But instead, she eloped with Baldwin I. Charles was furious and tried to have the Church excommunicate them but Church leaders refused and calmed him down. The end result was that he forgave them and they were remarried in another ceremony. Baldwin was given a northern territory in Flanders to defend against the Vikings. He was expected to fail, but he excelled in this assignment. Flanders is in the coastal area of present-day Belgium. He was made Margrave of Flanders. Margrave is a title given to Princes within the Holy Roman Empire. They apparently had a happy and successful marriage. Judith reigned as the 1st Countess of Flanders. Quite an interesting story. They had three children. Baldwin II was their middle child.

36 Baldwin II, Margrave of Flanders (c865–918) m 36 Aelfthryth of Wessex (877–929)

Baldwin II assumed his position upon his father's death and continued the struggle against Viking raids into Flanders by building a series of wooden fortifications. By marrying Aelfthryth of Wessex, the youngest daughter of Alfred the Great, an Anglo-Flemish alliance was established to further the defenses. Alfred was also fighting off the Vikings. Baldwin's mother, Judith, we must remember, was previously married to Alfred's older brother, Aethelbald, so the alliance was almost a family mutual protection pact. They had four children.

Aelfthryth of Wessex gives us a firm blood connection to our line in Chapter 1: Wessex.

35 Arnulf I, Count of Flanders (890–965) m Adele of Vermandois (915–960)

Arnulf I was named after St. Arnulf of Metz (582–640) (see 45 above) and assumed his position upon his father's death. As the attacks by the Vikings were more defended and subsided, Arnulf turned his attention southward to accrue more territory. Eventually he met strong resistance from the Normans and in the conflict Arnulf's men murdered William Longsword, Duke of Normandy, who of course was Arnulf's cousin.

Arnulf had a daughter with an unknown first wife. Adele was Arnulf's second wife with whom he had five children. She carried a noble heritage descending from both noble Carolingians and Franks.

Chapter 5: The Franks (580–1087)

34 Baldwin III, Count of Flanders (940–962) m Mathilde of Saxony (939–1008)

Baldwin III was the fourth child, but oldest surviving son, so was appointed co-ruler in 958. But Baldwin died in 962 where upon Arnulf I appointed Baldwin's infant son, Arnulf II, to be the next succeeding ruler. During Baldwin's short co-rule he established the woolen industry in Flanders.

Mathilde was from Germany and married three times. Baldwin III was her second husband and they had one child together, Arnulf II. Mathilde had many other children by her first and third husbands.

33 Arnulf II, Count of Flanders (960/1–987) m Rozala of Italy (950/60–1003)

Arnulf II was an infant when his father died and about five when his grandfather Arnulf I died, so even though he was heir, others ruled for him and in the process much of Flanders was taken away. After coming of age at 16 he married Rozala of Italy, daughter of the King of Italy, with whom he had two children. Arnulf II died at the young age of 26. Upon Arnulf II's death, Rozala as Countess of Flanders ruled for their son until he was of age to fully reign. Rozala then remarried to Robert II, King of France.

32 Baldwin IV, Count of Flanders (980–1035) m Ogive of Luxembourg (995–1035)

Being protected by his mother, Rozala, until of age gave Baldwin IV a foundation to assume his reign. Instead of continuing to fight for territory southward, he turned to the east pressing successfully to expand into Zeeland and other areas.

He married Ogive of Luxembourg with whom he had one son, Baldwin V. Ogive died and he remarried to Eleanor of Normandy, with whom he had a daughter, Judith.

31 Baldwin V, Count of Flanders (1012–1067) m St. Adela of France (1009–1079)

Baldwin V married Adela, daughter of Robert II, King of France. He had differences with his father, Baldwin IV, but they were resolved and he inherited his title upon the death of his father. Baldwin joined forces against the Holy Roman Emperor, Henry III, but lost battles and some territory. After Henry's death things stabilized. Later, Baldwin married off his son to merge and regain some of the territory that had been lost.

He gave sanctuary to Queen Emma of England when she was exiled, supplying security and entertainment. Baldwin supported the King of France, but also supported William I, Duke of Normandy, since their daughter was married to William I. Baldwin probably operated as an international envoy. He was certainly assisted by his wife, Adela, in these endeavors.

Adela was the second daughter of Robert II, King of France and Constance of Arles and should not be confused with others by that name. She was first married in 1027 to Richard

III, Duke of Normandy, who died shortly thereafter. She married Baldwin V in 1028. She worked with Baldwin on church reforms and established colleges and abbeys. She also assisted her husband with international diplomacy. After Baldwin died, she entered a convent in Ypres and was later given sainthood.

30 Matilda of Flanders (1031–1083) m William I, the Conqueror, Duke of Normandy (1027/8–1087)
Matilda's Frankish heritage and widespread royal family as shown here was a major help to her husband, William.

See William I and Matilda in Chapters 4 and 6. This provides us with a major bloodline connection to the Plantagenet in Chapter 6.

Chapter 6

The Plantagenet to Smith (1027–2021)

After invading and conquering England in 1066, William ruled both England and the Normandy area of France. But he let each country manage separately and for the most part continue their customary dislike for each other. This set up, or let's say allowed to continue, a belligerence between the two countries which lasted for the next 500 years.

The Norman takeover of England changed things, but it seems to me that they had been changing continuously and would continue to change. The English had been fighting among themselves and against foreign invaders for centuries. After 1066 and the arrival of the Normans, there were the Plantagenets, the Wars of the Roses, the Tudors, the Hanovarians, the Magna Carta and the wars with the French, the conquest of empire, the World Wars, the European Union and now Brexit — a series of governmental changes and conflicts that have never stopped. Perhaps that's the way the world turns. Along the way our family members continued to spread their genes and live lives as best they could — as we all try to do.

However, the Norman invasion of England in 1066 was different and a very major change. It created a rather large migration to England and a transformation within England by these new leaders and followers in their midst. It also explains why my DNA shows only 12% British ancestry, even though more than 90 percent of my known ancestors who migrated to America came directly from Great Britain. We have family members in several branches showing birth in France and death in England. Did they come with William in 1066 or follow afterward? We think of America as a melting pot, but England was a melting pot for centuries before Europeans were even aware that North America existed.

Chapter 6: The Plantagenet to Smith (1027–2021)

This line continues from the Normans in Chapter 4 and Franks in Chapter 5 through William I (the Conqueror) and Matilda to their son Henry I, King of England, and then into the Plantagenet family for 331 years before continuing through other family names down to the Smith family and myself in America.

I am indebted in this chapter to a great resource, a book titled *Plantagenet Ancestry of Seventeenth Century Colonists* by David Faris. The book is a thorough encyclopedia of Plantagenet Ancestry and is so logically organized and helpful in understanding the complexity of these royal family relationships.

The Plantagenet family was a complex group. Through marriage, alliances and belligerence they maintained royal power throughout western Europe for quite some time. Their relationships were very strategic and they often intermarried, which creates multiple genetic lines and complicates orderly genealogy research — at least for me. I have added the Plantagenet surname to some, where applicable, for clarity.

Although the Plantagenets go back many generations in Europe they were not recognized as a family under that name until Geoffery of Anjou married Matilda/Maud, daughter of Henry I, King of England. In fact, I read where historians only started using the Plantagenet name in the late 17th century. However, Richard of York did begin using it in the 15th century to distinguish his lineal heritage.

30 William I, the Conqueror, Duke of Normandy (1027/8–1087) m Matilda of Flanders (1031–1083)

William I, with solid support from his wife, Matilda, started this line by invading England and making their son Henry I, King of England. Their granddaughter marrying Geoffery Plantagenet established it.

29 Henry I, King of England (c1068–1135) m Matilda of Scotland, Court of Argon (1080–1118)

Henry was the youngest and fourth son of William I and Matilda. He became king upon the death of his older brother William II Rufus who was not liked by the English. Henry I was born in England and married Matilda of Argon/Edith of Scotland who was the daughter of Malcolm III King of Scotland. This endeared Henry to the English population and enabled him to continue solidifying the control of Great Britain begun by his father. Matilda was never crowned "Queen," but was known as the "Good Queen."

However their two sons died so their daughter Matilda was designated his successor. This caused great consternation — that a woman would dare be allowed to become the ruler. So, when Henry died the Council gave the throne to Henry's nephew, Stephen, a grandson of William I. Civil war resulted.

Chapter 6: The Plantagenet to Smith (1027–2021)

28 Matilda/Maud of England, the Empress, (1102–1167) m Geoffrey Plantagenet (1113–1151)

Matilda/Maud married Geoffrey who is considered the first of the Plantagenets. Geoffrey was from Anjou and inherited the title of Duke. Matilda was in line to become the first queen of England; however, those in power did not feel a woman could properly reign, so they crowned Stephen instead.

Forces loyal to Matilda were irate at Stephen getting the Throne and so they invaded England. Their forces captured Stephen. The end result was that Stephen's people agreed that, in exchange for freeing Stephen, they would allow Matilda's son, Henry II, to become King of England when Stephen died.

27 Henry II Plantagenet, King of England (1133–1189) m Eleanor of Aquitaine (1122–1204)

Henry II did become King of England when King Stephen died. His reign was marked by many accomplishments. Among them was the installation of trial by jury of your peers in a system of courts in each county shire. Prior to Henry's reign, each Sheriff ruled as both the law and the court, in his shire, with total power under the King. This was in addition to the Sheriffs having full authority to levy and collect taxes. Henry II revised the power of the Sheriffs. He divided authority and responsibilities between civil administration, the law and the courts.

Eleanor of Aquitaine's marriage to Henry II brought with it control of large areas of France which extended their vast lands. Henry spent less than half of his 34-year reign in England.

Henry II put the church under civil law which caused great argument between him and his close friend Thomas Becket. A misspoken declaration of "Will no one rid me of this turbulent priest?" caused followers to murder Thomas Becket. For this Henry II mourned and did penance probably the rest of his life.

26 John Plantagenet, King of England (1167–1216) m Isabelle d'Anglolene (1188–1246)

John was Henry II's youngest son and became acting King of England when his brother, King Richard I, the Lionheart, was away on Crusade. Richard was only in England less than one year of his ten-year reign. John is known as a wicked person, a bad king and was responsible for the Magna Carta being drawn up and he being forced to sign it. The Magna Carta brought some civility however badly John ignored it.

Chapter 6: The Plantagenet to Smith (1027–2021)

25 Henry III Plantagenet, King of England (1207–1272) m Eleanor of Provence (1217–1291)

Henry III became King at age 9 upon his father's death. At age 28 he married Eleanor, who was 12 at the time. By that marriage he attempted — with only limited success — to recover the holdings in France which his father had lost.

Henry III did succeed in restoring some semblance of order to the Kingdom of England in spite of Baronial uprisings. He established the Parliament with the two houses for lord and commoner representation. But, members were selected and called to Parliament by the King–not elected.

24 Edward I Plantagenet, Longshanks, King of England (1239–1307) m Eleanor of Castile (1244–1290)

Edward I was on the 9th Crusade to the Holy Land when informed his father had died and he was the king. His return took two years before he was crowned. His reign is noted for his attention to improving royal administration, legal reform of the common law and making the Parliament permanent.

By force and good management Edward brought Wales solidly into the fold of England. Pledging to the Welsh that they would have a Welsh-speaking leader, he arranged for his first son, Edward of Carnarvon, to be born there. To this day the first son of the King of England is titled the Prince of Wales.

Edward I is a key connection in linking our family. See Edward I in chapters 7, 8 and 9.

23 Edward II Plantagenet, King of England (1284–1327) m Isabella of France (1292–1358)

Edward II inherited much unfinished business from his father. War continued with Scotland and there were baronial uprisings as well as continued feuding with France over English holdings in France. His marriage to Isabella, the daughter of Phillip IV, King of France, was arranged to encourage good relations. Edward was criticized for not subduing the Scots, taxing highly to support wars, and maybe some ineptitude also. After having four children together, Isabella came to despise Edward for favoring an alliance with the de Spenser family. She and her lover, Roger Mortimer, an exiled Baron, raised forces to invade from France, execute the de Spensers, depose Edward and become the de facto rulers. Edward was sequestered in Berkeley Castle. He was forced to agree to his son becoming king and was later murdered by Mortimer.

Chapter 6: The Plantagenet to Smith (1027–2021)

22 Edward III Plantagenet, King of England (1312–1377) m Philippe de Hainault (1311–1369)

Edward III was crowned at age 14 when his father was deposed, but then had to lead a coup at age 17 to gain control of his reign from Mortimer. Mortimer was then executed.

Reigning for 50 years, Edward III was known for his prowess in war. He fought against the Scots and their French supporters in a series of altercations that ultimately evolved into the Hundred Years War with France. See Chapter 8.

21 Lionel Plantagenet, Duke of Clarence (1338–1368) m Elizabeth de Burgh (1332–1386)

Lionel was born in Antwerp and by marriage to Elizabeth inherited lands in Ireland. He was conferred the title of Duke of Clarence, moved to Ireland and attempted to administer Ireland by establishing a parliament. After very little success he returned to England. They had one child, Phillipa.

20 Phillipa Plantagenet, of Clarence (1355–1382) m Edmund de Mortimer, 3rd Earl of March (1351/2–1381)

It is somewhat ironic that Phillipa married a Mortimer when her grandfather had executed his grandfather. Phillipa was the 5th Countess of Ulster and continued the Irish connection. It is through Phillipa and her descent from Edward III that the Yorkist elements later claimed their right to the crown in the Wars of the Roses.

19 Lady Elizabeth de Mortimer (1370/1–1417) m Sir Henry Percy (1364–1403)

Elizabeth and Henry were both descendants of Edward I. This is so typical of the confused relationships of leading families of that time. The Percy families had supported the kings for several decades. Sir Henry (called "Harry Hotspur"), held the title of 4th Lord Percy, and also was rewarded as Earl of Northumberland. As a knight, he fought for King Henry IV against the Scots and in Wales, but then apparently fell out with the king. Henry Percy accused King Henry IV of not delivering on promises made after their hard-fought victories. He led forces against the king which led to a meeting at Shrewsbury where they parlayed and exchanged insults before engaging their forces in combat, where Sir Henry was slain. See Chapter 8.

18 Sir Henry Percy (1393–1455) m Eleanor Neville (1398–1472)

After his father's death, Henry became the 5th Lord. This Henry Percy continued rebellion against King Henry IV. He remained in hiding in Scotland until King Henry V came to the throne in 1413. King Henry V wanted to reconcile with the Percy family and provided for

Chapter 6: The Plantagenet to Smith (1027–2021)

Sir Henry Percy to regain the title of 2nd Earl of Northumberland by grant of Parliament. Sir Henry supported the King in the wars in France but his main assignment was to guard the border lands in defense against Scotland, which he did. King Henry VI assumed the throne upon his father's death in 1422 and Sir Henry Percy worked in many capacities under the new king. As King Henry VI's reign progressed toward eventual civil war, the Percys and the Nevilles began to have differences and to choose sides. In general, the Percys were for Lancaster and the Nevilles for York, but with many changes, twists and turns. As a knight, Sir Henry Percy fought for the Lancaster forces in the battle of St. Albans where he was slain. See Chapter 8.

17 Sir Henry Percy (1421–1461) m Eleanor Poynings (c1422–c1484)
Henry became the 6th Lord Henry Percy, 3rd Earl of Northumberland. He was also summoned to Parliament as Lord Poynings, a title he acquired by marriage to Eleanor whose father held the title until his death. Henry became a leading Lancasterian during the Wars of the Roses. As a knight at the battle of Wakefield he led the central section of the Lancasterian Army. He was killed in the battle of Towton. This was the fourth Sir Henry Percy in succession to be slain in battle. See Chapter 8.

16 Margaret Percy (1437–1486) m Sir William Gascoigne V (1445–c1486)
Margaret and William were both descendants of King Edward I. They had six sons and seven daughters. Sir William was a knight and the Justice of the Peace for West Riding, Yorkshire.

15 Elizabeth Gascoigne (1471–c1559) m Sir George Tailboys (c1467–1538)
Elizabeth was George's second wife. They had one son and four daughters. George was Sheriff of Lincolnshire. He was knighted at the Battle of Blackheath in 1497 and given the title 9th Lord Kyme de Jure. In 1517, he was judged a lunatic and taken into custody. All his lands were taken into custody.

14 Anne Tailboys (1520–1566) m Sir Edward Dymoke (1508–1566)
Edward was Sheriff of Lincolnshire and a knight as was his father-in-law. They were descended from Edward I, King of England. Edward Dymoke was "Champion" at the coronations of King Edward VI, Queen Mary and Queen Elizabeth. His father, Robert Dymoke, was Champion to Kings Richard III, Henry VII and Henry VIII. This demonstrates the nepotism which was very common with those in power.

The position of King's Champion as explained as follows in Wikipedia:
"The Dymoke family of the Manor of Scrivelsby in the parish of Horncastle in

Chapter 6: The Plantagenet to Smith (1027–2021)

Lincolnshire holds the feudal hereditary office of King's Champion. The functions of the Champion are to ride into Westminster Hall at the coronation banquet and challenge all comers who might impugn the King's title.

A member of the Dymoke family, Lieutenant Colonel John Dymoke served as the Queen's Champion at the Coronation of Queen Elizabeth II in 1953.

13 Frances Dymoke (1539–c1610) m Sir Thomas Windebank (1548–1607)
Thomas had the good fortune to be hired by a neighbor, to travel with their son through Europe, to keep him straight and teach him French. Upon their return and with that connection he became a clerk of the Signet to Queen Elizabeth and to King James I, who knighted him. He also was occasionally Clerk of the Privy Council.

12 Helen Windebank (1596–c1656) m Rev. Richard Denton (1603–1662)
Richard was born in Yorkshire, England, and ordained a priest after studying and teaching at St. Catherine's, Cambridge, which was a breeding ground for Reform and Puritan thought. After several years as a priest in Lancashire and Halifax he split from the Church of England and joined the reform movement. Around 1638 to 1640 he and his family joined a reform minded Puritan group coming to America. He preached in Watertown, Massachusetts, then later in Weathersfield and Stamford, Connecticut. In 1644 he moved with his followers to Hempstead, Long Island, New York, presumably to escape the Puritan restrictions in New England on religion and political freedoms. In early years, many towns in New England would only allow Puritans to vote. Reverend Richard Denton, as part of the reform movement, moved to avoid the restrictions placed upon him and his followers. In Christ's First Presbyterian Church, Hempstead, New York, he established what is recognized as the first Presbyterian Church in America. Reverend Richard Denton is credited, by many, with establishing the Presbyterian Church in America–even though the formal organization of the Presbyterian Church was many years forthcoming.

Reverend Richard Denton was an extraordinary preacher. While short in stature and with only one eye, in the pulpit "he was nine feet tall." He championed baptism for all, which at that time was only allowed for children of church members.

After many years in America, Richard returned to England in 1658 due to financial hardship, his wife's health issues and to claim a 400-pound inheritance from a friend. He continued living in England, doing writing, until his death in 1662 in Hempstead, Essex, England.

Richard's wife, Helen, is credited with bearing all of his children, although very little is known of her. This lack of information establishes alternative theories of her death and his remarrying, which I think is very probable.

Chapter 6: The Plantagenet to Smith (1027–2021)

Richard and his wife had between eight and eleven children according to varying sources. All of his children were born in England, came with him and remained in America after he and his wife left. Richard and his children are credited with the origin of most all the Denton families in America. Also see Denton in Chapter 27.

11 Samuel Denton (1631–1713) m Mary Rock Smith (1640–1713)
Samuel was born in Halifax, England, and came to America with his parents at the age of four. Mary was born in Dorchester, Massachusetts. Her father, John Rock Smith, was born in Halifax, England, and died in Hempstead, Long Island, New York. Presumably he was part of the group of followers of the Rev. Richard Denton. Samuel and Mary married in Hempstead and had eleven children. They owned 240 acres which presumably they farmed, but he is also listed as an administrator.

10 Abraham Denton (1675–1729) m Martha Thorne (1679–1730)
Abraham was born in Hempstead, New York, and moved to Orange County, New York

9 Martha Denton (1710–1763) m Hezekiah Gale (1710–1784)
Hezekiah was born in Jamaica, New York, and moved to Orange County, New York.
   The Gale family was from Bedfordshire, England. Edmund Gale arrived in America in 1630, settling in Cambridge, Massachusetts. Edmund's son, Abel, moved with his family to Long Island and then to Orange County, New York. Hezekiah is Abel's grandson. See Gale in Chapter 27.

8 Hannah Gale (1731–1817) m Derrick Smith (1730–1790)
We arrive at Derrick Smith in America, my 5th great grandfather. See Smith in Chapter 14.
   This provides a 50-generation direct bloodline from Cerdic in Wessex to the Franks, to the Normans, to the Welsh and down to the Smiths and myself.
   And it also provides another 50-generation direct bloodline from Cerdic in Wessex to the Franks to the Plantagenets and down to the Smiths and myself.

Chapter 7

Edward I to Spencer to Smith (1239–2021)

This chapter shows another continuous bloodline back to Edward I. While this is a direct connection, it also illustrates the intertwining of relationships that existed within the elite families in power.

This line is interesting because it establishes our connection to Cedric in only 48 generations, since the line to Edward I is only 22 generations.

22/24 Edward I Plantagenet, (Longshanks) King of England (1239–1307) m Eleanor of Castile (1244–1290)

See Edward I Plantagenet in Chapter 6.

21 Elizabeth Plantagenet of Rhuddlan (1282–1316) m Humphrey de Bohun (c1276–1322)

As a daughter of the king, Elizabeth was contracted, at the early age of about three, to marry John I, Count of Holland. They were actually married when Elizabeth was fifteen, but she refused to go to Holland with her husband. After a while, Elizabeth's father took her with him on an extended trip, through European countries, intending to end up in Holland with John. During the few months of their travel, and before their arrival in Holland, John died.

Elizabeth married a second time at age twenty to Humphrey de Bohun, 4th Earl of Hereford, 3rd of Essex and Constable of England, with whom she had around ten children. Elizabeth received Powderham Castle as a wedding gift.

Humphrey, or Hereford as he is sometimes called, as Constable under Edward I, engaged in many campaigns in Scotland. His lands were adjacent to those of Robert Bruce. The Bruce and Bohun families had a good relationship for years. Bruce alternated allegiance for and against the King of England. In the end he was defeated by the English and Bohun was awarded some of his forfeited lands.

Humphrey was saddened and depressed after the death of his wife, Elizabeth. Six years later, at the Battle of Bouroughbridge, Humphrey insisted on leading the charge against forces holding the bridge and was slain.

20 Margaret Bohun (1311–1391) m Sir Hugh de Courtenay (1303–1377)
Margaret Bohun, Countess of Devon, is my favorite heroine among my female ancestors based upon the history of events during her life. As a granddaughter of the King, she was contracted for marriage before the age of four. Her mother died when she was six. She became an orphan at eleven when her father was slain at Bouroughbridge. In spite of this, she did inherit the lands originally promised in her dowery. She and her siblings received a classical education and she became a scholarly collector of books. Per the contract, Margaret was married at age fourteen and bore seventeen children with her husband Hugh. Their children include an Archbishop of Canterbury and four knights. It certainly must have been a busy castle to have so many under foot. Winston Churchill was a descendant.

Hugh de Courtenay was contracted, at about age eleven, to marry Margaret, and apparently it was a successful union. He inherited the title of Earl of Devon and held various positions including being summoned to Parliament in 1337. He served in several battles alongside King Edward III during the Hundred Years' War.

Margaret and Hugh are buried in the Cathedral of Exeter.

Among their children, daughter Margaret provides the following line which is not our bloodline, but illustrates the continual connectivity of these people.

Margaret Courtenay (1328–1395) m John Cobham (1320–1408)
Margaret was the eldest daughter and married at a young age. She and John were both minors. As the 3rd Baron of Cobham, John was given a license to build a Cooling Castle at Cowling, Kent, which was their family seat. He was called to Parliament in 1355 and served in various expeditions against the French. John led an impeachment action against some of the King's favorites. And then later he was impeached himself and sentenced to be hanged. But, he was pardoned on condition of banishment to Jersey.

Joan Cobham (1340–1388) m John de La Pole (1335–1380)
Joan and John were married around 1362. Not much is known of them, however their La

Pole descendants were very much involved in the Wars of the Roses on the York side during the next century.

Joan de La Pole (1372–1434) m Sir Reynold/Reginald de Braybrooke (1356–1426)
Joan was married very young and had five husbands. She had the misfortune to lose four husbands before marrying one who did outlive her.

Reynold or Reginald was husband number two, whom she married while she was still underage. They had two sons and one daughter. Only the daughter survived to adulthood and marriage. Reynold was a knight and was wounded in battle during an attack on a citadel in Sluys, Flanders (present day Belgium). He died a few months later in 1405 from the wounds received in the battle.

Reynold or Reginald might be the same person or may have been two different people depending upon whom you believe. Much more study is needed here.

This line connects to Reynold's or Reginald's brother, our Gerard III Braybrooke, in Chapter 2.

Our line connects from daughter Elizabeth as follows:

19 Elizabeth De Courtenay (??–1395) m Sir Andrew Luttrell (before 1330–1378)
Elizabeth was one of her mother's seventeen children. Elizabeth and Andrew made a pilgrimage to Santiago in Spain with an entourage of 24 others. Elizabeth served in attendance to her cousin, Edward, the Black Prince, and his wife, Joan.

18 Hugh Luttrell (before 1364–1428) m Katherine Beaumont (??–1435)

17 Elizabeth Luttrell (??–??) m John Stratton (c1390–c1439)

16 Lady Elizabeth Stratton (c1410–1485) m John Hotoft Andrews, Sheriff of London (1410–1456)
John was a lawyer and admitted to Lincoln Inn in 1453 to practice the law. They most probably lived in London. She died there.

15 Lady Margaret Elizabeth Anne Andrews (1445–1485) m Thomas Windsor de Merrill (1440–1485)
Thomas was a constable at Windsor Castle. His parents were Miles Windsor and Joan Greene.

Chapter 7: Edward I to Spencer to Smith (1239–2021)

14 Sir John (The Elder) Merrill (1470–1529) and Anne Belchum (1475–1528)
Sir John and Anne were born, married, lived and died in Bedfordshire, England.

13 Ann Agnes Merrill (1509–1560) m John Spencer II (1505–1558)
John and Ann also were born, married, lived and died in Bedfordshire, England.

12 Michael Spencer (1531–1599) m Elizabeth Agnes Limer (1540–1599)
Michael and Elizabeth Agnes were born, lived and died in Bedfordshire, England.

11 Gerard Spencer I (1576–1646) m Alice Whitebread (1583–1628)
Gerald and Alice were born, married, lived and died in Bedfordshire, England.

10 Ens. Gerard (Jared) Spencer II (1614–1685) m Hannah Joanis Hills (1618–1692)
See Chapter 25.

9 Sgt. Nathaniel William Spencer Jr. (1658–1722) m Lydia Bailey (1658–1728)
See Chapter 25.

8 Daniel Spencer (1694–1769) m Abigail Clark (1715–1771)
See Chapter 25.

7 Elias Spencer (1750–1828) m Abigail Sexton (c1750–after1828)
See Chapter 25.

6 Sally Spencer (1783–1852) m William Prout (1779–1822)
See Sally Spencer and William Prout in Chapter 21.

5 Ruth Lucrecia Prout (1821–1898) m Watrous Ives Miller (1822–1885)
For Ruth Prout and Watrous Miller see Chapter 18: Miller.

4 Virginia Ruth Miller (1848–1939) m Halsey Horatio Blake (1843–1930)
See Part 3, Chapter 18: Miller and Chapter 16: Blake.

3 Genevieve Blake (1879–1933) m Charles Herbert Smith (1878–1967)
See Part 3, Chapter 16: Blake and Chapter 14: Smith.

Chapter 7: Edward I to Spencer to Smith (1239–2021)

2 Charles Clement Smith (1904–1980) m Carolyn Clark Kaddeland (1907–1966)
See Part 3, Chapter 14: Smith and Chapter 15: Kaddeland.

1 Watson Christen Smith (1936–) m Linda Knoop (1939–)
See Parts 5 and 6.

Chapter 8

Wars of the Roses (1339–1509)

In the beginning of the fifteenth century, England and France were involved in the Hundred Years' War. As that series of conflicts wound down the English found that they could continue fighting–among themselves. This was partly a result of the disastrous loss of lands across the channel and of course placing the blame on others for their loss of fortune and family members.

The Wars of the Roses, between the House of Lancaster (the red rose) and the House of York (the white rose) had been brewing for several years, but according to most historians it began with the first Battle of St Albans in 1455 and lasted until 1487.

Our family's connections and involvement in the events leading up to and during those years of the Wars of the Roses sparked my interest. My Smith family direct-line connection to the Plantagenets is discussed in Chapter 6. The Plantagenets were the royal family at that time and the wars ended their rule. The Plantagenets discussed here were mostly cousins. Several were direct line, others not. But most all were swept up in the political wars of the time over land, money, power and who controlled the throne of England.

This discussion also involves two family lines, the Nevilles and the Percys who were both major powers during this time. And they were also our ancestors. Some of them were direct line and others were cousins. Originally the Nevilles and the Percys were friendly neighbors residing a few miles apart in northern England. They even intermarried. Later the families started squabbling and became bitter political opponents. They supported various kings, sometimes on the Lancaster side and then on the York side. Sometimes the families were on the same side and sometimes on opposite sides. At some times, members of the same family found themselves on opposite sides. This is very confusing and very hard to follow. Suffice it to say, the Wars of the Roses was a gigantic family feud which involved many of our ancestors and resulted in the deaths of thousands of people who had nothing to gain from it.

Chapter 8: Wars of the Roses (1339–1509)

We begin with Edward III, King of England (1312–1377) from Chapter 6. Edward III's grandfather and wives had 17 children. His parents had 4 children. Edward III and his wife, Phillippe, had 12 children. If all their siblings had done similarly, the mathematics show 816 Plantagenet children vying for position and power within the Royal family not even to mention all the other Plantagenet cousins from previous generations who sought their share of power and position. We can readily see the coming of conflict.

Because of their Norman heritage, the Plantagenets and their followers still had most of their original family holdings in France and collectively laid claim to the throne of France. Edward III began the Hundred Years' War with France by reinforcing and expanding control of the Plantagenet holdings in France. They wanted it all.

Edward's grandson and successor, Richard II (1367–1400), became King of England at ten years of age. He quickly matured into leadership, but faced difficult times with multiple political sides offering different counsel as he matured–and afterwards also. He eventually reached a treaty with the French, but later was deposed due to claims of instability and unworthiness. Henry Bolingbroke, who also was a grandson of Edward III, was crowned King Henry IV.

Henry IV (1367–1413), King of England, founded the Lancaster House (the white rose) of the Plantagenet family because of his mother's Lancastrian heritage. He had a strong supporter in Ralph Neville (1364–1425), 1st Earl of Westmorland, who married his half-sister, Joan Beaufort (1374–1440).

The Neville family was native to England but came to noticeable leadership in the government only after the Norman invasion of 1066. They were one of only a few families that retained their lands which was probably partly due to their location in the northern part of the country. The family originally was centered in the county of Durham and had steadily gained land and influence in the late 14th century. By marriage they also accrued more land and titles. There were several branches of the Neville family, but mainly they were in two groups, descended from Ralph Neville's two wives. The Nevilles of Raby were descended from Ralph's first wife, Margaret Stafford, who descended from Edward I through his daughter, Joan of England. And then the Nevilles of Middleham were descended from Ralph's second wife, Joan Beaufort, who descended from Edward I through Edward III and John of Gaunt. The Nevilles were very intertwined on both sides.

Ralph Neville (1364–1425) had sons by his first wife, Margaret Stafford before she died. Joan Beaufort (1374–1440) was Ralph Neville's second wife and a pivotal figure in this complex family. Joan was one of four children born out of wedlock to John of Gaunt and Katherine Swynford. John and Katherine later married thereby legitimizing the children. The children were given the surname Beaufort which came from former French lands owned by John. John of Gaunt was the third of five sons of Edward III. As a Prince and

Chapter 8: Wars of the Roses (1339–1509)

Duke of Lancaster he was an influential statesman and military leader.

Ralph Neville (1364–1425) and Joan Beaufort (1374–1440) had nine sons and five daughters. Their son Richard Neville (1400–1460) was given land and made Earl of Salisbury, much to the objection of Ralph's sons by his earlier marriage to Margaret and the feud began. The family was strongly supporting their Lancastrian heritage and, therefore, Richard opposed the Yorkists. Richard, as Earl of Salisbury, worked with the Percys and was later killed at the Battle of Wakefield. Richard's son, Richard Neville (1428–1471), the Kingmaker and Earl of Warwick, married Anne Beauchamp and strongly supported the York side. And, so, the wars went on, with the Nevilles fighting on both sides.

The Percy family also were initially supportive of Henry IV on the Lancastrian side. They fought alongside Henry Bolingbroke (before he was king) against King Richard II and later with then King Henry IV in Wales against the rebellion of Owain Glyndwr. But then they became opponents when promises of rewards of lands for battle performance were not kept. Henry "Hotspur" Percy (1364–1403) publicly renounced allegiance to Henry IV, calling him out for false promises–perjury. In turn, Henry Percy was charged with perjury for various questionable infractions. Henry Percy gathered a force which met King Henry at the Battle of Shrewsbury in 1403, where Henry Percy was killed. Henry IV and his son, Henry V were both wounded in the battle. Henry "Hotspur" Percy's body was dismembered and his head put up on the north gate in York. Henry Percy being slain in the battle caused a bad relationship to continue between the king and the Percy family. (Also see Henry Percy (1393–1455) in Chapter 6.)

Henry V (1386–1422) came to the throne, as a Lancastrian, upon his father, Henry IV's death in 1413. Even before he came to the throne Henry V was a warrior. He was only 16 when he had led an army during the battle of Shrewsbury where he was wounded with an arrow in the side of his face.

Henry V endeavored to rule a united England, letting past sins be forgiven. In this regard he restored lands and family honors to the Percys by making Percy's son, Henry Percy (1393–1455) the 2nd Earl of Northumberland and some say obtained their loyalty to the Lancastrian side. The Percy family still retains title in Northumberland to this day. Henry V's reign was relatively short but he is known for several things including his victory at Agincourt utilizing long bow archery against French forces and establishing English as the official language. English was decreed for the government and promoted throughout the country.

A significant rebellion effort, called the Southampton Plot, was put down. This plot again involved some of the Percys which again shows the splits within the families. But at this point Henry Percy (1393–1455), 2nd Earl of Northumberland, remained supportive of King Henry V and the Lancastrian side.

Chapter 8: Wars of the Roses (1339–1509)

Henry V died young from an illness contracted during his campaign in France. Some describe it as dysentery; others say possible heat stroke from wearing armor in the hot sun.

Henry VI (1421–1471), a Lancastrian, came to power at eight months of age upon Henry V's death. Others ran the government until he was of age to assume control at sixteen. During those years, divisions began to build in England and the situation in France was deteriorating. Henry was not the strong forceful leader his father was. He was shy and passive and occasionally mentally unstable. He sought peace and to that end married Margaret of Anjou, the daughter of the French King Charles VII. Upon Charles's death, Henry, through his wife's heritage, and English control of areas of France, became the only king to rule both as King of England and King of France. But his reign was short-lived. Continued unrest in England, multiple battles lost in France and his wife's dominating efforts to favor France led Henry to basically crumble and become unfit to rule. Henry's periods of instability resulted in his Queen, Margaret of Anjou, effectively running the country of England and what they still held in France. They had lost military campaigns in France, which allowed French factions to regain control and rule France.

In England there was still considerable unhappiness with so much loss of life, power and treasure during the Hundred Years' War. Add to that the loss of lands across the channel in continental Europe, and you have perfect fuel for a royal family feud and an opening for the opposition. The wars between the House of Lancaster, the Red Rose, and the House of York, the White Rose, had been smoldering for several years, but the beginning was the Battle of St Albans in 1455.

Richard, 3rd Duke of York (1411–1460) was Henry VI's nearest adult relative and had fomented opposition to Henry VI including perpetual rebellion and outright civil war activities. While the Battle of St Albans was a comparatively small battle, it was decisive and the Duke of York's forces defeated the Lancastrian forces of Henry VI. Henry VI was captured by the Yorkists and held captive for a while and then released. Henry Percy, 2nd Earl of Northumberland, was killed in the battle fighting on the Lancastrian side. (Also see Henry Percy (1393–1455) in Chapter 6.)

Richard Neville, 16th Earl of Warwick, was an ardent ally and supporter of Richard, Duke of York. At the same time his father, Richard Neville, 5th Earl of Salisbury, supported the Lancastrians, illustrating how families sometimes split to support opposing sides. Things went on in a confused state for a few years until 1460.

The daughter of Ralph Neville (1364–1425) and Joan Beaufort (1374–1440) — Cicely Neville (1415–1495) — had married Richard, 3rd Duke of York, and two of their sons were possibly in line to become king.

In October 1460, Parliament enacted the Act of Accord by which Richard, 3rd Duke of York, was again appointed Lord Protector, king in all but name, and granted authority to govern the country. The act also provided that Richard's line would actually inherit the throne upon Henry's death. Henry in his weakened condition accepted this. Richard did not have sufficient support to become king. Henry was still king.

The contest continued until December 1460 at the battle of Wakefield where Lancastrian forces prevailed. Henry Percy, 3rd Earl of Northumberland, led the central section of the Lancastrian forces. Richard, 3rd Duke of York, was killed. The promise of the future crown being passed to Richard's son, Edward of March, was fulfilled.

Margaret, the wife of Henry VI, refused to accept this, wanting the throne for their son, Edward. This led to the Battle of Towton in 1461, the largest battle ever fought on English soil, with 28,000 deaths and the decisive defeat of Henry VI's forces. Henry Percy (1421–1461), 3rd Earl of Northumberland, was killed in the battle fighting for the Lancastrian side. As a result of this battle many things happened.

Edward of March (1442–1483) took the throne in 1461 to become Edward IV, King of England. The Yorkists were now fully in power, with the support of the Nevilles. Ralph Neville, Earl of Warwick, became the second richest man in England after the king. He was given the nickname "the Kingmaker."

Since Henry Percy, 3rd Earl of Northumberland, and several other Percys were killed in the battle, the Percy family was defeated as a major political power and influence. The Nevilles were still viable on both sides.

Queen Margaret had taken refuge in France, but continued to rally forces, retaking power in 1470 and reinstalling Henry VI in power. It turned out to be a short-lived and highy contested recovery of the throne. Forces built up against Henry VI, resulting in the Battle of Tewkesbury in 1471 which was again a decisive victory for the Yorkists. Margaret was captured and imprisoned. Henry VI's son, Edward, was executed on the battlefield. And Henry VI was imprisoned in the Tower of London, where he died, some say murdered. The Yorkists prevailed and Edward IV resumed power with the Lancastrian male line very decimated.

Edward IV died in 1483, leaving two sons. His older son Edward V was heir but Edward IV's marriage was declared to be illegitimate and his sons were never to be crowned. Edward IV was succeeded by his younger brother, Richard, who was crowned Richard III. And later Edward V and his brother, it is thought, were murdered by Richard III so there would be no chance of a change of mind.

Richard III assumed the throne and the unrest continued. Several Lords were still opposed to the Yorkists ruling. And Richard III made several decisions which alienated the power brokers.

Richard III married Anne Neville, daughter of Richard Neville (1428–1471), 16th Earl of Warwick (the Kingmaker). Richard III and Anne had one son who died suddenly of an unknown cause in 1484 at age ten. So there was now no heir to the throne on the York side.

Henry Tudor was born in Pembroke Castle in Wales and was a direct descendant of Edward III as shown here.

    Edward III (1312–1377) King of England m Philippe de Hainault (1311–1369)
    John of Gaunt (1340–1399) m Katherine Swynford
    John Beaufort (1371–1410) 1st Earl of Somerset m Margaret of Holland
    John Beaufort (1404–1444) 1st Duke of Somerset m Margaret Beauchamp
    Margaret Beaufort (1443–1509) m Edmund Tudor
    Henry VII Tudor (1457–1509)

He therefore had a claim to the throne as shown, particularly since Richard now had no living issue.

Henry Tudor brought French troops to England and rallied remnants of the Lancastrian forces from Wales to form an Army with which to attack Richard. They met in August 1485 near the town of Market Bosworth in Leicester. The Battle of Bosworth Field was essentially the end of the Wars of the Roses.

Various stories abound about the battle and Richard III, including Shakespeare's play Richard III. In Act V he wrote the line, "My horse, my horse, my kingdom for a horse." Richard lost his horse, his kingdom and his life in the battle. Richard III was the last English king to die in battle.

Henry Percy, 4th Earl of Northumberland, was on Richard III's Yorkist side, leading an army during this battle which needs some study and explaining. Henry Percy's father, the 3rd Earl of Northumberland, had died in 1461 supporting the Lancastrian side as described above. As a young teenager Henry Percy and his family had lost all land and title and he was even imprisoned in the Tower of London in 1464. Young Henry Percy eventually swore allegiance to Edward IV and was released from prison in 1469. He petitioned to recover his land and title and this was granted by Parliament in 1473. For the next twelve years Henry worked in various Yorkist government positions in Northern England. At the Battle of Bosworth Field, Henry commanded a reserve of Yorkist troops but he and other commanders withheld forces that might have made the outcome of the battle very different. Various theories have been put forward as to why, and whose side he really was on. As I have tried to explain, in family feuds people take sides and sometimes change sides.

Henry Tudor was victorious and became Henry VII, King of England. He married Edward IV's daughter, Elizabeth of York, in an effort to reconcile the two houses.

The Wars of the Roses were over in 1487, but remnants existed for another two years. The House of Tudor replaced the Plantagenets. The Tudors continued their reign through Henry's son, Henry VIII, and down through Queen Elizabeth's death in 1603.

Chapter 8: Wars of the Roses (1339–1509)

Above we have discussed the Percys and the Nevilles and their deep involvement in the struggle for power in the Wars of the Roses, including changing sides and losing key family members.

Our family genealogy bloodline which follows is interesting here since it intersects and includes a few of the main characters in this family feud.

25 Edward I, King of England (1239–1307) m Eleanor of Castile (1244–1290)

24 Joan of England (1272–1307) m Gilbert de Clare (1243–1295)

23 Margaret de Clare (1292–1342) m Hugh de Audley (c1289–1347)

22 Margaret de Audley (c1325–1348) m Ralph de Stafford (1301–1372)

21 Hugh de Stafford (1342–1386) m Philippa Beauchamp (??–c1386)

20 Margaret de Stafford (before 1364–1396) m Ralph Neville (1364–1425) 4th Lord of Raby, 1st Earl of Westmorland

19 Ralph Neville (1392–1457) m Mary de Ferrers (1394–1457)

18 John Neville (1416–1482) m 1st Elizabeth Newmarch (1416–1482)

17 Joan Neville (1443–1486) m Sir William Gascoigne (1428–1463)

16 Sir William Gascoigne V (1445–1486) m Margaret Percy (1437–1486)
Sir William and Margaret were cousins and both descendants of Edward I. They had seven sons and six daughters. So maybe love conquers all–when we take time to stop fighting each other.

This connects us to the Plantagenet line in Chapter 6 which continues down to Smith.

Chapter 9

Edward I to Linda Knoop (Smith) (1239–2021)

I had expected to end my searching through the Europeans in Chapter 8, but I plodded on with my wife Linda's ancestors, thinking that a few more names could be added to her tree. Most of her ancestors were of German descent and I didn't feel capable of research in that area so I concentrated more on her Anglican ancestors. Names kept getting added, but I ran into several brick walls. After fruitless searches of the Nance and Gookin families which turned out to be cousins but not direct-line ancestors, I came upon the Wootens. A string of Wootens got me back to the Throckmortons and it kept going on to Edward I. This of course meant that my wife, Linda, and I are cousins. We are connected not only by 62 years of marriage, but also 24 generations back with a common ancestor in Edward I. And, of course, she shares all the other ancestors back the full 50 generations to Cerdic in the late 5th century. See previous chapters for generations 25 through 50.

24 Edward I Plantagenet, Longshanks, King of England (1239–1307) m Eleanor of Castile (1244–1290)
See Edward I Plantagenet in Chapter 6.

23 Joan of England Plantagenet, of Acre (1272–1307) m Ralph Monthermer (1262–1325)
Joan was born in Acre in the Holy Land while her parents were on crusade. She was the seventh of fourteen children. On her parents' travel back to England, Joan was left with her maternal grandmother in France to be raised, educated and spoiled. The grandmother did well in all three areas. Her father, King Edward I, planned to arrange her marriage in order

to gain in power and wealth. His first candidate died before even meeting Joan, who was five years of age at the time. When Joan was twelve, he arranged a marriage with Gilbert de Clare whom Joan did marry, at about age eighteen. Gilbert died five years later, after they had three children together. Edward was busily planning another marriage for Joan when she secretly married Ralph Monthermer, a squire in the King's household. Edward was furious and seized Joan's properties inherited from her first husband. He imprisoned Ralph in Bristol Castle for a while, but finally relented. Ralph paid homage to Edward and was given titles of Earl of Glouchester and Earl of Hereford. Joan had five additional children with Ralph. He became the 1st Baron of Monthermer.

Upon Joan's death and Edward I's death, Ralph's titles were taken back and given to Joan's son by her first marriage who was considered the rightful heir. Ralph was then given a nominal earldom in Scotland.

22 Thomas Monthermer (1301–1340) m Margaret Teyes (??–1349)
Thomas became the 2nd Baron of Monthermer. He and Lady Margaret had one child, a daughter, Margaret. He fought in the Battle of Sluys and later died from wounds received in the battle.

21 Margaret Monthermer (1329–1394) m John de Montagu (c1330–c1390)
Margaret became the 3rd Baroness of Monthermer at age 10 upon her father's death. John was the youngest son of William Montagu, 1st Earl of Salisbury, and John later became the 1st Baron Montecute.

20 John Montagu, 3rd Earl of Salisbury (1350–1400) m Maud Francis (??–1424)
John Montagu grew up as heir to the Montagu and Monthermer positions of power and prestige. He distinguished himself early in war with the French and in Prussia. In 1391 he was summoned to Parliament and became a favorite of King Charles II. When Charles was arrested and imprisoned, Montagu was also arrested and put in the Tower of London along with several other of the King's councillors. He was released, but joined a plot to kill King Henry IV. The plot failed and a mob in Cirencester caught John Montagu and, without a trial, beheaded him. The authorities then stripped the family of their lands.

19 Sir Thomas Montagu, 4th Earl of Salisbury (1388–1428) m Allinor II de Holand (1387–1405)
Thomas inherited his title of Earl of Salisbury upon his father's death and over the years was able to recover several of the lands forfeited by his father. He was summoned to Parliament and formally invested as Earl in 1421.

Chapter 9: Edward I to Linda Knoop (Smith) (1239–2021)

During the Hundred Years' War, Sir Thomas joined King Henry V in France and fought in several battles and campaigns over thirteen years including the Battle of Agincourt. He was wounded by a cannonball striking the tower he was in at the Siege of Orleans in 1428 and died of his wounds a week later.

Allinor was his first wife and their only child, a daughter Alice, is our line.

18 Alice Montagu (1398–1462) m Richard Neville, 5th Earl of Salisbury (1400–1460)
Richard and Alice had twelve children who left their mark in English history. Richard became the 5th Earl of Salisbury by his marriage to Alice who inherited the right to the title. See Neville in Chapter 8.

17 Alice Neville (1431–1503) m Henry Fitzhugh (1429–1472)
Henry inherited his position as the 5th Baron Fitzhugh of Ravensworth, but he accumulated an additional position as Master Forester and a title in Parliament of Trier of Petitions. Alice and Henry had eleven children.

16 Lady Elizabeth Fitzhugh (1460–1513) m Sir Nicholas Vaux (1460–1523)

15 Anna Catherine Vaux (1488–1571) m Sir George Throckmorton (1480–1552)

14 Sir Nicholas Throckmorton (1515–1571) m Mary Margaret Whorlwood (1535–1626)

13 Sir Arthur Throckmorton (1557–1626) m Lady Anne Lucas (1561–1629)

12 Lady Mary Throckmorton (1588–1658) m Thomas, 2nd Baron of Marley, Wotton (1585–1630)
Their son changed the name to Wooten.

11 Thomas Wooten (1612–1669) m Sarah Jennings (c1620–1699)
See Chapter 38 for Thomas Wooten and Sarah Jennings.

10 Richard Wooten Sr. (1647–1687) m Frances Joyce Albrighton (1654–1688)
See Chapter 38 for Richard Wooten and Frances Joyce Albrighton.

Chapter 9: Edward I to Linda Knoop (Smith) (1239–2021)

9 Richard Wooten Jr. (1678–1738) m Lucy Hardy Council (1676–1738)
See Chapter 38 for Richard Wooten and Lucy Hardy Council.

8 Pvt. Samuel Wooten (1726–1814) m Sarah Elizabeth Callaway (1729–1761)
See Chapter 38 for Samuel Wooten and Sara Elizabeth Callaway.

7 Martha Wooten (1756–1851) m Lt. Josiah Tanner (1754–1807)
See Chapter 37 for Martha Wooten and Josiah Tanner.

6 Elizabeth Tanner (1780–1848) m William Tracy (1781–1846)
See Chapter 36 for Elizabeth Tanner and William Tracy.

5 George Tracy (1803–1860) m Susan Puckett (1812–1897)
See Chapter 36 for George Tracy and Susan Puckett.

4 Emily Francis "Fanny" Tracy (1845–1886) m Pvt. Charles William Sheets, CSA (1841–1903)
See Chapter 34 for Emily Francis Tracy and Pvt. Charles William Sheets.

3 Mary Francis Sheets (1876–1931) m George Hund Sr. (1861–1935)
See Chapter 34 for Mary Francis Sheets and Chapter 32 for George Hund Sr.

2 Ruth Hund (1909–2008) m Robert Fridolin Knoop (1908–1983)
See Chapter 32 for Ruth Hund and Chapter 31 for Robert Fridolin Knoop.

1 Linda Knoop (1939–) m Watson Christen Smith (1936–)
See Part 6: The Last Word for Linda Knoop and Part 5: My Story for Watson Christen Smith.

In Part 1 we came from our earliest known ancestors and traced some bloodlines down to the coming to America. We did not explore all the known European branches holding approximately six thousand names that are shown in our family tree in Ancestry.com. There could be many more.

So ends my exploration of Those Europeans. On to America.

Part 2

On to America — Jamestown and Plymouth

It is quite a jump from Europe and Great Britain to America. Why did they come to America? It is interesting to look back at how and why our ancestors took such an arduous and dangerous two- or three-month voyage in a cramped ship to begin a hard new life. Some were seeking financial gain and others endeavoring to avoid being forced to fight wars. Many others were escaping religious restraints or persecution. Some came because they were hired and others because they were forced by bondage. There are so many reasons, but I think most wanted a new beginning and/or opportunity.[14]

England was late in attempting to settle in the "New World." The first early Native Americans came from Asia more than 15,000 years ago. And before the English set foot on North America to establish a permanent settlement, several other European nations were well ahead of them. The Vikings left remnants of attempted settlements in Canada. The Spanish and Portuguese had been at it for many years after Christopher Columbus first arrived in1492 in the West Indies and brought back clear knowledge about what was here. The Spanish explorers were conquering and settling areas as well as bringing back the gold and other treasures. And even the French made an early attempt to settle Quebec City in 1541.

The jealous British began by turning loose privateers to harass and capture Spanish and Portuguese ships in order to plunder and bring home some of that treasure from the New World. This culminated in the Anglo-Spanish War ranging from 1585 to 1604 and of course included Spain's failed Spanish Armada attack on England and the heroics of Sir

---

14 Philbrick, Nathaniel, *Mayflower*, Penguin Group, New York, copyright 2006

Francis Drake. The war had cooled and ended in sort of a tired stalemate by 1603. As a result, they negotiated with Spain and signed the Treaty of London in 1604.

This negotiated peace opened the door for English interests to claim part of this New World for England and themselves. Starting by 1605, groups of prominent men in England organized to establish English colonies. In 1606, King James issued a Charter to two joint-stock companies who together have been referred to as the "Virginia Company" with coastal jurisdiction from present day Maine to Northern Florida. Their Charter reads in part:

"That they should devide themselves into twoe collonies, the one consistinge of divers Knights, gentlemen, merchaunts and others of our citte of London, called the First Collonie; and the other of sondrie Knights, gentlemen and others of the cittes of Bristoll, Exeter, the towne of Plymouth, and other places, called the Second Collonie." The old English spelling in this government document leaves me thinking about how words and meanings change over time.

The "First Collonie" became the Virginia Company of London or the "London Company" with jurisdiction from Long Island to North Florida. The "Second Collonie" became the Virginia Company of Plymouth or the "Plymouth Company" with jurisdiction from Maine to the Chesapeake Bay. There was intentional overlapping of territory. Both companies began organizing and seeking investors.

The London Company began by hiring people to come, settle, work and earn a profit for the company. They prepared three ships for the voyage and left Blackwall, London, England, in December of 1606. The three ships sailed to Virginia and arrived in May 1607. They were commanded by Captain Christopher Newport. After much sorting of wives and children, I connected Capt. Christopher Newport as a direct ancestor on a Virginia branch within my wife, Linda's family. We discuss the captain in Chapter 11.

The early settlement of Jamestown failed. They failed because the hired settlers had no motivation or incentive and really no involved management. Their selection of Jamestown's location in a swampy area contributed to disease. In addition, they encountered Native American tribes with whom they failed to interact well, and who objected to their territory being invaded. The Indian uprisings and massacres were very disruptive to settlement of the Virginia Colony. Later, the wealthy owners came to settle plantations with the help of contractors, employees, indentured servants and slaves. The land grants and governmental institutions were arranged by favor of the King. This was more successful because the plantation owners were essentially big agricultural businesses with on-site management and they were managing their own investments. Further development and expansion in Virginia and the South occurred mostly through the industry of agriculture from these early plantations.

The 1620 development at Plymouth, Massachusetts, and afterward throughout New England and the Northeast was very different. The people that came to New England and the Northeastern part of America, in general, were not the landed elite or wealthy. Some were wealthy, but most were not from the upper crust. They were from many walks of life, many backgrounds and many occupations, looking for opportunity and a new beginning. Most were of strong religious belief and willing to take risks and work hard to build a future. The Pilgrims, of course, were a close group of like-minded, very religious individuals who wanted to practice their beliefs as they saw fit, without any government direction or control.

The British Government did allow a significant degree of self-government to the colonists, which set the stage for American independence in years that followed. Also, in these early days the stark difference between the two settlements set the stage for many later developments in America. These included the differences between John Adams and Thomas Jefferson, the eventual abolition of slavery, states' rights and local government versus big government and currently socialism versus capitalism.

A common item of major importance here also was the relationship of the settlers with the Native Americans. These relationships both in Virginia and New England vacillated between friendship and hostility. The settlers were clearly squatting on occupied territory, but the concept of property ownership was foreign to the Native Americans and they were taken advantage of while trying to be accommodating to these foreigners. The Indians occasionally fought among themselves, as most tribal groups have for centuries, but they also got along and respected each other. The settlers upset the native communities and bought or took more and more land for keeps. Eventually there was war, and the Indians generally lost in the end–even as many settlers tried to be fair.

I have been very interested to see who our earliest settlers were and when they arrived in America. As you will find out while reading this book, I have gotten excited and maybe at times even obsessed to find certain ancestral connections, sometimes successful and sometimes not. Our stepmother, Eleanor Richmond (See chapter 14), easily found her Richmond family *Mayflower* ancestors. I was sure I would also easily find a direct connection. Such has not been the case. What I have found, and I share in Chapter 29, is that John Alden and Priscilla Mullens, who came on the *Mayflower* are definitely cousins. That fact is sufficient to satisfy my obsession in this area on the Smith side.

I was so very certain to have a direct descendant in the Brewster, Hopkins and Gookin families, only to find inaccuracies in the connections. I currently do not have any documented connections to confirm that they are relatives, but the stories of their adventures in coming to America are so interesting that I thought I must share them.

Chapter 10

Newport — The Founding of Jamestown

Christopher Newport (1561–1617) is the star of this chapter. There is very little known of the other members of his family who certainly must have participated in helping to form his character and who also shared in the fame and riches from his accomplishments.

15 Thomas Newport (1491–1551) m Joanna "Anna" Corbet (1495–1538)
Thomas and Anna were Christopher's grandparents and lived their lives in Shropshire, England.

14 Capt. John/Christopher Newport (c1536–c1591) m Dorothy Jane Hatton (c1536–c1591)
I give this gentleman his first two names because of the uncertainty of what is known of him. John and/or Christopher Newport is noted differently in accounts about his son Christopher. So, without any further research I use both names.

John/Christopher and Dorothy Jane lived in the Limetown area of London which at that time was a docking area for cargo ships on the north side of the Thames River a few miles down from central London. Limetown derived its name from pottery kilns that were in the area.

John/Christopher was reported to have been a "shipmaster" on the eastern coast of England. A "shipmaster" is a Captain of a ship transporting cargo between ports and therefore I have added the "Capt." to his name here. He certainly was responsible for imparting the skills and leadership qualities to his son, which definitely enabled his son to achieve a

Chapter 10: Newport — The Founding of Jamestown

degree of greatness.

13 Capt./Adm. Christopher Newport (1561–1617) m Elizabeth Glandfield (1565–1616)

Christopher was born in Limetown, London, England, and lived there until 1595.[15] He obviously was introduced to boats, ships, navigation and the maritime trade at an early age through his father as well as his neighborhood. He went out to sea on a major ship voyage at about age 19 and quickly gained rank and experience to became a master mariner dealing in trade with London.

In 1587 Christopher was with Sir Francis Drake during the raid on Cadiz and also fought against the Spanish Armada attempt to invade England in 1588. For the remainder of the Anglo-Spanish War, he commanded several ships owned by John Watts, a London merchant, which operated as privateers. As Captain of a privateer, operating throughout the Caribbean, Christopher captured Spanish and Portuguese shipping and is said to have captured more ships than Sir Francis Drake. During this period, he became an expert navigator of the Caribbean and eastern coast of North America. This activity brought him considerable wealth, as his share of the plunder, but at the cost of an arm which was shattered during a battle.

When the war came to a close and the London Company organized to begin settling Virginia, Capt. Christopher Newport was selected to be in sole command of the three ships, including the people and cargo, while they were at sea, traveling to settle in Jamestown. They left in December 1606 and arrived to begin the Jamestown Settlement in May of 1607. This arrival was after several stops along the way for water and food supplies in the Azores, the Caribbean and even the coast of America, before selecting the site for the Jamestown Settlement.

Christopher carried a sealed box from the London Company on the ship which was only to be opened upon arrival in Virginia. In it were instructions as to how a Council of the Colony was to be formed to govern and a President to be chosen to lead and that Christopher was one of the men to be on the Council.

As a member of the Jamestown Council, Christopher was active in decisions and served to explore the James River which they named for King James. He went upriver to the falls at present day Richmond, sparred with and later negotiated with the Indians. In about a month, after a fort was built, he left for England to begin the first of several supply trips he made from England to the Jamestown Colony.

---

15 K.R. Andrews, *Christopher Newport of Limehouse, Mariner,* William and Mary Quarterly 3d ser., 11, no. 1(January 1954):28.

Chapter 10: Newport — The Founding of Jamestown

On his third supply trip, Christopher was a Vice Admiral of the fleet of nine ships. They encountered a three-day storm in which their ship, *Sea Venture*, was in danger of sinking. The ship captain fortunately was able to ground their ship on the shore of the Bermuda islands, saving all 150 persons aboard and most of their provisions. During the next ten months they worked to salvage from the ship, survive and to build two smaller ships which they used to sail on to Jamestown. Also on this ship was Stephen Hopkins, whom we discuss in Chapter 11.

In 1611 Christopher left Jamestown Colony for the last time. He returned to England and received a commission in the Royal Navy. He joined the English East India Company and commanded three long voyages to the East Indies. On his third voyage in 1617, he became ill and died of an unknown cause in Java, Indonesia. His son, Christopher Newport III, was with him on this last voyage to the East Indies and also died there of illness.

Christopher had two or three wives and the history of his immediate family is not very clear or well documented. He married his first wife, Katherine Proctor, in 1584 and they had one child, Molly, before Katherine died in 1589. He married a second wife, Ellen Ade, in 1590 with whom he had one child, William, who died in infancy. Ellen died in 1593 at age 28. Finally, Christopher married Elizabeth Rose Glanfield with whom he had several children. Our line is from his wife, Elizabeth, through their daughter, Marian Newport.

12 Marian Newport (1611–1646) m William Hatcher (1614–1680)
William and Marian were born, raised and married in England. They immigrated to Jamestown Colony in 1636 or 1637, obtained a grant of land, settled in Henrico County and were probably progenitors of most Hatcher families in Virginia. He was quickly elected to the House of Burgesses and served intermittent terms. He was known for strong rhetoric and at one time was fined 10 Pounds for verbally attacking another member.

11 Edward Hatcher (1633–1711) m Mary Ward (1640–1711)
Edward and Mary were born in Varina Parish, Henrico County, Virginia. "Varina" was the particular type of tobacco which was liked and grew well in Virginia. This tobacco became the main cash crop to ship back to Europe, saved the economy of the Virginia Colony and rewarded the investors. Edward established a successful plantation there, called "Neck of Land Plantation." He was known for making risky investments.

10 Sarah Hatcher (1665–after1706) m 2 Joseph Tanner Jr. (1662–1698)
This was a second marriage for both. See Chapter 37 for Sarah Hatcher and Joseph Tanner.

Chapter 11

Hopkins — An Extraordinary Life

This connection between England and America is unique and is included mainly due to the extraordinary experiences of Stephen Hopkins. He came early on the ship *Sea Venture* which wrecked on Bermuda, eventually made it to Jamestown, returned to England and then came again later with his immediate family on the *Mayflower* to Plymouth.[16]

Stephen Hopkins (1581–1644) m 1) Mary Kent m 2) Elizabeth Fisher (1596–1639)
Stephen Hopkins was born in Hampshire, England, to John and Elizabeth Hopkins. His father died when he was about 12 years of age. He married first to Mary Kent and they had three children. They owned an alehouse in Hampshire, which he operated with Mary and her mother, Joane. He also worked as a reader for the church and worked for the Jamestown Company. In 1609 he left the alehouse to be run by his wife and mother-in-law, to join a group of Jamestown Company employees sailing for the new settlement in Jamestown, Virginia, bringing supplies, workers and additional settlers.

Their ship, the *Sea Venture*, was part of a fleet of nine ships that encountered a severe storm. Our Christopher Newport, the Vice Admiral of the fleet, was aboard the *Sea Venture* but not the captain of the ship. The *Sea Venture* was separated from the others and foundered in the storm taking on water. The ship captain made it to the shores of the Bermuda islands where he grounded the ship and saved all aboard. Being safe but marooned on Bermuda they were fortunate for the abundance of game and fruits to sustain themselves.

---
16 Philbrick, Nathaniel, *Mayflower*, Penguin Group, New York, copyright 2006

Chapter 11: Hopkins — An Extraordinary Life

They built two smaller vessels from the remains of their ship and nine months later set sail for Jamestown in 1610. They arrived in Jamestown in 11 days.

Stephen worked in Jamestown for three to four years during which time his wife back in England died, leaving his three young children alone. Upon receiving word of this, Stephen left Jamestown and returned to England to care for his children. One of his children, Elizabeth, apparently died since there is no record of her. He lived in London and remarried to Elizabeth Fisher. He worked as a tanner and was a merchant of some kind.

Stephen, his two young children, Constance and Giles, along with his wife, Elizabeth, and one of their children, Damarius, joined a group planning to go to Virginia to start a new colony north of Jamestown. Stephen and Elizabeth were not Pilgrims. Some say he was sought out because of his previous experience in Jamestown and especially his experience dealing with the Indians. They originally left on the *Mayflower* in July of 1620. A companion ship developed leaks so they all had to turn back. They left again on the *Mayflower* in September 1620.

Stephen's wife, Elizabeth, delivered a male child during the voyage, whom they named Oceanus. This was the only childbirth during the voyage of three months.

Stephen was the 14th signer of the 41 signers of the Mayflower Compact which bound the signers to collectively work together and help each other to establish an orderly community. This Compact was created, before they landed, as they realized the extraordinary task they had before themselves.

Arriving on Cape Cod in November 1620, they were far north of Virginia but decided to settle anyway and, after a month of exploring the coast, chose the location at Plymouth. They spent the winter living on the *Mayflower*, while building homes on the land. They moved into their new homes on shore in March 1621. Over the winter about half of the people died.

Stephen had experienced hardship while shipwrecked on Bermuda and during his time at Jamestown, he had learned how to deal with the Indians. Therefore, his advice was sought during the early days of the settlement. His services as an adviser to the Governor continued through 1636.

In Plymouth and the surrounding area he accumulated sizable land holdings and was considered wealthy at the time of his death. Wealth in those days was quite different than our values today. Today multimillionaires and billionaires are the wealthy. I consider all Americans wealthy just to be here and enjoy the benefits of freedom and opportunity. In 1620 and shortly thereafter in America they must have felt lucky and blessed just to have survived the voyage and the first few years of hunger, struggle and death. The colony grew, prospered and appreciated their religious freedom.

By 1635 the Plymouth Colony was growing both by new family members and by new

Chapter 11: Hopkins — An Extraordinary Life

arrivals. As their numbers grew they purchased more land along the coast to establish new towns. Stephen received permission, in 1638, to build a new house in Mattacheese (now Barnstable County) where he wanted to cut hay to feed his cattle. But he was required to still maintain his house in Plymouth. The town of Eastham was established farther east on the cape in 1644. Stephen's son Giles moved to Eastham in 1645, as did his daughter Constance, after her marriage to Nicholas Snow.[17]

Reviewing Stephan's inventory of possessions after his death in 1644 reveals what wealthy meant at that time. Thirteen cows, two oxen, normal household items, clothing, 4 silver spoons, a horse, and a house all seem successful, but normal to us today. Stephen also owned considerable land compared to others, perhaps that is what made him "wealthy." Wealth was a comparative evaluation as it is for us today. Miles Standish did the inventory.

Stephen and Elizabeth had seven children together. Of Stephan's total of ten children, seven reached adulthood and married. In Stephen's will, he divided most of his possessions equitably between his children, except that he left most of the land to son Caleb. Caleb in turn gave his step-brother Giles 100 acres of land. Caleb died not long afterward and left most all the rest of the land to Giles.

Elizabeth pre-deceased Stephen by a few years. In Stephen's will he asked to be placed next to Elizabeth when he was buried. He was so buried.

---

[17] Deyo, Simeon L., *History of Barnstable, Massachusetts*, H.W. Blake & Co., New York, New York, 1890

Chapter 12

Brewster — Steady Faith and Leadership

The Brewster family is from Nottinghamshire, England, as far as we know. Not much is known about them except their titles until we get to Elder William Brewster (1536–1644). Then he suddenly brings his family to be a significant part of history. Many dates are questionable for the earlier people. And again, these are not our relatives as I currently have not documented a connection. But Elder William Brewster was vital to the Plymouth Colony and for that fact alone he and his family are included here.[18]

Sir John Brewster (1325–1379)

Galfridus Brewster (1350–1410)

Sir James Brewster, Knight (1380–1441) m Margaret (1381–??)

Humphrey Brewster (1410–1443) m Velma Ruth McGhee (1414–1481)

Sir Robert Brewster, Knight (1440–1505) m Ann Mary Harvey (1440–1504)

Sir William Brewster, Knight, Oxford Univ. (1470–1510) m Lady Mary Harvey (1470–1510)

---

18 Philbrick, Nathaniel, *Mayflower*, Penguin Group, New York, copyright 2006

Chapter 12: Brewster — Steady Faith and Leadership

William Brewster II, Archbishop of York (c1505/10–1558) m Lady Maud Mann (c1500/15–c1558/88)

William Brewster (1536–1590) m Mary Smythe (1535–1627)

Elder William Brewster, "Mayflower Compact," "Chief of the Pilgrims" (c1566/8–1644) m Mary Love Wentworth (c1569–1627)

William Brewster was born in Scooby, Nottinghamshire, England, to a long line of apparently important people. He married Mary in 1591 or 1592. Her last name remains uncertain. He studied at Cambridge which was a center of thought for religious reform at that time. This movement apparently could not get the Anglican Church to reform or change and therefore they looked toward splitting away from the Church. The English authorities did not agree and applied pressures and regulations. This drove the reformers to seek a friendlier neighborhood, which they found in the Netherlands. However, it was illegal to leave England without permission and the group was arrested in 1607 trying to leave. In 1608 Brewster, his family and his group were successful in getting to the city of Leiden in the Netherlands. Brewster served as an assistant to their Pastor John Robinson and in 1609 was elected Elder of the Congregation of the Pilgrims. He taught English at Leiden University during their stay in Leiden and began writing and publishing pamphlets and books in order to make a living. These writings were critical of the English King and Bishops, prompting King James to order his arrest. Brewster went into hiding for several years until the time for the *Mayflower* departure in 1620.

The Separatists finally received permission to leave England for America to establish a new colony north of Jamestown and the *Mayflower* departed Plymouth, England, in September 1620. Elder William Brewster and his family, which included his wife, Mary, and two sons, Love and Wrestling, were on board. He was the highest positioned layperson on board and without a pastor in the colony he became the group's spiritual leader until a clergyman arrived in 1629. Among the passengers on board were four unaccompanied children, two of whom were assigned under the care of Elder Brewster and his family and for whom the two children were to be servants. The 100-foot-long *Mayflower* carried 102 passengers and a crew of 30 to 40 causing very cramped conditions. The ship ran into foul weather and took on water which added to their discomfort. One passenger and one seaman died on the voyage.

William Bradford and William Brewster drafted the Mayflower Compact which 41 of the male passengers signed on November 21, 1620. This document bound them to mutually work together, supporting a common effort for the community. It is considered a major document in the development of freedom, self-determination and constitutional government in the United States. William Brewster was the 4th signer.[19]

They were among the survivors of that first winter at Plymouth. Living on the *Mayflower* in very crowded conditions with sickness and death around them could not have been what they were expecting upon arrival in America.

Their son Jonathan arrived in November 1621 and their daughters, Patience and Fear, arrived in July 1623.

Since Brewster was the only university educated person of the group, until the pastor arrived in 1629, he led them spiritually and also was an advisor to Governor Bradford. Brewster continued as Chief Elder until his death in 1644. He was given farm land in Duxbury, and four islands in Boston Harbor still bear his name.

Patience Brewster (1600–1634) m Gov. Thomas Prence (1600–1673)
William and Mary's daughter Patience arrived in Plymouth 2-½ years after her parents and therefore avoided the initial difficulties incurred by the Pilgrims, but I'm sure she had her share of work to do in the new colony. In 1624 she married Thomas Prence who arrived in Plymouth in 1621 and they had four children. In 1634 smallpox and influenza hit the colony and the local Indian population. Patience died that year of "petulant fever." Thomas Prence remarried three more times and had several more children.

The Plymouth Colony was a joint venture of the religious separatists and a group of investors. The investors intended to profit from funding the settlement of the colony. By 1626 it was apparent that there was insufficient return available from their investment. Thomas Prence was one of eight leaders of Plymouth who stepped forward to assume the debts of the Plymouth Colony for which they were given an exclusive right to trade furs. This was marginally successful and some of the eight withdrew. Prence had to sell his house and then renegotiated the deal with the investors. Eventually things worked out for him and he became a very successful landowner.

Thomas Prence was very active in the leadership and affairs of the colony. He served in several positions and became Governor of Plymouth after Bradford refused to run for another term. He stayed active in the Plymouth government until his death in 1673.

Mercy Prence (1631–1711) m Maj. John Freeman (1622–1719)
Mercy was three years old when her mother died and had two new stepmothers before reaching adulthood. Since her second stepmother's first marriage was to a Samuel Freeman, I suspect that is where John Freeman came from. Also, her husband John's brother Edmund Freeman Jr. married Mercy's sister Hannah. Major John Freeman was active in the Indian

---

19 Deyo, Simeon L., *History of Barnstable, Massachusetts*, H.W. Blake & Co., New York, New York, 1890

wars and in colonial government. As the mass migration into Plymouth and the Boston areas happened over several years the colony spread out from Plymouth to establish many towns along the shore of the cape. John Freeman helped found the town of Eastham, Massachusetts, out on Cape Cod.

Deacon Thomas Freeman (1653–1716) m Rebecca Sparrow (1655–1740)
Thomas and Rebecca were born in Eastham, Massachusetts.

Rebecca Sarah Freeman (1694–1757) m Patrick Tracy (1689–??)
I had thought this couple connected to my wife, Linda, and her ancestors in Maryland. They have identical names of Rebecca Freeman married to a Patrick Tracy. I was only to be disappointed after my research found no connection. See Tracy in Chapter 36.

Chapter 13

Gookin — A Servant to Mankind

I asked my grandson Blake Andrew Smith to assist me in some research on Daniel Gookin, who at the time, I thought was firmly a direct bloodline ancestor to my wife, Linda. A subsequent correction in our tree placed him outside of our family as we know it. But, General Gookin is a very interesting individual, who had an important life as a public servant and deserves to be included here. His origin in England, migration to Virginia and Maryland, move to Massachusetts for religious reasons and his humanitarian work with Native Americans all shed light on the struggles the immigrants to America had and their efforts to survive, prosper and associate–both among themselves and with the Native Americans. His life shows some of the differences between Virginia, the First Collonie, and New England, the Second Collonie.

Major General Daniel Gookin Jr. (1612–1687) by Blake Andrew Smith
Major General Daniel Gookin was a fascinating early American settler during the 17th century. During his lifetime Gookin was many things including a soldier, a settler, and indentured servant, and a writer. Gookin's writings on Native Americans are perhaps what he is best remembered for but there was much more to him.

Daniel Gookin was born in 1612 in Ripple, Kent, England, by most accounts, though some sources believe he was born in Ireland as his father was living there at the time of his birth. Most of Gookin's early life is unknown; it is believed he was educated in England and immigrated to Virginia in 1621 where his father owned a plantation. Shortly before he turned 18, Daniel was indentured to another local plantation manager, Thomas Addison. A year later Addison retired and granted Gookin 150 acres. Gookin returned to England during the 1630s but there is little to no indication of exactly when.[20]

---

20 Wikipedia contributors, "Daniel Gookin," *Wikipedia, The Free Encyclopedia,* https://en.wikipedia.org/w/index.php?title=Daniel_Gookin&oldid=859406087 (accessed February 12, 2019).

Chapter 13: Gookin — A Servant to Mankind

Daniel Gookin returned to Virginia in 1641 shortly before the outbreak of the English Civil War which lasted from August 1642 to September 1651. It is said that Daniel was a Puritan sympathizer which has been suggested as his primary motivation for returning to the colonies. When Gookin returned to Virginia he brought with him his wife and young son. Daniel had been busy during his years in England; he had been a soldier and married twice. While no record of his first marriage has been discovered, it was stated on his marriage license when he married Mary Dolling in London on November 11, 1639, that he was a widower. It is also believed that Gookin performed military service while in England as he is often referred to as a soldier and even a Captain in some sources. While much of Daniel Gookin's early life seems to be shrouded in mystery it is of little importance. It is what he did after his return to the colonies that is most significant.[21]

Upon Daniel Gookin's return to Virginia in 1641 he was made a Burgess to the Virginia House of Burgesses in Upper Norfolk, Virginia. A Burgess, while having several meanings throughout history was, in Virginia at this time, a title for a member of the legislative body for the Virginia Colony. During this time Gookin was also granted 2,500 acres of land near the Nansemond River in Norfolk, Virginia. Between 1642 and 1643, Puritan ministers were invited to the Virginia Colony from the Colony of Massachusetts but were poorly received. One of the ministers, William Thompson, became friends with Daniel Gookin. Shortly after arriving in Virginia most of the ministers returned to Massachusetts. Thompson and Gookin decided to relocate to the Colony of Maryland in the summer of 1643. The Colony of Maryland was predominantly Catholic but was tolerant of other religious beliefs.[22]

In the spring of 1644 Gookin and his family decided to relocate once again, this time to Boston. It seems that Gookin had always wanted to go to Boston but did not want to leave his brother behind. Daniel Gookin's brother, John Gookin, still lived in Virginia and must have had a strong bond with his brother as Daniel wanted to remain close to him. John Gookin died in November of 1643 followed by Daniel's young son Samuel in early 1644 (it should be noted that Daniel Gookin had two sons named Samuel, the second being born in 1652 Massachusetts). Daniel, feeling that he no longer had anything tying him to the area, decided to leave for New England. Gookin did not sell his land in the Virginia Colony but instead left it in the care of servants.[23]

After moving to New England, Daniel Gookin and his family settled at Cambridge, Massachusetts, in 1648. Gookin must have had exceptional leadership skills combined

---

21 Ibid
22 Ibid
23 Ibid

Chapter 13: Gookin — A Servant to Mankind

with his military service in England because shortly after his arrival, he was made Captain of the Cambridge Militia, a position he maintained for forty years. The following spring Gookin was once again made a government official when he was elected as the Deputy to represent Cambridge in the General Court of the Massachusetts Colony, held in Boston. Daniel continued to rise in the political world when he was elected as a Speaker for the Colony in 1651 and eventually became an Assistant in 1652. An Assistant was one of 18 magistrates who governed the Massachusetts Colony alongside the Governor and Deputy Governor. Gookin held this position almost continuously for the next 35 years except for the year 1676 when he lost re-election due to his sympathy toward Native Americans during King Philip's War. [24]

During the 1650s, Daniel Gookin made several trips to London as a representative of the Massachusetts Colony. During this time the English Civil War (1642–1651) was coming to an end and King Charles I was executed by Oliver Cromwell. Cromwell assumed the title of Lord Protector and assumed power in England. Many of the colonists in North America wanted to know what was happening back in England and so Gookin made the journey back to England several times as a representative. After King Charles II was restored to the throne in 1660, Gookin ceased his voyages to England.[25]

Following the restoration of King Charles II, Daniel Gookin continued working to improve the Massachusetts Colony. Between 1660 and 1672 Gookin was a Selectman and was made the First Superintendent of Praying Indians. Praying Indians referred to Native Americans who had converted to Christianity. It was through his role as Superintendent that Gookin came to respect and sympathize with Native Americans. Gookin even wrote about them and their culture. During his time as Superintendent of Praying Indians, Gookin wrote two books on Native Americans in New England as well as a history of New England, though few of his writings survive today.

Daniel Gookin was elected to a committee between 1665 and 1668 to determine the location of a new settlement in the Massachusetts Colony. The committee submitted their report in 1668, and building of the settlement began in 1673. Gookin was granted land in the settlement along with three other committee members: Captain Daniel Henchman, Captain Thomas Prentice, and Lieutenant Richard Beers. The settlement was never completed as it was raided and burned during King Philip's War. Lieutenant Beers was killed during the raid and the settlement was quickly abandoned. In 1683 Daniel Gookin and the committee would try again to establish the settlement with Captain John Wing replacing the fallen Beers. This settlement would suffer the same fate and was burned during

---

24 Ibid
25 Ibid

Chapter 13: Gookin — A Servant to Mankind

another raid by Native Americans. Daniel Gookin would not live long enough to see the settlement finally succeed after a third attempt in 1713, establishing the town of Worcester, Massachusetts.[26]

Between the years of 1675 and 1678 Daniel Gookin participated in King Philip's War. As the conflict raged throughout much of New England, the colonists' resentment toward Native Americans was high. King Philip's War was named after Metacomet, a Wampanoag Chief, who was the son of Massasoit, who had helped the *Mayflower* Pilgrims. Metacomet took the English name Philip due to his father's close relationship with the English settlers. Metacomet was not able to maintain the same relationship with the English colonists as his father and after many negotiations failed war broke out between the colonists and their former native allies. King Philip's War was the first major conflict between Native Americans and European settlers and is considered by some historians as the start of the Indian Wars which lasted until the turn of the 20th century.[27]

Despite the war, Gookin was sympathetic toward the Native Americans, having spent time with them as Superintendent of Praying Indians. Gookin took several steps to protect the Native Americans under his care and relocated many of them closer to Boston. He feared that angry European settlers might mistake the converted Native Americans for combatants, or that they might be killed just out of hatred. Gookin also feared that, if left isolated, the Native Americans under his care might be subject to raids by King Philip's warriors. So Gookin took steps to move them to the Boston Harbor area which made him very unpopular with the Massachusetts colonists and he lost re-election as Assistant the following year, in 1676. Despite losing re-election and his sympathies toward Native Americans, Daniel Gookin was promoted to Major General of the Massachusetts Colony Militia. Gookin also participated in the Great Swamp Fight which was considered one the most significant and bloodiest battles in King Philip's War.[28]

Daniel Gookin died in Cambridge, Massachusetts, on March 19, 1687, at the age of 75. He is buried in the Old Cambridge Burial Ground which is across from Harvard University's Johnson Gate. Daniel Gookin was married three times and had nine children of which five survived to adulthood. All of Daniel Gookin's adult children were from his second marriage to Mary Dolling. Gookin had two sons named Samuel and two sons named Daniel. The first of each name died before reaching adulthood. The first Samuel

---

26 Ibid
27 Wikipedia contributors, "King Philip's War," *Wikipedia, The Free Encyclopedia,* https://en.wikipedia.org/w/index.php?title=King_Philip%27s_War&oldid=882981856 (accessed February 13, 2019).
28 "Yale University." Danforth, Thomas, 1623–1699 | Yale Indian Papers Project. Accessed February 13, 2019. https://yipp.yale.edu/bio/bibliography/gookin-daniel-1612-1687.

Chapter 13: Gookin — A Servant to Mankind

Gookin was born in England in 1640 and died in Maryland in 1644. The second Samuel Gookin (1652–1730) was thought to be our ancestor line. [29]

Maj. Gen. Daniel Gookin (1612–1687) m. Mary Dolling

Capt. Samuel Gookin (1652–1730) m. Mary Larkin (1652–1707)

---

29 Wikipedia contributors, "Daniel Gookin," *Wikipedia, The Free Encyclopedia,* https://en.wikipedia.org/w/index.php?title=Daniel_Gookin&oldid=859406087 (accessed February 12, 2019)

Part 3

My Smith Side of Our Family — In America

Starting in this part we are exploring American ancestor families on my Smith side of the family. We explore each family branch from earliest known ancestors down to the present. Starting with the Smith family we then follow the branches of our spouse's families and proceed family-by-family, taking each family with their subsequent branches. I include as many as practical.

We Smiths are not all that special, but every individual and family does things during their lifetime that are important to themselves and those close to them in their allotted time. And we affect people around us much more than we realize. It's human nature and part of what makes the human species unique. It is also the special privilege of the freedom that we have been given in America which allows us to seek new ventures and take advantage of opportunities available to us. This is what motivates us and separates us from other countries. I have tried to learn and understand how our various ancestors lived and what they accomplished. And, why they did so.

As I explored the various ancestors and family branches of our tree and got back six to ten generations, I became quite surprised by the number of branches that were connected and how they were connected. Some were connected by marriage of cousins and some others by obvious friendly social connections. I found several marriages between subsequent generations of founding families in a community. People do stick together and are tribal. We have some family friends, Alan and Ruth McCoy, who have six children. They introduced four of their six children to their eventual spouses. Close families tend to do this and I can see this in many of our early American ancestors.

And then I see there are those others who are very private or independent who strike out to carve their own destiny. Some are successful while others are not. Linda and I encouraged our children to seek their own individual interests, friends and opportunities. Which approach is better and makes for more happiness, I really don't know. I do find it very interesting to see how our ancestors lived. Here is the Smith side of our family.

Chapter 14

Smith — The Most Common of Names

Smith is a very common last name found everywhere. Tracing any particular branch of such a family name can be tedious with many certain dead ends. My father, Charles Clement Smith, discovered how difficult tracing the surname Smith was, when he tried to sort through the several Daniel Smiths who were around in Orange County, New York, in the late 1700s. Back then, most documents were handwritten, but, even with good penmanship, Daniel looks very much like David. So care must be used in searching and deciphering the accuracy of the facts surrounding certain names.[30]

Why were they there? Orange County, New York, established in 1683 is on the west side of the Hudson River 60 miles up from New York City. I visited New York City in 2014 and walked along the long, wonderful park beside the Hudson River that has walking, skating and biking paths. On a plaque I read about how the tidal surge extends all the way up the Hudson to that area. Upon researching further, I found that the lowest elevation in Orange County is sea level in the Hudson River. So, it's very apparent that a boat could easily ride the incoming tide up the river with maybe a little wind at their back and also return with the river flow as the tide went out. In fact, when Henry Hudson first explored the New York Harbor he sailed up the Hudson River to about that area.

The Wallkill River valley is an area between the Hudson River and the Delaware River valleys. It is known as the "Black Dirt Region" for its fertile soils. The Wallkill flows north into the Hudson. Certainly, travel and trade occurred with the short distance to New York City, since the farmers and merchants in those areas depended on each other. Verra

---

30 "The Surname 'Smith' and its Scottish Significance," Author and Publisher Clan Smith Society, Inc.

Chapter 14: Smith — The Most Common of Names

Hill Jacob, A.G. (a research genealogist) wrote in a letter to my father, Charles C. Smith, "At the time of … 1791, boats had regular schedules from Manhattan to Kingston (and) Newburgh day and night so travel was not that uncommon for immigrants to not remain overnight in Manhattan." Benjamin Franklin, as Postmaster General for the British colonies, had established daily mail shipments between New York City and Montreal, Canada, by 1760. So traveling up the Hudson River was very common.

"The original land patent for the town of Wallkill was dated 1724, but little was done for decades to develop and settle the region. The town was established in 1772, but part of the town was lost upon the formation of Ulster County, New York." The word "town" here is not what we normally think of as a small village. In the 2010 census Wallkill encompassed 62.8 square miles in Orange County, and that is long after the Ulster County area and other city areas were removed. In the Midwest we would call it a large township, or an organized area in between the incorporated areas of villages and cities. Another confusing thing is that town and county names and boundaries have continually shifted over the years making documentation more difficult.

We had solid sources to trace our lineage back to Floyd Smith Sr. (1791–1874) born in Ulster (now Orange) County, New York, but my father, when he died in 1980, had not firmly connected Daniel to be Floyd Smith Sr.'s father. However, his searching did pay off when a letter came a month after his death from a paid researcher who found a newspaper death notice of Juliet Nicholson tying together the Nicholsons with Daniel, and Floyd Smith.

Since then, we have found Derrick Smith (1730–1790) who was born in Glasgow, Scotland, and his parents. Until this fact was found we had no knowledge of where these Smiths came from. There was even speculation they could have come earlier, as the area was initially settled by Dutch families, and perhaps the Dutch "Schmidt" had been anglicized to Smith. But not so. In early Scotland there was a "Gow" or "McGowan" meaning Smith Clan around Loch Lomond, but also each of the many Scottish clans had a smith to make plowshares, horseshoes, tools, knives, swords and armor. I firmly suspect we Smiths are from an early metal worker named for his occupation in Scotland. Many Smith families originated this way (and remain), very disassociated from one another and in separate locations.[31]

Earlier history states that Scotland was "pioneered by Vikings, Celts, Picts, Norsemen and Irish." Early records also show a Roman station located there. Some say Hibernian Scots came to settle from Ireland. Maybe some future DNA testing will prove from which and where we all came. [32]

---

31 "The Surname 'Smith' and its Scottish Significance," Author and Publisher Clan Smith Society, Inc.
32 "Glasgow, Lanarkshire, Scotland/History" Family Tree Memory Search

Chapter 14: Smith — The Most Common of Names

Why did they leave Scotland? History books tell us that England finally culminated its domination of Scotland with the battle of Culloden in 1746. In that battle Bonnie Prince Charlie was defeated and subsequently fled back to France. As a result, there was quite a bit of migration to America from Scotland at that time either by choice or by force of the English Crown. Glasgow was a major port of departure. Many Scottish families settled in the Wallkill Valley area of New York between 1680 and 1750. So, there was a cultural attraction to the area as well as the good soil and opportunity. We know that Derrick Smith and Hannah Gale were there, so we know of eight generations for sure, but there is certainly more to know about the Smiths.

More recently we have a recognized connection to a second, earlier Daniel Smith who may be our Daniel (1710–1786). I present it because it does fit into our time line, but the documentation is speculative at this time. If it is correct and factual, it opens up our whole Scottish heritage back for several more generations to a Duncan Smith in Buchanan, Stirling, Scotland. Buchanan is now a Parish in the southwest of the Stirling Council Area (like a county) of Scotland on the eastern shore of Loch Lomond. It is named for the clergyman, Sir Absalon of Buchanan, who obtained a grant of lands in 1225. Clan Buchanan is also claimed to be much older, but in any event, the lands were sold for debts and all that remains are ruins of a country estate home, which was built much later in the 18th century. The hamlet of Buchanan Smithy was built at that time to house workers building and working on the estate and named after three blacksmiths. Were they our ancestors?

12 Duncan Smith (1635–after 1665) m Jonet Govan (??–after 1665)
Duncan was born in Buchanan, Stirling, Scotland. Jonet was born in Glasgow, Scotland. Her family is documented back many more generations in our tree.

11 John Smith (1665–after 1687) m Gresell Robinson (1665–after 1687)
John was born in Boreland, Stirling, Scotland. Boreland is a name associated with an estate or landed property, so we assume he may have been was born on the Buchanan estate. Gresell was born in Stirling (council area). They married in 1681 at age 16 in Boreland, Stirling, Scotland, and later died in Scotland.

10 John Smith (1687–1751) m Elizabeth "Elspie" Bryce (1686–1734)
John and Elizabeth were both born in Buchanan, Stirling, Scotland, and married there. Their son, Daniel, was born there also. Was John one of the three blacksmiths? John died in Perth, Perthshire, Scotland. Elizabeth died in Scotland.

9 Daniel Smith (1710–1786) m. Elizabeth Frazier/Fraser (1710–??)

Daniel and Elizabeth were both born in Buchanan, Stirling, Scotland. They moved to Glasgow where their son, Derrick, was born and then on to America. They came to America as a family about 1750 which was four years after the Battle of Culloden and a period when the British were consolidating their takeover of Scotland and may have been a good time to leave.

Daniel Smith's wife, Elizabeth Fraser, is interesting because of her presumed ancestry with the Fraser Clan. The Fraser Clan inhabited an area near Inverness in the Highlands and had sided with Bonnie Prince Charlie. After the battle of Culloden and the British takeover of Scotland, all clans were disbanded. Wearing of kilts, tartans and even use of bagpipes was forbidden. The Fraser soldiers were given choice of jail, deportation or joining a special Fraser Regiment in the British army as only foot soldiers. If they joined the British army they could keep their kilts, tartans, bagpipes and weapons. This regiment has developed into the famous Highlanders with a notable history in the British Army over the years. Daniel Smith and Elizabeth Fraser's specific historical connection to the Fraser Clan is unknown.

Elizabeth's parents were Thomas Fraser and Mary Lowery. They were married in St. Boswells, Roxburgh, Scotland, which is in southeastern Scotland. Further back the family was in Cannongate, Midlothian, Scotland, which is a parish in the City of Edinburgh. Midlothian was rural at that time.

Daniel died in Vermont. We presume Elizabeth died there in Vermont also.

8 Derrick Smith (1730–1790) m. Hannah Gale (1731–1817)

Derrick was born in Glasgow, Lanarkshire, Scotland. Glasgow at that time was developing into a shipbuilding city with an excellent natural harbor which later became a major international trading center. Again, why did they leave? Was it because of the Jacobite uprising or the English takeover of Scotland? If so, it may have been a good time to leave.

He came to America about 1750 with his parents. In 1756, at age 26, he was in Orange County, New York, where he married Hannah Gale who had been born in Wallkill, Orange County, New York. Wallkill at that time was the Precinct of Wallkill. They had seven or ten children. Their children were baptized at the First Presbyterian Church in Goshen. He died in Hamptonburgh, Orange County, New York, a small town on the eastern boundary of the current town of Wallkill.

There is a record of a Derrick Smith, who served in 1779 under Brigadier General Robert Van Rensselaer in his 2nd Brigade of the Albany County Militia. In 1779 they fought the British at the Battle of Klock's Field in Palatine Bridge, New York. Is this our Derrick, a son or someone else?

Derrick's wife, Hannah Gale, came from a long line of Gales. Edmund Gale (1602–1648) was from Oakley, Bedfordshire, England, and came as an early settler to the Boston area. See Chapter 27: Gale. She died several years after Derrick in Goshen, Orange County, New York. Derrick and Hannah are both buried in the Hamptonburg Cemetery in Campbell Hall, Orange County, New York.

7 Daniel Smith 2 (1763–1810) m. Ann Nicholson (1768–??)
Born in Goshen, Orange County, New York, he grew up among many brothers and sisters.

The family moved to Montgomery at some point while he was growing up. He was about 12 years old when the Revolutionary War activity broke out in 1775. From Revolutionary War widow's pension records we learn that Daniel served as a private in the Revolutionary War from Montgomery, Ulster County (now Orange County), New York. While it is not clear what his actual dates of service were or where he served, we do have some clues.

Daniel served in the 3rd Regiment of the 4th Brigade of the New York State Militia. The 4th Brigade was organized under a law passed by the Provincial Congress of New York in 1775. Of the 5 Regiments authorized, the 3rd Regiment was formed by Ulster and Orange Counties. It was also called the Goshen Regiment. Recruiting was aimed at men aged 16–50. Daniel was 16 in 1779, so probably missed the 3rd Regiment's early action along the Hudson River from below West Point up to Kingston. But in 1779 he very well could have participated in the Battle of Minisink.

The town of Montgomery was named after the fallen General Richard Montgomery who led American Continental Forces in the invasion of Canada in the fall of 1775 and was killed at the battle of Quebec on December 31, 1775. An interesting thing here is that the town of Montgomery was not named for the General until 1782. The town originally was named Hanover by the first German and Dutch settlers in the area. Perhaps a simple explanation would be that it was named Montgomery by the time Daniel joined up and certainly by the time the application for Daniel's pension was submitted.

Alternately, we might assume that Daniel was inspired by Colonel John Nicholson. Col. Nicholson, of neighboring Maybrook, was a local military hero. Col. Nicholson had served under General Richard Montgomery in the 1775 invasion of Canada and at the battle of Quebec in late 1775. After the American military defeat at Quebec, Nicholson returned to New York and obtained authority to organize and recruit a new regiment called Nicholson's Regiment. Daniel may have gone to war earlier, at about age fourteen, inspired by Colonel Nicholson. The regiment campaigned mainly in the Mohawk Valley and western New York. Also see Chapter 23: Nicholson.

Daniel married the colonel's daughter, Ann Nicholson, at the First Presbyterian Church in Goshen. They lived in Wards Bridge, which is now a part of Montgomery. They had four children, Floyd, John Nicholson, Juliet and Elmira. He was a carpenter and a landowner with three horses. The three horses indicate a modest amount of wealth at that time. The 1790 census shows three adult males and three adult females in the home. It would be interesting to know who the six adults were in the household. They also operated a tavern or inn in Wards Bridge. It was reported to be a meeting place for the locals to have the revolutionary discussions.

After Daniel's death in 1810, his wife, Ann, continued living in the Middletown area as deed transfer records show. She later lived with their son, Floyd Smith Sr., in New York City, as the 1850 census shows. The pension law for widows was passed in 1832. As a widow Ann received a continuation of Daniel's Revolutionary War pension.

6 Floyd Smith Sr. (1791–1874) m. Catherine Ritter (1796–1869)
Born in Wards Bridge (now Montgomery), Ulster (now Orange) County, New York, Floyd grew up as one of four children in the Wards Bridge–Hamptonburgh area. He went to New York City at age 19 and worked for the Ritter family in their hardware business at Broadway and Maiden Lane. He lived with the Peter Ritter family which leads to the speculation that he may have had a family relationship to Deborah Smith (1742–1832), Peter Ritter's mother-in-law.

Floyd married their daughter, Catherine, in Christ Church when it stood on Ann Street between William and Nassau Streets in 1812. Catherine's uncle William Post had been a founder of the church in 1793. Floyd and his wife, Catherine Ritter, had fourteen children and lived at various addresses in New York City. After Peter Ritter died in 1811, the Ritter family moved to Greenwich Village and Floyd and Catherine lived on Barrow Street around the corner from Hudson Street. According to the 1822 City Directory they lived on "Bedford Street near Arden Street." As Chelsea developed, they moved from Greenwich Village to 251 West 19th Street and then to 435 West 21st Street where Floyd died in 1874.

In the War of 1812, Floyd served two tours of duty. He served one in 1812 and another in 1814. He was a Sgt. Major in Lt. Col. Simeon Fleet's 9th Regiment of New York Artillery, a militia unit, from 15 September 1812 to 15 December 1812 and received pay of $9.00 per month. Later, Floyd served as Staff Pay Master in Major Daniel D. Smith's 1st Battalion (formerly 9th Regiment) of New York State Artillery and later as a 2nd lieutenant and Pay Master in Capt. Benjamin Cooper's Company of Artillerists within the 1st Battalion, 6th Regiment of the New York State Artillery from 2 September 1814 through 2 January 1815 for which he received pay of $35.00 per month plus $8.00 per month forage pay (for his horse). One monthly pay record shows no forage pay with a note "kept no horse this month." It appears that his place of duty was New York City and that he saw no military

Chapter 14: Smith — The Most Common of Names

action. His unit was for the defense of New York City should the British attack. About 1850 he received 80 acres of "Bounty Land" for his service in the War of 1812. In 1855 he applied and received an additional 80 acres of "Bounty Land" for that "war service."

Later, in 1833, he was one of the founders and a vice president of the Manhattan Gas Light Company. This business grew as the city grew and was very successful. There were several gas companies that produced gas initially by heating resin rich wood and later in 1849 by heating coal or coal tar, thereby driving the gas out of the coal and pumping it through pipes to their customers. As these gas businesses grew, they competed for territory and space under the streets for their pipes. The term "gas house gang" derived from the work crews actually fighting for space to lay their pipes under the streets. He continued as vice president of the company until his death in 1874. In 1884, Manhattan Gas Light and five competitors merged together into what is today the Consolidated Edison Company, the major utility serving the New York City metropolitan area.[33] [34]

Catherine's parents, Peter Ritter and Catherine Post, were very active in the Episcopal Church. See Chapter 22: Ritter. Floyd and Catherine were also. They presented St Luke in the Fields with their first silver communion set in 1823 and contributed to the salary of their first rector. Floyd served as a Vestryman and Warden. Later, they were quite active at St. Peter's Church on 19th Street and the Church of the Annunciation on 14th Street, which has since been razed. Their children put up a plaque in their memory in that church. When Church of the Annunciation was torn down, the plaque was relocated to the tower of the chapel on the grounds of the Protestant Episcopal Church General Theological Seminary which was nearby. Floyd served as treasurer of the Episcopal

Floyd Smith and Catherine Ritter plaques in the tower of the Seminary Chapel.
Photo by W.C. Smith

---

33 American Oil and Gas Historical Society–Con Ed–America's Largest Utility
34 Website "ConEd.com–history–gas" accessed November 2018

Church Diocese of New York City, a voluntary elected position. See Chapter 22 for more on the Ritter and Post families.[35] [36]

5 Floyd Smith Jr. (1823–1893) m. Margaretta Oliver (1820–1881)

Floyd was born and raised in New York City. He was a tall man as we see in a picture of him with other Civil War soldiers. Early records show he joined the 59th Brigade of the New York State militia as a "member" in 1845 and served for years thereafter. At this time, his residence is listed on a militia membership receipt as 114 Chambers (Street). He married Margaretta Oliver, daughter of John and Maria Oliver of Philadelphia. They were married on October 12, 1848, in the Church of the Annunciation, at 142 West 14th Street, New York City, by the Rev. Samuel Seabury, DD. Reverend Samuel Seabury was a namesake and I presume related to Bishop Samuel Seabury (1729–1796), the first bishop of the Episcopal Church of America. Around 1853 they lived at 171 Second Street in Williamsburg, Long Island, where their son William was born. Later they purchased a house at 167 West 17th street in Chelsea from Clement Clarke Moore. They had six children. Two of their young children died in 1857 perhaps during one of the cholera epidemics prevalent about that time.

At the beginning of the Civil War, New York military units were called up and sent off to war. Many New Yorkers including those at the Manhattan Gas Light Company were concerned for the safety of New York City, their families (and their property) with the mainline troops being absent from the area. At a dinner meeting of employees gathered by an engraved invitation and held in the company offices on May 10, 1861, they set out to establish a militia guard from among their employees. The company president, Charles Roome, a man with military experience, agreed to be the Commanding Officer if elected, and the Manhattan Gas Light Company gave $5,000 toward their uniforms. After discussions and with approval from Governor Morgan and military leaders on September 7, 1861, it was opened to all qualified men and named the State of New York 37th Regiment of the 3rd Brigade, 1st Division.[37]

Floyd Jr. was a company employee and became a private in the 37th Regiment, Company A. He had multiple short tours of active duty during the Civil War: They left the state May 29, 1862, for three months of service and then returned and mustered out on September 2, 1862. This tour of federal service was to Camp Balger near Baltimore, Maryland, as part of the emergency defense of Washington DC.

---

35 Rev. Floyd Appleton, "Ritter and Post Family Records and Reminiscences of our Forbears," manuscript in the library of the New York Genealogical and Biographical Society.
36 Tuttle, Mrs. H Croswell, History of Saint Luke's Church in the City of New York 1820–1920, Publisher Unknown, 1926
37 Smith, Floyd, Jr., "37th Regiment Historical Scrapbook," Compiled by Floyd Smith Jr., c1868

Chapter 14: Smith — The Most Common of Names

He was promoted to the rank of corporal on April 3, 1863. On June 16, 1863, they were ordered to Harrisburg, Pennsylvania, for 30 days service, to assist with defense against Confederate forces moving north to capture that city. They left New York on June 18, 1863, arriving by train in Harrisburg at midnight June 20, 1863, with 585 officers and men. They immediately were assigned to Camp/Fort Washington for defensive duties. Beyond that, they participated in driving the confederates back, which precipitated the Battle of Gettysburg. During that battle, the 37th Regiment was in defensive positions around Chambersburg. They then returned to New York and mustered out on July 22, 1863.

The regiment was mustered in May 6, 1864, for 30 days of "in state" service at Fort Richmond. During this tour at Fort Richmond, which was a fort guarding the New York harbor, he wrote an interesting diary. This is a very detailed record of his daily activities. It is interesting that, as a senior non-commissioned officer, he was detailed to go into New York City at times. On these excursions he visited his family and also made collection calls on various customers of the Manhattan Gas Light Company for whom he was still employed. Such activity would be very frowned on by active-duty military personnel today.

Floyd was promoted to Fourth Sergeant, Company A, on September 2, 1864, then to Sergeant Standard on December 20, 1864, and then to Sergeant Standard Bearer, Company A, on September 19, 1866. On November 22, 1867, about the time of his retirement from his involvement with the Regiment, he was appointed Historian of the Regiment. In that position he made a scrapbook about the outfit. It is a collection of letters, military orders and announcements from the beginning of the regiment through the end of the war. The book is quite interesting, and provided much detail for the narrative above. His Honorable Discharge is dated November 20, 1868. The scrapbook belongs in a museum.[38]

The official record of the 37th Regiment Infantry in federal service during the Civil War as documented:

> 37th regiment; left state May 29th, 1862; service 3 months; mustered out Sept. 2nd, 1862.
>
> 37th regiment; left state June 19th, 1863; service 30 days; mustered out July 22nd, 1863.[39]

---

38 Smith, Floyd, Jr. "37th Regiment Historical Scrapbook," Compiled by Floyd Smith Jr., c1868

39 Phisterer, Frederick, New York in the War of Rebellion 1861–1865, F.R. Lyon Company, State Printers, Albany, 1912, p. 79

Chapter 14: Smith — The Most Common of Names

(left) Market in Harrisburg, PA 1863 — from left Shannon (our cook), Futchwanger, Floyd Smith Jr., R. H. Disbrow, Grotodoss and Morris. (above) Camp Seymour, PA 1863
Photos from Floyd Smith Jr. scrapbook of c1868

Troops of the 37th New York Regiment in 1864 (left) Fort Richmond, New York Harbour (right) Bay Ridge, S.I. — Probably Bay Ridge, Brooklyn, NY
Photos from Floyd Smith Jr. scrapbook of c1868

Floyd's wife, Margaretta, was the daughter of John and Maria Oliver of Philadelphia, Pennsylvania. Her father, John Oliver, died. We have no other records of this Oliver family other than the names of her parents and that they lived in Philadelphia.

Maria Oliver remarried to C. N. S. Rowland of New York City. C. N. S. Rowland adopted Margaretta and gave her away at her wedding. Also, he and Maria were sponsors at the baptisms of Floyd and Margaretta's children. At some point Floyd Jr. and family moved to Queens, Long Island, as census records show. Floyd's wife, Margaretta, died in 1881.

Sometime after that Floyd moved to New Haven, Connecticut, to live with his son, William, as evidenced in census records. He returned to the New York City area where he died in 1893. The family gravestone in the Westville Cemetery, New Haven, Connecticut, lists their names and death date. However, Floyd's death date on the stone, 1899, is incorrect. Could it be a later burial date? More detail work for family genealogists.

4 William Clement Smith (1853–1912) m. Eva Elizabeth Lehr (1856–1938)
I always wondered where the middle name Clement came from. While I don't have a firm source, I can easily assume that it came from association with Clement Clarke Moore as he was a prominent person, church organist and family acquaintance. While Clement Clarke Moore is most noted for his writing of "A Visit from St. Nicholas" also known as "T'was the Night Before Christmas," he was a very active and involved individual.

The family had an association and I presume friendship with Clement Clarke Moore as evidenced by several property deeds from Moore to our Smith family members including Floyd Smith Jr. Moore's father, Benjamin Moore, Anglican Bishop of New York, married Charity Clarke whose family owned a country estate. This estate consisted of the large area known today as Chelsea in New York City. At that time, it was rural and many families owned such rural estates north of Houston Street and up along the Hudson River, north of Greenwich Village. Charity Clarke and Clement Moore inherited the property and lived in the country home with their children. They donated land for the Protestant Episcopal Church General Theological Seminary to be located there, and he taught history and Latin at the Seminary for many years. As the city grew and developed northward, Moore established a real estate company, Chelsea Moore, which developed the Chelsea property and sold off the lots in the area around the Seminary.

Moore also donated land for the building of St. Peter's Chelsea Episcopal Church on West 20th Street, where he served as a Vestryman, warden and organist for many years. Several stained-glass windows in the church were donated by Floyd Smith Jr.'s siblings and their families. I have a strong feeling that Moore influenced William in his decision to leave home at age 16 to go to New Haven, Connecticut, to be an apprentice pipe organ maker.

William Clement Smith was born and raised in New York City. He was a tall man just like his father. We have some drawings of his that show his special inventive and mechanical abilities at some early age. The following passages are from a New Haven Fire Department booklet printed in 1888.[40]

He came to "… finish learning his trade as a pipe organ maker, but never worked a

---

40 Unknown, "Pamphlet from the New Haven Fire Dept.," Publisher unknown, c1888

minute in the business after completing his term of apprenticeship. He joined the fire department as a steamer driver in 1869, and filled various positions on the call and permanent force until he was transferred to the fire alarm telegraph service."[41]

William was away from home and driving a team of horses which were pulling a steam generator for fire fighting at age 16.

"During this time as a call man Mr. Smith manufactured various devices of his own invention, among them being a lightening hitch, for instantaneously hitching a horse to any vehicle with shafts or pole. At an early age he developed an inventive talent, especially in the line of electrical machinery."[42]

"In 1883 he was appointed superintendent of the fire alarm telegraph, and began at once to thoroughly transform the system then in vogue into the present. New methods and appliances were adopted and all the old signal stations remodeled to meet the requirements of the non-interference system of fire alarms. … Much of the wonderful mechanism now in use is his invention. He is the electrician of the police department also, and the joint inventor with Detective Brewer of the Brewer and Smith visual signal system. … Mr. Smith is a courteous official, popular with both firemen and the public."

Photo from Fire Dept. pamphlet c1888

He became a fireman and rose to become an assistant fire chief of the New Haven Fire Department. His inventions include patent number 191,081 "Apparatus for Attaching Harness to Shaft" patented May 22, 1877. The fire horses were trained to respond to the alarm of a fire by moving into place in front of the fire wagons. His invention was a mechanism to cause the harnesses to automatically drop onto the horses and easily connect once they stepped into place, saving response time to a fire.

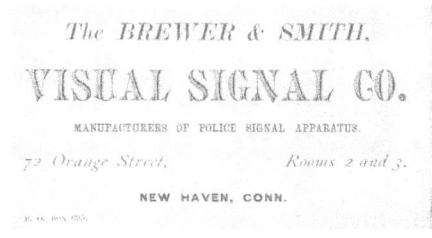

---

41 Ibid
42 Ibid

Chapter 14: Smith — The Most Common of Names

Another invention (patent number 343,863 "Electric Alarm Apparatus") was patented June 15, 1886. This was a system of alarm bells to signal calls to the station. And another of his inventions was patent number 347,318 "Apparatus for Signaling Policemen," patented August 17, 1886. This was a police call box, which stood on a sidewalk where a policeman could call his station house. This system also allowed a central station operator to trigger an electromagnet in the lamp to drop a red lens over the lamp to notify a beat policeman to call his station from the call box.

In the course of his work with the fire department he was injured and crippled for life when an excited horse suddenly backed up a fire vehicle just as he jumped off the rear of the vehicle and it backed up over his legs. He received a modest pension from the fire department and was bedridden the rest of his life. My father recalled how he would crawl up on his grandfather's bed to sit with him during visits.

Chief A. C. Hendrick (leading), Fire Marshal Kennedy (behind Chief), William C. Smith (tall man in the right photo)

William Clement Smith married Eva Elizabeth Lehr. She was the daughter of German immigrants, J. Gottfried Lehr from Shierstein near Weisbaden and Eva Barbara Kirchmer from Edelsheim, Bavaria. They arrived by ship from Antwerp, Belgium, with 4 pieces of luggage. Gottfried and Eva Barbara lived at 902 Grand Avenue in New Haven where he was a tailor. Eva Barbara Kirchmer died young and Gottfried remarried. Gottfried had more children by his second wife, many of whose descendants continue to reside in New Haven.

Chapter 14: Smith — The Most Common of Names

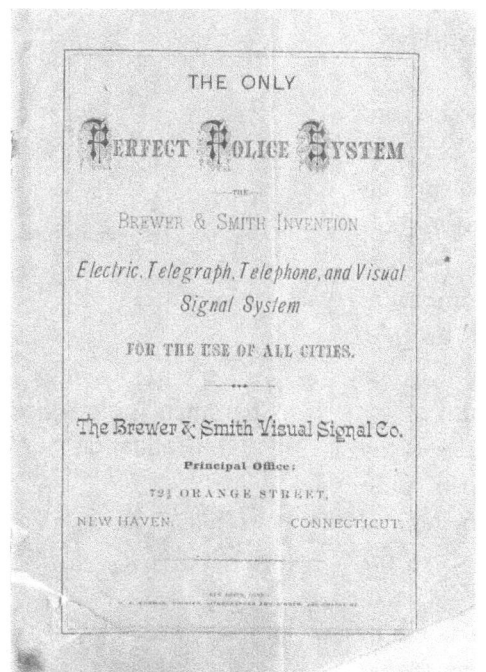

The Brewer and Smith Visual Signal System 20 page sales pamphlet explaining its operation.

William and Eva Elizabeth lived at 725 State Street in New Haven. They had two boys, Samuel William "Will" Smith and Charles Herbert Smith. William and Eva are buried in Westville Cemetery in New Haven, Connecticut.

Brothers — Will and Charles H. Smith

3 Charles Herbert Smith (1878–1967) m. Genevieve Blake (1879–1933)

In the 1880s and 1890s growing up in New Haven, Connecticut, was good for middle class youth. The city had not become far flung. The factories were humming and industry was not yet producing unusual pollution such as the steel industry in Pittsburgh. The Connecticut River still had good shad run fishing and in Long Island Blue fishing was good. Charles Herbert Smith and his brother Will had a good childhood. When we lived with Charles during WWII and a few years thereafter, we would sit by the fireplace some evenings and he would tell stories of his growing up and the boats he built and fished with. One story related that, when the circus came to town, he and his friends would get free tickets for hauling water to the animals.

Boardman Trade School Graduation

He attended Boardman Trade School, the equivalent of a vocational high school, in New Haven where he played football and learned mechanical and technical skills. After graduating from Boardman, he found employment in the early auto industry.

On July 28, 1902, Charles married Genevieve Blake in her parents' home at 134 Cedar Hill Avenue in New Haven. Genevieve, or "Genie" as she was called, was a strong influence in the family and "got things done" as my mother told me several times. They had two children, Charles Clement Smith born in 1904 and Susie Virginia Smith born in 1907.

Charles and Genevieve

Charles and Genevieve ensured that their children got good schooling including good college educations. Charles served on the Shelton School Board, but removed his son when he felt he needed a better school. Or maybe he needed a school that made him apply himself.

He worked for the Kidder Motor Vehicle Company in New Haven and Boston, a firm that manufactured an early steam-powered automobile called the Kidder Steam Wagon. Apparently, they were only in business in 1900 and 1901. He

Susie Virginia Smith and Charles Clement Smith

also said he worked in a Pierce Arrow auto agency's repair shop and told me how he "scraped-in" bearings for engines, among other jobs. This was a particularly skilled job of hand-fitting the engine bearings to the size of the crankshaft. New Haven was active early in the auto industry, as many cities were before Detroit and Henry Ford became dominant. In 1901 New Haven passed a speed limit law of 12 mph in the city and 15 mph in the countryside.

**1901 Kidder Steam Automobile
Charles H Smith standing - 2nd from left**

**1901 Kidder Steam Automobile
Photo from New England
Historical Society Website.**

Next, he worked at Yale University in New Haven as a laboratory technician, setting up sound experiments in their Psychology Dept.

Charles H. Smith of New Haven, Connecticut, was issued patent number 343,862 for the design of a "Snap Hook." The application was filed on April 26, 1886. The patent was issued June 15, 1886, and assigned to O. B. North & Company of New Haven. Whether this patent is his, at eight years old, I don't think so. But, my grandfather was very creative, intuitive, and excellent with mechanical machinery of all kinds. He also designed a drinking water fountain, the advertising for which says it was patented.

In 1905, Charles was recruited by his uncle, Watson J. Miller, to become Assistant Shop Superintendent of the Derby Silver Company in Shelton, Connecticut. See Watson J. Miller in Chapter 18. The company

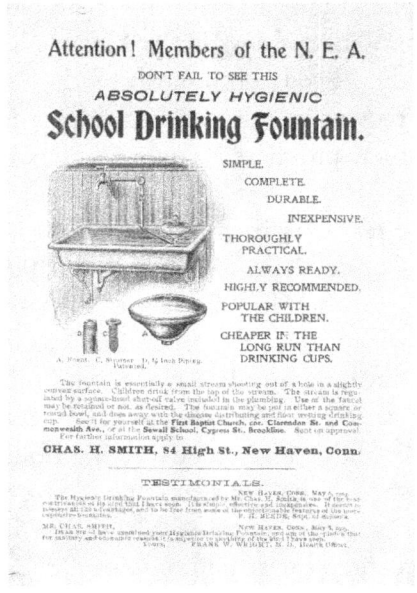

was a subsidiary of the International Silver Co. of Meriden, Connecticut, and manufactured plated silverware, tea sets, platters, and serving dishes. It was located in a large three-story brick factory building on the southeast corner of Canal Street and Bridge Street, adjacent to the bridge connecting downtown Shelton to downtown Derby. Canal Street in Shelton was a long street parallel to the Housatonic River. Water was diverted from the river by a dam far above the city into the canal, which also ran parallel to the river and served as a reservoir to turn sophisticated turbine water wheels in the sub-basements of the long row of factories that faced on Canal Street. From the sub-basements, the power would be transferred up to the machinery on upper floors by belts, pulleys and line-shafts. When the valve was opened, water flowed and the machinery

Charles H. Smith c1920

turned. There were many stories of the canal and the machinery including a story that said someone had to clean the eels out of the water turbines periodically. Another interesting story he told me was that the floor consisted of two layers of wood flooring and every few years they would tear up the top layer of the factory floor and replace it. They would then send the removed wood flooring boards to a company in Bridgeport to reclaim the silver metal dust and shavings that had fallen to the floor and become imbedded in the wood.

Charles and his family moved to Shelton where they lived temporarily with his Uncle Watson on Howe Avenue in the south end of Shelton. They then purchased a two-story house across the street at 108 Howe Avenue. About 1925 they bought Great Oak Farm at 962 Grassy Hill Road in Orange, Connecticut. A beautiful 300-year-old oak tree gave the farm its name. It sat high on Grassy Hill with views of "Derby Hill" to the north and across the Housatonic River to the hills of Shelton in the west. The farm consisted of 88 acres of fields, apple orchards and woods with a house, garage, barn and sheds. The house was good size with three stories, 6 bedrooms and 3-½ baths. The 1-½ story garage was a three-car structure with a basement that was used

for garden produce storage. Apples and potatoes would keep for 6 months in the cool, dark basement environment. The upstairs of the garage served as his daughter Susie Virginia's art studio and later his grandson's playroom and clubhouse.

The garage upstairs became our playroom and clubhouse. It was allowed to get us noisy grandsons out of the house. Along with our play areas in that upstairs there was also a small room with a locked door. We wondered what was in that room that grandpa kept locked. Curiosity got the best of us and my brother got a skeleton key, from where I don't know. He was always good at coming up with items we needed. We unlocked the door and perused through grandpa's things stored in the room and found nothing of interest for young boys. But we must have left something out of place for shortly thereafter the garage upstairs was placed off limits and our grand ideas for our clubhouse were vacated.

House at Great Oak Farm — Genevieve Blake (right) with their daughter Susie Virginia Smith about 1925

After accumulating considerable net worth in the 1920s, he was hit hard by the 1930s. He lost heavily in the stock market crash of 1929–1932. His wife, Genevieve, died of leukemia in 1933. The silver company closed about 1933 due to the Depression since few people were buying silverware items. They had even added a line of pewter products, which were lower priced, but no one was buying much of anything they made. The beautiful 300-year-old oak tree which gave the farm its name blew down in the famous 1939 hurricane.

Charles's mother, Eva Elizabeth Lehr (Smith), and his mother-in-law, Virginia Ruth Miller (Blake), lived with him at the farm, until their respective deaths in 1938 and 1939, as did his daughter, Susie Virginia Smith, who lived with him and cared for them all until she married Edward Carl Spahr Jr. in 1939.

Chapter 14: Smith — The Most Common of Names

Four generations in summer 1934 in yard at Great Oak Farm. From left: Susie Virginia Smith (my Aunt Virginia), Virginia Ruth Miller (dad's Gramma Blake), Charles Herbert Smith (my Grampa Smith), Charles Rosfjord Smith (my brother), Carolyn Clark Kaddeland (my mother), Eva Elizabeth Lehr (dad's Gramma Smith)

After the silver company closed, he started Smith Manufacturing Co. in the barn on his farm where he manufactured steel tote boxes for parts-storage in factories. His son, my father, Charles C. Smith, helped him get the shop started by working weekends with him and getting the electrical wiring material from General Electric Co. where he was working as an engineer at the time. My grandfather worked at this business for about 25 years, along with tending a large vegetable garden and his 350 apple trees. Most of the time he worked alone or with a part-time helper or two. During WWII he was very busy with orders from the U.S. Navy and employed some fellows who worked second jobs for him. Since he had military contracts, these employees were now working on war effort jobs and would have otherwise been drafted into military service. In 1943 when my father went overseas, we — that is my mother, brother and I — moved to live with grandpa since he was alone and we needed a home. As a kid, I was a little bitter that my father was away and these men got to stay home only because they worked on "war production" on a part-time second job. This was a bit self-centered on my part, since my father had chosen back in college to be a reserve officer and had gotten called up in 1939 even before WWII was declared for the United States.

Charles was a 32nd degree mason and belonged to the Scottish Rite. The Scottish Rite was an outlet for him, away from his solitary little shop in the barn, where he could meet and have lunch with his old friends every so often–usually once a week.

For some reason, he and his brother Will had a falling out and did not talk to each other for several years. His brother was executor of their parents' estate and I believe Charles thought his brother slighted him in the estate settlement. However, upon learning that his brother's health was failing, he quickly went to visit his brother to put aside whatever it was. He told us they had reconciled their differences.

Upon our father's return from the war, we continued to live at the farm. Our Aunt Virginia, Susie Virginia Smith, returned with her daughter, Virginia Miller Spahr, to live with us at the farm, after her (Aunt Virginia's) divorce about 1948. So, it was a busy place. See Appendix C: Spahr.

In 1951 my father took a new job, so we moved away to Louisville, Kentucky. It was a sad departure for all. Aunt Virginia taught school, raised her daughter and looked after her father for those many years until his death in 1967. He fell, broke a hip and was hospitalized, to his great disliking. He missed his home at the farm and surroundings of so many years and passed away in just a few weeks. Charles and Genevieve are buried in Eastlawn Cemetery in East Haven, Connecticut, along with her parents, the Blakes. Also see Chapter 16: Blake.

The farm was sold after his death. The house, garage and barn, being in disrepair, were torn down. The farming area was subdivided into home sites. Orange at that time was gradually changing from a farming community into a suburban town with housing subdivisions. The town of Orange purchased the area of the house and erected a large above-ground water tank on the site. The two stone pillars at the head of the old driveway on 121 Grassy Hill Road still stand with a gate at the entrance to the water tank area.

Life with my grandfather was all a young boy could ask for. He taught us how to raise a victory garden and sell the vegetable produce, cut and haul firewood, work on the apple trees, handle a gun to hunt rabbits and squirrels, and cut a live Christmas tree. We could also roam the woods, play on the remains of the great oak tree or get together with neighborhood playmates. On some rainy days he would drive us around on our newspaper route and vegetable produce deliveries. He even paid us to work in his shop where he taught us how to run machinery and equipment at age 13, much against the child labor laws but with our mother's permission. Looking back on that experience, I know it was good for us. He was the father we didn't have at the time and we were the company he needed also. I'm grateful for that.

Chapter 14: Smith — The Most Common of Names

2 Col. Charles Clement Smith (1904–1980), m. Carolyn Clark Kaddeland (1907–1966)

Charles was born in New Haven, New Haven County, Connecticut. When he was very young, the family moved to Shelton, Fairfield County, Connecticut, where he grew up and had his formative years. Charles had a dog named Bubbles, who like all dogs was always ready to eat something. Charles's mother always preceded feeding Bubbles with a narrative that went, "Bubbles, you should not be hungry today. You had big meal yesterday."

As a boy growing up during WWI, he was impressed by the military and kept newspaper clippings of the war news. At the close of World War I, the family went to New York to see a military homecoming parade featuring General John Pershing and some of his troops.

**c1904 Left Picture
(four generations from left)
Gottfried Lehr, Charles H. Smith,
Eva Elizabeth Lehr (Smith) and
Charles C. Smith**

**Right Picture
(four generations from left)
Gottfried Lehr, Genevieve Blake
(Smith), Eva Elizabeth Lehr
(Smith) and Charles C. Smith**

Not living up to his parent's expectations in grade school in the Shelton Public Schools, even though his father was on the school board, he was sent for high school to the private Hopkins Grammar School, where he became a better student. He attended Wooster

Chapter 14: Smith — The Most Common of Names

Polytechnic Institute for one year and then transferred to Massachusetts Institute of Technology where he graduated in 1927. Through an early version of Army ROTC at MIT he obtained a reserve officer's commission in the U.S. Army.

In 1928 Charles was diagnosed with tuberculosis and was sent to Gaylord Farm Sanitorium. Nine months later, in 1929, a new doctor examined him to discover that he did not have TB but another very curable ailment. He was treated and released.

About age 4

With sister

Hopkins Grammar School

Boy Scout

Model T Ford

1927 MIT graduation

Gaylord Farm Sanitorium c1930

Working at GE

Chapter 14: Smith — The Most Common of Names

During the 1930's he worked for several different companies, obtained his Professional Engineers License and served as President of the Bridgeport Engineers Club. He married Carolyn Kaddeland, a childhood next-door neighbor and also a close friend of his sister, Susie Virginia Smith. They had two sons, Charles Rosfjord Smith and Watson Christen Smith.

During the 1930s he went to Army Reserve camps for a week or two each summer to stay active in the reserve. Being an Active Reserve Officer, he was called up in 1939 for the Lend-Lease Program, supplying arms, equipment and munitions to Great Britain before our entry into WWII. He was assigned to inspect ammunition at the Springfield Armory in Springfield, Massachusetts, and commuted weekly to Springfield. In 1940, he was transferred to the Pentagon in Washington, DC. The family moved to 201 Raymond Street, Chevy Chase, Maryland. Prior to the Japanese attack on Pearl Harbor, military personnel in Washington were to wear uniforms only occasionally, in order to minimize the military appearance in the city. Many of the officers shared uniforms to reduce their expenses by taking turns wearing the same uniform on different days of the week. After Pearl Harbor was attacked on December 7, 1941, everyone was ordered to wear full uniforms. Since officers are not furnished their uniforms, but must buy their own, that week they spent most of their paychecks on new uniforms.

He was sent to Command and General Staff School at Fort Leavenworth, Kansas, for training as a field grade officer. He often spoke of the intensity of that program and how many men washed out. After graduating from the program and being promoted to the rank of major, he was assigned to command an ordnance battalion in Mississippi in preparation for shipment overseas.

We packed into the 1940 two-door, six-cylinder Packard and rode with him to Jackson, Mississippi, where he put my mother, brother and me on a train back to Washington. I contracted measles along the way and my mother was afraid we would be put off the train as it was full of soldiers. I was kept hidden in our roomette until we arrived safely back in Washington. I recovered from the measles in due time without any additional problems.

The 140th Ordnance Base Auto Maintenance Battalion trained at Camp Flora, near Jackson, Mississippi, and then packed up to ship out to England. Our father returned with the car to Washington, said his goodbyes and then left to catch up with his outfit at its port of embarkation in New Jersey. Part of his responsibilities included standing at the top of the ship's boarding ramp to receive his troops. No pets were allowed on board. As the Battalion Senior Sergeant stepped on board, the head of the battalion's mascot, a small dog, poked his head out of the sergeant's pocket. My father quickly turned his head to avoid having to deny the mascot's boarding.

Chapter 14: Smith — The Most Common of Names

Until then, our mother did not drive. She took driver training and quickly became proficient enough with the manual gear shift on the 1940 Packard to drive us from Washington, DC, through New York City to Connecticut. The trip was successful with only the loss of one hubcap on the curb of a tight corner in New York City. The family moved to Great Oak Farm in Orange, Connecticut, to live with Charles's father, Charles H. Smith, for the duration of the war. Our mother had the adjacent very nice picture taken of us to send to Charles in England to remember us.

In England, the 140th Battalion set up shop assembling war equipment and vehicles from parts and subassemblies shipped from the States and England. One interesting job they had was to rebuild landing craft which had been used in the invasion of North Africa. The battalion had been thoroughly trained in gasoline engines, but these craft had diesel engines. Fortunately, they had an officer named Gray from Salt Lake City, Utah, who knew enough about diesel equipment to be able to train the battalion to handle the job. We visited officer Gray at his Hudson automobile dealership in Salt Lake City in 1949 on our trip to California. Our father and he reminisced for an hour before we got back on the road.

The officers of the 140th Base Auto Maintenace Battalion, Camp Flora, Jackson, Mississippi. Major Charles C. Smith front row center with arms folded. 1943

Chapter 14: Smith — The Most Common of Names

The battalion and maybe the regiment held a large parade to donate an American flag to the Salisbury Cathedral which they hung during the war. In 1976, Linda and I along with the kids vacationed in England and visited Salisbury. In a second-floor room we found the flag along with a copy of the Magna Carta and other historical items.

Presentation of the American Flag to the Salisbury Cathedral 1943/4

Charles C. Smith at Salisbury Cathedral 1943 & c1975

As more troops arrived in England and in preparation for the D-Day invasion, Charles was reassigned to command a marshaling area, a large camp for transient troops and equipment. After D-Day he was again reassigned as Director of Port Services of the Port of Southampton, England, which shipped more troops and equipment during WWII than any other port in the world except New York City.

He kept a dairy of his day-to-day events and interesting thoughts while serving overseas in England during the war. We received many V mails from him which were always exciting even if he could not tell us much due to wartime security. V mails were a photo reduction of the original letter, reduced in order to conserve shipping volume during the war. He also shipped a crate which contained 2 German helmets, a German overseas cap and a German gas mask which we proudly showed off to our playmates.

He achieved the rank of full colonel for which he was justly proud. His chronological military experience of assignments and promotions are as follows:

Reserve Officer Training Corps.–MIT 1927.
Appointed 2nd Lt. 16 July 1931
  Promotions:
    17 Nov. 1936 to 1st Lt.
    1 June 1941 to Capt.
    2 Jan. 1942 to Major
    12 Nov. 1943 to Lt. Col.
    8 June 1945 to Col.
  Active Duty:
    Aberdeen Proving Ground, MD   26 Jul 1931–8 Aug 1931
    Connecticut Nat'l Guard, CT   29 Jul 1934–11 Aug 1934
    Mass Inst of Technology, MA   16 Aug 1936–29 Aug 1936
    Springfield Armory, MA   1 May 1938–14 May 1938
    Hartford Ordnance District, CT   27 Nov 1939–
    Office of Chief of Ord., Pentagon, DC
    Ex Off. 2nd Bn 126 Ord. Regt.
    12th Div. Class Command & General Staff School
    CO 140th Ord. Bn. Jackson, MS to England
    CO Marshaling Area C, Salisbury, England
    Director of Port Services, 14th Port, Southampton, England
    Return to Camp Devon, MA, USA — Discharged — 17 May 1946

After returning from WWII, Charles desired to start his own business. His experience of working a few years in wire and cable at the General Electric Company in the 1930s interested him in starting a copper wire company. He had purchased a building on Canal Street in Shelton, Connecticut, and was in the process of buying equipment when a copper strike put a stop to his endeavors. The frozen wages and price controls during the war years had created a pent-up inflationary movement and an accompanying demand for wage and salary increases. This broke loose after the war. It led to several strikes in key industries, in the years following the war, until a balance of supply and demand evened things out.

Chapter 14: Smith — The Most Common of Names

Charles returned for a visit to MIT and conferred with a former professor about what he should do. The advice was that his background and experience was very suitable for management consulting in the engineering and manufacturing fields. He obtained such a consulting position with Ebasco Services in New York City. Commuting from Orange every day by train, he was able to read during the hour-long trip each way. Some client assignments took him away on month-long trips, which did not sit well with the family as we missed him.

One such trip resulted in our moving to San Diego, California. Our father, as part of a team of consultants from Ebasco Services, had spent a month there evaluating Consolidated Vultee Aircraft. Floyd Odlum, the financier-owner, accepted their report and now wanted them to implement their recommendations. This necessitated several families on the consulting team, including us, to uproot their lives and move to San Diego for a year. Our family rented a California bungalow house on 1st Avenue up toward Old Mission and the family got to see their father every evening. The trip to California and back from Orange in our 1946 two-door, six-cylinder Packard was a grand adventure thoroughly planned by our mother. It was her chance to see the country, while Charles did the driving. This was the day before 4-lane interstate highways. Every road was two-lane west of New Jersey. We took a northern route traveling west which included the Dakota Badlands, Wyoming, Yellowstone Park and Salt Lake City. On holidays while in California we traveled to Los Angeles to see the Rose Bowl Parade, to Yosemite National Park and the redwoods, San Francisco Fisherman's Wharf and down into Mexico. After our one-year stay, we took a southern route back to the east with stops at Boulder Dam, the Grand Canyon and the Petrified Forest. It was a memorable year for the family.

About 1951, Charles took a position with General Electric Co. as Superintendent of Manufacturing of the Range Division's new plant at a new "Appliance Park" industrial complex to be built in Louisville, Kentucky. The family moved to Dorsey Lane near Anchorage, Kentucky, a move that made us Midwesterners. It was a good move for the family, but it was bittersweet to leave our grandfather and Great Oak Farm. This was the first home that my parents owned after moving around in rental houses and living with my grandfather. It was on 5 acres with a two-car garage, a small barn, fruit trees, a garden area and 3 acres of woods. They finished the second floor into two bedrooms and added a second bath before my brother came home from college. The house was well suited for us.

Dorsey Ln., Anchorage, KY.

After about 5 years, Charles and GE parted ways and he went back to management consulting with several different companies that took Charles and Carolyn to homes at 506 Arlington in Erie, Pennsylvania, and at 14260 Larchmere Blvd. in Shaker Heights, Ohio. Our mother, Carolyn, was a loyal wife and a good trooper, enduring these moves, upheaval of the family and parting from friends without complaint.

Charles never lost a desire to own his own business. An opportunity came in 1964 to purchase a small business in Cincinnati, Ohio, in which their two sons, who were now out of college, could join him. They moved to 6780 Tupelo Lane, Indian Hill, Ohio, near Cincinnati. The company, The Harvey P. Bertram Company (later Industrial Air Inc.), was a manufacturer of industrial fans of 12 inch to 12 feet in diameter sold to a wide variety of industrial customers. This business engaged Charles and he applied himself to the many tasks of running it. The business grew and expanded to enable him to bring both sons into the company management. The sons took over running the business day to day, while he served as Chairman of the Board and provided wisdom from his broad and extensive business experience.

Carolyn Clark Kaddeland, his wife, our mother, was very typical of executive's wives during that era. Although she had a college degree, her duty was to manage the household, bear and raise the children, and support her husband, the breadwinner of the family. She handled things very well and raised us while our father was very busy and away from home in the Army during WWII and on various consulting projects around the country. Just when retirement years approached, Carolyn fell ill with ovarian cancer and passed away in 1966 at age 57. See Chapter 15: Kaddeland.

A few years later, while at a reunion at MIT in Boston, he looked up an old friend from his college days, Eleanor Richmond. She had just retired from teaching, had never married, still lived in the same house and even had the same license plate number. Needless to say, they were married within a year. Eleanor tore up her New England roots, and moved to Cincinnati. She got Charles to eat healthy, travel, not worry about the business, to eventually move

Eleanor cranking dad's model T Ford. c1927

Chapter 14: Smith — The Most Common of Names

to a retirement village and to spend winters in Green Valley, Arizona. His interest in supporting military training continued and since his military training began with Reserve Officer training at MIT, he established a fund for a saber to be given annually at the spring

MIT saber presentations by Charles, myself and Aunt Virginia

military banquet. He gave the saber for the first few years and after that family members made the presentation.

These were well deserved good years. Eleanor provided needed companionship and extended his life by many years.

He devoted his remaining years to the Smith family genealogy and wrote many letters searching historical records in Connecticut, New York and Massachusetts which have provided a wealth of data for me to build upon. Today it is quite a bit easier with a computer and internet use.

He wrote a very nice, interesting memoir of his life, *Autobiography of a Connecticut Yankee*, which he finished just a few months before he died. The memoir was published, as a hardbound book, by Eleanor and his sons.[43]

Charles and Eleanor working on Genealogy

---

43 Smith, Charles C. *Autobiography of a Connecticut Yankee* (Cincinnati: Charles C. Smith Family 1980)

Chapter 14: Smith — The Most Common of Names

A 75th birthday party for Charles and Eleanor in late spring 1979 at our home in Terrace Park.

From left rear: Robert Knoop, Ruth Hund (Knoop), Marilyn Neuhaus (Smith), Charles R. Smith, myself, Mable Rebstein, Wally Sarran, Helen Bertke, Don Bertke, William Hartman, Blake Smith, Margaret Hartman, Nellie Loch, Al Rebstein, Millicent Bender, Estel Sarran, Dad, Matthew Smith, Eleanor, Linda Bermudez, Linda, Charles T. Smith, Nancy Smith, William Smith, Todd Bermudez, Todd's friend, Paula Smith, Eleanor's Friend

Charles passed away in his sleep in Green Valley, Arizona, in 1980. He is buried in our family plot in Spring Grove Cemetery, Cincinnati, Ohio, along with both of his wives, Carolyn Clark Kaddeland and Eleanor Barnes Richmond.

1 Watson Christen Smith (1936–) m Linda Knoop (1939–)
See Parts 5 and 6.

Chapter 15

Kaddeland — A 20th Century Viking Connection

Norwegian genealogical research is difficult to follow. Until recent generations the use of last names was not common. If anything, they followed the custom of using the town they were from as last names. And the custom of adding "sen" or "datter" to parents' names for sons or daughters was widely used.

In 2015, Linda and I had a wonderful trip to Norway and after two weeks of exploring the country we visited Vest Agder and Mandal. Through my niece, Katie Dreisbach, we had been introduced, online, to Jan Landers, a distant cousin, in Portland, Oregon, whose grandmother had come to New York City in America from Norway a month after my grandfather in 1900. Jan gave us the name of Svein and Snnove Haddeland, who invited us to come and stay with them in Holme, Vest Agder and visit Mandal. Svein and Snnove could not explain the origin of the Kaddeland name, so I can only presume it is the farm location that yields the name Kadde land, at the end location on Kaddeland Street. Svein Haddeland, Jan

Karl Kaddeland Home Mandal, Norway

Chapter 15: Kaddeland — A 20th Century Viking Connection

Landers and I have a common great great grandfather, Christen Christensen Kaddeland. We thoroughly enjoyed our visit with Svein, Snnove and their daughter Anna, who went out of their way with kind hospitality to show us the area and specifically Karl Andreas Kaddeland's home, in Mandal, where my grandfather grew up. It was like we had known them all our lives.

9 Knud
All we have is a name.

8 Morten Knudsen (??) m. Gunlaug Aslaksdatter (1683-1775)
Morten was Knud's son.

7 Knud Mortensen Mjaland(1752–1823) m. Ase Jansdatter Hoye (1752–1817)
This Knud was Morten's son from Mjaland, which is north of Vest Agder.

6 Christen Knudsen Mjaland (1790–1816) m. Targjer Torelsdatter Aurebekk (1788–1858)
Christen is Knud's son.

5 Christen Christensen Kaddeland (1815–1896) m. Gunhild S. J. Brindsdal (1814–1891)
Christen is Christen's son from or of Kaddeland. Christen and his wife lived and worked on the farm where they raised six children. According to family legend, at some point he lost half the original farm to pay a gambling debt. The original farm buildings no longer exist. Only the Haddeland's very nice home, beautiful gardens and fields going back to nature are there now. Svein and Snnove Haddeland's son, Frank, now owns the remaining farmland.

Christen Christensen Kaddeland and his wife, Gunhild.

4 Karl Andreas Kaddeland (1856–c1920) m. Jette Oline Samuelsdtr Olsen (1853–1880)

Karl left the farm and moved to Mandal where he ran a bicycle and/or sewing machine shop. In 1879 he married Jette and they had one child, a son, Christen. Jette died a few months later, in October. The Olsen family was from a nearby town one mountain and one fjord west of Mandal.

Karl Andreas Kaddeland

We visited Mandal and found their home at Kastell Gata 2, Sanden, Mandal. Snnove Haddeland told us that at one time Karl had owned the whole block. No one seemed to know where his shop was. The home is a small modest one-and-one-half story home on a busy town street. Svein knocked on the door and we found that Snnove knew the occupant of the home. She invited us in and was kind enough to have us for a cup of coffee and a delicious piece of cake. This lady had grown up in the house as her family rented the second floor from the Kaddelands when she was a child. It was interesting to see the interior which now has plaster removed to expose the square log construction of the original house. We sat in the room where Karl and his second wife had posed for a picture, back when the room was plastered over the face of the logs.

Karl and Tomine

Svein, Anna and Snnove Haddeland with us in the former Karl Kaddeland home.

Chapter 15: Kaddeland — A 20th Century Viking Connection

Karl remarried to Tomine. Tomine corresponded with my grandfather and also my mother until she was 92. She had beautiful handwriting and perfect English. I recall my grandfather telling us that he had a letter from her saying that the fishermen brought her fish during the German occupation in the war when food was very scarce. The present occupant of the house had rented from Tomine and knew her very well. She said Tomine was a wonderfully happy person. The letters we have also reflect this.

Karl, Tomine and Christen

3 Christen Rosfjord Kaddeland (1880–1958) m. Daisy Selkirk Shelton (1886–1959)

Since his mother died a few months after he was born, he could have been cared for at first by grandparents and then by Tomine who raised Christen after his father remarried. Growing up in Mandal, Norway, Christen probably was technically trained by his father who in his sewing machine and bicycle business was very involved with mechanical things. There is a story told to me by my mother, that Christen had gone to a technical school in Denmark. Reportedly, he wanted to be a shipbuilding engineer and decided to come to America to pursue that career. At that time (1900) in Norway, the area around Mandal was very depressed economically. The conversion from wooden to steel boats was causing a depressed market for timber which was their main industry. Severe unemployment caused approximately fifty percent of the population to emigrate to Europe and North America. At age 20, Christen left Norway, went to England and then came to America, arriving through Ellis Island in New York in May 1900.

Christen R. Kaddeland

Locating in Brooklyn, New York, he found work as a "draughtsman" with a printing press company. A year or two later he moved to Shelton, Connecticut, to work for Premier

Chapter 15: Kaddeland — A 20th Century Viking Connection

and Potter Company, another printing press company. Apparently, he liked the printing press business because he spent the rest of his life at it. And he must have been good at it, as shown by his rising to the position of Vice President with Premier and Potter.

Christen liked mechanical things, including automobiles. We have several pictures of him driving early automobiles with Daisy Shelton riding alongside him. They married in 1905 and lived their early years in Shelton and then Ansonia, a nearby town. They purchased a lot in "south-end" Shelton at 21 Spring Street, and had a house built which Christen designed. Edward Carl Spahr Sr., a quality Derby builder, constructed the home. See Appendix C: Spahr. I particularly liked the house because it was on a fair-sized lot on a hill. The edge of the hill was rocky and a great place for a young boy to climb and explore. They had two daughters, Carolyn and Marcia, who grew up there. Life in Shelton was good for them.

21 Spring Street, Shelton, Connecticut

The Premier and Potter Company prospered and grew. They developed several gravure printing press designs. In 1926 they merged with Harris to become the Harris-Seybold-Potter Company headquartered in Cleveland, Ohio. The old plant on Canal Street in Shelton was closed in 1928 with their operations moved to the nearby newer plant on Housatonic Avenue in Derby. Both plants were sold by 1935 and all operations moved to Cleveland. Christen's job moved to Cleveland, so Christen had to go with it. Daisy would not leave her Shelton home, so Christen commuted between Shelton and Cleveland as best he could. I can only guess that Daisy clung to the security of her home and would not budge because she had experienced her mother's passing during her teen years and had moved around as a young girl. This long-distance marital relationship continued through the remainder of their lives. See also Daisy Shelton in Chapter 17: Shelton.

Chapter 15: Kaddeland — A 20th Century Viking Connection

During Christen's working career he was well known and well thought of. During WWII he was a member of the War Production Board. The Board's purpose was to strategically allocate material and production resources from civilian uses to the needs of the war effort. He traveled frequently to Washington, DC, and while there he often visited his daughter, Marcia Kaddeland (Dreisbach), who worked in Washington during the war and later also.

 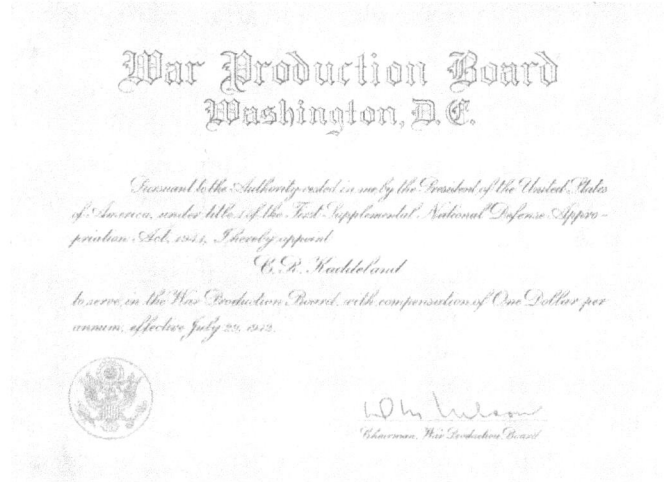

After we moved from Connecticut, Grandpa Kaddeland, as we knew him, would visit us a few times a year in conjunction with his business travels. It was always a short visit overnight and then he would be on his way. I recall my parents staying up late talking with him after I was long in bed. Our mother had a steady pattern of writing to him every month or so and he to her also. I remember we would buy him silk pajamas every Christmas and get them in the early mail to him. He would send my brother and me each a $5 check for birthdays and Christmas.

At some point he changed jobs to go with the Mielhe Company, another printing press manufacturer, in Chicago, Illinois. He stayed with Mielhe until he retired. He had several patents and I remember him telling me how they got the perforations on the printing of US postage stamps to stay lined up in between the stamp face. The problem was that as the sheets of paper rolled through the presses, small movement or paper slippage would cause the perforations to be not exactly between the faces of the stamps and constant adjustment was needed. Replacing the mechanically activated perforating with a photocell activated perforation corrected the alignment. This was part of new thinking in the printing press industry. That was the change from everything mechanical in the machinery to the inclusion of electronic control devices. He was always an innovator and I'm glad some of that rubbed off on me.

Chapter 15: Kaddeland — A 20th Century Viking Connection

He retired in the early 1950s and moved to Hendersonville, North Carolina. His former employer sent plans and drawings for his expert review. He enjoyed having something active to do in his lifelong field of work, since his entire being was wrapped up in the printing press business. While in college, I had a co-op job with DuPont in Kinston, North Carolina, and arranged to visit with him on my way back to college in Louisville, Kentucky. We met at the Battery Park Hotel in Asheville, just north of Hendersonville. Upon my arrival, I found him in the hotel lobby, smoking his cigar and reading the newspaper. We enjoyed dinner together, breakfast the next morning, and then I got back on the road. We talked family, engineering, college and printing presses. One quite interesting story he told involved some work he did on a Mielhe press at the US Mint in Washington, DC, that was printing US currency. It seems they were changing the plates that the bills were printed from and upon removing the old plates he put them in his suit pocket or brief case to get them out of the way. Upon returning to his office in Chicago he was visited by secret service agents, asking if he happened to see what happened to the plates. He promptly produced the plates for the agents.

Christen R. Kaddeland in retirement with a bow tie (I never saw him without a coat and tie on)

He was a very industrious and hardworking person who was honest and respected in his field, and received recognition for that. To illustrate this, he told me if I was in Washington, I should go to the US Treasury, ask for the Secretary of the Treasury, and tell him that I was Chris Kaddeland's grandson. He assured me I would get a personal tour of the US Mint. I never followed this up, but I'm sure what he said would have happened.

Retirement Dinner

Chapter 15: Kaddeland — A 20th Century Viking Connection

The Rosfjord name always perplexed me as it was my brother's middle name and my grandfather's middle name. I knew it was important from our Norwegian heritage, but why was it used? My mother and grandfather never shed light on it and I never thought to ask. During our Norwegian trip I found that the name originates on a fjord of that name just west of Mandal and a specific location on that fjord. Some ancestors came from there. So many Norwegian names originate on the place where a person is from. This solves the question somewhat, but there is still more to learn here.

He was a 32nd degree Mason and member of the Scottish Rite. I'm sure it was a good social and sincere activity for him, since his family was not with him for those last several years. He seemed very content with his life. I asked him why he retired in Hendersonville, North Carolina. He told me it reminded him of Norway.

In those years, traveling by train was easy and convenient and even if it took a little longer, it was usually his means of travel. Daisy at this time was in a nursing home and comatose, but he would still visit her in Connecticut perhaps twice a year to ensure she was cared for. He died of a heart attack on Christmas Eve 1958 getting into a cab at the New Haven, Connecticut, railroad station on his way to visit Daisy. Daisy died two weeks later. They are buried together in a family plot at Riverside Cemetery in Shelton, Connecticut. See Chapter 17: Shelton.

2 Carolyn Clark Kaddeland (1907–1966) m. Charles Clement Smith (1904–1980)

The Charles H. Smith family lived next door to the Kaddeland family in southend Shelton, Connecticut. Their son, Charles, was three years older than Carolyn and their daughter, Susie Virginia, about her same age. Growing up, Carolyn and Virginia were friends and playmates. Charles was just an older brother.

Carolyn worked hard and was a good student. I believe that is why her parents sent her to Derby High School in the adjacent town of Derby, Connecticut–so she would be challenged. She continued to work hard, got good grades and graduated from Derby High School in 1924 with honors.

At Vassar College she did well, graduating with her class in 1928. She was a member of the "Daisy Chain," an honor for which she was quite proud. "Historically, Vassar sophomores would attempt to sabotage the annual senior class tree planting ceremony by stealing the tree before or after it was planted. As a formal apology, they would in turn participate in honoring the seniors during graduation. Fifteen sophomores, dressed uniformly in white, would be chosen by the senior class to

Chapter 15: Kaddeland — A 20th Century Viking Connection

escort the graduates to and from the ceremony. Together, the members carry an intricately woven chain of daisies, handpicked from the surrounding Hudson Valley."[44]

Vassar at that time was an all-woman college. They had some association with Yale where the Yale men would come for dances and vice versa. For some reason she had no use for the Yale men. Yale, in New Haven, Connecticut, was close to Orange where I grew up. One day, I suggested to her I would like to consider going to college at Yale. She informed me that I could not go to Yale under any circumstances. That was the end of the discussion and the subject.

Carolyn had a younger sister, Marcia. Marcia married William Dreisbach and they had two children, William Shelton Dreisbach and James Dreisbach. See Appendix D: Dreisbach. My Aunt Marcia, Carolyn's sister, also attended Vassar College. Years later, she received an inquiry from the Vassar College Alumni asking if by chance she had gone to Derby High School as they had information about a Derby High School ring being found. She had gone to Shelton High School, but remembered that Carolyn had graduated from Derby. Carolyn had since passed away, so she passed the inquiry on to me. Contacting the alumni president, I was informed that an individual, with a metal detector, was searching in a hockey field that was to have a new building constructed on it, found the ring and wanted to return it to the owner. I contacted the man and arranged to meet him on my next business trip to the Poughkeepsie, New York, area the following month. We met and he gave me the small gold ring with Derby HS 24 on it. What a treasure. I tried to reward him for his efforts, but he refused, saying his pleasure was getting the ring to its owner. The ring is plain without any stone and so small compared to the large class rings with stones that are worn today. It carries memories of my mother, and my wife, Linda, now wears it almost constantly. Apparently, Carolyn played field hockey, which I never knew. Now we

---

44 Rubinstein, Merrick, miscellanynews.com, The Miscellany News, Vassar College student newspaper of record since 1869, 4/22/2021

Chapter 15: Kaddeland — A 20th Century Viking Connection

know why she always encouraged us to play ice hockey.

After graduating from Vassar, Carolyn returned home to Shelton. She took a job doing family counseling with Bridgeport Family Services, commuting there every day. By chance, Charles was working at General Electric Company in Bridgeport and it seems he offered her rides to work. A relationship developed and they married in 1932 at the Church of the Good Shepherd in Shelton. Their honeymoon trip was by train to New York City and steamship to Bermuda. The honeymoon trip was fine and wonderful except for the small fact that Carolyn was very seasick on the boat rides to and from Bermuda.

Charles and Carolyn's wedding party and aboard boat to Bermuda

They rented a house in Devon and then Fairfield. They had two boys, my brother Charles in 1934 and me in 1936. With two children, Carolyn became a stay-at-home mom. She was a good mother, always pressing us on different things that she felt were important for us, but letting us find our own way on most everything else.

Our family moved around quite a bit. During WWII the moves were caused by different military assignments, but afterward it was our father's various job moves. Our mother, Carolyn, I believe, had a say in those job changes, but was supportive of her husband's career and the family's future prosperity. One of those moves included going to San Diego, California, for a year in 1948 as described under Charles C. Smith in Chapter 14. This was an opportunity for her and the family to see the country and in particular California and Mexico. She planned various trips for weekends and holidays. We visited most everything there was to see in California and also on the way out there and the way back to the east. Our father did the driving of our 1946 2 door, 6 cylinder Packard automobile. Our mother rode in the front passenger seat and my brother and I fought over space in the back seat. But we all thoroughly enjoyed the traveling and seeing so much of the country.

Moving brought the opportunity to improve her home. They bought a good-sized Cape Cod style home on 5 acres on Dorsey Lane, Anchorage, Kentucky, where we lived for about 5 years and then a very comfortable two-story new home at 506 Arlington Road, Erie, Pennsylvania, where they lived 3 years.

Carolyn holding baby Charles R. Smith with his Great Grandmas Blake and Smith

They then moved to Cleveland where they purchased a large, very comfortable, Tudor-style home at 14260 Larchmere Boulevard, Shaker Heights, Ohio. The house had 6 bedrooms, 3-½ baths and a second-floor solarium off the master bedroom. This home was our mother's dream and she really loved it, but by then her children were off on their own and they were empty nesters. She fully enjoyed our visits, but you could tell she wished we were closer and around more often.

A family decision to purchase a business in Cincinnati, Ohio, caused another move for Carolyn, this time to a large ranch-style brick home at 6780 Tupelo Lane in Indian Hill, Ohio, where she could be near her children and grandchildren. It was a comfortable home for them and many good family outings occurred there. That was a consolation for Carolyn. She appreciated being near to her sons and grandchildren, but she still missed the Shaker Heights home which understandably was her favorite.

Carolyn died before our children really got to know her. It's interesting what memories last. Our daughter, Nancy, was only three, but remembers her grandma's gingerbread cookies. Carolyn saved sour milk for weeks to make the cookies. She was very thrifty and the cookies were delicious.

In October of 1965 she became ill with ovarian cancer. An operation and chemotherapy only prolonged her decline. She died in October of 1966 at Christ Hospital in Cincinnati. She was a conscientious and serious person who tried to have a good life for her family and do things honestly and properly. Outside of a good home there was very little she did for or spent on herself. Although she was not known to drink anything but water, the last thing she said was, "I think I would like a cup of tea." She was given a cup of tea and died shortly thereafter. My wife, Linda, thinks that if she had lived longer, and gotten to know and relate to her granddaughters, her life would have been very much different and enjoyable. Probably so. I have to agree.

Chapter 16

Blake — A Very American Family

According to Wikipedia, the surname "Blake" could have one of several origins before it became a common name in England. It could be Old Norse (Viking) from a people who came to Yorkshire, England, or from Blaker, a town east of Oslo, Norway. Alternatively, it could be from the word "Blac" meaning dark hair or skin or from dark earth area, meaning good farming.

Early use of the name back to 1286 sometimes refers to Blakeland, a Parish in Wiltshire County, England. Early family names from there used "de Blakeland," meaning "of or from there" and maybe meaning black dirt land. Subsequent generations dropped the "de" and the "land" and used the remaining "Blake." In any event it is an old name in England. Our branch comes from there and way back this may be an additional Norwegian connection.

10 Capt. Blake (1604–??) m Elizabeth Lyker (1632–1691)
Not much is known about the Captain except that he married Elizabeth Lyker of Somerset, England, and they had a son, John. Captain Blake died shortly thereafter and his widow, Elizabeth, remarried to George Durant, a blacksmith in Malden, England. They emigrated about 1660 or 1661 to Malden, Massachusetts, where they rented a farm for a year or more and then moved to Middletown, Connecticut. Elizabeth died in Middletown.[45]

9 John Blake Sr. (1652–1690) m Sarah Hall (1654–1726)
John Blake was born in Malden, Surrey, England, and came to America with his mother and stepfather, George Durant, when he was about nine or ten years old. He married Sarah

---

45 Blake, George Matthew, *Our folks–Blakes,* Second Preliminary Draft, Printer W. P. Lamb, Rockford, Ill., 6/1/1895, page 3

Hall in Malden, Massachusetts, in 1673 and they had nine children including a daughter, Sarah Blake (1675–1737). See Chapter 25 for daughter Sarah Blake. John and Sarah lived in Middletown, Connecticut. They are buried in Old Farm Hill Cemetery in Middletown, Connecticut.[46]

Sarah Hall's family came from England to Maine and then to Massachusetts. After John's death in 1690, Sarah remarried an Edward Turner and had three more children.[47]

8 Stephen Blake (1687–1755) m Annah Lucas (1712–1752)

Stephen was born, lived and died in Middletown, Connecticut. His first wife, Hannah Cole, from Hartford died with no children. Two months later he married Abigail Hubbard with whom he had four children. Abigail died and then he was remarried to Annah Lucas with whom he had six additional children including our Freelove. After Annah died he married a Mary Brown.[48]

7 Freelove Blake (1745–1825) m Rachel Fairchild (1749–1815)

Freelove was born and raised in Middletown. He served in the Revolutionary War as a private in the 1st Regiment, 9th Company of Connecticut Militia under General Wooster of New Haven. The Company was organized after the British attack on Lexington in April 1775. He was discharged on December 28 of 1775. He served in the North Department, which means he most likely was in the Montreal–Quebec Campaign and was one of the many soldiers whose enlistment ran out at the year-end, prompting General Montgomery to make his ill-fated attack. General Montgomery had Quebec surrounded. The British were shipping in large numbers of fresh troops from Boston. Montgomery knew that his diminishing advantage, due to the ending of enlistments, would only get worse. He decided to attack, led the attack himself and was killed in the opening salvos. Freelove's enlistment expired three days before, so he probably was marching home to Middletown, Connecticut, when Montgomery and the remaining troops made the fatal attack on New Year's Eve.[49]

Freelove was a farmer and landowner. He was married three times and seven children were named in his will as recipients of his land and possessions. Some children were by his first wife, Sarah, who died in 1776. Some, including our Richard, were by Rachel, his second wife, who died in 1815. He married Olive, his third wife in his later years when

---

46 Ibid, pages 3 & 4
47 Ibid, pages 3 & 4
48 Ibid, page 6
49 Blake, George Matthew, *Our folks–Blakes*, Second Preliminary Draft, Printer W. P. Lamb, Rockford, Ill., 6/1/1895, page 6

Chapter 16: Blake — A Very American Family

he was seventy or older. All three wives are buried together with him in the Old Farm Hill Cemetery in Middletown.

There was another Freelove Blake, who was a cousin and lived about the same time in Middlefield, Connecticut. Some genealogy records incorrectly confuse the identically named cousin.

6 Richard Blake (1780–1857) m Patience (1789/90–1856)
Richard was born, lived and died in Middletown, Connecticut. He and his wife Patience had two sons we know of, Edwin and Albert. Edwin was about four years older than Albert. Richard was a farmer and we know naught of Patience.

5 Edwin Blake (1818–1875) m Lucretia Polly Andrew (1817–1865)
Edwin and Lucretia had three children we know of: Adeline, Halsey and Joanna. He worked as a machinist in his younger years. They lived in Middletown, Connecticut. Their daughter Joanna probably preceded Lucretia in death since she is not mentioned in Lucretia's will which does include Adeline and Halsey. After Lucretia died Edwin apparently remarried a widow named Annie with a daughter also named Annie and moved to Elkhorn, Kansas, where in the 1870 census he is listed as a farmer. He died there and is buried in Lincoln, Kansas.

Lucretia Polly Andrew's ancestors were as follows:
    Thomas Andrews (1539–1593) m Constance Sandrenham (1543–1593)
    John Andrews (1575–1663) m Esther Cherington (1575–1616)
    William Andrews (1595–1659) m Mary Abigail Savage (1602–1639/40)
    Samuel Andrew (1620–1701) m Elizabeth Ann White (1631–1687)
    Rev. Samuel Andrew (1656–1738) m Abigail Treat (1660–1727)
    Jonathan Andrew (1701–1739) m Elizabeth Smith (1702–1740)
    Jonathan Andrew (1715–1797) m Eunice Baldwin (1738–1764)
    John Andrew (c1759–1789) m Sarah Ann Beers (1760–1818)
    Jonathan Andrew (1786–1848) m Chloe Gilbert (1787–1872)
    Lucretia Polly Andrew (1817–1865) m Edwin Blake (1818–1875)

Rev. Samuel Andrew (1656–1738) was born in Cambridge, Massachusetts, in 1656, graduated from Harvard College in 1675 and continued there as a "Tudor and Fellow." He became an ordained Congregational Church minister and moved to Milford, Connecticut, in 1689, where he served as pastor for the next 50 years. In 1701, he and nine other ministers combined their books and other resources to found the Collegiate School. Under his tenure as Rector there, this later became Yale College

Rev. Samuel Andrew's wife, Abigail Treat, was the daughter of Governor Robert Treat and Jane Tapp also of Milford, Connecticut. Another of the Treat daughters, Abigail Treat's sister, Elizabeth Treat, married Rev. Timothy Cutler who followed Rev. Samuel Andrew as Rector of Yale. They kept it in the family.

Abigail's father, Gov. Robert Treat, was governor following our ancestor Gov. William Leete. See Chapter 26 for Gov. William Leete. Robert Treat was born in Pitminster, Somerset, England, and immigrated with his parents to Massachusetts in 1630 at age six. The family moved to Wethersfield, Connecticut, in 1637 and then to Milford, Connecticut, in 1639. Robert Treat and Jane Tapp met in Milford and married there. They had eight children. Robert became a leader in the New Haven Colony and opposed the merger with the Colony of Connecticut. He moved his family to a part of the colony in New Jersey (New Ark/Newark) for a while but returned to remain in Milford. He led the colony's militia for several years including the King Philip's War of 1676. He became governor in 1683 and served through 1698 except during the years when Connecticut was part of the Dominion of New England, an effort which failed. He is credited with saving the Connecticut Royal Charter of 1662 by having it hidden in the hollow of a large old white oak tree to keep it from the English Governor General, hence the "Charter Oak" narrative for Connecticut.

Originally there were several colonies in Connecticut. The Milford Colony was located just west of New Haven and eventually merged with the New Haven Colony. The town of Orange where I grew up was part of the town of Milford until 1804 when Congregational Church members, in Orange, petitioned for the establishment of their own parish and the area become North Milford. In 1822 the area of North Milford was divided into West Haven and Orange, Connecticut. The Andrew and Treat families were still prominent and numerous around Milford and Orange, Connecticut, when I was growing up there as a boy in the 1940s. At that time, we had no knowledge of any family relationship several generations back.

4 Halsey Horatio Blake (1843–1930) m. Virginia Ruth Miller (1848–1939)

Halsey was born in Watertown in Litchfield County where his mother, Lucretia, was from. So she probably went home to have her baby, Halsey. He grew up in Middletown and married Virginia in the Baptist Church there in 1873. They had two daughters, Genevieve and Betsey. Both he and Virginia were very short from pictures we have of them. One pension document lists him as 5 foot 4 inches tall, blue eyed, light hair and complexion. He worked in Middletown as a mechanic and lived at home in his younger years as noted in the 1860 census. After the war years, the 1870 census

Virginia Ruth Miller

lists him as a "Life and Fire Agent" which is an insurance agent. Then the 1880 census lists him as a "Tin Peddler." A man of many talents. He apparently understood mechanics, which is probably how he later became a "Traveling Agent" selling sewing machines. And eventually he became a real "Yankee Peddler," complete with horse and wagon, traveling door to door through the countryside and also had a store. As mentioned above, he was a small man. At age 74, the 1917 military census taken during WWI lists him as still 5 foot 4 inches tall and weighing 127 pounds.

Halsey served thirteen months in the Civil War with the 24th Connecticut Infantry Regiment, Company G, later company I. He joined as a musician, served the duration of the war and was discharged as a Private. One of their major engagements was the siege of Port Hudson on the Mississippi River below Vicksburg, Mississippi. From some notes in the family files for Halsey Blake and some further research, I can narrate his travels as follows:

The 24th Connecticut Infantry Regiment was organized on November 18, 1862, in Middletown, Connecticut, at "Camp Trench Hill," where he was either drafted or enlisted for nine months. They traveled by boat to Jamaica, New York, on Long Island where they boarded a steamship which took them to New Orleans, Louisiana. (The steamship was wrecked off Cape Hatteras, North Carolina, on its return voyage.) They then traveled by boat up the Mississippi River to Baton Rouge, Springfield Landing and Port Hudson among several engagements with the Confederates in Louisiana. At some point he was ill and sent to a convalescent camp to recover. He particularly noted the "Springfield Landing fight." The Regiment mustered out on September 30, 1863. The Regiment had lost only 18 men to enemy action, but 57 men to disease. He received a pension in later years for his service.

Halsey Blake at Lookout Mountain, Tennessee c1900

Halsey served in the Civil War and the adjacent picture looks like Lookout Mountain, Tennessee, from the view and the curve of the river. He is not in uniform, but it appears that he might have a medal on his left chest, suggesting that he may have returned there after the war during a veterans' reunion.

After many years in Middletown, Halsey and Virginia Ruth moved to 7 Cedar Hill

Chapter 16: Blake — A Very American Family

Avenue and then to 134 Cedar Hill Avenue, New Haven, Connecticut, where in 1902 their daughter, Genevieve, was married to Charles H. Smith, my grandfather. In New Haven, Halsey operated a retail

H.H. Blake sign from his Peddler Wagon or Store

store, selling the same items he sold out of his Yankee Peddler Wagon. Our son, Blake, has the H.H. BLAKE sign from the store or wagon.

After he retired and in his later years, they lived in a shore cottage on Main Street or Bungalow Lane in Short Beach, Branford, Connecticut (just east of New Haven). After Halsey's death Virginia Ruth moved in with their daughter, Genevieve, at Great Oak Farm, Grassy Hill Rd., Orange, Connecticut. After Genevieve's passing her care was in the hands of Genevieve's daughter, Susie Virginia, who also lived at Great Oak Farm. Upon Susie Virginia's marriage to Carl Edward Spahr Jr., they moved her to Ed and Susie Virginia's new home at 44 High Street, Milford, Connecticut. Virginia Ruth died there in 1939. Halsey and Virginia Ruth are both buried in Eastlawn Cemetery in East Haven, Connecticut. Also see Chapter 18: Miller.

Blake Short Beach Cottage

Grandma Blake and Aunt Virginia at Great Oak Farm c1935

An added note here is that the adjacent picture of Grandma Blake, as Virginia Ruth Miller was called, is in the yard at Great Oak Farm and the glass reflecting ball in the background was very pretty, but was destroyed by two young boys who thought it was a great target for BB guns. Needless to say, we were properly punished and made restitution to our grandfather.

3 Genevieve Blake (1879–1933) m. Charles Herbert Smith (1878–1967)

While my grandfather was a smart, industrious, hard-working man, Genevieve, or Gene (pronounced Genny) as she was called, was the driving force in the family, according to my mother who knew her well as a next-door neighbor and later daughter-in-law. She was the spark of the family and when we lived at Great Oak Farm you had a feel for what the house, farm and gardens had been like in years past before she died.

Chapter 16: Blake — A Very American Family

They had two children Charles C. Smith (our father) and Susie Virginia Smith (Spahr) (our Aunt Virginia). They raised them well and gave them good educations up through good colleges. She took in and cared for her mother, Ruth Virginia Miller (Blake) (Grandma Blake) and for her mother-in-law, Eva Elizabeth Lehr (Smith) (Grandma Smith). Genevieve died of leukemia before we were born so we never got to know this grandmother.

Great Oak Farm originally was a quite nice country home with gardens, orchards, etc. Genevieve was the energy that kept it beautiful and in order. Her death and the financial reverses of the Depression caused it to be neglected and to deteriorate. When we were there at Great Oak Farm, our mother did what she could to get us to work on the gardens and we helped our grandfather around the place. But much was needed and we young boys had other interests. She had rooms repainted and papered, but there was a major refurbishing needed by then–much beyond her budget.

When we lived with her widower husband, our grandfather, during the WWII years at their Great Oak Farm home in Orange, even though we were young, we knew she was missed. I feel our grandmother, Genevieve, would have been a good influence on us.

Chapter 17

Shelton — Early Strong Roots in England, Virginia & Connecticut

The name Shelton comes from the word shelter or an enclosed group of shelters in very early days. In that regard the name is very generic and many unrelated Shelton families could become established. The Connecticut Sheltons originated with Daniel Shelton and are certainly from England; most feel we are tied along with the Virginia Sheltons possibly as far back to a Robert De Sheldonne (1033–1070).[50][51][52] The Shelton ancestry connection is thought to be as follows:

32 Robert De Sheldonne (1033–1070) m Isabel De Sheldonne (1035–??)

31 Robert De Sheldonne (1055–1107) m Sarah Beavis (1057–1105)

30 Sir John De Shelton (c1080–c1150) m (??)

29 Sir John II De Shelton (c1100–c1145) m (??)

28 Sir John III De Shelton, Lord Mayor of Stradbrooke, 1st Lord of Shelton (c1140–c1190) m Dalta De Shelton (1128–??)

---

50 Nelson, Karen J., "Shelton Family History–and RelatedFamilies," Shelton-Family-History.com 6/21/21
51 Unknown, "Descendents of John de Shelton/Lord of Shelton Manor," Unknown
52 Shelton, Jane de Forest, *Reunion of the Descendants of Daniel Shelton at Birmingham, Connecticut*, Printers E.M. Ruttenber & Son, Newburgh, New York; June 14, 1877. Repository DAR Library, Washington, DC

Chapter 17: Shelton — Early Strong Roots in England, Virginia & Connecticut

27 Sir John IV De Shelton, 2nd Lord of Shelton (c1160–c1225) m Lady Beatrice De Record (1150–1200)

26 Sir Ralph De Shelton, 4th Lord of Shelton (1180/1200–1245) m Lady Catharine De Elleigh (1204/5–c1260)

25 Sir Ralph De Shelton, 6th Lord of Shelton (1229–??) m (??)

24 Sir John Shelton, 13th Lord of Shelton (c1249/53–c1333) m Agatha Gedding (1284–??)

23 Sir Ralph Shelton, 14th Lord of Shelton Manor, built Old Shelton Hall and St. Mary's church in Norfolk (c1315–c1358) m 2nd wife, Joan De Plais (1326–1405)

22 Sir Ralph Shelton, 15th Lord of Shelton Manor (c1330/34–c1385) m Alice Uvedale (1351–??)

21 Sir Ralph Shelton, 16th Lord of Shelton Manor (c1361–1429) m (??)

20 Sir John Shelton, 17th Lord of Shelton Manor (c1380–1431) m Lady Margaret De Brewes (c1412–1479)

19 Sir Ralph Shelton, 19th Lord of Shelton Manor (1430–1497) m Margaret Clere (1433–1498)

18 Sir John Shelton, 20th Lord of Shelton (1451–c1499) m Margaretha Saxony Wettin (c1433–c1500)

17 Sir John William Shelton, 21st Lord of Shelton, High Sheriff of Norfolk (1472–1539) m Lady Anne Boetler Boleyn — Aunt of Anne Boleyn (1475–1555), the 2nd wife of Henry VIII

16 Sir John Shelton, 22nd Lord of Shelton (1504–1558) m Lady Margaret Parker (c1509–1558)

15 Sir Ralph Shelton, 23rd Baron of Shelton, High Sheriff of Norfolk (c1530/5–1580) m Mary Amy Wodehouse (1534–c1565)

Chapter 17: Shelton — Early Strong Roots in England, Virginia & Connecticut

14 Sir Ralph Shelton, 26th Baron of Shelton (1560–1628) m Lady Jane De West (c1558–c1606)

13 "Gentleman" James Shelton (c1585–c1668) m Ann Herbert (1588–c1639)
James came to Virginia in 1610 with Lord De la warr/Delaware, later moved to Bermuda.

12 Thomas Shelton (1606–1683/5) m Hannah Wood (1606–1684)

11 James Shelton (1629–1716) m Mary Jane Bathurst (1630–1682)

10 Lt. Daniel Shelton (c1668–1728) m Elizabeth Welles (1670–1747)

There are existing references to other lines, but they are without clear documentation at this time. Many dates are not specific, but I am very comfortable with the above ancestral line at this time. Further research, back before Daniel, is needed and is beyond the scope of this book.

Being a Connecticut Shelton descendant tied to Daniel Shelton has been a lifelong learning experience for me. As a boy, my mother told me we were Sheltons even though our name was Smith and we didn't know any Sheltons (or at least they didn't associate with us, for whatever reasons). Then I learned my grandmother's maiden name was Daisy Shelton. And I learned that the town of Shelton, Connecticut, was named for the family and that my parents had grown up as childhood neighbors in Shelton. And we went to the dentist and church in Shelton. And my father owned a factory building on Canal Street in Shelton. But who were and where are these Sheltons?

Many years later, I picked up working on the family tree and the Shelton branch. I was able to get back two more generations to John Douglas Shelton (1813–1894), Daisy's grandfather, and learned he lived in Ansonia, Connecticut, and worked at the Star Pin Co. on Canal Street in Shelton. And, his son, Daisy's father, Charles Frederick Shelton (1845–1919), was a Civil War veteran. But I hit the proverbial "brick wall" as they say in genealogy research. A Daniel Shelton (1668–1728) had emigrated from England and was the origin of the "Connecticut" line of Sheltons. I was facing a search through the spread of many generations down to find the connection to John Douglas Shelton. This meant searching through and organizing about 1000 male Shelton descendants. Would I live long enough to do this?

At a Christmastime gathering in 2012, my cousin Bill — William Shelton Dreisbach, who is also a Shelton descendent — informed me that his daughter, Katherine "Katie" Dreisbach, was into the Shelton genealogy and had the connection. She gave me the line

Chapter 17: Shelton — Early Strong Roots in England, Virginia & Connecticut

connecting us back to Daniel Shelton and possibly a long way back in England. She was so full of information I just had to follow this up. Her source was a person named Tracy Gabbard (Shelton) who has a "Shelton Family Tree." Katie provided me with an email address.

Contacting Tracy turned out to be more than an interesting connection in that she and her husband, Roland Frederick Shelton (1954–), live about 20 miles from where my wife and I had lived in Cincinnati for 45 years. She provided the source document: A 100-page document from a Shelton family reunion organized by Edward N. Shelton (1812–1894) and held June 14, 1877. It is titled *Reunion of the Descendants of Daniel Shelton* and although no author is indicated, it most likely was drafted in part and organized for printing by Edward's daughter, Jane de Forest Shelton. The reunion document is a wonderful source of genealogical information, which clearly ties us back to Daniel Shelton.[53]

Jane de Forest Shelton (1843–1914) later became an accomplished author by writing for *The American History Magazine and Harper's Monthly Magazine*. Later, in 1900, she wrote the book, *The Salt Box House*. This book is still in print and sheds wonderful insight into the lives of the people in those early days. Although she doesn't specifically call it a history of the Shelton family, it is recognized as having been written from family letters and documents about how colonists lived in the 1700s, using some Shelton family members as characters.[54]

So, after 76 years I find that we are indeed Sheltons. I also learned that my grandmother, Daisy Shelton, had a brother John Frederick Shelton (1879–1967) and a sister Abbie B. Shelton (1868–1944). So, I had an uncle and an aunt as well as cousins that I had never met or knew anything about. Roland Shelton is descended from Daisy's brother John.

In May of 2014, my wife, Linda, and I met Tracy, her husband, Roland Frederick Shelton, their son, Nathan, and Roland's two sisters, Nancy and Becky, for dinner at the Golden Lamb near Cincinnati. It was quite a joyous occasion to meet and realize how family members and generations go in many different directions. After years of being unknown to each other, suddenly you feel a family closeness. Needless to say, many photos and family information were exchanged with firm promises to meet again.

---

53 Shelton, Jane de Forest, *Reunion of the Descendants of Daniel Shelton at Birmingham, Connecticut,* Printers E.M. Ruttenber & Son, Newburgh, New York; June 14, 1877. Repository DAR Library, Washington, DC

54 Shelton, Jane de Forest, *The Salt Box House,* Revive Books, Westport, Connecticut; Originally Published by Baker and Taylor, 1900

Chapter 17: Shelton — Early Strong Roots in England, Virginia & Connecticut

Plumb Library Visit 2014 — (From top left) Katie Dreisbach, Virginia Spahr, Bill Dreisbach

(From left) Nathan Shelton, Tracy Gabbard (Shelton), Linda Knoop (Smith), Roland Shelton, Becky Shelton, Nancy Shelton, W. C. Smith

More research and an October 2014 trip to the Plumb Memorial Library in Shelton, Connecticut, with Virginia Spahr, and Bill and Katie Dreisbach, brought out a load of information. This trip filled a lot of blanks in my understanding of the Sheltons. Daniel Shelton was the first Shelton in Connecticut and he certainly established himself by his vast holdings, as you can read below. The area where he lived was first inhabited by the Paugussett Indians who called the area Pootatuck. When Daniel arrived, it was called Coram and then Long Hill in the town of Stratford, then Ripton Parish and then in 1789 named Huntington after the Connecticut Lieutenant Governor, Samuel Huntington. The Ripton name certainly was Daniel's use of his childhood home in England. The name of Shelton was applied much later to a new industrial area, a few miles away along the Housatonic River that was developed in the late 1860s by and named after his descendant, Edward Nelson Shelton (1812–1894). Shelton incorporated as a city in 1915. The town of Huntington and city of Shelton were consolidated as the city of Shelton in 1919.[55]

I'm getting a better understanding of the Sheltons. I was always told that they were loyalists during the revolution, but they were in patriot territory. I don't have any record of them signing the "Oath of Association" so I expect they were not rabid patriots. I did find where William Shelton served in the militia, so I suspect there may have been more patriot participation. The more I read about the general population at that time, I realize

---

55 Shelton Historical Society, *Images of America–Shelton,* copyright 2002 by Shelton Historical Society; Arcadia Publishing, Charleston, South Carolina

Chapter 17: Shelton — Early Strong Roots in England, Virginia & Connecticut

there were loyalists, there were patriots and there was a very large group of people in between. And there were people who shifted toward one or the other side depending on who was winning the latest battles. This is a natural reaction for people who are trying to live their lives as best they can in the midst of a war. I think the Sheltons might have been among those in between, who sold their produce and goods to both sides. The family had about 9,000 acres of land and was in the farming, lumbering, warehouse and shipping business. Stamford was an active port and ships could come up the Housatonic River to the Huntington Landing. After Daniel, his sons and grandsons inherited and operated the farming, lumbering and shipping enterprises. Under British rule, colonists were discouraged from manufacturing, as Britain wanted the finished product trade. So manufactured items mainly came from England. It is well known that during the revolution, farm goods were shipped the short distance from Connecticut across the Long Island Sound and traded to the British. British manufactured goods were brought back to be sold to the colonists in Connecticut who still wanted nice things and utilitarian items even though it was forbidden by the Continental Congress to buy British goods.

From page 1004 of *A History of the Old Town of Stratford and the City of Bridgeport*, found in the old section of the Plumb Library, written in the 1880s: "Shelton is a new and prosperous manufacturing village on the west side of the Housatonic opposite Birmingham, in the town of Huntington, and was named in honor of Mr. Edward N. Shelton, who was very prominent in starting and pushing on the manufacturing enterprises which have caused the city to be built. … Some of the manufactories are very large and produce an immense amount of goods. The great dam across the Housatonic River just above the village secures such an immense water power as will give opportunity for a great enlargement of the place." Birmingham was the downtown area of the adjacent town of Derby, Connecticut. While by today's standards the canal and factories were small, in 1860 the dam, canal and factories were quite foresighted and an enormous undertaking. The company was formed in 1863 but construction was delayed by the Civil War. The 800-foot-long dam was completed in 1870. Canals on both sides of the river served waterpower to new factories in both Shelton and Derby. Although it was washed out by an ice jam in early 1891, it was rebuilt and back in service in 10 months. The dam and canals continued to serve customers until the 1950s and are still in place. Edward N. Shelton, who founded the Ousatonic Water Power Company that built the dam and canal for waterpower, was a cousin of our Alfred Shelton (1792–1857), although Alfred was 20 years older. And, yes the spelling of "Ousatonic" is correct. Wouldn't you have liked to have heard the discussion of using that name in 1870.

Edward Nelson Shelton

Chapter 17: Shelton — Early Strong Roots in England, Virginia & Connecticut

The canal was what brought my great, great uncle Watson J. Miller (my "Watson" namesake) and The Derby Silver Company to Shelton and subsequently the Charles H. Smith family.[56][57][58]

After WWII my father bought an old factory building on Canal Street. When I was 14, my brother and I worked there all one summer scraping and painting the interior of a part of the building that had been damaged by a fire in a tenant's space. Our father employed us for 25 cents per hour. Of course, we explored the building, as kids do, and way down in the sub-basement was a turbine waterwheel which had been used to drive the line-shaft machinery on the three or four floors above. It was very dark and spooky down there and I never wanted to stay long, however interesting it was. At that time, 1950, most of the factories had converted to electric motors, and only one or two still used water power from the canal.

Shelton is an area rich in history and from which many Shelton branches have spread with interesting lives and stories to tell. It's time for another reunion.

10 Lt. Daniel Shelton (c1668–1728) m. Elizabeth Welles (1670–1747)

In the Genealogy Appendix of the *Reunion of the Descendants*, written about 1880 by Jane de Forest Shelton, is the following about Daniel Shelton.[59]

> "Daniel Shelton, the founder of the New England branch of the family, was born at Deptford, Yorkshire, England. He and his brother Richard emigrated to this country before 1690. Daniel settled in Stratford, Connecticut and Richard in Virginia.
>
> "The earliest mention of Daniel Shelton, on the Stratford Records, is in 1687, when he is described as 'Merchant.' On his tombstone he was styled 'Lieutenant Daniel Shelton,' but in which country he served, or from which he received his commission, is not known. There is no record of his having served in this country.
>
> "He was one of the non-resident proprietors of Waterbury, as appears

---

56 Orcutt, Samuel. *A History of the Old Town of Stratford and the City of Bridgeport, Connecticut.* New Haven, CT: Press of Tuttle, Morehouse & Taylor, 1886.

57 Committee of Shelton Historical Society, *Images of America–Shelton*, Arcadia Publishing, Charleston, South Carolina, 2002

58 Wilcoxson, William Howard, *History of Stratford, Connecticut, 1639–1969*, Stratford Tercentenary Commission, Stratford, Connecticut, Second Edition 1969, pages 206–209

59 Shelton, Jane de Forest, *Reunion of the Descendants of Daniel Shelton at Birmingham, Connecticut,* Printers E.M. Ruttenber & Son, Newburgh, New York; June 14, 1877. Repository DAR Library, Washington, DC

Chapter 17: Shelton — Early Strong Roots in England, Virginia & Connecticut

by grant of G. Saltonstall, Governor, dated 28 Oct., 1720. He owned lands in Stratford, Stamford, Farmington, Oxford, Woodbury, Corum, Ripton and Derby. He settled in that part of Stratford called Long Hill. His land there was a tract about two miles square, extending from Long Hill through Corum to the Housatonic river, and on which three of his sons settled.

"He married 4th April, 1692, Elizabeth Welles, dau. of Hon. Samuel Welles of Wethersfield, Conn., and Elizabeth Hollister. Samuel Welles was son of Hon. Thomas Welles, one of the first settlers of Hartford, and one of the early Governors of Connecticut. Elizabeth Hollister was dau of John Hollister Jr., of Wethersfield, and Joanna, dau of Hon. Richard Treat.

"Mrs. Elizabeth (Welles) Shelton was born in 1670; died 1st April, 1747, a(g)e 77.

"Daniel Shelton died early in 1728, and is supposed to have been about 60 years old."[60]

That gives you a snapshot of Daniel Shelton and you would think that Jane de Forest Shelton would certainly know all about him, but there are some questions and discrepancies and there is more to know. First of all is the fact that there is no Deptford in Yorkshire County, England. Deptford is in Kent County, southeast and across the Thames River from London. The area was the home of the Royal Navy and there was considerable dockage in that location during the 17th century.[61]

Daniel is definitely linked to the Virginia Sheltons and probably as I have previously delineated above. Certainly DNA will eventually discern the truth of all that. Another story says he was shipwrecked off the coast of Connecticut. There is more to learn here.

From all I have read, my conclusion is: Daniel was born in Ripon, Yorkshire, England, where his family lived at the time, and that he emigrated from Deptford near London, probably with other family members. He arrived in Virginia and due to a family disagreement over his brother Ruben's will, where Ruben left his estate to Daniel and his brothers were jealous. Daniel left and went to Connecticut, which was opening up new colonies with inviting opportunity.

His exact birthdate is unknown, but most writers have selected 1666 or 1668. I think 1668 is probably more accurate. That makes him about 19 years of age when, in 1687, he

---

60 Shelton, Jane de Forest, *Reunion of the Descendants of Daniel Shelton at Birmingham, Connecticut,* Printers E.M. Ruttenber & Son, Newburgh, New York; June 14, 1877. Repository DAR Library, Washington, DC
61 Wikipedia Website, "Deptford, England"

Chapter 17: Shelton — Early Strong Roots in England, Virginia & Connecticut

is in Stratford, Connecticut, applying for permission to build a warehouse and wharf as a merchant. The permission was granted in May, 1687 and thus begins this history of the Sheltons in Connecticut. He was quite an enterprising young man–I strongly think he had substantial family backing or an inherited nest egg.[62]

Daniel's marriage to Elizabeth Welles indicates a very fortunate connection since her family was instrumental in the early settlement of the colony of Connecticut and the city of Hartford. This gives me reason to believe the Sheltons were somehow connected with the Welles, Hollister, Wyatt and Treat families in New England and there may have been connections back in England also.

Daniel obtained a large acreage of land in the northern area of the town of Stratford where he built his home and farm. This area was still mainly unsettled at that time and his accumulation of additional properties as Jane DeForest Shelton describes could have been land grants or investment purchases. He farmed, sold timber from his lands, and it is believed he operated a merchant and shipping business.

There were several separate original plantations or colonies started in Connecticut including Windsor, New Haven, Guilford, Stratford, Saybrook and Connecticut River Colonies. Each negotiated and purchased land from the Indians and established their own government and settlement. Slowly, they merged and combined to become the Connecticut Colony and later the State of Connecticut. The founders of Hartford and the Connecticut River Colony were the strongest group and basically absorbed the others. Daniel Shelton's wife, Elizabeth Welles's family was among the leaders in Hartford. Her grandfather, Thomas Welles, was Deputy and then Governor of the Connecticut River Colony for several years, from 1654 through 1659.

Some writers have speculated that Daniel engaged in the rum/slave trade, although I have not seen any documentation to prove that. He did have slaves, as did most large farmers, as Jane de Forest Shelton writes about them in her *Salt Box House*. Depending upon the character and disposition of the farmer or business owner, as she describes, they were sometimes almost part of the family. I would suspect there may have been indentured servants also.[63]

Living in a relatively unsettled area there was a need for security. According to the *A History of Stratford*, Daniel was appointed "Lieutenant of the Train Band" organized as a kind of local militia to provide a defense against possible Indian attacks.[64]

---

62 Orcut, Reverend Samuel, *History of the Old Town of Stratford and the City of Bridgeport, Connecticut*, Fairfield County Historical Society, 1886 Page 960 -966

63 Shelton, Jane de Forest, *The Salt Box House*, Revive Books, Westport, Connecticut; Originally Published by Baker and Taylor, 1900

64 Wilcoxson, William Howard, *History of Stratford, Connecticut, 1639–1969*, Stratford Tercentenary

Chapter 17: Shelton — Early Strong Roots in England, Virginia & Connecticut

A History of Stratford also tells of an interesting story about Daniel. He was a strong Anglican churchman. Local government in Stratford required all landowners to pay a church levy or tax. The local Congregational Church was the beneficiary of those funds. Being an Anglican, he refused to pay the tax. They sent men to arrest Daniel, tied him to a horse and took him to jail in Stratford. They would not release him until he paid the tax. He continued to refuse, saying the tax was unlawful. His family petitioned the Governor. The final solution was that they paid the amount as a fine to the Governor for his release. The governor gave the money to the church. Later, he and a group petitioned the Anglican diocese to have a separate Parish established from Stratford since it was a long way to go to church in Stratford, They were successful in that endeavor and the Ripton Parish was established.[65] [66]

Daniel Shelton was obviously a man of principle and good character, as well as a very successful businessman. The honors and recognition bestowed on him at the reunion were quite deserved.

His Long Hill home still stands as a private home. A few artifacts of Daniel's are on display at the Plumb Library.

9 Joseph Shelton (1696–1782) m. Mary Hollister (1704–1782)

Joseph was born in Wethersfield, near Hartford, about 40 miles from Long Hill. Apparently, his mother had gone "home" to her parents to have her child. Carriages were not common at that time in those remote farming communities according to Jane de Forest Shelton. Horseback or horse and wagon were the normal means of traveling any distance of more than a few miles. This is certainly an indication of the hardiness of these people.

In any event, the Welles family connection proved very interesting to Joseph and he probably traveled that road many times before he married. Mary was his second cousin from Glastonbury, Connecticut.

Mary Hollister's great grandfather, Lt. John Hollister, had settled in Weathersfield in 1643 and was an original founder of Glastonbury in 1644. He had received a land grant for work done for the Colony and held over 900 acres of land.

"Joseph Shelton lived at Long Hill, not far from his father's house."[67] Joseph and Mary

---

Commission, Stratford, Connecticut, 1939, pp 206–7

65 Wilcoxson, William Howard, *History of Stratford, Connecticut, 1639–1969,* Stratford Tercentenary Commission, Stratford, Connecticut, 1939, pp 206–7

66 Orcut, Reverend Samuel, *History of the Old Town of Stratford and the City of Bridgeport, Connecticut,* Fairfield County Historical Society, 1886, pp 957–9

67 Shelton, Jane de Forest, *Reunion of the Descendants of Daniel Shelton at Birmingham, Connecticut,* Printers E.M. Ruttenber & Son, Newburgh, New York; June 14, 1877. Repository DAR Library, Washington, DC

Chapter 17: Shelton — Early Strong Roots in England, Virginia & Connecticut

had seven children. Being the oldest son, he inherited twice the acreage of land than that which each of his brothers received. This was a British custom continued by many colonists. By all indications he continued the business operations of his father on his share of the inherited properties.

8 William Shelton (1739–1812) m. Susannah Strong (1743–1816)
"William Shelton lived at Long Hill, near his father's house."[68] William is the only member of our line of the Shelton family who was "of age" to serve during the Revolutionary War.

He married Susannah Strong on 1 Oct. 1764 and that association might have made him very patriotic. How she met William Shelton we don't know, but I suspect their family social and business connections, including trade across Long Island Sound or patriotic endeavor caused them to intersect.

William (DAR #A102830) served in the militia during the Revolutionary War during 1777 and 1778, so at least on his side of the family the patriotism was sincere. The Lineage Book of the Charter Members of the DAR, Volume 017, page 197 lists "William Shelton served from Norwich as a private in the Burgoyne Campaign, in Capt. Eben Lathrop's Company, Col. Johnathan Latimer's regiment of militia." This was part of the mustering of militia called up to stop Burgoyne's British invasion forces from Canada, which culminated with Burgoyne's defeat at the Battle of Saratoga.

Susannah was born in Setauket on Long Island within the town of Brookhaven, Suffolk County, New York. Her great-great-grandfather, Elder John Strong, had come from Taunton, Somersetshire, England, to Massachusetts in 1630. Her grandfather, Selah Strong Sr. (1680–1732), had come to Long Island from Northampton, Massachusetts, in 1700. She had an uncle named Selah Strong Jr. Her brother, Selah Strong III (1737–1815) married an Anna Smith (1740–1812). Selah Strong III was a captain in the Battle of Long Island, was captured by the British and imprisoned on the British prison ship *Jersey*. Anna got permission to bring him food, which probably saved his life and through Tory family members got his release. After the British captured Long Island in the Battle of Long Island and New York City, many patriots left and went to Connecticut or New Jersey. Selah III went to New Haven, Connecticut, for the duration of the war. Anna stayed behind to protect their home from destruction, as many women did since they were seen as non-combatants. The couple had nine children and there are conflicting stories of whether they went with Selah or stayed with Anna. Maybe some children went with each parent. Anna became part of General George Washington's famous Culper spy ring, which spied on the British in New York City and Long Island. She acted as a courier and signaled message

---

68 ibib

Chapter 17: Shelton — Early Strong Roots in England, Virginia & Connecticut

pick-ups by hanging laundry on the line. A black petticoat meant a message was waiting to be picked up. The number of handkerchiefs on the line indicated in which of six coves the message was secretly located. The coded messages were transferred to couriers who then rowed them across the Long Island Sound to Connecticut. From there they were carried by horseback up the western shore of the Housatonic River. The Shelton home was precisely along that route. The route then went up to Waterbury and then west to Washington's headquarters at Newburg, New York, near the Hudson River above West Point.[69]

Since New Haven was only six miles from Huntington, I expect Susannah might have provided considerable assistance to her brother and the Strong family when they migrated to Connecticut as part of the war refugee contingent and also may have assisted in the support of the movement of spy messages.[70]

At the end of the war in 1783, Selah Strong III with his children returned to their home and Anna on Strong's Neck, near Setauket within the town of Brookhaven. He became a judge and he and Anna lived out their lives there.

William and Susannah had eight children including a son named Selah Shelton born in 1770. Thus, she continued the use of the first name "Selah" on to a fourth generation. This also indicates the closeness of the families.

7 Selah Shelton (1770–1831) m. Phoebe French (1768–1831)

Selah was born in Huntington, Connecticut. Phoebe's parents, Joseph French (1730–1781) and Charity Beardsley (1731–1780), were both from Fairfield, Connecticut, and had moved to Huntington. Phoebe was born in Huntington. Selah and Phoebe married on October 18, 1787, in Huntington, Connecticut, and had ten children. They moved west to Berkshire Township, Delaware County, Ohio. The main reason for migration to Ohio at that time was bounty land in the west given to soldiers of the Revolutionary War and the War of 1812. I find no records of his service in either the Revolutionary War for which he was too young or the War of 1812.

---

69 Rose, Alexander, *Washington's Spies*, Bantam Books, Random House LLC, New York, Copyright 2006
70 Mather, Frederick Gregory, *The Refugees of 1776 from Long Island to Connecticut*, J.B. Lyon Company, Printers, Albany, New York, 2013

Chapter 17: Shelton — Early Strong Roots in England, Virginia & Connecticut

Was Huntington getting too crowded, or the opening of new land in the west a lure? There is more to learn about Selah Shelton and Phoebe.

As I researched further, I found that some of their older children, including our Alfred, stayed in Huntington, probably because they were already married and had settled down. Selah, his wife, Phoebe, and their younger children moved to Ohio. I found them in Berkshire Township, Delaware County, Ohio.

Ohio became a territory in 1799. A state legislature first met on March 1, 1803, which later became the official date of its statehood. Many Revolutionary War veterans obtained bounty land in Ohio for their service in the revolution. Ohio at that time was probably a place of perceived opportunity. Colonel Moses Byxby, a wealthy entrepreneur from Lenox, Berkshire County, Massachusetts, purchased 8,000 acres of land and led a group of settlers to central Ohio in 1804. At one point he owned or co-owned 38,000 Acres. He apparently was a very persuasive promoter. He recruited Easterners to migrate to his new town and purchase his land. The town was formally called Berkshire Township in 1806. An 1808 poll book listed 32 names of people from a wide variety of places including all the New England states, New York, Virginia, Maryland, Kentucky, Pennsylvania, Bavaria and Wales.[71][72][73]

I found Selah and part of his family in Berkshire Township, Delaware County, Ohio. I haven't found any record of when they migrated there, but I'm assuming after the War of 1812 and certainly prior to their daughter Abigail's marriage there in 1819. So, let's say about 1815. For some reason they are not included in the 1820 census, but they do show up in the 1830 census.

Two of their daughters we know went to Ohio with them. Abigail (Abby) (Nabby), born in 1800, married a Joseph Prince on December 12, 1819, and they had one child who died. Abigail died roughly four years later, at age 23, on September 12, 1823. Her sister, Polly, born in 1806, then married Joseph Prince on June 10, 1824, and they had five children: Henry, Abigail, Charles, Charles and Frederick. It seems only Charles and Frederick lived to adulthood. Polly died December 30, 1841, at age 35. The fact that Jane Shelton lists Abby as "died unmarried," and does not say anything more about them, further indicates she was unaware of Selah's family happenings in Ohio.[74][75]

Joseph Prince was born about 1785 in Connecticut, and moved to Delaware County,

---

71 Perrin, William Henry, *History of Delaware County and Ohio*, O.L. Baskin & Co., Historical Publishers, Delaware County, Ohio, 1880
72 U.S. Dept. of Interior, National Park Service, National Register of Historic Places, Northwest District Delaware Ohio
73 Wikipedia website: Delaware, Ohio, accessed October 2018
74 Delaware Patron Newspaper; Delaware, Ohio, June 10, 1824
75 Ibid

Ohio, with his brother, Daniel, about 1808. During the War of 1812, Joseph served from September 20 to November 19, 1814, as a private in Captain Elias Murray's Cavalry Company, a State Militia, along with his brother who was the Company Lieutenant. "Each man furnished his own Horse and equipments and over his shoulder was slung the inevitable canteen of whiskey." Their service mainly included harassing the British countryside in the area of Detroit. He became a successful farmer owning several hundred acres of land. An 1830 map of Berkshire Township shows Joseph Prince owning 200 acres of land. (Selah Shelton is not shown to own any land acreage.) At the 1834 Delaware County Agricultural Exhibition Joseph won $5.00 for the "Best Cow" and also $1.50 for the "Best Spring Calf." He and his brother were also hog brokers and drove them to market at Baltimore, Ohio. After Polly's death, Joseph Prince married a third time to a widow, Mary Meeker Sprague. Joseph Prince died in July 1866 and is buried in the Berkshire Township Cemetery. Mary received Joseph's war pension and cared for his son Frederick who was somehow handicapped or impaired. Mary lived to age 89 and is buried in Oak Grove Cemetery, Delaware, Ohio, with her first husband.[76]

Selah's wife, Phoebe, is buried in the old section of the Berkshire Township Cemetery, as are their two daughters and Joseph Prince. Their graves are marked in a row of family graves. No date of death is noted for Phoebe as the gravestone is unreadable.

According to Family Links website, "Ther(e) is a death record for him Aug 1830 in CT," but more likely he is buried in the row of family graves in Berkshire Township Cemetery in Delaware, Ohio. He is listed in the 1830 census in Ohio. There is a court record in Delaware stating he died in August 1831 in Ohio. I firmly believe he died in Delaware County, Ohio, in August 1831 and is indeed buried, near Phoebe, in one of the unmarked or unreadable graves in the old section of the Berkshire Township Cemetery, Delaware County, Ohio. Jane Shelton's write-up of Selah in the 1877 Reunion document, mentions only that he went to Ohio. I think she would have known if he had returned, died or was buried in Connecticut.[77]

6 Alfred Shelton (1792–1857) m. Ruth Beardsley (1789–1854)

Even though his father, mother and several siblings went to Ohio, Alfred stayed home in the Huntington area. According to available census records he continued to live in Huntington all his life. He was a cousin of Edward Nelson Shelton but 20 years older.

---

76 Ibid
77 Shelton, Jane de Forest, *Reunion of the Descendants of Daniel Shelton at Birmingham, Connecticut,* Printers E.M. Ruttenber & Son, Newburgh, New York; June 14, 1877. Repository DAR Library, Washington, DC

Chapter 17: Shelton — Early Strong Roots in England, Virginia & Connecticut

His life in Huntington most likely paralleled that of the family detailed in Jane de Forest Shelton's book, *The Salt Box House,* before the industrial development in Shelton. Alfred and Ruth are buried in the Old Cemetery of Huntington.

Very little is known of Ruth Beardsley and her family.

5 John Douglas Shelton (1813–1894) m. Mary Hanser Clark (1815–1906)
Records show they lived in Huntington and Ansonia, an adjacent town. John worked at the Star Pin Company, which was one of the larger factories along Canal Street in Shelton.

An engraved 50th Wedding Party invitation survives to let us imagine a very nice party and celebration of family and friends commemorating their earlier vows and life together.

John's wife, Mary Clark, was descended from a Waterbury, Connecticut, Revolutionary War "hero," Captain Timothy Clark. When my grandmother, Daisy Shelton, applied for membership in the DAR she used Timothy Clark as her veteran. Why did she use Timothy Clark and not William Shelton? Probably because of the Captain rank versus Private rank and Clark's "hero" status. But William Shelton probably saw more action at Saratoga than Timothy Clark did at New Haven. See Clark in Chapter 25.

4 Charles Frederick Shelton (1845–1919) m. Georgia Ann Christopher (1847–1902)
Charles was born in Orange, Connecticut, a town just east of Derby and Shelton. Why he was born there is unknown, as the census records show his family in Huntington and Ansonia. However, all the towns there are just a few miles apart.

During the Civil War he served in the 1st Connecticut Heavy Artillery, Company B. This outfit served in or near action during the entire war including Gettysburg, Petersburg, and Appomattox.

Georgia was from Jacksonville, Florida. They married in 1867 at St. Paul's in Huntington, Connecticut, but then, after a few years, moved back to Jacksonville, Florida. They had four children, one of whom died as an infant.

It is understood that he tried citrus farming, but failed due to climatic conditions in Jacksonville However, we have no certain information on this. He did have a very successful uncle, General Henry Shelton Sanford, who after many years of government service, in 1870, invested

Charles Frederick Shelton

Chapter 17: Shelton — Early Strong Roots in England, Virginia & Connecticut

in an area south of Jacksonville by purchasing 12,548 acres of land, building the town of Sanford, Florida, and planting large areas of orange groves. That region became the largest shipper of oranges in the world. However, Wikipedia states, "In 1887, the city suffered a devastating fire, followed the next year by a statewide epidemic of yellow fever. When the Great Freeze of 1894 and 1895 ruined the citrus industry, farmers diversified by growing vegetables as well." After that Sanford was nicknamed "Celery City." We don't know of any business connection between Charles and Henry Shelton Sanford, but I'm sure they both faced the same problems growing citrus in that area of Florida.[78][79]

Georgia died in 1902 and was buried in Florida. Charles returned to Connecticut with his three children, Abbie, Daisy and John. It is unknown what happened to Abbie, the oldest. John, a young man by then, married and returned to Florida where he lived in Miami until his death at age 89. Daisy, the youngest child, was placed with relatives in Connecticut. Charles was not able to care for her.

Charles then traveled the country from New England to California and stayed much of the time in "old soldiers homes." He married a 2nd wife, Anna Ruff Compton, in Boston, Massachusetts. Nothing is known about that marriage. He died at Frick's Old Soldiers Home in Norton Heights, Connecticut.

Charles Frederick Shelton is buried in Riverside Cemetery in section "O" in South End Shelton. He is in the same plot where we found the Kaddeland headstone and the graves of Daisy and her husband Christen Kaddeland. It's a fairly large plot 8–12 places with only three taken, so some are most likely still available. Other Sheltons are buried nearby.

3 Daisy Selkirk Shelton (1886–1959) m. Christen Rosjford Kaddeland (1880–1958)
Daisy grew up in a family with widely separated children. Abbie was about 18 years older and John about 8 years older. Daisy was about 15 years old when her mother died and they moved to Connecticut. Daisy lived with an aunt. I don't remember ever being told their name or having them visit. My mother had told me that her mother, Daisy, had been treated poorly by this relative, like a stepchild, but she had no choice in the matter and maybe there was a reason she was treated so. She was close to a cousin named Carl Hubbell who stayed in touch for many years.

Daisy's father, Charles, was very near the same age as an uncle, Edward DeForest Shelton, who ran The Shelton Company. Edward was the brother of Jane DeForest Shelton, the author. The Shelton Company, as best I can determine at this point, was a fabric distributor

---

78 "General Henry S. Sanford Biographical Notes," Sanford Historical Society, Sanford, Florida accessed October 2018
79 Wikipedia Website; Sanford, Florida; Accessed October 2018

Chapter 17: Shelton — Early Strong Roots in England, Virginia & Connecticut

with offices in Shelton and New York City. Daisy worked as a clerk for this great uncle, Edward, until she married.

In 1905 Daisy, at age 19, married Christen Kaddeland, a Norwegian who had emigrated to the United States in 1900. Christen, who had received technical training in Mechanical Engineering in Norway and Denmark, wanted to design ocean-going steamships. However, he only found work with printing press manufacturers, first in Brooklyn, New York, and then in Shelton, Connecticut. His occupation was listed as "draughtsman," but he was far more than that. Before computer aided design, engineers always started out on a drafting board. I inherited my grandfather's drafting instruments and used them when I started out in engineering on a drafting board.

Daisy with daughter Carolyn

They built a very nice house on a small hill, in the south end of Shelton, at 21 Spring Street, which Christen designed. From my childhood, I always remembered it as barn red in color and in 2014 it was still barn red. See pictures in Chapter 15. They had two daughters, Carolyn and Marcia, ten years apart.

The 1920 census shows an Edward age 79 living with them. The only Edward I can readily find of that age is Daisy's great uncle, Edward de Forest Shelton, who was a contemporary of Daisy's father, Charles. Charles had died the previous year. Maybe the families were a lot closer than I ever knew.

The Kaddelands bought a shore cottage in Madison, Connecticut. It was relatively small, with living, dining and kitchen areas downstairs and with three small bedrooms upstairs. Daisy moved there for the summers. We were allowed to visit for a week or two in the summer,

Daughter Marcia

which my brother and I enjoyed. We were sent outside mostly and explored the beach and adjacent rocky areas. Daisy was very stern, allowing no sand to be brought in. We cold showered outside before entering the cottage. When inside we were under orders not to be noisy. Needless to say, we enjoyed the outside.

Christen Kaddeland rose to be Chief Engineer and Vice President of the Premier and Potter Company, a printing-press manufacturer. The company merged with the Harris Company and moved to Cleveland, Ohio. Christen's job moved to Cleveland. Daisy

Chapter 17: Shelton — Early Strong Roots in England, Virginia & Connecticut

refused to leave their home in Shelton. Christen went to Cleveland and later on to Chicago, commuting home on holidays for many years. Even though they were apart, Christen supported Daisy in her comfortable lifestyle. She even wintered many years in St. Petersburg, Florida.

In the late 1940s Daisy suffered three strokes, the last of which placed her in a nursing home in Madison, Connecticut, for 12 years. Christen retired and moved to Hendersonville, North Carolina. He died of a heart attack on Christmas Eve 1958 getting into a cab at the New Haven, Connecticut, railroad station on his way to visit Daisy. Daisy died two weeks later. Also see Kaddeland in Chapter 15.

Daisy Selkirk Shelton

Chapter 18

Miller — Early Rowley, Middletown and Middlefield

Our Miller family knowledge begins with some vague information of several connecting Millers in Bishops Stortford, Hertfordshire, near London, England. But we really begin with John or Martin Miller and his wife Mary or Priscilla (nobody seems to have documentation) in that location and quickly move to focus on Rowley and East Riding of Yorkshire, England. There, an Anglican priest, by the name of Ezekial Rogers, the Rector of St. Peter's Church in Rowley, England, since 1621, was suspended in 1636 for "his non-conformist beliefs." After his suspension, he continued ministering to a local following, which grew and led to twenty families emigrating to America with more to follow. Little remains of the once vibrant little village of Rowley, Yorkshire, England, but St. Peter's Church is still standing. It is protected by being on the National Heritage List of England.

Thomas Miller and his family sailed with this group from Hull, England, in June 1638 aboard the ship *John of London* and arrived in Boston, Massachusetts, in August 1638. In the hold of the ship was the first printing press to be brought to America. Over the next year, in Boston, Reverend Rogers gathered a total flock of fifty-nine families. In 1639 they obtained land, for 800 pounds, north of Salem by a grant which read "Mr. Ezekiel Roger's [sic] Plantation Shall be Called Rowley, Mass."

The following is from a 1976 article by Ian Beckwith, Senior Lecturer, Bishop Grosseteste College of Education: "The early years were a struggle to survive which tested the endurance of the fold who had uplifted themselves, lock, stock and barrel from Rowley in the East Riding. In 1643 supplies from England failed to arrive and the Rowley settlers, many of whom had been cloth workers at home, set to work to make the first cloth ever produced in the New World, using cotton from Barbadoes [*sic*]. Indian raids became more troublesome and the settlers formed a company of soldiers to protect themselves."

Ian Beckwith continues concerning Reverend Rogers's control on the community: "His regime was maintained by overseers, or informers, chosen to see that the Sabbath was maintained and each one responsible for the moral welfare of ten families. Every evening he would call some of his people up to his house to examine how they spent their time, what books they read and whether they prayed without ceasing. Not surprisingly some failed to conform to this strict way of life and they were condemned to be kept in irons and put to hard labor."

Thomas Miller and his family are the origin of our Miller family line in America, first in Rowley, Massachusetts, and later Middletown and Middlefield, Connecticut. I can understand why they moved on to Connecticut.

11 John/Martin Miller (c1560–1633) m Mary/Priscilla Pylston ?? (c1589–??)

All we know of John and his wife Mary is that they were in Bishops Stortford, Hertfordshire, England where their son, Thomas, was born.

10 Thomas Miller (1609–1680) m. Sarah Nettleton (1642–1728)

Thomas was born in Bishops Stortford, Hertfordshire, or maybe Birmingham, England. Thomas married his first wife, Isabel (1613–1666), How they located from Hertsfordshire (or Birmingham as others say) to Yorkshire or joined the Rogers group to leave from Hull is unknown.

Thomas Miller, Isabel and daughter Ann were part of the original group in Rowley, Massachusetts, in 1639 and apparently very active. In New England, "freeman" was an honor given to settlers who had proven themselves to the community, paid their debts, joined the church and behaved themselves–and only then could take an oath of allegiance and were allowed to vote. It had nothing to do with slavery. Thomas was made a freeman and took the oath.

Thomas worked as a carpenter. They obtained a 1-½ acre lot on Pleasant Street in the original town layout and built a substantial, garrison-style house which was later called "the fort" and used as "the block house" for defense against the Indians. In 1646 he obtained a license to sell wines the following year.

Rowley was a unique area and I think these settlers were fortunate to have located there. The Indians had used the salt marshes for hunting waterfowl, fishing, and collecting shellfish. The settlers did likewise and also harvested the salt marsh hay for roofing, insulation and animal bedding. The salt acted as a fire retardant and was much safer to use. Each original family was given their own area of an equal size for harvesting the salt marsh hay. Thomas was allocated two acres of salt marsh. He also had four-and-a-half acres of "upland" for planting. I suspect everyone farmed, in addition to the other skills, to keep food on the table.

Reverend Rogers obviously ran a tight ship and I suspect Thomas was, although a good carpenter and hard worker, a bit of a nonconformist. This put him, in occasional trouble, as various records indicate. But the record is not too specific about his misdeeds, so I expect they were minor.

About 1651, after roughly a dozen years in Rowley, Thomas with his first wife, Isabel, and daughter Ann moved to Middletown, Connecticut. Middletown at that time was to be a new community. Thomas and his family were part of the first 23 families in Middletown. Middletown is on the Connecticut River about 35 miles up the river from its mouth on Long Island Sound. The river is navigable up past Middletown to Hartford where there are falls. It is presumed they sailed from Boston to Middletown as overland travel through wilderness would have been an ordeal. He brought letters of recommendation from his church in Rowley. In 1653 their daughter Ann married Nathaniel Bacon. Ann and Nathaniel were the progenitors of the Bacon family in Connecticut.

In 1655, Middletown granted Thomas a "mill privilege" to build the town's first gristmill with community assistance to operate it. I'm not quite sure what that means, but Thomas built the mill and in 1658 they approved his damming the river to provide a more consistent water flow for the mill. Thomas was more than a carpenter. He was a builder. Thomas built the gristmill on Miller's Brook. Whether he owned the land and stream is not clear.

Sarah Nettleton was the daughter of Samuel Nettleton and Maria Mary Lucas, of Branford, Connecticut, and was working as a servant for Thomas Miller and his family. She was younger than his daughter Ann, but Thomas had an affair with her and she was with child. This of course caused a major problem within the family. Thomas and Isabel separated and Isabel died very shortly after Sarah's child was born, in early 1666. He was excommunicated by his church back in Rowley and imprisoned in Middletown for a short period of time. Thomas married Sarah Nettleton on June 6, 1666, and later on traveled back to Rowley to make penance. They had eight children and thus began the growth of the Miller family in Connecticut.

The parting of Thomas and Isabel must have been very bitter within Thomas's family and I suspect caused differences between the Bacon and Miller families also for a few generations. An example of some of the fallout of this was a lawsuit filed later, after Thomas had died, against Thomas Miller's estate by his daughter Ann and her husband Nathaniel Bacon for a share of the inheritance. They won a judgment against the estate and received a share of the inventoried assets.

Chapter 18: Miller — Early Rowley, Middletown and Middlefield

Polly McLean (Bassett) connection

Examples of connectivity in genealogy continually are found. So, I'll relate this one. Kenneth and Polly Bassett were good friends of ours in Terrace Park, Ohio. In talking with Polly one day, we discussed growing up in Connecticut and our family roots. After a little research I confirmed that we have common ancestors in both Thomas Miller and Nathaniel Bacon. She by Thomas Miller's first wife, Isabel, whose daughter Ann married Nathanial Bacon. I by Thomas Miller's second wife, Sarah Nettleton. And as you will discover below, Nathaniel Bacon's great-granddaughter, Elizabeth Bacon, married into the Miller family which gives us a line to Nathaniel Bacon also.

Such a small world.

Linda and Polly enjoying an early morning coffee at the cabin

From left: Ken Bassett, Linda Knoop (Smith), Polly McLean (Bassett), W.C. Smith

Other Middletown connections[80]

In the original settlement at Mattabesset around 1650 there were 23 early "first settlers" or "original proprietors." The name Middletown was approved for the town in 1657. Of those 23 founding families we have a direct ancestral connection to nine. They are as follows with the location of more information:

    Nathaniel Bacon Sr. (1630–1705) m Ann Miller (1633–1680) — See above
    William Cornwell (1609–1678) m Mary Hyanno (c1618–1695) — See Chapter 19
    Capt. John Hall Sr. (1584–1673) m Esther Willicke (1590–1673) — See 8 Deacon

---

80 Bacon, Reginald W., *Early Families of Middletown, Connecticut, Vol. 1:1650–1654*, Variety Arts Press, Newberryport, Massachusetts

Ichabod Miller and Mary Elton below
Richard Hall Sr. (1620–1691) m Mary Anthony (1622–1691) — See 8 Deacon Ichabod Miller and Mary Elton below
Capt. Daniel Harris (1615–1701) m Mary Weld (1627–1711) — See Chapter 26
Thomas Miller (1609–1680) m Isabel (1613–1666) — See Above
John Savage m Elizabeth Dubbin — See 8 Deacon Ichabod Miller and Mary Elton below
Rev. Samuel Stow (1623–1704) m Hope Fletcher (1624–1704) — See Chapter 26
Thomas Wetmore (1615–1681) m Sarah Hall (1622–1664) — See 8 Deacon Ichabod Miller and Mary Elton below

It is very interesting to me how these families connected and intermarried, but sometimes it gets very confusing to keep everyone straight and organized, much less try to explain it. Suffice it to say they were a homogeneous group seeking opportunity and endeavoring to make a new community in the wilderness.

9 "Gov." Benjamin Miller (1672–1747) m Mary Johnson (1674–1709)

Benjamin was the youngest son of Thomas Miller and his second wife, Sarah Nettleton. Benjamin must have been an impressive individual. Reportedly, he was a large man "of fine physique and strength." Benjamin married his first wife, Mary Johnson, with whom he had eight children. She died bearing her eighth child, Ichabod. Benjamin married a second wife, Mercy Bassett (1676–1756), of North Haven, Connecticut, and they had seven children.

In 1700, Benjamin Miller with his wife, Mary, and three children, at that time, moved from the Miller Farms in Middletown to Middlefield. Benjamin was one of the first three settlers of Middlefield, Connecticut, a new area just west of Middletown, where he established himself as a large landowner. Thomas Adkins in his *History of Middlefield and Longhill* in 1883 writes, "The country then was wild, the soil unbroken by white man's hand. Benjamin was a stout, athletic man, and capable of enduring hardships. All settlers in new countries have to endure much, and he was fitted by nature to be a pioneer. Forests were cleared, roads made, and bridges built while surrounded by Indians and wild beasts. The first settlers scarcely left home without taking their guns and dogs. Tradition says the title of "Governor" was conferred upon Benjamin by the early settlers partly because of his influence with the Indians, partly on account of his being a large landowner and of influence in the settlement, and no doubt partly because of his character, which appears to have been of a dominant type. It is plain that Benjamin Miller .... was a man of great influence in the early history of Middlefield. ..."

Chapter 18: Miller — Early Rowley, Middletown and Middlefield

There is a story of his shooting a bear that was attacking his cattle on a Sunday. This resulted in his being charged with "desecrating the Sabbath" and put in jail.

Benjamin and his wives are buried in the Old North Burying Ground Cemetery in Middlefield.

8 Deacon Ichabod Miller (1709–1788) m Mary Elton (1710–1739)
Ichabod Miller was the eighth child of Benjamin Miller and Mary Johnson. His mother, Mary Johnson, had died on the day of his birth. Ichabod and Mary Elton had four children before she died in 1739 giving birth. Mary Elton's family tree gives a picture of the intertwining of the early settler families. All of people are original founders of Middletown or direct descendants down through three generations and further in many cases.

Capt. John Hall (1584–1673) m Esther Willicke (1590–1673)–Founders
Capt. Richard Hall (1620–1691) m Mary Anthony (1622–1691)–Founders
John Elton (1648–1686) m Jane Hall (1653–1724)–Daughter of Founders
Richard Elton (1679–1765) m Elizabeth Wetmore (1687–1743)–Granddaughter of Founders
Mary Elton (1710–1739) m Deacon Ichabod Miller (1709–1788)–Great-Grandchildren of Founders
Thomas Wetmore (1615–1681) m Sarah Hall (1622–1664)–Founders and sister of Jane Hall
John Wetmore (1646–1696) m Mary Savage (1663–1723)–Son and Daughter of Founders
Elizabeth Wetmore (1687–1743) m Richard Elton (1679–1765)–Grandchildren of Founders
John Savage (1627–1684) m Elizabeth Dubbin (1631–1696)–Founders
Mary Savage (1663–1723) m John Wetmore (1646–1696)–Son and Daughter of Founders

Ichabod remarried Elizabeth Cornwell (1716–1787), a widow of Jeremiah Bacon (1717–1746)–all descendant of Founders. Elizabeth Cornwell brought three or four children to the marriage and Ichabod brought four children to the marriage. They then proceeded to have ten additional children by my understanding. That must have been a busy household with eighteen children.

Another interesting observation here is that Elizabeth Cornwell's first husband, Jeremiah Bacon, was the grandson of Ann Miller and great-grandson of Thomas Miller through his first wife, Isabel. Ichabod was the grandson of Thomas Miller through his second wife, Sarah Nettleton.

Chapter 18: Miller — Early Rowley, Middletown and Middlefield

In 1758, Ichabod served in the 9th Company, 2nd Regiment of Connecticut Militia during the French and Indian War. He also has been recognized by the DAR as being in the Revolutionary War, but I think that may be an error in confusion with his son, Ichabod, who definitely did serve in the American Revolution.

Ichabod was a Deacon in the Congregational Church. He certainly could have held a Sunday School without leaving home. He must have farmed to feed all those hungry mouths.

7 Capt. Ichabod Miller Jr. (1739–1824) m Elizabeth Bacon (1738–1831)
Ichabod Miller Jr. was also born on the day his mother died. It is very interesting that he married his stepsister and distant cousin Elizabeth Bacon. Since they grew up together in the same household they must have known each other quite well. It took me awhile to study and figure all this out.

The Bacon line from Miller and back to Miller is as follows:
Thomas Miller (1609–1680) m Isabel (1613–1666)
Ann Miller (1633–1680) m Nathaniel Bacon Sr. (1630–1705)
Lt. Nathaniel Bacon Jr (1674–1758) m Hannah Wetmore (1681–1722)
Jeremiah Bacon (1717–1746) m Elizabeth Cornwell (1716–1787)
Elizabeth Bacon (1738–1831) m Capt. Ichabod Miller (1739–1824)

Ichabod and Elizabeth had seven children together. He was a farmer.

Ichabod served as a Lieutenant and then Captain in the Revolutionary War as commander of the 8th Company of the 23rd Regiment from April 1 to November 1, 1779. This was an Alarm Company responding to a British attack on New Haven, Connecticut, in July 1779.

6 Jeremiah Miller (1780–1848) m Mary Hall Ives (1792–1863)
Jeremiah was the last of seven children and grew up on the farm. He and Mary had six children together. The 1840 census shows his household had three males engaged in agriculture. We presume that was he and his two sons, who were in their twenties, and at the time engaged in farming.

5 Watrous Ives Miller (1822–1885) m Ruth Lucrecia Prout (1821–1898)
Watrous grew up on the farm in Middletown, Connecticut, married Lucrecia and they had three children. Lucrecia's Prout family is more fully detailed in Chapter 21.

But, Watrous did not stay on the farm; instead, he ventured out into other lines of work. He is listed as a farmer and manufacturer. The American Silversmiths website lists

Chapter 18: Miller — Early Rowley, Middletown and Middlefield

Watrous as a "Pewtersmith." Pewter is an easily worked metal and something that could be entered into with minimal investment and readily learned skills. The 1850 census lists him as a peddler. The 1860 census shows him back as a farmer with real estate valued at $30,000. The 1870 census lists him as a Britannia salesman living in the South Farms area of Middletown. In the 1880 census, he is shown as a "Tin Peddler" in New Haven, Connecticut. So, Watrous obviously was a very industrious individual and an entrepreneur. After Watrous's death in 1885, the New Haven City Directory for both 1891 and 1898 lists Lucrecia as a widow living in New Haven.

Their second child, Watson John Miller (1849–1911), was an entrepreneur and also my Watson namesake. He had a fondness for books, inventions and sports. He attended Middletown High School, Chase Institute in Middletown and then New Haven Business College. The American Silversmiths lists Watson as a "Silver Plater." In 1868 he started in the silver business. In 1872 he helped found the Derby Silver Company in Derby, Connecticut, which manufactured silver-plated houseware items including serving platters, tea sets, bowls, dishes, flatware, loving cups, combs, brushes, etc. and sold them through the Sperry and Hutchens stamp stores. I remember them as "S and H Green Stamps." In 1873 they built "Factory B," just across the Housatonic River, at the corner of Canal Street and Bridge Street in Shelton. It was a large, multistory brick building located on the canal to obtain waterpower for running its equipment.

Watson J. Miller

American Silversmiths lists Watson as obtaining a patent number 10,277 for a dessert set which he assigned to E G Webster & Brother of New York City. He apparently worked for a few years for Webster Manufacturing as a silver plater prior to the Derby Silver Co. Or, maybe they were partners.[81]

---

81 Committee of Shelton Historical Society, *Images of America–Shelton*, Arcadia Publishing, Charleston, South Carolina, 2002, Page 4

In any event they prospered and Watson sold his shares in the Derby Silver Company to the International Silver Company of Meriden, Connecticut, a consortium of silver companies, as reported in a *New York Times* article on January 14, 1899. Shareholders of Derby Silver could cash out or receive preferred stock in International Silver. Watson continued as an executive of the combined companies. He was a favorite person to our immediate family because he was looked up to as a successful business person. And, also, because he hired his nephew, my grandfather, Charles Herbert Smith, as his plant superintendent for "Factory B" in Shelton. The company was successful for many years, but closed in 1933 due to the effects of the Depression. See also Charles Herbert Smith Chapter 14.

Watson and Susie

Watson lived in a large home on Howe Avenue in South Shelton. He and his first wife, Susie Waite, had no children but they enjoyed having my father and his sister Susie Virginia over to visit as if they were their own grandchildren. My Aunt Susie Virginia Smith (Spahr) was named after her Aunt Susie. Aunt Susie died in 1907. Watson remarried a year later to Maude Patchen of Derby. Maude was not into having the children around.

Watson served on the staff of several governors. He was an aide to Gov. Cobbin in 1895 and Gov. McLean in 1901. In 1902 he was Quartermaster General on the staff of Gov. Chamberlain. For this he was given the rank of Colonel, which I understand was mainly ceremonial. Watson later served in the Connecticut State Legislature in 1904, 1905 and 1906.

Watson built a good-sized mausoleum in Riverside Cemetery in South Shelton for himself and his immediate family. He and his two wives are buried there. His parents, Watrous Ives Miller and Ruth Lucrecia Prout, are also buried in the mausoleum.

4 Virginia Ruth Miller (1848–1939) m Halsey Horatio Blake (1843–1930)

Virginia Ruth was oldest of the three children. She was close to her brother, Watson, but they led very different lives. The 1870 census lists her as a bookkeeper. This was most probably before she married Halsey. She met and married Halsey Blake, a humble "Yankee Peddler," similar to her father, but quite different from her wealthy brother.

From pictures and stories "Gramma Blake" as she was called was a spry little woman. Halsey and Virginia Ruth had two daughters, Genevieve and Betsey. Our mother told the story of how she would always ask "How's the baby?" referring to my brother or myself. I, being very young, don't remember her at all. After Halsey died in 1930, she lived with her daughter Genevieve and son-in-law Charles at Great Oak Farm in Orange, Connecticut. When Genevieve died in 1933, our Aunt, Susie Virginia Smith, who was still living at home, cared for her at the farm. And when Aunt Susie Virginia married, she took Virginia Ruth into her home in Milford, Connecticut, and continued to care for her until she died at age 89.

3 Genevieve Blake (1879–1933) m Charles Herbert Smith (1878–1967)
See Genevieve Blake in Chapter 16.

Chapter 19

Cornwall — Early Middletown and a Native American Connection

This chapter has a special flavor all to itself. It centers around Sgt. William Cornwall, about which much is known, and then his wife, Mary, and other family members about which little is known and much is speculated.

The Cornwall family originates in the southwestern tip of England. The Cornwall name came from the "Old English" tribal name Cornwealas. In Old English, wealas meant stranger or foreigner. The name later on might have been Cornwell or Cornell (without the "w"). The English pronounce it "Cornell." Our early ancestors had the name "de Cornwall" or "of Cornwall" which indicates the name became Cornwall. Originally they were from that Cornwall County area in southwestern England. Many surnames originated in that way by using their town name and thereby confusing us in later generations. So, we will use Cornwall until we get to Sgt. William who used Cornwell — except he omitted the "w" in signing his will "Cornell."

Sgt. William Cornwell

Various narratives have been written about this branch of the family being part of the landed gentry and having had ties to the English King. But, in becoming Puritans, many of the landed gentry lost everything under the religious and civil discord of the time. Charles I, King of England, confiscated many properties during this period before he was confronted and beheaded.

Chapter 19: Cornwall — Early Middletown and a Native American Connection

Our branch of the Cornwalls were of Burford and a newer or younger branch of the ancient Cornwall family. The overall family owned considerable properties in Devon, Shropshire and Herefordshire.

18 Richard de Cornwall (1360–1443) m Celillia/Alice Dau Merbury (1364–1417)
Richard was born and died in Burford, Shropshire, England.

17 Sir Edmund de Cornwall (1382–1443) m Lady Elizabeth de la Barre (1402–1468)
Edmond was born in Burford, Shropshire, England. He was the 5th Baron of Burford. He died in Cologne, Germany. What venture was he on there?

16 Sir Thomas Plantagenet de Cornwall (1407–1472) m Elizabeth Lenthal (1424–1489)
Thomas was born in Burford, Shropshire, England. He was the 6th Baron of Burford. He died in Hereford, Herefordshire, England.

15 Edmund Cornwall (1422–1498) m Maria Hoorde (1425–1498)
Edmund was born in Shropshire, England. He died in London, England.

14 Lord Thomas Cornwall (1467–1537) m Anne Juliana Corbet (1470–1548)
Thomas was born and died in Shropshire, England. He was the 8th Baron of Burford, Shropshire, and through that title he also held the office of Sheriff of Shropshire and Herefordshire.

13 George Cornwall (1532–1594) m Joana Martyn (1537–1567)
George was born, lived and died in Essex, England. Essex is in the east of England. What took him so far from Shropshire? Not much is known of George and Joana.

12 William Cornwall (1562–1625) m Margery Haywarde (1561–1616)
William and Margery were born, lived and died in Terling, Essex, England.

11 Sgt. William Cornwell (1609–1678) m Mary "Little Dove" Hyanno (c1618–1695)
William was born in Terling, Essex, England. He married his first wife, Joane Ranke, and worked as a farmer, perhaps on land inherited from the residual of a larger family estate. At some point they joined the Puritans and immigrated to America. They arrived in Roxbury (now Boston), Massachusetts, in 1633. Roxbury was one of the first towns in the Massachusetts Bay Colony. William and Joane are listed as members of the Reverend John Elliot's church in Roxbury. Joane, died in Roxbury in about 1635. They had no children.

Chapter 19: Cornwall — Early Middletown and a Native American Connection

In 1636, he migrated with a group of over one hundred settlers in the "Great Removal" from Massachusetts to Hartford, Connecticut. They traveled by land over old Indian trails on the journey. He is listed as one of the early settlers and is listed on the Founders Monument. Several families listed on the Founders Monument such as the Pecks, Hales, Welds, Barnes, Andrews and others show up in our tree branches. Too many to fully explore in this volume, but very interesting that the group of families stayed socially close and intermarried. And it was an influential group. In May 1637 William joined others from Hartford to fight the Pequot Indians.

From the first settlements in Jamestown in 1607, Plymouth in 1620 and New Amsterdam in 1624, there existed a variable relationship between the multiple Indian tribes and the waves of newcomers who began taking possession of the land through purchase or force. The Indians had always settled and moved as they desired with occasional aggressive disputes over territory, while the colonists firmly believed in possession and ownership. The Indians were at a disadvantage in that they did not recognize immediately what their future fate was and organize to meet it. The tribes operated independently, freely gave up or traded the land at first, and then began to realize how they were being taken advantage of. By then it was too late, partly because the colonists were better organized, but also because they had better weapons and tactics and had experience using them in recent European wars. There were many attacks, skirmishes, and even small battles leading up to this time. The Pequot War, between 1636 and 1638, was a result of these misunderstandings and their belligerent outcomes, but also of the dominance of the Pequot in Connecticut. By 1635 the Pequot had achieved dominance over the other tribes and in effect controlled the Indian population throughout Connecticut. The other tribes resented this and sought to be free from this control. Colonial settlements throughout southern New England were continually being attacked by the Pequots with continuous looting, killings and burned property. The Massachusetts Governor called forth men from across southern New England to attack the Pequot Indians. They were led by Capt. John Mason from Windsor, Connecticut, and Capt. John Underhill from Massachusetts. William Cornwell joined Capt. Mason, and they were joined by many Indian warriors from the Mohegan and Narragansett tribes who were at odds with the Pequots. Their major attack on the large Pequot fort at Mystic was a surprise since they approached by boat. This resulted in a massacre of the Indian village and ultimately destruction of the Pequot as a tribe.

For his service in the Pequot War, William Cornwell received the rank of Sargent and was also granted a plot of land in the Hartford "Souldier's field." In 1639 he is listed as owning 8 acres in the village and that year he also was remarried to a woman named Mary. There is no public record of their marriage even though at that time records of marriages were being kept. Was it a common-law marriage or an Indian ceremony? They had several

Chapter 19: Cornwall — Early Middletown and a Native American Connection

children, all born in Hartford.

There is no record of Mary's last name. In several documents where wives' names are mentioned with complete last names, Mary is only listed as Mary. In his will William only uses her first name Mary. Many Cornwall genealogies list Mary as Mary "Little Dove" Hyanno for which there is little documentation. This is interesting because another family named Bearse or Be Arce in Cape Cod also claim her and again with no acceptable documentation.[82][83] Much is written about Mary "Little Dove" Hyanno but little is really known and documented. As most Cornwall genealogies list Mary Hyanno as William Cornwell's wife Mary, I will join the crowd, but with reservations. It's popular and exciting to have some Native-American heritage. We welcome Mary Hyanno to our Smith family tree.

The Wampanoag Indians are probably of Asian Mongolian origin, one of the many waves that migrated across a land or ice bridge from Asia to North America about 12,000 years ago. The Wampanoag Indians at the time of the Pilgrims had about seventeen villages located in the area of Plymouth, Cape Cod, and Rhode Island. They were part of or sometimes allied with the Narragansett tribe. The Wampanoag were organized and friendly and were known as the "white Indians" because of their lighter skin color and red hair. Speculation has it that they have part Irish or Viking heritage. Perhaps so. Mary "Little Dove" Hyanno (1618–1678) was the daughter of Sachem (Chief) John Hyanno (1595–1680) and his wife, Princess Mary Noepe (1600–1624). She had light skin and red hair. Some say Mary Little Dove was Sachem John's sister, but the dates do not match for that.

William Cornwell and Sachem John Hyanno knew each other since they had fought together against the Pequot at the Mystic massacre. In 1638 William accompanied an expedition and helped negotiate a land acquisition for the Stratford Colony from the Indians through Sachem John Hyanno. I feel the Cornwells have as much of a claim to Mary Hyanno's heritage as do the Bearses.

Around 1650, William and Mary moved 15 miles down the Connecticut River where he obtained land on the east side of the river described as "a great lot over the Great River" and located at Hocanum, an Indian village. Being in that location, in 1650 or 1651 they were one of the original founding families of Middletown, Connecticut. There he obtained land, the deed of which was recorded as 903 acres in 1652. In addition, as an "Original Proprietor" he was allotted a share of the undivided lands, which his descendants received later whenever a division was made. It is unclear if the 903 acres includes these shares, but in any event, he was a large landowner.

---

82 Bearce, Franklin, *Who Our Forefathers Really Were–From out of the Past–The Be Arce Family*, New York, NY, 1935

83 Jacobus, Donald Lines, M.A., of New Haven, Connecticut, "Austin Bearse and His Alleged Indian Connection," *The American Genealogist*, 1935

Chapter 19: Cornwall — Early Middletown and a Native American Connection

In 1654, 1664 and 1665 William was the representative from Middletown in the Colonial Legislature. In 1664 he was Constable for the town. In 1670 he was the fifth largest taxpayer of fifty-two households in Middletown. As he aged, I suspect his land holdings gave him stature and certainly financial security.

William made his will in 1674 stating he was "well stricken in years and much abated in natural strength." He died in 1678. Mary lived many more years before dying in 1695.

10 Sgt. John Cornwell (1640–1707) m Martha Peck (1641–1708)
Being the son of a notable father is sometimes hard. John Cornwell grew up in Hartford and Middletown obviously in the shadow of his father. His occupation is listed as Sergeant, presumably in the local militia. He married Martha Peck in Middletown in 1665. They had ten children and lived next to his parents in Middletown. Martha was the daughter of Deacon Paul Peck Sr. and Martha Hannah Hale, one of the founding families of Hartford. Martha's ancestors are as follows:

    John Peck III (1530–1619) m Margery Passion (1532–1570)
    Stephen William Peck (1562–1619) m Mary Cave Melton Mowbray (1564–1603)
    Edward William Peck (1582–1686) m Grace Green (1586–1686)
    Deacon Paul Peck (1608–1695) m Martha Hannah Hale (1618–1695)
    Martha Peck (1641–1708) m Sgt. John Cornwell (1640–1707)

9 Capt. Joseph Cornwell (1679–1742) m Abigail Harris (1656–1723)
Joseph grew up in Middletown. In 1710 he married Abigail Harris from Middletown. The Harris family were early settlers in Middletown. Abigail died in 1723 and Joseph remarried Elizabeth Hall in 1726. The Hall and the Harris families were part of the original founders of Hartford. See Harris in Chapter 26.

Following in his father and grandfather's footsteps Joseph was commissioned as Captain of Middletown Militia in 1628.

8 Elizabeth Cornwell (1716–1787) m Jeremiah Bacon (1716–1746)
Jeremiah Bacon died at an early age and Elizabeth remarried to Ichabod Miller Sr. It was a second marriage for both Elizabeth and Ichabod. Two of their children, Elizabeth and Ichabod, that they brought to the marriage, grew up together and married. See Chapter 18 for Jeremiah Bacon.

7 Elizabeth Bacon (1738–1831) m Capt. Ichabod Miller Jr. (1739–1824)
See Chapter 18: Miller.

Chapter 20

Christopher — Early in Florida

This family certainly moved around until they got to Talbot Island, Florida. Were they seeking opportunity and a new life? Were they seeking the warmer climate?

Talbot Island, Florida is located about 20 miles east of Jacksonville, Florida. Talbot Island today is divided into a Big Talbot Island and a Little Talbot Island and due to erosion Little Talbot Island is larger than Big Talbot Island. Both islands are now all state park and wildlife preserves.

The history of the area around Talbot Island follows that of Florida. Early Native American tribes settled there with abundant wildlife including plentiful shellfish and sea otters. The Spanish arrived and claimed Florida in 1531. The French established a settlement on nearby Amelia Island. They were driven out by the Spaniards, who were driven out by the British in 1663, who lost it back to the Spanish in 1783 after our Revolutionary War. In 1821 it became a U.S. Territory. Before, and in between, the area of Northeast Florida was traded back and forth so many times I gave up trying to follow it all. The Christophers were there early and were there for several of the governmental control changes.

Why they came from Germany to New Amsterdam to Virginia to Maryland to Florida is a good question for someone to figure out.

13 Peter Christopher (1590–1620) m Barbara Menn (1597–1644)
Peter and Barbara were born, lived and died in the Hessen area of Germany.

12 Johannes Hans Christopher (1626–1688) m Tryntje Barents (1636–1705)
Johannes was born in Hessen, Germany, but immigrated to the Dutch colony of New Amsterdam. Tryntje was born in either Netherlands or Sweden and immigrated to New Amsterdam with her parents. Johannes and Tryntje apparently married and lived in New

Chapter 20: Christopher — Early in Florida

Amsterdam and then New York City as the British took over New Amsterdam in 1664. They both died on Staten Island, New York.

11 John Christopher Sr. (1650–1720) m Anna Marie Melchior (c1650–1709)
John Sr. lived and died in Orange, Virginia.

10 John Christopher Jr. (1669–1750) m Hannah Chavez (c1670–c1760)
John Jr. lived and died in Maryland.

9 Clement Christopher (1709–1769) m Sarah Shockley (c1718–1761)
Clement lived in Maryland. Various sources list Sarah Shockley as his wife but her birth date of 1728 is obviously incorrect so I have arbitrarily established the c1718 date. Their son was reportedly born in Duval County, Florida, so they were in Florida for a while. I am assuming that is when the Christophers began to establish their holdings there. Clement and Sarah died in Maryland.

8 John Bluet Christopher (1730–1800) m Martha Watson (1739–??)
John was born on Talbot Island, Florida, so the family was definitely getting established there. Martha was born in Maryland. They lived in Florida for a while since their son Spicer may have been born there, or at least grew up there. It is believed that John was raising horses for the British military in Florida. The change in government control back to the Spanish could have driven them back to Maryland. Both John and Martha died in Maryland.

7 Spicer Samuel Christopher (1759–1811) m Mary Greenwood (1763–1806)
Spicer was born either in Maryland or in northeast Florida. Since the British took control of Florida in 1763, it is possible he was born in Maryland, but it is definite he grew up in Florida. It is written that he was very wealthy, owning Talbot Island and about 1500 acres of five plantations with cattle and pedigreed horses. It seems apparent that the family had been building wealth for several generations both in Maryland and Florida. During the British years of 1763 through 1783, the Christophers and the Greenwoods built sizable neighboring plantations on the St. Johns River. Spicer was a loyalist and was First Sergeant in the local militia and cavalry. For this he suffered repercussions from the rebels. When the British lost and the Spanish resumed control of Florida in 1783, Spicer was married to Mary Greenwood and they built their home and plantation on Talbot Island. Being a large landowner he got along with the Spanish. Since the Spanish controlled this area of Florida at this time, they required everyone to become Catholic, so Spicer converted to Catholicism.

Chapter 20: Christopher — Early in Florida

Mary Greenwood was the daughter of William Clyde Greenwood and Isabel Bryan. The Greenwood family were prominent very early settlers in Virginia. Isabel was born in Georgia. They had moved to Nassau County, Florida, where they owned a large plantation. Mary was born there.

According to Spicer's will he owned 55 slaves which certainly didn't hurt his accumulation of a large estate. He died in Crandall, Florida, on the St. Mary's River where he had an estate. This is just north of Jacksonville on the Georgia border. Upon his death, his will distributed the estate, plantations and slaves among his wife and children. His instructions in his will requested the burial service be from the Anglican liturgy. Mary died on a part of the estate in Crandall, Florida.

6 William Bluet Christopher (1785–1815) m Elizabeth Edwards (1791–1845)
William was born on Talbot Island, Florida. Elizabeth was born either on neighboring Amelia Island or in South Carolina. She was the daughter of John Edwards (1776–1818) and Mary Ann Braddock. Her grandfather and great grandfather were both named Capt. John Braddock and of Revolutionary War fame.

William inherited his share of the plantations, but died at a relatively early age. Elizabeth remarried to Thomas J. Reynolds. She died in Lloyd, Florida, which is way west near Tallahassee.

5 William Greenwood Christopher (1814–1880) m Mary Floyd (1825–1868)
William was born on Talbot Island, Florida. According to the 1860 census he was a planter with 17 slaves. According to the 1870 census he was a farmer with 180 head of cattle and 7 various horses–and no slaves. The Civil War had made a difference.

Mary Floyd was his first wife and our line, but we don't know much about her. Only that she was born in Florida and was replaced by a 2nd wife Louisa Elizabeth Ward (1836/7–1883), who was born in Alabama. William had several children with each wife. Upon his death everything was auctioned off. William is buried in the New Berlin Cemetery, Jacksonville, Florida.

4 Georgia Ann Christopher (1845–1902) m Charles Frederick Shelton (1845–1919)
See Chapter 17: Shelton.

3 Daisy Selkirk Shelton (1886–1959) m Christen Rosfjord Kaddeland (1880–1958)
See Chapter 17: Shelton and Chapter 15: Kaddeland.

Chapter 21

Prout — A Long Line from England to America

13 Thomas Prout (1528–1561) m Joane Lucas (1512–1610)
Thomas was born in Bideford, Devon, England. Joane was probably born in Launceston, Cornwall, England. They married and died in Bideford, Devon, England.

12 Hugh Prout (1556–1619) m Agnes Phesy (1540–1610)
We presume Hugh and Agnes were born, married and died in Bideford, Devon, England.

11 William Prout (1588–1654) m Susan Lambert (1590–1637)
William and Susan were born, married and died in Bideford, Devon, England.

10 Capt. Timothy Prout (1620–1702) m Margaret (1623–1685)
Timothy was born in Bideford, Devon, England and came to America in 1635 during the Great Migration. He married Margaret in Boston in 1643. In 1657 he was Master of the ship *Increase*. In Boston he was a surveyor of the Port of Boston in 1682, Captain of forts and artillery in 1683, on the Committee for Settlement of Deeds with Indians in 1685, a Selectman in 1684 to 1690 and a Representative to the General Court 1685, 1686, 1689 and 1692.

Little is known about his wife, Margaret. They had seven children. Margaret died at age 62. Timothy remarried to an Elizabeth Upshall. Timothy outlived Elizabeth also, lived to the age of 80 and is buried in the King's Chapel Burying Ground in Boston, Massachusetts.

Chapter 21: Prout — A Long Line from England to America

9 Dr. Ebenezer Prout (1656–1735) m Grace Sherman (1659–1712)

Ebenezer was born in Boston, Massachusetts, and was the youngest of seven siblings. He married first an Elizabeth Wheeler who died in 1683 in Charlestown, Massachusetts.

Ebenezer's second wife, Grace, was born in Watertown, Massachusetts. Ebenezer and Grace were the first generation of their families born in America. They married in 1678 in Concord, Massachusetts, where their son, William, was born as one of seven children.

Ebenezer was Clerk of the House of Representatives of Massachusetts in 1689, a Representative from Watertown in 1693 and Town Clerk and Selectman in 1694. In 1711 he received a license from Yale University in New Haven, Connecticut, to practice Physics and Surgery. Grace died the following year in Watertown, Massachusetts. He moved to Middletown, Connecticut, where he lived until he died many years later.

Grace was the daughter of the Rev. John Sherman (1613–1685) and Mary Launce (1625–1710). John Sherman was born in Dedham, Essex, England, and attended Trinity College of Cambridge University where he received AB and AM degrees. He preached in England, but his Puritan views caused him persecution. John came to America in 1635 with his parents and several siblings to Boston where they settled in Watertown. John did not stay in Watertown very long, but moved on to Wethersfield, Connecticut, where he became a magistrate for several years. Later he moved to Branford in the New Haven Colony and then moved to a church in Milford, Connecticut. In 1639, probably in New Haven, he married his first wife, Abigail Mary Gibbs. They had six children. Abigail died in 1644 in Milford.

In 1646 John Sherman married second wife, Mary Launce. Mary Launce was the daughter of John Launce (1597–1639) and Isabella Darcy (c1600–c1669). In 1647 he left Milford to move back to Watertown, Massachusetts, where he lived and preached–until he died. He gave lectures at Harvard College. He was known for his great preaching as well as a controversial individual throughout New England. John and Mary had many children. There are records for six children, but also statements that they had twenty children which is questionable. Also see John Launce and Isabella Darcy in Chapter 2.

8 William Prout (1699–1789) m Rachel Harris (1707–1799)

William was born in Concord, Massachusetts. Rachel was born in Middletown, Connecticut. They married in 1729, in Middletown, Connecticut. In 1717 he "taught school in the Upper Houses" which I presume means he was hired by wealthy families to educate their children. He was also a merchant for several years. He apparently was unsuccessful in some business ventures, particularly a shipbuilding venture where his partner absconded, leaving William with a loss.

They lived in "South Farm" on a farm that his wife inherited from her family. In 1723 the family donated part of the farm to the town for use as a cemetery, which is now Old Farm Hill Cemetery in Middletown, Connecticut.

In 1744, while crossing the Connecticut River at night on ice, he fell into the river. He swam for about 40 minutes before being rescued, suffering hypothermia and shock. He survived, but remained an invalid for the rest of his life.

Several of their sons served in the Revolutionary War. William and Rachel are buried in the Old Farm Hill Cemetery. Also see Harris in Chapter 26.

7 Harris Prout (1732–1822) m Priscilla Roberts (1736–1810)

Harris is obviously named for his mother's family of Harris. Harris and Priscilla were born, married and died in Middletown, Connecticut. Harris served in the Revolutionary War as a private in Capt. Ebenezer Johnson's Company 23 of the Connecticut State Militia. They are buried in Old Farm Hill Cemetery in Middletown, Connecticut. Also see Roberts and Harris in Chapter 26.

6 William Prout (1779–1822) m Sally Spencer (1783–1852)

William was born in Middletown, Connecticut. Sally was born in Haddam, Connecticut, to a family of Spencers who had been there for several generations.

William Prout died on July 12, 1822, in a house fire at his father's home. His father had died earlier in February of that year. William and Sally are buried in Old Farm Hill Cemetery in Middletown, Connecticut. Also see Spencer in Chapter 25.

5 Ruth Lucrecia Prout (1821–1898) m Watrous Ives Miller (1822–1885)

For Ruth Prout and Watrous Miller see Chapter 18: Miller.

Chapter 22

Ritter and Post — In New York City

In Chapter 14 our discussion of Floyd Smith's wife, Catherine Ritter, became voluminous and needed more of its own space. Catherine's family had been in New York City for only a few generations. Catherine was the fourth generation in America for her father's Ritter family. She was the third generation of her mother's Post family in America–as far as I can document.

There is conflicting information on the Post side here and I have endeavored to sort it out to the most reasonably accurate record of facts. Some family trees show the Post family back many more generations in America, to the early Dutch settlers under Peter Stuyvesant in New Amsterdam and before that in Europe. But I feel the footnoted reference here to be more factually reliable for our line, even if it excludes some other Post family records of history in America. [84]

The Post name sounds very British, but the name is thought to originate with "Postmael," which was the Dutch name for a postman. So, as an occupation it was added to their name. We know naught of our John Post's family in the Netherlands. Only that John Post emigrated from the Netherlands to New York with his parents in 1750.

The name Ritter is German for "knight" and is the second low rank of nobility–above "Elder" and below "Baron." But, since we know nothing of these Ritters in Germany and we try not to have class distinctions in America, we will move on.

Catherine's Ritter family is fairly straightforward. Her grandfather and great grandfather came in 1741 when they emigrated from the Rheinland area of Germany. They seem

---

[84] Tuttle, Mrs. H. Croswell, *History of St. Luke's Church in the City of NY 1820–1920*, Appeal Printing Co., 1927

to have been an industrious, entrepreneurial family with a typical German work ethic.[85]

10 Johan Petrus Ritter m Ann Catherine Fauth (??–1717)
Johan and Ann Catherine were supposedly born and died in Spalmheimerthal, Germany. But, I have not found that town on any map. They had a son John Peter born in Geissen, Germany.

9 John Peter Ritter (1698–1747) m Maria Elizabeth Fox or Wogen (1705–??)
John Peter was born in Geissen, Germany. Maria was born in Germany. They married in 1722 in the Lutheran Church in Germany and immigrated in 1741 to New York with their immediate family which at that time included 6 or 7 of their 10 children. Several of their children were baptized in the Dutch Reformed Church.

8 John Michael Ritter (1734–1799) m Margaret Bandt (1736–1805)
John Michael was born in Germany and immigrated with his parents and siblings to New York at age 7. Margaret was born in New York since her family had been here for several generations. John Michael and Margaret married in New York in 1757 and had 8 children. He was a merchant and had a store on Chatham Street. Their son Peter was the oldest.

7 Peter Ritter (1758–1811) m Catherine Ann Post (1766–1828)
Peter Ritter was born in New York City. Peter's first wife, Lucretia Dash, died in 1783, three years after their marriage. They had no children. He remarried to Catherine Ann Post

Portraits of Peter Ritter and Catherine Ann Post

---

85 Appleton, Rev. Floyd, *Ritter and Post Family Records and Reminiscences of our Forbears*, manuscript in the library of the New York Genealogical and Biographical Society

Chapter 22: Ritter and Post — In New York City

in the same year, 1783. Catherine Ann Post was also born in New York City. They had 9 children, but only 5 lived to adulthood.

I am assuming Peter Ritter, as the oldest son, entered the father's business. Peter is variously listed as a jeweler, a hardware merchant, an iron monger, and as a goldsmith. That's quite a variety of occupations. But it appears they had a clearly established and apparently successful business.

We have no record of their activity during the Revolutionary War. As a merchant in New York did they trade with the British? I imagine they had to in order to survive. About half the city burned during the war. How were they affected? We just don't know.

A framed pair of pastels on paper that show portraits of Peter Ritter and Catherine Ann Post by painter Gerrit Schipper was recently for sale at Elliot and Grace Snyder Antiques in South Egremont, Massachusetts for $4,500. How did those portraits get to the Berkshire area of Western Massachusetts?

Catherine Ann Post's parents, John Post (1740–1817) and Deborah Smith (1742–1834) are an interesting study. John arrived in New York City with his parents in 1750 from the Netherlands at age 10. Deborah was born in New York City. We know nothing of any of their parents. They married in 1765 and had 10 children–all born in New York City. Catherine Ann was the oldest child. They lived at 8 Cherry Street which, at that time, was a well-to-do address.

John Post held a position of Inspector of Provisions and he also was a re-packer of beef and pork. In those occupations he must have used a lot of barrels to become the "leader of the Association of Coopers." It's also good to see the enthusiasm for the new Constitution.

> "On July 26, 1789, there was a grand procession in New York, celebrating the Ratification of the Constitution of the U. S. * * * John Post was the leader of the Association of the Coopers. He is said to have had a Float on which the staves of a barrel fell apart until bound together by a hoop representing the Constitution which bound the Thirteen States together. On this occasion the Association gave John Post two pitchers with his name on them as a Souvenir."

The Posts were very active in the Anglican Church before the Revolutionary War and afterward with the evolution to the Episcopal Church in America. Prior to the conclusion of the Revolutionary War, the Church of England, or Anglican Church, was organized with Bishops in America under the direction of the Archbishop of Canterbury in England. Upon conclusion of the war the Anglican Church withdrew all of their Bishops from America which prevented the church from being able to confirm new parishioners or to ordain new priests. This caused an uproar within the church in America. They would not allow Bishops in America who would not swear allegiance to the English king. It was solved

Chapter 22: Ritter and Post — In New York City

by sending Rev. Samuel Seabury to Scotland in 1784 where he was consecrated as a Bishop in the Anglican communion of the Episcopal Church of Scotland to return to establish the new Episcopal Church of America. John Post supported the controversial Bishop Samuel Seabury's action.

Portraits of John Post and Deborah Smith

John Post and his brother William Post were among the founders of Christ Church in New York City. They were later originally buried in a family vault at the old St. George's Church on Beekman Street but still later moved to Trinity Church Cemetery.

Peter Ritter and Catherine Ann Post moved to Greenwich Village in New York City and were founding members of St. Luke in the Fields Church on Hudson Street in Greenwich Village. They were very involved in the starting of St. Luke's Church. While the church was under construction, services were held in a room over a nearby firehouse. After services,

Catherine Post (Ritter) plaque or vault in an originally exterior south wall (now interior wall) of St Luke in the Fields Church, Greenwich Village, New York City.

they visited the church site to check on the progress and work. It was a "family affair" and even the children helped.

Catherine Ann Post was very active in St. Luke's, where a wall bears a stone plaque for "Catherine Ritter," Catherine Ann Post's married name. Her descendants gave a new high alter in her name which was dedicated on Ascension Day, May 13, 1923.[86]

About one hundred and seventy years later, our daughter Nancy joined St. Luke's and two of our grandchildren were baptized there.

6 Catherine Ritter (1796–1869) m Floyd Smith Sr. (1791–1874)
I have never heard why Floyd Smith Sr. lived with Catherine's family. Is there a Smith family connection here through Deborah Smith that we don't know anything about? Floyd Smith came to New York City from Orange County and lived with the family. He later married into this family and seems to also have prospered. See Catherine Ritter and Floyd Smith Sr. in Chapter 14.

---

86 Tuttle, Mrs. H. Croswell, *History of St. Luke's Church in the City of NY 1820–1920*, Appeal Printing Co., 1927

Chapter 23

Nicholson — Col. John at Quebec and in the Revolution

There are several Nicholson families in America. I have not found a connection of our line to any other Nicholson group, but I'm sure they exist. Our Nicholsons settled in New Windsor, Ulster County, New York. I presume they were of Scottish or northern English origin as were the majority of Presbyterian settlers in that area at that time.

9 John or Daniel Nicholson m Mary?
The Nicholsons had four sons: John, Thomas, Daniel and Andrew.

8 Col. John Nicholson (1743–1811) m. Elizabeth Moffat (1740–c1794)
John Nicholson grew up in Little Britain, now called New Windsor, New York. At age twenty-two he had a job called a "Fence Sitter" which was a tax assessor position. People were taxed on the number of animals they owned and his job was to count the number of various animals on farms. He became a prosperous farmer on his own, with a large acreage in a church community called the Goodwill Community, later called Maybrook, and now part of the town of Middletown. The census of 1790 showed he owned one slave. He married Elizabeth Moffat from nearby Blaggs Cove and they had four children: John, Samuel, Ann and Margaret.

  John C. Nicholson (1765–1852)–Rev. War Veteran
  Ann Nicholson (1768–??) m Daniel Smith (1763–1810)–Four Children
  Margaret Nicholson (1769–1834) m Jacob F. Bookstaver Jr. (1750–1821)–Ten
   Children
  Samuel Nicholson (c1770–??)–??

Chapter 23: Nicholson — Col. John at Quebec and in the Revolution

When the Continental Congress decided in 1775 to invade Canada in order to befriend the predominantly French settlers and keep the British, who controlled Canada, from accessing the Lake Champlain corridor to New York, John Nicholson was part of the Invasion force. He was commissioned a Captain in Colonel James Clinton's 3rd New York Battalion. His original enlistment was from 28 June to November, 1775. The campaign was delayed and moved slowly north. Sickness, desertions and expiration of 90-day enlistments decimated the American forces. Delays by the Congress to fund the operation aggravated the situation by causing shortages of food, arms and ammunition. Forced extensions of enlistments, recruitment of Canadian sympathizers and sheer determination by the patriots kept them going. They captured Lake Champlain, Fort St Johns, Montreal and then set siege to Quebec City. With most enlistments expiring on December 31, General Montgomery decided to attack Quebec City on New Year's Eve. He led the charge and was killed in the first broadside from the defenders. The attacking colonials fell back in disarray, retreated and settled into winter quarters. Many, fed up with the whole thing, did not reenlist and returned home to their families. Nicholson and some of his troops remained near Quebec City. He was now promoted to Colonel and transferred under the command of General Benedict Arnold.[87][88]

In Canada, Arnold was an excellent field commander, whose forces were well-disciplined and performed well. However, he was always an opportunist and not generally liked or trusted by his fellow commanders. His much later defection came at a time when the success of the patriots was seriously in doubt and he thought he could gain stature, success and financial gain by going to the other side. He died penniless years later in England.

As spring of 1776 came, the British brought in shiploads of troops and the remaining Patriots fled. Nicholson was faulted for abruptly retreating, but they had no choice. They retreated all the way back home to New York.

The Continental Congress initiated an inquiry into the performance of many officers, including Colonel John Nicholson. Nicholson saw that this might take years to be resolved and petitioned General George Washington for an immediate hearing to clear his name. This was granted. The charges against him could not be substantiated and therefore were dropped.

This cleared Nicholson to be able to recruit his own regiment, which was called Nicholson's Regiment of Continental Forces. This regiment operated from March to

---

[87] Wikipedia Contributors, "Battle of Quebec (1775)," Wikipedia, The Free Encyclopedia. (accessed September 2018)

[88] Anderson, Mark R., *The Battle for the Fourteenth Colony: America's War of Liberation in Canada, 1774–1776*, University Press of New England. ISBN 1-61168-497-8

Chapter 23: Nicholson — Col. John at Quebec and in the Revolution

November 1776, mainly in the Hudson and Mohawk Valleys and in western New York state. By the summer of 1776, Nicholson was in ill health and returned to his farm in Wallkill. His regiment was later reorganized into the 5th New York Regiment. Today there is a group doing reenactments of "Nicholson's Regiment" in Orange and Ulster County, New York.

In 1809, Colonel Nicholson served as a member of the New York State Legislature from Orange County, New York, and served on that body with a Selah Strong also from Orange County. My father descended from Colonel Nicholson, and my mother descended from Susanna Strong, a sister of Selah Strong III from Long Island. My parents were married 123 years later in 1932 in Connecticut. What a small world it is. See William Shelton in Chapter 17.

At some point his wife, Elizabeth Moffat, died. See Chapter 24: Moffat. John Nicholson remarried to a Jane McCaughry. They are buried in the Brick Church Cemetery in Neelytown, New York.[89]

Col. John Nicholson home

Nicholson's home stood on a hill overlooking the farm acreage. The wood-frame, two-story home still stands with a state historical marker out front. The house is in very good condition and still in use today over 200 years later. Down the hill where the farm was is now a major railroad transfer yard containing a maze of railroad tracks.

---

89 "Brick Reformed Church, Montgomery, Orange County New York," Brochure copied, typed and indexed by Mrs. Jean D. Worden including "The Independent Republican, Goshen, N. Y. ;" issue of November 1925 Graves of Revolutionary War Soldiers by Robt. O. Thompson, Campbell Hall, N. Y.

7 Ann Nicholson (c1768–??) m. Daniel Smith 2 (1763–1810)
Very little is known of Ann Nicholson other than she was the daughter of Col. Nicholson and his first wife, Elizabeth Moffat. We have no birth or death dates. We can presume that she grew up in a household centered around the farm and the Revolutionary War. With her father very much involved in the war, she likely helped in keeping the home and farm running. After the war she married Daniel Smith.

They had four children:
- Juliet Smith (1786–1836) m Joseph Gregg
- Floyd Smith Sr. (1791–1874) m Catherine Ritter (1796–1869)
- Elmira Smith (1794–1877) m Levy Hedges (1791–1874)
- John Nicholson Smith (1796–1839) m Alice Fielding

See more on Daniel and Ann in Chapter 14: Smith.

Chapter 24

Moffat — From Scotland to Orange County, New York

The name Moffat or its alternate spellings of Moffatt, Moffitt, Moffett and Morphet has several possible origins, which may represent totally different families. Various stories exist that the 1066 Norman Conquest brought several persons of this name from France, Italy and even Nordic origin to England and Scotland. The earliest is a Norwegian knight, Willam de Moffett who came to England with William the Conqueror. We will leave it to others to sort out the very original source of the name Moffat.[90][91]

Our Moffats come into visibility at the English/Scottish border area. "… the family appears to have flourished as minor barons and freeholders … possessing a fair share of power and influence, and leading the usual life of such 'Border' families. They served Wallace until his fall, then transferred their allegiance to Bruce, whose fortunes they followed till the culminating victory of Bannockburn … and finally established the independence of Scotland."[92]

This didn't last long, however, as the English again took control and inter-clan feuds with the Johnstones left the Moffat Clan "broken" or leaderless. "The final overthrow of the Moffats appears to have been brought about by the Johnstones taking advantage of an assembling together of the Moffats in a large building wherein they had met for council or prayer. The Johnstones set fire to the building and, on the Moffats attempting to escape

---

90 Moffat, Hector, *The Story of Blooming Grove and the Tribe of Samuel Moffat*, Washingtonville, NY, October 1, 1907
91 Wikipedia, "Clan Moffat Genealogy" as of 5/14/2009
92 *The Moffats of Earlier Days*, Found in Moffat Library, Washingtonville, NY, page 18

Chapter 24: Moffat — From Scotland to Orange County, New York

from the flames, attacked and killed many of their principals. This disaster deprived the clan of its leaders and ultimately led to its breaking up."[93]

Firm knowledge of our Moffat branch begins in Ayrshire, Scotland, around the 17th century. In the 17th century, conflicts between the Presbyterian Scots and the English Anglicans continued. A battle was fought on June 22, 1679, which more or less ended the rebellion of the militant Presbyterian Covenanters. Our ancestor Samuel Moffat was there. Approximately 6,000 Covenanters faced 5,000 British regular troops at the Battle of the Bothwell Bridge. After some initial success in the battle, the rebels lacking artillery and sufficient ammunition fell back and were routed. Those captured were treated sternly and fairly, but retained in Edinburgh at a place now called the Covenanters Prison. Many were deported to the colonies. The Moffat Clan was generally dispersed at that time. Some continued to move and spread, while many stayed deeply involved in their communities. Samuel went to County Antrim in Ireland.[94]

11 Samuel Moffet (before 1679–after 1710)

Samuel is the earliest Moffat we can firmly document anything about. He lived in Ayrshire, Scotland, married, and had two sons, William and Samuel.

He became involved in the 1679 Covenanter uprising at Bothwell's Bridge against the King.

"Samuel Moffet had to flee from Scotland to Ireland. His wife and son/s remained in Scotland for a period of time and then went to Ireland. He remained in Ireland a generation. He, and his son, William, and grandson Samuel emigrated to Woodbridge, New Jersey." At that time there were other Moffats already in Woodbridge. We don't know who in his immediate family came first or if the family group came together. It is speculated that son William came to America first and then sent for the father, Samuel. Samuel joined the Woodbridge Presbyterian Church in 1710. It is presumed that Samuel died in Woodbridge. His son, Samuel, stayed in County Antrim, Ireland, for the rest of his life and his descendants are still there.[95]

10 William Moffat (1675–1748) m. Margaret Gregorie (c1682–1746)

William was born in Ayr, Scotland. At some point, his mother with her two sons moved to join his father in County Antrim, Ireland. All except William's brother Samuel moved

---

93 Ibid
94 McLaughlin, Edward J. *Around the Watering Trough*, Publisher: Washingtonville Centennial Celebration, Inc.; Printed by Spear Printing Co., Inc. Washingtonville, NY, Copyright 1994
95 Ibid

on to America in 1710 where they settled in Woodbridge, New Jersey. William and his wife, Margaret, had five children, one girl and four boys, and are buried in the Woodbridge Presbyterian Church graveyard.

9 Samuel Moffat (1704–1787) m. Anne Gregg (1716–1794)

Samuel was born in Balleleag, County of Antrim, Ireland, while his family were "refugees" from Scotland. In 1710, when he was six years old, they migrated to America, settling in Woodbridge, New Jersey. That must have been a grand adventure for a six-year-old, to travel across the vast ocean for many weeks.

Samuel grew up and married a Ruth Burns (1711–1734) who apparently died without bearing any surviving children.

Samuel married a second time to Anne Gregg in Woodbridge, New Jersey, on June 5, 1735. Anne Gregg was the daughter of Hugh Gregg, and born in Sluh Hull, County of Fermanaugh, Ireland. Anne was 19 when she married. Samuel was 31.

Several years later, in 1752, Samuel and his wife bought land from Edward Blagg and moved to Blagg's Clove, Orange County, New York. They were probably the first settlers of Blagg's Clove. There they carved a homestead and farm out of the wilderness. They had twelve children, seven girls and five boys. Samuel and his five sons all signed the New York Association Pledge of 1775 to support the Revolutionary War. Samuel and Anne died at Blagg's Clove and are buried in the Bethlehem Presbyterian Church Graveyard. Notice of the probate of his will listed him as a "yeoman," which indicates him as being a farmer of some means.

8 Elizabeth Moffat (1740–c1794) m. Col. John Nicholson (1743–1811)

Betsy as she was called, was most likely born in Woodbridge, New Jersey, since the family did not move to Blagg's Clove, Orange County, New York, until 1757. But all my sources list her as being born in Blagg's Clove. She married John Nicholson and had two daughters and two sons. During the Revolutionary War days, when her husband was away, she had to run the farm as many other wives did. She apparently did it well, for the farm prospered. Also see Nicholson in Chapter 23.

Moffat Library

A little added information includes Samuel Moffat III (1744–1807) who married Hannah Chandler.

This Samuel III was a nephew of Elizabeth (1740–1794) above, an early influential settler in Little York, New York. He established a trading post store there and was instrumental in changing the town name to Washingtonville, New York. Although many

Chapter 24: Moffat — From Scotland to Orange County, New York

wished to name the town Moffatville, he persuaded them to name the town after General Washington since there had been a large Revolutionary War Camp nearby which included Washington's headquarters.

Samuel III's grandson David Moffat went west, and was very successful in railroad and mining investments. David returned and donated funds to build the Moffat Library in Washingtonville, New York. This library organization and the structure he funded stands today serving the community. Much of my Moffat family information above came from a very helpful visit there in 2014.

Chapter 25

Spencer — Another Long Family Line and Founders in Hartford and Haddam, Connecticut

At first, I thought that these small, short branches of the family tree were of minor interest and could quickly be reviewed. But how mistaken I was. It certainly shows that everyone is significant if we just get to know and understand them.

This chapter originated with an interest in exploring a statement that said the Spencers probably went back to a Robert de Spencer, who was a steward to William the Conqueror. Well, I never discovered any facts to confirm that, though it still may exist. However, I certainly found two Spencer lines that needed further development and are worthy of the time spent perusing their lives and relationships.

First is Lady Margaret Spencer (1495–1524), wife of James Denton (1492–1532). See Chapter 27.

Second, Ens. Gerard (Jared) Spencer II (1614–1685) married Hannah Joanis Hills (1618–1692) and was of interest as an early settler in Hartford, Connecticut. Ens. Gerard (Jared) Spencer gave us another solid line back through King Edward I and the Plantagenets for an additional bloodline connection back to Cerdic. See Chapter 7.

First–Lady Margaret Spencer's line is as follows:
    Galfridus Geoffrey Despencer (1190/1200–1242) m Emma De Harcourt (c1200–1265)
    John Despenser (1235–1274) m Anne de Lou (1240–1275)

Chapter 25: Spencer — Another Long Family Line and Founders in Hartford and Haddam, Connecticut

William Spencer (1264–1328) m unknown (1281–c1350)
John Spencer (1300–1386) m Alice Deverell (1305–1386)
Nicholas Spencer (1340–1395) m Joan Polard (1344–c1362)
Thomas Spencer (c1366–1435) m Dorothy Hills (1370–1408)
Sir Henry Badby Spencer (1392–1476) m Isabelle Lincoln (1394–1462)
John Hodnell Spencer (1418–1479) m Lady Elizabeth Joan Warsted (1422–1445)
Thomas Spencer (1441–1475) m Margaret Matilda Smith (1450–1487)
Sir William Spencer III (1470–1532) m Lady Agnes Heritage (1478–c1557)
Lady Margaret Spencer (1495–1524) m James Denton (1492–1532) See Chapter 27

And Second–Ens. Gerard (Jared) Spencer II's line is as follows:

10 Ens. Gerard (Jared) Spencer II (1614–1685) m Hannah Joanis Hills (1618–1692)
Gerard (or Jared as he was also called) emigrated from England in 1632 to settle in Cambridge, Massachusetts. Gerard was one of four Spencer brothers to arrive in America. William arrived in 1631. Thomas arrived in 1633. Michael arrived in 1634. They all moved to Lynn, Massachusetts, about 1634 where Gerard met and married Hannah in 1636. Around 1639 Gerard obtained a license to operate a ferry there for two years. Gerard and Hannah moved to Hartford, Connecticut, in 1660 along with two of the brothers, William and Thomas. They were part of the Founders of Hartford. William and Thomas Spencer were part of the Founders of Hartford and are recognized on the Founders Monument. Gerard moved on in 1662 to a new area as part of a group who bought 100,000 acres from the Indians called Thirty Mile Island. Gerard and Hannah moved there and the area was later renamed Haddam, Connecticut. In Haddam he was appointed Ensign of the Train Band. He also served as a State Legislator from Haddam for 8 years.

Hannah was born in Great Burstead, Essex, England, and had immigrated to Massachusetts with her parents. She was descended from the Plantagenet line in Chapter 6 as follows:

16 Margaret Percy (1437–1486) m Sir William Gascoigne V (1445–c1486)
Dorothy Gascoigne (1476–1526) m Ninian Markenfield (1474–1528)
Alice Markenfield (1506–1563) m Robert Mauleverer (1495–1541)
Dorothy Mauleverer (1528–1590) m John Kaye of Woodsome (1528–1594)
Richard Kaye (1564–1597) m Anne Speght (1568–1598)
Isabel Kaye (1595–1638) m Henry Dunster (1592–1646)
Rose Dunster (1603–1650) m John Hills (1602–1688)
Hannah Joanis Hills (1618–1692) m Ens. Gerard Spencer II (1614–1685)

Chapter 25: Spencer — Another Long Family Line and Founders in Hartford and Haddam, Connecticut

Hannah's uncle, Henry Dunster (1609–1658/9), Rose Dunster's brother, was the first president of Harvard College. He had emigrated from England in 1640 to Boston and was almost immediately selected to be the head of the college. The previous Master had been discharged the previous year. Henry set up and taught all subjects, the entire curriculum, alone, for several years and graduated the first college class in America in 1642. In 1650, Henry Dunster obtained Massachusetts Bay Colony Court approval of a Corporate Charter for Harvard College as the first Corporation in America. The Charter is still in effect at Harvard University. He served as president of Harvard for fourteen years before departing over the issue of infant baptism.

Henry Dunster is said to have inherited, from his first wife, Elizabeth Harris, the first printing press in America. If true, this was the same printing press brought to America on the ship *John of London* which brought our Thomas Miller to America in 1638. See Chapter 18: Miller.

Gerard and Hannah had about 12 children. They both died in Haddam, Connecticut.

9 Sgt. Nathaniel William Spencer Jr. (1658–1722) m Lydia Bailey (1658–1728)

Nathaniel was born in East Haddam, Connecticut. He and Lydia married, lived and died in Haddam.

Lydia was either the daughter of Thomas Smith or John Bailey and Lydia Backus. Records show both, but I favor the Bailey side since the mother and daughter have the same first name.

8 Daniel Spencer (1694–1769) m Abigail Clark (1715–1771)

Daniel and Abigail were born, married, lived and died in Haddam.

Abigail's Clark family is known back many generations as follows:
Sir John Richard Clark (1503–1559) m Lady Margaret Walker Sweet (1513–1567)
John Clark (1541–1598) m Katherine Carew Cooke (1541–1601)
Thomas Clark (1570–1627) m Rose Kerrick (1572–1627)
William Clark (1610–1681) m Katherine Bunce (1610–1683)
Joseph Clark (1652–1716) m Ruth Spencer (1654–1744)
Daniel Clark (1683–1732) m Mary Tully (1681–1738)
Abigail Clark (1715–1771) m Daniel Spencer (1694–1769)

An interesting note here is that Ruth Spencer's parents are Ens. Gerald Spencer II (1614–1685) and Hannah Joanis Hills (1618–1682). This means that Daniel and Abigail share half of the same ancestors.

Chapter 25: Spencer — Another Long Family Line and Founders in Hartford and Haddam, Connecticut

7 Elias Spencer (1750–1828) m Abigail Sexton (c1750–aft 1828)
Elias was born in Haddam, Connecticut. Abigail was born in Connecticut, but nothing is known of her Sexton family. According to the 1820 census Elias was a farmer. They married, lived and died in Haddam.

6 Sally Spencer (1783–1852) m William Prout (1779–1822)
See Sally Spencer and William Prout in Chapter 21.

Chapter 26

Roberts — Very Involved in Early Connecticut

This chapter began as a simple page to contain the ancestors of Priscilla Roberts and the Roberts family without adding too much confusing detail in Chapter 21 on the Prouts. But it grew significantly when I began looking into all the spouses and their families. Some very interesting family branches and individuals with their various life stories are included.

14 Sir John Roberts of Burway (1510–1610) m Elizabeth Piggot (1536–1590)

13 Sir William Thomas Roberts (c1548–c1648) m Lady Elizabeth Whitton (1555–1621)

12 Lord William Roberts (1576–1675) m Thosamine Harry (1581–1641)
William and Thosamine lived their lives in England.

11 Samuel William Roberts (1608–1690) m Sarah Hinman (1608–??)
Samuel William was born in England and immigrated to America. Sarah was born in England or Stratford, Connecticut. He died in New Haven, Connecticut. She died in Middletown, Connecticut.

10 Samuel Roberts (1638–1726) m Catherine Leete (1642–1693)
Samuel and Catherine were both born, married, lived and died in Middletown, Connecticut. Since Samuel outlived Catherine, they apparently divorced somewhere around 1670, since

Chapter 26: Roberts — Very Involved in Early Connecticut

Catherine remarried Thomas Wetmore in 1673 and had three additional children with him. It was Thomas Wetmore's third marriage. Also see Thomas Wetmore in Chapter 18.

Catherine's ancestors were prominent in England and were as follows:
  Thomas Leete (1520–1582) m Lady Dorothy of Warde (1528–1587)
  Thomas Leete II (1554–1616) m Maria Slade (1553–1610)
  John Leete (1570–1648) m Anne Shute (1557–1650)
  Gov. William Leete (1612–1683) m Anna Payne (1621–1668)
  Catherine Leete (1642–1693) m 1) Samuel Roberts (1638–1726)
              m 2) Thomas Wetmore (1615–1681)

Catherine's father was William Leete. He and his wife, Anna Payne, were both born in Huntingtonshire, England, and migrated to the New Haven Colony in Connecticut, where they married and lived in Guilford, Connecticut. William was educated as a lawyer in England and held successive administrative and judicial positions in the New Haven Colony. He was Deputy Governor of the New Haven Colony in Connecticut from 1658 to 1661 when the King sought the capture of the two judges, William Goffe and Edward Whaley. He successfully delayed the King's agents until the judges could get into hiding and avoid capture. He was Governor of the New Haven Colony when it merged with the Colony of Connecticut in Hartford which had a charter to exist. He became Governor of the Colony of Connecticut from 1676 until his death in Hartford in 1683. Records show he had seven wives.

9 John Roberts (1668–1721) m Sarah Blake (1675–1737)
John and Sarah were born, married, lived and died in Middletown, Connecticut. For Sarah Blake's ancestors see Blake in Chapter 16.

8 Jonathan Roberts (1707–1788) m Mary Gilbert (1713–1757)
Jonathan and Mary were born and married in Middletown, Connecticut. Mary died in Middletown. Jonathan died in New London, Connecticut.

Mary Gilbert's family was from England and her ancestry is as follows:
  Richard A. Gilbert (Gylbryde) (before 1550–1626) m Margery Morken or Morton (1553–1637)
  Thomas Gilbert Sr. (c1559–before 1659) m Elizabeth Lydia Bennett (1586–1654)
  Jonathan Gilbert Sr. (1617–1682) m Mary White (1626–1650)
  Jonathan Gilbert (1648–1698) m Dorothy Stow (1662–1710)
  John Gilbert (1683–1727) m Mary Harris (1692–1742)
  Mary Gilbert (1713–1757) m Jonathan Roberts (1707–1788)

Chapter 26: Roberts — Very Involved in Early Connecticut

Thomas Gilbert and Elizabeth Bennett were born in England, married in Yardley, Worcestershire, England, and migrated to New England before 1639. Their son Jonathan Sr. was born in England and came with them.

Mary White is the daughter of Elder John White and Mary Levit, who were all born in England, arrived in Boston, Massachusetts, in 1632 and settled in Cambridge. Their house stood where Gore Hall of Harvard University stands today. Elder John White and his family moved to Hartford most likely with the initial group of Founders of Hartford in 1636. Elder John White is listed on the Founders Monument in Hartford, Connecticut.

Dorothy Stow (1662–1710) was the daughter of Rev. Samuel Stow (1623–1704) and Hope Fletcher (1624–1704), who were one of the 23 founding families of Middletown, Connecticut.

Mary Harris's Harris family was as follows:
John Harris (c1540–c1650) m Jone Erburon (c1540–c1640)
Walter Harris (1556–1618) m Joan Carter (1556–1632)
Thomas Harris (1580–1634) m Elizabeth Cutter Hills (1601–1670)
Capt. Daniel Harris 1615–1701) m Mary Weld (1627–1711)
Capt. William Harris (1665–1751) m Martha Collins (1666–1750)
Mary Harris (1692–1742) m John Gilbert (1683–1727)

Thomas Harris and Elizabeth Hills were born in Heatherop, Gloucestershire, England, married in Bedfordshire, England, and emigrated to Massachusetts with their son Daniel.

Mary Weld was the daughter of Capt. Joseph Weld and Elizabeth Shatswell who came from England early and were married in Roxbury, Massachusetts. Their daughter, Mary, was born in Roxbury. Mary and Daniel Harris were married in Roxbury. Capt. Weld died in Roxbury and is buried in the Old Burial Ground on Eustis Street. Capt. Daniel Harris was a wheelwright in Roxbury, Massachusetts. He was granted a house lot in Rowley, Massachusetts, in 1643 and settled there in 1651. His father, Thomas, died in Rowley in 1651. Daniel left Rowley in 1652, moving his family, including his mother, Elizabeth, to Middletown, Connecticut. The Rev. Ezekial Rodgers, the essential "master" of Rowley, must not have worn well with Daniel and his family either. If you will recall from Chapter 18, this is the same time that Thomas Miller and his family moved from Rowley to Middletown. I'm sure the families knew each other and what a small world it was–and still is. In Middletown Daniel operated an ordinary and an inn. He became a lieutenant and then captain of the train band. Daniel died in New Haven, Connecticut. Mary died in Middletown, Connecticut.

Capt. William Harris and Martha Collins were born, married, lived and died in Middletown and are buried in the Old Farm Hill Cemetery in Middletown, Connecticut.

As a side note here, I was sure that the Gilbert family were the ancestors of A.C. Gilbert who founded the AC Gilbert Company in New Haven, Connecticut. That company provided so many pleasures for my childhood such as the erector set, chemical sets for children and American Flyer electric toy trains. Those toys certainly initiated my interest in a future vocation in engineering. I was sure I would find a connection to our Gilbert ancestors, but alas he was born in Portland, Oregon, came to New Haven to attend Yale University and stayed there to build his toy company. I have not found any connection — yet.

7 Priscilla Roberts (1736–1810) m Harris Prout (1732–1822)
For Priscilla Roberts and Harris Prout see Chapter 21.

Chapter 27

Gale & Denton — England to Boston to Orange County, New York

The Gale and Denton families have long histories back into England. Our connection of course is Hannah Gale's union with Derrick Smith in Orange County, New York, in the mid-1700s. Of the many Gale spousal branches, the Dentons seem to have a large amount of data available. So they are presented here in more detail also.

There are many branches of the Gale family both in England and America. Our branch originates, as far as we know, with three generations of Thomas Gaels in Edwardstone, Suffolk, England, a small village in the east of England just northeast of London. It originated as "Eadweard's farm" or settlement and was listed in the Domesday Book as Eduardestuna.[96] These Thomas Gaels were born, married, lived, died and were buried in Edwardstone until the third generation when they started relocating.

There is quite a bit of mistaken and fragmented information on various websites which I have endeavored to collect, interpret and clarify as follows:

16 Thomas Gael (1506–1546) m Mary Lord (1506–1546) or Joan Skinner (1510–1580)
They were born, married, lived, died and were buried in Edwardstone, Suffolk, England.

15 Thomas Gael (1522–1588) m Maude Manda Cooke (1526–1588)
Thomas and Maude Manda also were born, married, lived, died and were buried in Edwardstone, Suffolk, England. They had 11 children.

---

96 Wikipedia Contributors, "Edwardstone," Wikipedia, The Free Encyclopedia

Chapter 27: Gale & Denton — England to Boston to Orange County, New York

14 Thomas Gael (1552–1606) m Grace Tunstall (1540/50–1617)

Thomas was born in Edwardstone, Suffolk, England. Grace was born in Scruton, North Yorkshire, England.

About this time the area of Scruton was in rural agriculture. In 1678 a Dr. Thomas Gale from York purchased 1,100 acres to form an estate which included the few small buildings of the village. Later still, in 1705, a manor house was constructed and named Scruton Hall by a Roger Gale.

I suspect our Thomas Gael/Gale was an early family member hunting or farming in the area. And that he met Grace there. They were married in 1572 in Edwardstone, Suffolk, probably at the family home. They had 10 children, five of whom were born in Scruton, North Yorkshire. Three children were born in Oakley, Bedfordshire, so they apparently lived there for a while. Thomas died in Edwardstone, Suffolk. Grace died several years later in Scruton, North Yorkshire, where half of her children lived. She is buried in the churchyard of the church in Scruton, North Yorkshire. There is no gravestone. My thanks to Trevor Howe from the scrutonhistory.com website for confirming some of these facts for me.

13 John Gale (1571–1650) m Margery Wadam (1575–1608)

John and Margery were both born in Oakley, Bedfordshire, England. They married and had five children. Margery died in Oakley, Bedfordshire. John died many years later in Scruton, Yorkshire, England.

12 Edmund Gale (1602–1642) m Constance Ireland (1602–1665)

Edmund and Constance were born in Oakley, Bedfordshire, England, where they were married in 1631 and some of their eight children were born. They immigrated to Boston, Massachusetts, about 1634. Edmund died in 1642 and is buried in Cambridge, Middlesex, Massachusetts.

As their eight children grew up and married, several moved away from the Cambridge area. Two brothers had gone to New Haven, Connecticut, and another to Schenectady, New York. Constance died later in Marblehead, Essex, Massachusetts, an area where some of their children had moved.[97]

Their son Abel left and went to Long Island, New York.

---

[97] Reynolds, Cuyler, *Hudson-Mohawk Genealogical and Family Memoirs: Gale,* Lewis Historical Publishing, Schenectady County Public Library, Schenectady, New York, Copyright 2020, Volume I, pp 419–23

Chapter 27: Gale & Denton — England to Boston to Orange County, New York

11 Abel Gale (1635–1721) m Dinah Smith (1635–1730)
Abel was born in Oakley, Bedfordshire, England, and came to America with his parents in 1641 when he was about seven years old. After growing up in the Boston area, he moved to the Long Island area of New Amsterdam where he married Dinah in 1659. She was born in Jamaica, Queens, New York, and after marrying they settled there where Abel was a husbandman (farmer). He was active in the First Presbyterian Church in Jamaica.

10 John Gale (1670–1750) m Miriam Stacey (1683–1746)
John was born and married in Jamaica, Queens, New York. He was in the milling business and owned mills in the Jamaica area. He sold the mills in 1721 for 1,500 pounds and moved to Goshen, New York. Goshen was then a new town in Orange County, New York with good farmland. He became a "proprietor" in the town. We are not quite sure exactly what he was a proprietor of.

Moving to Goshen must have pleased Miriam who was born in Goshen. John died in Goshen, Orange County.

9 Hezekiah Gale (1710–1784) m Martha Denton (1710–1763)
Hezekiah was born in Jamaica and moved with his parents to Goshen. Martha was born in Wallkill, Orange County, New York. They had 6 children.

Martha Denton's family has a very long history back in Yorkshire and the midland counties or shires of England as follows:

    22 Thomas Denton (c1332–??)
    21 John Denton (c1345–??) m Johanne De La Launde ?? (c1345–??)
    20 John Denton (1375–Aft1401) m Johanne De La Launde (1378–Aft1401)
    19 Thomas Denton (1401–1427) m Lady Agnes Baldington (1403–1428)
    18 Sir Thomas Denton (1427–1453) m Alison Dauncy (1429–1453)
    17 Sir Robert John Denton (1445–1497) m Isabell Brome (1435/45–1513)
    16 James Denton, 14th Dean of Litchfield (1470–1532) m Sarah Jane Webb (1468–1560)
    15 James Denton (1492–1532) m Lady Margaret Spencer (1495–1524)
    14 Richard Denton (1504–1548) m Gennett Banyster (1527–1561)
    13 Richard Denton (1557–1619) m Susan Sibella (1563–1655)
    12 Rev. Richard Denton (1603–1662) m Helen Windebank (1596–c1656)
    11 Samuel Denton (1631–1713) m Mary Rock Smith (1640–1713)
    10 Abraham Denton (1675–1729) m Martha Thorne (1679–1730)
    9 Martha Denton (1710–1763) m Hezekiah Gale (1710–1784)

See also Denton in Part 1, Chapter 6.

Chapter 27: Gale & Denton — England to Boston to Orange County, New York

Hezekiah and Martha died in Wallkill and are both buried in the Wallkill Cemetery in Phillipsburg, Orange County, New York.

8 Hannah Gale (1731–1817) m Derrick Smith (1730–1790)
See Hannah Gale and Derrick Smith in Chapter 14: Smith.

Chapter 28

Clark — So Many Branches

Clark is a common name and was so in the early days of America. The name originated from the Latin word clericus which meant scribe or secretary and then evolved into the English word clerk. So, we Smiths have something in common with the Clarks in that we could have come from everywhere since everyone needs a smith and a clerk. And there were many Clarks in early New England.

It seems they preferred to spell it with an "e" on the end as Clarke, but subsequent generations changed to Clark around 1700. It was common in those early times for an "e" to be on the end of a name for whatever reason. There also were a lot of Williams around. It was a very popular first name. So as a result, there were a lot of William Clarks, and subsequent generations kept using the name. I trust I have our line reasonably factual.

There were several Clark immigrants coming into America in the 1600s and many historians get them confused and maybe I have also. But we do our best to keep it straight and point out possible conflicts. The Clarks came from England. Our branch came specifically with Lt. William Clarke and Sarah from Dorset County, England. As "Puritans," they were being restricted in the practice of their religious beliefs by English Royal authorities and sought freedom and relief in the New World.

12 James Clarke (c1580–c1650) m Joane (c1580–c1645)
James and Joane were born, married, lived and died in Dorset County, England.

11 Lt. William Clarke (1609–1690) m Sarah (1613–1675)
William and Sarah were born in separate towns in Dorset County, England, and came as young adults in 1630 or shortly thereafter with the Puritan movement to Massachusetts. No one seems to know for certain Sarah's family name. There are many speculations but

Chapter 28: Clark — So Many Branches

I did not find any clearly documented information. They married in 1637 in Dorchester, Massachusetts.

Dorcester, Massachusetts, was a town, adjacent to Boston, founded by Puritans from Dorchester, Dorset, England, in 1630. William and Sarah were part of those early Puritans in Dorchester.

He was a sergeant in the militia and elected as a Selectman in Dorchester. They had ten children who were all born in Dorchester.

In 1653, William was one of 24 petitioners to request permission to purchase land from the Indians and establish a new town to be called Northampton and located about 100 miles west in Massachusetts on the frontier. The other petitioners were all original settlers of Dorchester, Massachusetts, who had since moved on to Windsor, Connecticut.

In 1659 William and Sarah left Dorchester and moved to Northhampton, traveling on a horse path to a new home in the wilderness–surrounded by Indians. Sarah is said to have traveled on horseback with two young boys in panniers and another child on her lap. The courage and determination of these ancestors continues to astound me.

The town at that time had about 200 inhabitants. He was granted or bought 100 acres of land including some of which now is part of Smith College. William was elected Lieutenant of the first militia company organized in Northampton and organized the town defenses during the King Philip's War.

Sarah died in 1675 and William remarried to a Sarah Russell in 1676. Sarah Russell died in 1688.

William died during an epidemic that swept through several communities in 1690. They are all buried in the Bridge Street Cemetery in Northampton, Massachusetts.

10 Capt. William Clarke Jr. (1656–1725) m Hannah Strong (1659–1694)

William was born in Dorchester, Massachusetts, and moved with his parents to Northampton, Massachusetts, at age three. He was one of the sons carried in a pannier on his mother's horse over the narrow path through the wilderness. William grew up and married in Northampton to Hannah Strong who was born in Windsor, Connecticut. Hannah Strong was the daughter of Elder John Strong and Abigail Ford. See Chapter 30 for the Strong family. William and Hannah had seven children together.

William and Hannah moved to Lebanon, Connecticut, when William joined 51 original purchasers in what was a large tract on the northern area of the town and called "The Clarke and Dewey Purchase." William was the first representative from the town to the Connecticut General Assembly and continued in that position for thirteen years. He was a Selectman for sixteen years and Town Clerk for twenty-five years. As Captain of the militia, he was involved in wars with the Indians. Hannah died at age 35 and is buried in the Old

Cemetery in Lebanon, Connecticut.

William remarried a year later in 1695 to Mary Smith (1667–1748). They had five children together. William and Mary are also buried in the Old Cemetery in Lebanon, Connecticut.

9 Thomas Clark (1690–1765) m Sarah Strong (c1696–1749)
Thomas and Sarah were both born in Lebanon, Connecticut. They married in 1717 in Waterbury, Connecticut, and lived their lives in Waterbury. She died in 1749 and is buried in the Grand Street Cemetery. He died 16 years later and is buried in the Riverside Cemetery in Waterbury, Connecticut.

Sarah Strong was the great granddaughter of Elder John Strong and his first wife, Margery Deane. Her line is as follows:
    Elder John Strong (1605/6–1699) m Margery Deane (1610–c1630)
    John Strong III (1626–1698) m Elizabeth Warringer (1640–1684)
    John Strong IV (1665–1749) m Hannah Trumble (1673–1747)
    Sarah Strong (c1696–1749) m Thomas Clark (1690–1765)

To confuse us even more, Thomas was the grandson of Elder John Strong and his second wife, Abigail Ford. His line is as follows:
    Elder John Strong (1605/6–1699) m Abigail Ford (1619–1688)
    Hannah Strong (1659–1694) m Capt. William Clarke Jr. (1656–1725)
    Thomas Clark (1690–1765) m Sarah Strong (c1696–1749)

See Chapter 30 for the Strong family.

8 Capt. Timothy Clark (1732–1824) m Hannah Bronson (1738–1783)
Timothy and Hannah both were born, married and died in Waterbury, Connecticut. Hannah was his second wife.

Timothy served during the Revolutionary War, initially as an ensign in the alarm company of Capt. Joseph Blague of Col. James Wadsworth's Connecticut regiment in 1776. In 1779, his company was called to New Haven by Governor Tyrone of New York to repel a British invasion there. Timothy served as a Captain in the 1779 activity.

Hannah's Bronson family tree goes back several generations as follows:
    Cornelius Brownson (1470–1560) m Anna Browme (1470–1560)
    Cornelius Brownson (1490–1550) m Abigail Jackson (1505–1616)
    Cornelius Brownson (1525–1560) m Elizabeth Hovell (1526–1616)
    John Brownson (1548–1623) m Joan (c1552–1617)

Chapter 28: Clark — So Many Branches

    Roger Brownson (1576–1635) m Mary Sudbury Underwood (1575–1623)
    John Bronson (1602–1680) m Francis Hills (1605–1680) First to move to America
    Sgt. Issac Bronson (1645–1719) m Mary Roote (1650–1701)
    Isaac Bronson (1670–1751) m Mary Morgan (1678–1749)
    Isaac Bronson (1707–1799) m Eunice Richards (1716–1749)
    Hannah Bronson (1738–1783) m Capt. Timothy Clark (1732–1824)

John Bronson and Francis Hills were the first of both of their families to emigrate from Essex, England, to America. They married in Essex, England, and arrived in Cambridge, Massachusetts, in 1633 or 1635. They promptly moved to Hartford and then Farmington, Connecticut, where John was a prominent citizen as a deputy to the court, constable, and church founder. Sgt. Issac Bronson and Mary Roote moved their family on to Waterbury, Connecticut. There is a long list of Bronsons and Clarks buried along with Timothy and Hannah in the Grand Street Cemetery in Waterbury, Connecticut.

Of all the people in her family tree, my grandmother, Daisy Shelton chose Capt. Timothy Clark as her Revolutionary War ancestor to use in her application for membership in the DAR. Why him? His role was rather minor and the action was a skirmish. Perhaps his rank or another family member used it. Anyhow I have a DAR number due to her application and successive family applications.

7 William Clark (1763–1814) m Sarah Carrington (1765–1844)

William was born in Waterbury, Connecticut. Sarah was born in Woodbridge, Connecticut, which is just west of New Haven. They grew up 40 miles apart which was two or three days' travel. They married in 1785 in Waterbury just after the Revolutionary War, which ended in 1783. It makes you wonder how they met and became acquainted. William and Sarah had ten children together. They died in Waterbury and are buried in the Grand Street Cemetery.

Sarah's Carrington family tree goes back a few generations as follows:
    John Carrington (1640–1690) m Elizabeth Clark (1653–1690)
    Dr. Peter Carrington (1669–1727) m Anna Wilmot (1669–1728)
    Noadiah Carrington (1706–1738) m Hannah Moulthrop (1709–1748)
    Samuel Carrington (1732–1815) m Mary Johnson (1741–1774)
    Sarah Carrington (1765–1844) m William Clark (1763–1814)

John Carrington and Elizabeth Clark become interesting people here in that they were both born in Simsbury, Connecticut, near Hartford. Their son, Dr. Peter, was born in New Haven and several successive generations continued to live in New Haven until Sarah went to Waterbury to marry and live. John and Elizabeth apparently moved on to Waterbury where they died. What was the draw or connection to Waterbury? I haven't found a connection from Elizabeth Clark to the other Clarks in this chapter.

6 Asahel Clark 2 (1789–1861) m Ruth Adams Selkregg (1791–1885)
Asahel and Ruth were both born in Waterbury, Connecticut. They married in nearby Morris, Connecticut, which at the time was called South Farms and is about 5 miles south of Litchfield, Connecticut. Asahel was a farmer. He died in Waterbury and is buried in the Grand Street Cemetery. Ruth lived another 24 years. Also see Selkregg in Chapter 29.

5 Mary Hanser Clark (1815–1906) m John Douglas Shelton (1813–1894)
See Mary Clark and John Shelton in Chapter 17.

Chapter 29

Selkregg — A Branch Connection to John Adams and also the *Mayflower*

Being an engineer by training and taught to think logically about things, I am curious about why people change the spelling of their names. But, much of the time I just don't figure it out. Such is the case with the Scottish name Selcraig to Selkrigg to Selkregg.

12 Johne Selcraig (1625–1650) m Christiane Kilgour (c1630–??)

11 Alexander Selcraig (c1651–1721) m Janet Neill (1647–??)

10 William Selkrigg (1671–??) m Helen Thomson (1678–??)

9 William Selkrigg (1710–1756) m Judith Mallory (1689–1760)

8 John Selkrigg (1734–1790) m Irene Hopkins (1742–1792)

7 Osee Selkregg (1768–1825) m Prudence Adams (1765–1842)
  Prudence Adam's family ancestry is as follows:
    Henry Adams Sr. (1583–1646) m Edith Rosamund Squire (1587–1672)
    Capt. Samuel Henry Adams (1612–1688) m Rebecca Graves (1630–1664)
    Capt. John Adams (1661–1702) m Hannah Webb (1665–1694)
    John Adams (1687–1729) m Esther Cady (1686–1734)
    William Adams (1714–1793) m Susanna Bronson (1718–1812)

Chapter 29: Selkregg — A Branch Connection to John Adams and the Mayflower

Samuel Adams (1740–1773) m Mary Tompkins (1748–1769)
Prudence Adams (1765–1842) m Osee Selkregg (1768–1825)

Henry Adams Sr. and Edith Squire grew up and married in Somerset County, England. They immigrated to Braintree, Massachusetts, in 1632 and joined the Thomas Hooker Puritans who came in 1633. He was a farmer. They had ten children of which their son, Captain Samuel Henry Adams, is our line. Another son, Joseph Adams (1625–1694), was great grandfather to President John Adams Jr. and great great grandfather to President John Quincy Adams. Therefore our William Adams (1714–1793) above was a second cousin to President John Adams.

Henry Adams Sr. (1583–1646) m Edith Rosamund Squire (1587–1672)
Joseph Adams (1625–1694)
Joseph Adams (1654–1736)
John Adams Sr. (1691–1761)
President John Adams Jr. (1735–1826)
President John Quincy Adams (1767–1848)

President John Adams's maternal grandmother Hannah Bass was the granddaughter of John Alden and Priscilla Mullins who came on the *Mayflower*. This maybe makes them cousins of some sort. Interesting.

The Adams farm in Braintree, Massachusetts, is now the Adams National Historical Park.

6 Ruth Adams Selkregg (1791–1885) m Asahel Clark 2 (1789–1861)
See Clark in Chapter 28.

Chapter 30

Strong — A Very Involved Family

The name Strong or Stronge gives one the impression of an ancestor being physically large and of superior strength. It most probably originally was Strang or Strange, but strang also meant strong. Some say the origin is Scottish and Irish. Others say it originated from a fellow named Lestraunge from Brittany in Normandy who came with William the Conqueror. There is also the French word L'Estrange, meaning stranger, which hints that it even could be Viking in origin. This all seems to be historical bits, speculation, wishful thinking and not lot of facts. Eventually our family of Strongs located in Shropshire, England, but then our particular branch moved to Taunton, Somersetshire, England, then to Charde, Somersetshire, England, where a few generations later Richard John Strong took the hand of Eleanor Deane to produce a child named John. He became known as Elder John (1605–1699).

Elder John Strong is the progenitor of most all Strong family branches in America. He and his offspring had many children which spread the family quickly throughout Massachusetts and Connecticut. Their several marriages with members of the Clark families keeps us connected in several relationships. Successive generations with first and second wives adds to the numbers and creates considerable confusion as to who is related to whom.

16 Robert Lestraunge/Strong (1440–1519) m Lady Ann Boyington (1495–1515)

15 John Strong (1515–1534) m Agnes Whitman (1519–1556)

14 George Strong (1556–1636) m Ann Bond (1563–1628)

Chapter 30: Strong — A Very Involved Family

13 Richard John Strong (1585–1613) m Eleanor Deane (1586–1654)
Richard and Eleanor lived in Taunton and Charde, Somersetshire, England, where their son, John, was born.

12 Elder John Strong (1605/6–1699) m Margery Deane (1610–c1630)
John was born and grew up in Chard, Somerset, England. John was an adventurer, a Pilgrim and a pioneer and following what is written about his life is interesting. He was the first of the Strong family to come to America.

Elder John Strong came, in 1630, on the ship, *Mary and John*, with his first wife, Margery Deane, and son, John Strong III (1626–1698), who was about four. They had another child born on the ship. The family settled in Hingham, Massachusetts which was a "New-Plymouth Colony." The infant child and Margery died not long after arrival.

Elder John Strong (1605/6–1699) remarried to Abigail Ford (1619–1688) who was sixteen years of age. Abigail had also arrived in 1630 on the ship, *Mary and John*, with her parents, Thomas Ford (1587–1676) and Elizabeth Abigail Charde (1589–1643). Thomas Ford and his family settled in Dorchester with most of the 1630 Pilgrims who had arrived on the same ship. Thomas was elected a Selectman in Dorchester. The Ford family moved to Windsor, Connecticut, where Thomas was a Deputy to the Connecticut General Court and later moved on to Northampton along with many of the 1630 Pilgrims.

Elder John and Abigail moved from Hingham to Taunton, Massachusetts, which was also a Plymouth Colony. In Taunton he represented the town for four years in the General Court of the Plymouth Colony. They then moved to Windsor, Connecticut, where Elder John became a prominent person in the new Connecticut Colony.

They moved next to the new settlement of Northampton, Massachusetts, in 1659. Northampton was a new frontier recently acquired from the Indian tribes in west-central Massachusetts. Located north of Hartford and Windsor, Connecticut, it also is on the Connecticut River. The river valley provided good farmland. Elder John was part of a group of eight who founded the First Church of Northampton in 1661. He helped defend the town against Indian raids during the King Phillip's War. He was chosen and ordained as Ruling Elder of the church he helped found.

Elder John Strong and Abigail Ford had 15 children together. He had a total of 18 children between his two wives. The spread of age difference between his youngest and oldest children was 39 years which causes some study to follow how the lineage aligns. His Strong family descendants have connected with other branches of our family in several places. There are major family connections which we can detail. Two are clearly detailed in chapter 28 with the Clark family. In Chapter 23 there is an association with a Selah Strong and Col. John Nicholson both serving together in the New York Legislature. And then there is the connection of the Shelton family in Chapter 17 which is detailed as follows:

12 Elder John Strong (1605/6–1699) m Abigail Ford (1619–1688)

11 Thomas Strong (1638–1689) m Rachel Horton (1650–1714)

10 Selah Strong Sr. (1680–1732) m Abigail Terry (1680–1706)

9 Thomas Strong II (1708–1760) m Susannah Thompson (1707–1783)

8 Susannah Strong (1743–1816) m William Shelton (1739–1812)

This closes Part 3: My Smith Side of Our Family — In America. For myself, I found it an interesting study of people's lives. Partly because they were relatives with whom I can easily attach emotion and empathy, but also because I saw in their lives the struggles we all find in the course of our existence. The effort to live and survive of course is primary, but we strive to associate well with those around us and bond to those we love, to have faith in God or a higher being, to provide for our families, to nourish our offspring, to seek freedom and opportunity and to build a better future. All that effort and progress is within a world of turmoil and strife. And, of course, this is despite our human frailties, limited skills and abilities, and the unexpected reversals that we all face in life. I am so proud and pleased to get to know them!

Part 4

My Wife Linda Knoop's Side of the Family — In America

Picking up from Part 1: Chapter 9, we continue with my wife Linda's side of the family. All our married life, of these many years, I continually heard of the limited ancestral knowledge in the Knoop family because no one knew of their ancestors beyond the Knoop family's arrival in America, which was in the mid- to late-19th century. My exploration of her family tree branches, particularly those other than the more recent arrivals in America, brought a much fuller ancestry to light on her side of the family. There is more to learn if others will pick up the task.

The Knoop name is one that draws people's curiosity — first, because it is not widely found and second, because they rarely pronounce the name as the holder expresses it. The most common pronunciation is "kanoop." We express it with a silent "K" as "Nooop." It is certainly German and/or Dutch. Our Knoop side of the family migrated mainly from Germany in the nineteenth century, and is now several generations into the melting pot.

Not everyone came from Germany as Linda initially thought. We have several very English branches which go back through early settlers in Maryland and Virginia prior to the American revolution. We find her ancestors involved as fairly early settlers in Kentucky and later with Southern sentiment during the Civil War.

As we did in Part 3, we are now exploring American ancestor families, but on the Knoop side of the family. We look at the family tree from the bottom or most present family and proceed up the tree to earlier branches. Starting with the Knoop family we then follow the branches of the spouse's families and proceed family by family, taking each family with their many subsequent branches. We explore each family branch from the earliest known ancestors down to the most recent connection.

Chapter 31

Knoop — A Louisville Family

There are many Knoop families in Louisville, Kentucky. Why don't we know more of them? I thought this was very similar to my Shelton family discussed in Chapter 17. People have many reasons, but with only five generations back at this time, we certainly can know more about the Knoop family in Louisville. So, I began to explore our line of the Knoop family one-by-one with what information I could find readily available. I put it forward for comment and correction as others can document.

Linda had an acquaintance with Jodi Knoop, who was an art teacher at Seven Hills School in Cincinnati. We met with her, but could not find any specific family connection. Paul Knoop, Linda's brother, has come across a Tracy Knoop, who is a saxophone musician, teacher and the Director of the Jazz Orchestra at the University of Puget Sound in Tacoma, Washington. So, the Knoop family is not as obscure as first thought. There is much more to know and I hope others will come forward to fully document the Frank Knoop family of Louisville. It's time for a Knoop family reunion.

5 Frank Knoop (c1826–1898) m Mary Agnes Bloecker (1833–1869)
There is a story told in the family, that Frank was married three or four times. It was originally told by Oliva Knoop (1903–1974) in her later years. But I can only document his marriage to Mary Agnes Bloecker. Frank and Mary Agnes were both born in Hanover, Germany, and immigrated to America. They married in 1849 in Kenton County, Kentucky, which is just across the Ohio River from Cincinnati, Ohio.

They moved 100 miles down the Ohio River to Louisville, Kentucky, where he worked as a tailor and had a business at 5th and Market streets. According to the stories told by Oliva Knoop (1903–1974), Frank Knoop may have been a foreman at the H & J Deppen Co., a merchant tailor and clothing company, located on Market Street between 13th and

14th streets. They raised nine children and are probably the progenitors of the various Knoop families in Louisville. Their nine children, as best I can decipher, are as follows:

Frank Clemens Knoop (1853–1936) m Elizabeth Risen (1832/3–1869)
They also had nine children. See 4 Frank and Elizabeth below.

Henry F. Knoop (1854–1937) m Anna R. Neeb (1856–1931)
Henry was a carpenter and worked up into his seventies. They had 3 children, but later divorced. Anna remarried James H. Wright who was a boarder in her house in the 1900 census. In 1920 Henry was living with his sister, Anna Knoop (Cummings), and her family. He died single and is buried in St. Michael's Cemetery in Louisville.

Rosa A. Knoop (1855–1856)
Rosa died as an infant. She is the Rosa that died in 1856 and is buried in St. John's Cemetery with her name and date on the monument.

Mary Agnes Knoop (1857–1928) m Charles Harold Smith (1858–1919)
Charles started as a painter in Louisville and then worked as a finisher at a carriage factory and also a coffin manufacturer in Indiana. They married in Louisville and had 4 children. They lived in Dearborn County, Indiana, and in Ohio and died in Cincinnati, Ohio.

Rosa Knoop (1859–??)
In 1879 Rosa Knoop was listed in the City Directory as a tailoress. In the 1880 census, Rosa was a seamstress at age 21. Presumably she worked for her father who was a merchant tailor at that time. I think she died as a young, unmarried woman.

Albert John Knoop (1863–1932) m Annie Belle Ziegler (1862–1954)
Albert worked as a tailor most of his life. They had 3 children. At age 69, Albert was struck by an automobile and died of a fractured skull. The young driver was charged with manslaughter. Albert and Annie are buried in Cave Hill Cemetery in Louisville.

Luella Knoop (1864–??)
I think she died young and unmarried. She may be the Lulu that died in 1871 and is buried in St. John's Cemetery with her name and date on the monument.

Chapter 31: Knoop — A Louisville Family

Anne Knoop (1865–1927) m Robert E. Lee Cummings (1868–1915)
Before marriage Anne was a "tailoress" in the footsteps of her father. After marriage she became a housewife and they had 7 children. Robert began his working years as a clerk, cashier and then a policeman. Robert and Anne are buried in the St. Louis Cemetery in Louisville, Kentucky, with names and dates on their headstone.

John William Knoop (1868–1955) m Carrie F. Harvey (1870–1960)
John married Carrie in Hancock County, Indiana. He became a farmer and they lived in Sugar Creek, Hancock County, Indiana. They had 3 children. John and Carrie are buried in New Palestine, Hancock County, Indiana.

Frank and Mary Agnes died in Louisville and are buried in St. John's Cemetery. St. John's Cemetery is known as a "German Catholic Cemetery" near the community of Portland. Portland is an area of Louisville adjacent to the falls of the Ohio River. The cemetery was established in 1851 and is located at 26th Street and Rowan Avenue in the west end of Louisville.

That is my best effort. Some of the above does not correlate with the legible markings on the Knoop monument in St. John's Cemetery. Some of that is weatherworn and undecipherable, but indicates the multiple wives theory may be correct and that other children may have existed who died young.

4 Frank Clement Knoop (1853–1936) m Mary Elizabeth Risen (1855–1935)
Frank was born and raised in Louisville, Kentucky. Mary Elizabeth was born in Hawkins County, Tennessee, near Kingsport. Her parents, A. B. Risen (1820–1859) and Olive Griffith (1838–1907) were from Tennessee. Her grandmother was Delilah Potter (1804–1860) who married an Arden Evans Griffith (1802–1870).

There is a claim that Mary Elizabeth's great grandmother was a full-blood Cherokee Indian. This was first disclosed to my wife, Linda, by her father, Robert F. Knoop, that his grandmother Risen was descended from Native Americans. While researching Mary Elizabeth's ancestors, I uncovered a record of applications made in 1907 for membership in the Cherokee Tribe by two of Mary Elizabeth's cousins. Their application was

for their common grandmother Delilah Potter (Griffith)'s mother to be recognized as a full-blooded Cherokee. Their applications indicate that her name was "unknown." And apparently the applications were not approved. I doubt that a new application would be viewed any differently.

From census reports we learn that Frank was a "Tobacco Manufacturer" or "Cigar Maker" during his working years, which brings us to ask whether he was an owner or worker bee in the business. Much later, at age 77, in the 1930 census he is listed as a "cemetery laborer." Was this a reversal of fortune due to the beginning of the Depression years or just casual employment during retirement?

Frank and Mary Elizabeth had 9 children who were as follows:

Frank Albert Knoop (1874–1951) m Emma Louise Meffert (1876–1941)
Frank and Emma were married in Jeffersonville, Indiana, and had 4 children. He worked many years as a packer for the Louisville Milling Company. They lived in Louisville and are buried in Eastern Cemetery.

John Henry Knoop (1877–1960) m Katherine "Katie" Faust (1879–1947)
Katie was born in Hesse, Germany, and came with her family at about age 5. John worked as a tobacco wrapper and then as a packer for the Louisville Milling Company along with his older brother. John and Katie married in Jeffersonville, Indiana, and had 7 children. They are buried in Cave Hill Cemetery.

Herman Edward Knoop (1880–1965) m Elizabeth Henrietta Lutz (1880–1962)
Herman and Elizabeth married in Jeffersonville, Indiana, and had 14 children. He worked first as a mail clerk for a dry goods store and then as an oiler for a corn milling company. Herman and Elizabeth are buried in Resthaven Cemetery.

William James Knoop (1881–1951) m Ernestine A. Reukauf (1879–1933)
They had 2 children. See Below.

Olivia Marie Knoop (1884–1968) m James Edward Bush (1880–1944)
Olivia married James Bush and they had 4 children. James was a paperhanger for a dry goods company, worked his way up to foreman and then was self-employed

as a decorator. He served as a private in WWI in the Army Artillery. They lived in Louisville and are buried in Evergreen Cemetery.

George Washington Knoop (1887–1970) m Maude Mae Huffman (1888–1952)

George and Maude married and had 11 children. There are many photos of George and his family that can be accessed on the Ancestry website. He apparently worked as a paperhanger his whole working life. They lived in Louisville and are buried in Evergreen Cemetery.

Minnie Lee Knoop (1889–1946) m Riley Wilson Harrod (1888–1957)

Minnie and Riley married and had one child. He was self-employed as an ice man and later worked for the Frank Fehrs Brewing Co. (I recall tasting a few of their products while in college at the University of Louisville.) They are buried in the Louisville Memorial Gardens.

Robert Elmer Knoop (1893–1971) m Eulah/Julia Stevens (1896–1967)

Although Robert Elmer Knoop was his name he frequently went by Elmer which confuses research into his history. Robert Elmer and Eulah grew up, married in Louisville and had 2 children. He worked as a self-employed photographer and photo finisher. Later he worked for the K & I Railroad Co. which operated one of the first railroad bridges to New Albany, Indiana, for light passenger rail service. He received a railroad pension. They are buried in Calvary Cemetery.

Louis Knoop-Schorch (1895–1962) m Viola T. Weis (1897–1986)

Louis Knoop changed his name to Schorch. I think this started when he registered for the draft for WWI in 1916. It appears he wrote his name as "Louis Schorch Knoop" and signed it "L.S. Knoop." However, the death certificate for their stillborn infant in 1917 is for "Infant Knoop." In registering for the draft for WWII he used the name "Louis Knoop Schorch." And the family continued using Schorch for their last name. There is a story to be told here?

They grew up in Louisville. I don't readily see anything about their marriage, but they had 6 children. Their later 5 children all use the Schorch last name. He began working in a drug store and later was self-employed selling barber supplies. They lived and died in Louisville and are buried in Calvary Cemetery.

Frank and Mary Elizabeth both lived into their eighties, died in Louisville and are buried in Calvary Cemetery.

3 William James Knoop (1881–1951) m Ernestine A Reukauf (1878–1933)

William was born and raised in Louisville, Kentucky. William and Ernestine had four children of record. A son, Henry, and an infant baby died very young. Two children lived to adulthood–a daughter, Oliva M. Knoop (1903–1974), and a son, Robert Fridolin Knoop (1908–1983). William worked in the boiler trade as a pipe fitter. They lived at 1104 Schiller Avenue in Louisville. Also see Reukauf in Chapter 33.

William James Knoop

Ernestine

Ernestine and son Robert Knoop

It appears that in our line, until this generation, the Knoop families were mostly Catholic and the Reukaufs were Lutheran. Succeeding Knoop generations in our line were strongly Missouri Synod Lutherans. This might be why my wife Linda's family did not gather with other Knoop families in Louisville. In those times families seemed to stick to their own church families and tended to be much more clannish than they are today.

My wife, Linda, has an early memory, at about age eight, of walking on a sidewalk in Louisville with her parents and her father leaving to go across the street and talk with a man. Her mother said nothing about it and her father returned back across the street and said nothing. Later, her mother told her the man was her grandfather, William James Knoop, whom her father had thrown out of the house years before for philandering and bringing home a contagious disease to her grandmother which caused her death.

Later, William and their son, Robert, reconciled. William died in Louisville. William and Ernestine are buried in Cave Hill Cemetery.

Their daughter, Olivia, inherited the home on Schiller Avenue. Later in life Olivia married Joseph Kaelin with whom she had had a long-term relationship. Oliva and Joe lived there the rest of their lives.

1104 Schiller Avenue

Olivia

2 Robert Fridolin Knoop (1908–1983) m Ruth Hund (1909–2008)

Robert and Ruth both were born and grew up in Louisville, Kentucky. Robert attended Concordia Lutheran Grade School and later graduated from the Ahrens Trade School, a vocational high school where he learned bookkeeping and printing. Ruth attended Atherton High School. Ruth was from a large family of 12 active brothers and sisters. The brothers had active jobs and the sisters tended the home and small farm. Robert and Ruth married at Concordia Lutheran Church on upper Broadway in Louisville in 1935. They were always active in Concordia Church. Ruth taught Sunday school and was on the Alter Guild. Robert worked on various activities, committees and in leadership positions. Their two children, Linda and Paul Robert, attended the Concordia Lutheran Grade School there through the eighth grade.

**Concordia Lutheran Grade Schhool
Robert Knoop middle of second row**

**Ahrens Trade School Graduation, June 1924
Robert F. Knoop in knickers on the right**

Chapter 31: Knoop — A Louisville Family

One of their first homes was on Cornell Place in the Crescent Hill section of Louisville. Linda specifically remembers that she was told they lived there during the 1937 flood which flooded most of the main area of Louisville. They were thankful to be on higher ground. During the 1930s, Robert worked for the telephone company. During WWII he worked for the military as a civilian employee in the supply section at Bowman Field. Ruth became ill with subacute bacterial endocarditis and required several long stays in the hospital. He did not enter military service due to his wife's medical condition and the need for care of their two young children. During the war years they lived in Fincastle which was a wartime government housing project in the southern area of Louisville.

Their son, Paul Robert Knoop, attended Camp Taylor Elementary for grades 1 and 2 and then attended Concordia Lutheran school along with his sister, Linda, up through 8th grade. He then attended and graduated from Southern High School, a Jefferson County High School. Paul went on to Western Kentucky State College, now Western Kentucky University, in Bowling Green, Kentucky, majoring in chemistry and in the Army ROTC. At Western Kentucky he met and married Nettye Jean Brown. Upon graduating and receiving an Army Officer's Commission, he entered military service. Paul served more than 29 years in the Army Chemical Corps rising to the rank of full colonel. During his Army career he had various assignment locations which drew us to visit them in many areas of the United States including Alaska.

Paul Robert Knoop

In the 1950s Robert and Ruth built a new 3-bedroom home at 607 Primrose Lane in the St. Matthews area of Louisville.

Because Ruth was ill for many years, Robert worked two jobs. During the day he worked in an office and then in the evening he had a part-time job in a specialty printing shop. Robert worked many years as a budget analyst in the accounting department of International

Harvester at their farm tractor plant at Standiford Field in Louisville and retired at age 65.

In retirement he took up woodworking in his garage and made many furniture pieces. We still have one of the bedside tables he made. I contracted with him to make approximately forty lineal feet of eight-foot-tall bookcases for our offices at Industrial Air to hold all our catalogs and sales literature.

About 1962, as empty nesters, they built a smaller two-bedroom brick home at 212 Fenley Avenue next to Ruth's sister, Christine, and her husband, Jacob Ossman. In the early 1980s Robert and Ruth moved to SEM Laurels Apartments, a Southeastern Ecumenical Ministry retirement community in Milford, Ohio, to be near their daughter, Linda, in their final years. They died while at SEM, and are interred in the columbarium wall at the Resthaven Cemetery in Louisville, Kentucky. For more on Ruth, see Chapter 32: Hund.

Robert Knoop and Ruth Hund (Knoop), c1974

1 Linda Knoop (1939–) m Watson Christen Smith (1936–)

Also see Part 6 for Linda Knoop and Part 5 for Watson Christen Smith.

Chapter 32

Hund — Another Louisville Family

The Hund family is German or Saxon as you might expect. A coat of arms dates back to March 1, 1664, in Austria and has many meanings such as hunter or hound, teacher or instructor, and also messenger or courier. Tracings of the name are found in England in the 13th century, but those are most likely Saxon in origin, either prior to 1066 or because of that invasion and the Normans winning the Battle of Hastings.

Our more recent Hund ancestors definitely came directly from Germany to America. That we do know.

5 Jurgen Andreas Hund (c1800–??) m Therese/Josephine Rohrbach (1798–1874)
Jurgen Andreas and Therese/Josephine lived in Baden-Wurttemberg, Germany, but we know very little about their lives. They signed papers to allow their son to leave Germany when he was 27 years old. We have no understanding of why this was necessary. This document is signed by Jurgen Andreas Hund and Josephine Hund. Other documentation shows the wife to be Therese. It might have been a second marriage.[98]

4 Sigmund Karl/Charles D Hund Sr. (1822–1897) m Anna Susanne Merkel (1824–1915)
Sigmund Karl Hund changed his name apparently upon arrival in America to Charles D Hund, and I believe he only used the D for a middle name. Charles and Susanne (as she was called) were both born in Germany and immigrated to America, but separately and apparently without their parents or family. Susanne was born in Auerbach, Hesse, Germany. Her parents, Johann Tobias Merkel and Anna Elizabetha Keil, remained in Germany.

---

98 Wiley, Judie Rhae, *Had A Grand Time*, currently being prepared for publication, Connecticut 2021

Chapter 32: Hund — Another Louisville Family

Charles was from Baden-Wurttemberg, Germany. He left aboard a ship from Bremen, Germany, and arrived in 1848 in Baltimore, Maryland. Susanne came from Hesse, Germany, and left from Le Havre, France, on the ship *Scioto*, to arrive in New York in 1854. They married in Louisville, Kentucky, in 1856. Charles was listed as a laborer on a Civil War draft registration in 1863. In the 1870 census he is listed as a coal laborer and as a clerk. In the 1880 census he is listed as a retired cart driver. At that time four of their children were living at home with them. Their sons Charles, age 23, and George, age 19, were working in a woolen mill. Daughter, Lizzie, as they called Elizabeth, age 21, was a dressmaker.

They lived in the Edwards Pond area of Louisville which was in the eastern area of present-day downtown. In those early days in Louisville ice was cut from the pond for use in local tavern drinks–a somewhat novel thing at that time. Later, as the city became more polluted in that area due to the meatpacking plants, they moved east to the Clifton Heights area of Louisville. Charles and Susanne died in Louisville, Kentucky, and are buried in Cave Hill Cemetery. Charles, who died earlier, was buried in Eastern Cemetery which is an earlier section of the same cemetery.

3 George Washington Hund Sr. (1861–1935) m Mary Frances Sheets (1876–1931)

George grew up in the east end of Louisville. Mary Frances grew up in Lexington. I am firmly of the opinion that they met because George worked on the railroad, as did Mary Frances's father, Charles W. Sheets. They married in 1892 in Jeffersonville, Indiana, just

George Hund **Mary Frances Sheets** **George Hund, railroad engineer 2nd from right**

across the river from Louisville. He was 31 and she was 16. Children shortly followed. In the 1900 census their first five children are listed. They had a total of 14 children. Twelve lived to adulthood and survived into their eighties. They were a hardy stock and several lived into their nineties.

Chapter 32: Hund — Another Louisville Family

**Twelve Hund siblings at a family picnic in Cherokee Park, Louisville, KY c1968
(From left - rear row)
Rosetta Hund (Rhea), Paul Emmett Hund, Harry Seabolt Hund, Roger Otis Hund, Charles William Hund, George Washington Hund
(From left - front row)
Gladys Julia Hund (Stafford), Ruth Hund (Knoop), Joseph Henry Hund, Christine Mae Hund (Ossman), Emily Francis Hund (Spangler) and Susie Elizabeth Hund (Redmon)**

Working in the Woolen Mill at 19 must have engaged George in machinery for he moved forward in responsible positions. In 1887 he was listed as a fireman and in the 1900 census as a Railroad Engineer. Railroading work was good at that time and Railroad Engineer was a prestigious position. His son Harry also worked on the railroad as did his son-in-law, Clarence Redmon "Red," who was a conductor. They all worked for the Louisville and Nashville Railroad.

George was also the master of the house and his children loved and respected him, calling him "Papa." No one picked up a fork at the table until Papa sat down and picked up his. His daughter Ruth told the story that one of her jobs as a child was to go to the local tavern with her father's beer bucket and

Chapter 32: Hund — Another Louisville Family

hand it in the door of the tavern. They would fill it, hand it out to her and she would carry it home so her father would have his cool beer at the end of the day.

They lived in rented houses at first in the east end of Louisville, first on Smyser Avenue and then at 143 Spring Street. By the time of the 1920 census they had moved to Landrey Avenue in the Indian Hill section. The 1930 census shows them living in Clifton Heights where we know they owned a small farm from his mother's family on Lindsay Avenue. As the children grew up, they all lived at home until they married. This was a very common situation in those days. The boys got jobs and went out to work each day. The girls helped care for the younger children and did the housework. Mary Frances died in 1931 after several years of illness. The children still at home cared for George until he died in 1935. Shortly after that all the remaining children married. George and Mary Frances are buried in Resthaven Cemetery, Louisville, Kentucky. Also see Sheets in Chapter 34.

Children clockwise Paul age 6, Christine age 8, Ruth age 4, Rosetta age 2

Mary Frances Sheets holding daughter Ruth with three older children

**Eleven of twelve Hund siblings at a family gathering at Greentree Manor, Louisville, KY c1946
(From left - rear row) George Washington Hund, Charles William Hund, Roger Otis Hund, Joseph Henry Hund, Paul Emmett Hund
(From left - front row) Susie Elizabeth Hund (Redmon), Emily Francis Hund (Spangler), Christine Mae Hund (Ossman), Ruth Hund (Knoop), Rosetta Hund (Rhea) and Gladys Julia Hund (Stafford)**

A Hund yard picnic

Chapter 32: Hund — Another Louisville Family

2 Ruth Hund (1909–2008) m Robert Fridolin Knoop (1908–1983)

Ruth was the third youngest of the fourteen children. She remembered living on the small farm in the Crescent Hill section of Louisville where she grew up and remembered the first car that drove by their house. She was warned not to cross the street if a car was coming, so she took it to heart and would not step in the street if a car was in sight.

After her mother died in 1931, Ruth and her unmarried siblings stayed at home to care for their aging father until he died four years later. She lived at home until she married Robert Knoop in 1935 at Concordia Lutheran Church in Louisville. They had two children, Linda and Paul Robert. See Chapter 31 for Robert F. Knoop and Paul Robert Knoop.

Ruth became ill with subacute bacterial endocarditis and required several long stays in the hospital. There was no cure for the disease, but her woman doctor would not give up until, after several years, the newly developed drug, penicillin, was available which saved her. Later one of the mycin drugs cured her completely. Ruth gave credit to God and the dedicated doctors, which certainly was the truth.

Ruth was close to her family and her siblings, especially her sisters Christine, Rosetta and Gladys. They were of course closest to her in age but also in a large family they probably had to stick together. On a daily basis Ruth and Christine were closest, with weekly dinners and later living next door to each other. Around 1961, after their children, Paul and Linda, moved away, Ruth and Robert built a new brick home at 212 Fenley Avenue, next door to Ruth's sister Christine and her husband, Jake.

Her sister Gladys was a person talented in arts and crafts, who connected with Ruth in things they were working on.

Ruth, about 18 months, and her father, George Hund.

Chapter 32: Hund — Another Louisville Family

Rosetta was close to Ruth at all ages since they were near in age and Rosetta had a daughter, Judie, close in age to Ruth's children. Rosetta and her husband, John, were very kind and hospitable in bringing the family together, particularly after John returned from his military chaplain's career and retired to Louisville. John and Rosetta had many gracious gatherings at their home and worked to keep everyone connected. The bond between Ruth and Rosetta seemed to become stronger as the years passed and continued even after Ruth and Bob moved to Cincinnati.

Rosetta and Ruth
Linda, Judie and Paul

Ruth's brother Paul was everyone's favorite brother. She and Bob visited him in Arizona at least twice. Even I remember him as a very engaging person when I first met him in Phoenix, Arizona, in 1960 and he encouraged me to join him in the real estate business in Phoenix after I got out of the service. I have no doubt that we would have been successful together as Phoenix has experienced phenomenal, continual growth in the years since that visit.

Ruth was a dedicated homemaker and superb seamstress. Her son Paul said, "Her work outside the home was wide and varied. She was a census taker, sold Avon products, and she and her sister Christine made ties at the Cavalier Tie Company. She used her sewing skills to make needlework purses for Maude Hundley Studios (in Middletown, Kentucky), and also made much of the clothing worn by her family and friends. She continued to make clothes and knit sweaters for many years. Her children, grandchildren and great grandchildren each have at least one as a reminder. Later, she made hundreds of lap robes and wheelchair bags for nursing homes and shut-ins. She seemed happiest when in the kitchen cooking, baking and canning for her family and friends."

In 1966, Ruth was next door visiting Christine and came home to find a burglar who said, "Lady, you scared the hell out of me." He was kind to her, loosely tied her up and told her to wait ten minutes, which she dutifully did because she was scared to death. Fortunately, as the adjacent news article states, he didn't find much to steal.

Ruth and Bob, her husband, were both involved in the activities of Concordia Lutheran Church until moving to

Thief Is a Gentleman To Housewife, Takes $5

Mrs. Ruth Knoop, 55, of 212 Fenley, returned home about 1:30 p.m. yesterday and was confronted by a gentlemanly burglar who, insisting he meant no harm, tied her up loosely and told her to wait 10 minutes before freeing herself and calling the police.

The man, who had entered the house by forcing open the front door, took $4 from a dime bank and $1 and some change from her wallet, Mrs. Knoop told police.

***Louisville Courier Journal,*
article 1966**

Chapter 32: Hund — Another Louisville Family

Cincinnati in 1980, after Bob's retirement, to be nearer Linda and her family. While at Concordia, she was a Sunday School teacher for many years and served on the Altar Guild. As an expert needlewoman, she embroidered altar cloths, cushion covers and vestments for their pastor, Rev. Dr. Carl Eberhard.

Our son, Blake, borrowed the Industrial Air company truck to move them from Louisville to Cincinnati. He was a college student at the time and I recall that I was proud of his initiative in helping his grandparents move to be closer to us. They certainly appreciated his help as Linda and I were busy working and not much assistance.

After moving to SEM Laurels Apartments, a Southeastern Ecumenical Ministry retirement community, in Milford, Ohio, they joined St. Paul's Lutheran Church in Madisonville. After Bob died, Ruth moved to the Lutheran Village, a retirement community, at St. Paul's where she gathered many close friends and was very happy for several years. After several years at St. Paul's Lutheran Village, she had a fall which broke her hip, causing her to return to assisted living at SEM where she spent her last years. They gave excellent care and she enjoyed being there. Especially the bingo. They played at least once a week and anyone could play. If you had no money, they would put in for you. At that time I was managing her checking and cash since she (in her nineties) could no longer balance her checkbook accurately. She asked for some quarters so she could play bingo without being on the dole, and I gave her an envelope full of quarters. Assuming she must be winning since she hadn't asked for more, I thought no more about it until the day when we cleaned out her room and found the quarters were still there. She was a very proud person, always wanting to do the right thing even if she was not quite able to do so.

Ruth and friends at St. Paul's Lutheran Village

Linda sent this note to Ruth's friends in December 2005:

> "Paul and Linda's mother, Ruth Knoop, celebrated her ninety-seventh birthday in August. It was a quieter affair than some of her past birthday parties that some of you might remember, but she seemed to enjoy it none-the-less.

"Mother sleeps more than she did last year, but overall her health is good. She still likes watching the birds that come to the feeders outside her window. She likes visits and cards and the occasional phone call … and thanks to all of you who have sent her cards and visited. If you do visit and find Ruth asleep, don't hesitate to wake her; she would much rather talk and visit than sleep. And if she seems a bit vague sometimes, not to worry, she'll remember in five minutes or an hour or the next day. The main thing is that she loves hearing from family and friends. So, Merry Christmas to you from Ruth."

Linda would have her in for dinner every Sunday evening and afterwards Ruth and I would play cards. Linda preferred to clean the dishes and kitchen rather than play and lose because Ruth would consistently win.

She never lost her beautiful black hair. It was still solidly black almost until her death. Even then it was only very slightly gray. Ruth passed away quietly at age 98. Linda was with her.

1 Linda Knoop (1939–) m Watson Christen Smith
See Part 6 for Linda Knoop and Part 5 for Watson Christen Smith.

Chapter 33

Reukauf — A Typical Immigrant Family

4 Frederick Fridolin Reukauf (1849–1934) m Wilhelmia Vierling (1850–1899)
Frederick Fridolin and Wilhelmia were both born in Sachsen, Germany, married in Germany and immigrated to America in 1882 from Bremen, Germany, on the ship *Leipzig* with two of their three children, Ernestine (1878–1933) and Adolph (1879–1968). Their third child, Louise (1890–1953), who was called "Lulu," was born in Louisville, Kentucky. We have no record of the Reukauf and Vierling families left behind in Germany.

In Louisville, they lived at 1304 Schiller Avenue, where they rented. After Wilhelmia died in 1899, the 1900 census shows Frederick living there with the three children. Frederick was working as a "tobacco presser" and their son, Adolph, was working as a day laborer. Next door, at 1308 Schiller Avenue, lived a John Vierling and his family. This John Vierling was about Wilhelmia's age so we presume he was her brother and their families emigrated from Germany together.

Adolph Reukauf, Fridolin Reukauf, Wilhemene Vierling Reukauf, Ernestine Reukauf

In the 1910 census Frederick was working as a laborer in a brewery. He lived with his daughter Ernestine and her husband, and later with his granddaughter, Olivia, at 1104 Schiller Avenue.

In the 1920 census he was working as a laborer in a factory. The census gives us conflicting information as to how educated he was. One report says he could not read or write, while another says he could. In any event, it appears that his English was not strong. This of course is very common in first generation immigrants.

The Reukauf and Vierling families were Missouri Synod Lutherans and attended Concordia Lutheran Church at the east end of Broadway in Louisville. My wife Linda recalls her father always going to talk with the family after church each Sunday. Their son, Adolph (Linda's uncle), was a solid person in the family, had married and had a good job. She also recalls going as a child to Lulu's funeral in 1953 and her Uncle Adolph crying, saying, "They're all gone. They're all gone. I'm the only one left."

Frederick Reukauf

He was referring to the fact that all of his parents and siblings had died by then. I think it also reflects how important family relationships are to us. While we know the Lord gives us only so many years, we are never quite ready to lose our lives or our loved ones. We also probably don't appreciate the additional struggles and fears that immigrants have in living, getting accepted and culturally adapting to their new country. Frederick and Wilhelmia are buried in Cave Hill Cemetery.

3 Ernestine A. Reukauf (1878–1933) m William James Knoop (1881–1951)

Ernestine was born in Germany and at age 3 in 1882 immigrated to America with her father, mother, and older brother. She grew up in Louisville and married William Knoop. For more on Ernestine Reukauf and William Knoop see Chapter 29.

Ernestine Reukauf (Knoop)

Chapter 34

Sheets — Early Kentuckians

Our branch of the Sheets family in Maryland migrated to Virginia sometime around 1700 and to Kentucky probably just before 1800. Each generation had several children, and, therefore, by the middle 1800s, there were many Sheets families in Maryland and Virginia and later in the central Kentucky area of Franklin, Shelby and Woodford counties. I found it difficult to distinguish between the various branches of the Sheets family with all of the repetitive and common first names and with no middle names. So, the Sheets family heritage is presented on a best-effort basis.

9 Peter Sheets (c1680–??) m Elizabeth
Peter Sheets was born in 1680. There is a record of a Peter Sheets immigrating in through Philadelphia, Pennsylvania, in 1740 and also a record of a Peter Sheets who was born in Anne Arundel County, Maryland. Records show nothing else. Peter and Elizabeth had at least two sons, twins, born around 1700 in Anne Arundel County, Maryland. They were Martin (c1700–c1782) and Frederick (c1700–c1782). I believe the immigration date to be incorrect.

8 Martin Sheets (c1700–1782) m Sarah B. Aldridge (c1700–c1740)
Martin and Sarah were both born in Anne Arundel County, Maryland. They married in 1733 in Fredericksburg, Maryland. Martin was a farmer.

Sarah's parents were Nicholas Aldridge IV (1653–1708) and Martha Besson (1662–1722). Nicholas had emigrated from England. Martha's parents had come from England earlier and she was born in Anne Arundel County.

Twenty-four ancestry family trees currently show Sarah died in 1740 in Kentucky. But, I find this cannot be true if their son Henry was born in 1740 in Maryland and married

Chapter 34: Sheets — Early Kentuckians

there in 1765. According to the 1790 census he was still there in 1790. I believe Sarah died during or from complications of childbirth in 1740 and that Martin and Sarah both lived and died in Anne Arundel County, Maryland. And, also, that they are buried in All Hallows Cemetery in Anne Arundel County, Maryland.

7 Henry Harrison Sheets (1740–1810) m Mary Dunkle (1745–1782)
Henry was born in Maryland. Mary was born in Maryland, but we have no other documentation on her or her family. Henry and Mary married in 1765 in Maryland and had six children together. Mary died leaving Henry with six children ranging in age from two to eighteen. Henry managed somehow, most probably with help from close family members. The 1790 census shows Henry eight years later living in Frederick, Maryland, with only two or three children. Three of their children married before then. The family migrated sometime in the 1790s west to West Virginia, which at that time was still part of Virginia, and then to Franklin County, Kentucky.

After the Revolutionary War there was a large migration to the west. Many war veterans were paid in land to the west for their service since the new government had very little in the way of funds to pay the debt from the war. Other members of the Sheets family, John and Jacob Sheets, had obtained a large Virginia Land Grant of 2,481-3/4 acres on Eagle Creek in Fayette County, Kentucky, in 1789. The Sheets family was large with many branches and very little documentation, but there definitely was a herd migration to Kentucky. Henry moved with the family.

The 1801 and 1810 censuses both show Henry living in Franklin County, Kentucky. Henry died in Franklin County in that year, 1810.

6 Benjamin Sheets (c1773–1842) m Sophronia Lena (Sener) (Sena) Litten (1780–1849)
Benjamin was born in Martinsburg, Berkeley County, West Virginia, which again at that time was still part of Virginia. Sophronia or Lena or Sener or Sena as she was called (are all recorded) was born in Berkeley Springs, Berkeley County, Maryland, as best I can determine. Benjamin married Sophronia in Martinsburg in 1793 and they joined the migration west to Kentucky before 1800. They settled first in Woodford County, Kentucky, and then moved to Benson in Franklin County, as noted in the 1800 census, where they raised seventeen children. In 1821 he is noted to hold 250 acres of land. In 1837 he had 470 acres of land. They obviously needed that large farm to employ and feed that large family.

His will was proved in Franklin County in 1842. Examination of the will might show more information. Benjamin and Sophronia are buried in Benson, Franklin County, Kentucky.

Chapter 34: Sheets — Early Kentuckians

In exploring Sophronia Litton's family I opened up a family line with very interesting colonial ties and experiences. Also see Chapter 35: Litton.

5 Charles Sheets Sr. (c1811–1876) m Malinda Rupe (c1811–1850)

Charles was born in Woodford County, Kentucky. He moved with the family to Benson in Franklin County. He married his first wife, Sara Edrington, in 1831, and she died shortly thereafter.

Malinda Rupe, Charles's 2nd wife, was born in Franklin County, Kentucky. Malinda married Charles in 1835. Her father's name was Nicholas Rupe. Nicholas and his wife, Mary McGinnis, had married in Philadelphia and migrated to Kentucky. Nicholas's family had emigrated from the Rheinland area of Germany. Mary was born in Virginia.

Charles and Malinda had six children together. Their son Charles William is our line. Malinda died in Franklin County, Kentucky.

Charles remarried a third time to Francis E. "Fannie" Truell (1827–1880). Francis was born in Virginia and migrated with her parents to Benson, Franklin County, Kentucky, at about age eleven. In 1851, at age 22 she married Charles. They had six children together.

The Civil War brought considerable activity to the Sheets family as well as the nation. In the summer of 1862, Kentucky was a neutral state but various factions in Kentucky leaned North or South. From what we can dig out, the Sheets in Kentucky leaned toward the South, probably due to their migration from Virginia. Descendants of their Pennsylvania and some Maryland ancestors obviously had northern leanings and there are records of them as Union soldiers during the Civil War. Charles and Francis saw their boys go off to war to fight for the Southern side during the Civil War.

4 Pvt. Charles William Sheets, CSA (1841–1903) m. Emily Francis Tracy, "Fanny" (1845–1886)

According to the 1860 US Census, Charles William Sheets was 21, single and living with his parents (father, Charles Sheets Sr. and step-mother, Francis Truell), on their farm in or near Frankfort, Franklin County, Kentucky. During August and September of 1862, the Confederates, under command of General Edmund Kirby Smith, entered Kentucky from Tennessee. On Sept. 2, 1862, the Confederates were cheered as they entered Lexington only to be driven out by Northern troops on September 8. Part of their entry into Kentucky was to gain territory and recruit troops. Charles William Sheets, "also known as Robert Sheets" and his older brother, John Sheets, signed up with Co. C, 7th Kentucky Cavalry CSA (Gano's Cavalry–mounted rifles) on 10 Sept. 1862 for 3 years. The 7th Kentucky Cavalry CSA had been organized in Sept. 1862 from Gano's Texas Cavalry as a nucleus. Confederate cavalrymen had to bring their own horses, so apparently, they were well off enough to own their horses.

Chapter 34: Sheets — Early Kentuckians

The reference to Charles William Sheets as Robert is confusing. Charles and his brother John had cousins named Charles T. Sheets and James Sheets who were sons of Granville Sheets. Charles T. Sheets was born in 1844 and at age 18 also joined Co. K, 7th Regiment KY Cavalry, CSA (ref. US Civil War Soldiers 1861–1865 film #M377, roll 12). He was in the same 7th Kentucky as Charles W. and John Sheets. Perhaps they called Charles W. by the name "Robert" to keep them straight. This could be all it was. Maybe they gave him the name "Robert" after Robert E. Lee. It would be interesting to know, but we don't.

The Regiment skirmished and had a few battles in Kentucky, but gradually pulled back into Tennessee as the Union forces got stronger and more organized. Robert Sheets and John Sheets later appear on Co. C, 2nd Regiment Kentucky Cavalry CSA muster rolls for Nov. and Dec. 1862. John Sheets appears also on the muster roll for Feb. 1863.

Sometime in 1863, they transferred into the 7th Cavalry under the command of Gen. John Hunt Morgan, one of the South's great cavalry generals. Morgan was from Lexington, Kentucky, and developed a great following and loyalty from his troops. They fought in several battles, skirmishes and raids in Tennessee and Kentucky and became known and feared as Morgan's Raiders. Their raids were designed to tear up union supply lines, mainly railroads, and divert union troops from advancing farther into the south. Since most of his troops were Kentuckians, they wanted to retaliate against the Union invaders of their homeland. In late June of 1863, such a raid took them to the outskirts of Louisville. Although orders forbid them from crossing north of the Ohio River, on 2 July Morgan and his men crossed into southern Indiana.

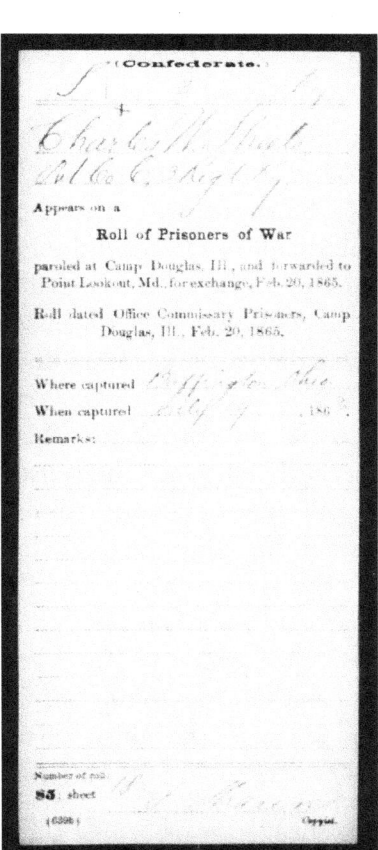

Pvt. C.W. Sheets CSA Camp Douglas Parole

The Raiders crossed the river and progressed eastward across southern Indiana and Ohio. On 19 July 1863 they were cornered and surrounded in southeastern Ohio near Pomeroy as they were trying to cross the Ohio River to return to the south through West Virginia. Morgan and part of his forces escaped to be captured later. Charles W. Sheets, known as "Robert," was captured near Pomeroy, Ohio, at Buffington Island as noted in his later parole documents.

Chapter 34: Sheets — Early Kentuckians

On 2 July 1863 Charles T. Sheets and his brother James were killed in Brown County, Ohio. They, somehow, were part of Morgan's Raiders, but the Raiders didn't reach that area until later that month. No other southern forces fought in Ohio so we still have many things to learn here.

Charles W. Sheets was taken to a prisoner of war camp, Camp Morton, in Indianapolis, Indiana. On 18 August 1863 "Robert" Sheets was transferred from Camp Morton, Indiana, to POW Camp Douglas, near Chicago, Illinois, on Lake Michigan. Treatment of prisoners there is reported to be not too much different than at Andersonville in the South. The record of prisoner treatment was very bad. September and November 1863 Muster Rolls show "Robert" at Camp Douglas. The parole record shows on 20 February 1865 he was paroled at Camp Douglas and sent to Point Lookout, Maryland, for prisoner exchange. The North only officially exchanged prisoners at two locations: Point Lookout, Maryland, and Vicksburg, Mississippi. We believe Charles probably confessed to being Charles W. Sheets under the alias of Robert Sheets to get early release and changed his outfit to 3rd Kentucky for the same reason. The parole record has a note saying, "See also Robert Sheets–Co. K, 7 KY Cav."

Exchanged prisoners were not to fight anymore and supposedly took a vow to that. They could work behind the lines, but they were not to fight. However, many ignored the vow upon being exchanged. Charles W. joined General Wheeler's 3rd Cavalry, CSA in their resistance against Gen. Sherman's March to the Sea. At the war's end, he surrendered with the Army of Tennessee at Augusta, Georgia, on 7 May 1865. On 15 May 1865, Charles W. Sheets took an oath of loyalty to the U.S. and was released.

After the war, Charles W. Sheets returned to his parents' home in Frankfort, Kentucky. In the 1870 census, he is listed as living in his father's home in Frankfort, Kentucky, and "working on railroad." All of his war travels by horse, train and foot probably interested him in the railroad job. Train riding is also a lot easier than farming.

The Tracy family lived in Frankfort and later Lexington, Kentucky. Charles W. Sheets married Emily Francis "Fannie" Tracy, widow of Harrison Williamson, on November 23, 1875, in Lexington. They were married by W. H. Felip, minister of the Baptist Church of Lexington. The 1880 U.S. Census shows them living in Lexington and he working as a brakeman on the railroad. They had 6 children, the eldest of them was Mary Frances Sheets who married George Hund, a railroad engineer.

Charles W. Sheets and Emily Francis Tracy are buried together in the Section "O" Lot 59 of the Lexington Cemetery in Lexington, Kentucky. Her gravestone says "Emily Francis–wife of Bob Sheets." Charles's grave is adjacent to hers. His grave is unmarked.

Chapter 34: Sheets — Early Kentuckians

A newspaper article found in the Sheets file in the archives of the Kentucky Historical Museum in Frankfort, Kentucky, states "Dixie–Played after funeral at last request of deceased–Secretary A.K. Storm of Saxon's band, wishes to make an explanation in regard to playing "Dixie" coming home from the funeral of C. W. Sheets. It was Mr. Sheets [sic] express wish that it should be played, as he made out the whole program of music to be played at his funeral, before he died. Mr. Storm feels that this explanation is due the public, as many might consider the piece inappropriate for such an occasion."

General John Hunt Morgan's grave is nearby. When visiting Charles and Emily's graves, my son, Blake, and I also visited General Morgan's grave where at the base of his headstone we noticed a small Confederate flag, a pack of cigarettes and a half bottle of Kentucky bourbon whiskey.

General John Hunt Morgan grave in Lexington Cemetery

3 Mary Frances Sheets (1876–1931) m George Washington Hund Sr. (1861–1935)

See Chapter 32 for Mary Frances Sheets and George Washington Hund Sr.

Chapter 35

Litton — Early Virginians

This Litton family in America seems to be centered around Caleb (the Elder) Polleckfield Litton and his descendants who dispersed from Rockville, Maryland, to several areas. Some connections are questionable and need more research for proper documentation, but this line held my interest and seemed the most probable Litton/Litten line. I feel reasonably certain that Sophronia is descended from Caleb and if not through this line of Lt. John Richard Litton, then through their close cousins in Maryland and Virginia.

10 Michael Litton (1647–1720) m Johanna Polleckfield (1655–1720)
Michael and Johanna lived and died in Devonshire, England.

9 Caleb Polleckfield Litton, the Elder (1678–1763) m Grace Hartley Burton (1703–1791)
Caleb was born in Autre-St. Mary, Devonshire, England. In 1700 he became a member of the British Royal Dragoons, a cavalry unit. He married Dorothy Teller in 1716, but she died two years later without children and is buried in Autre St. Mary, England.

In 1720 Caleb was sent to Saint Mary's City, Maryland, which at that time was the capital of Maryland. His duties were mainly policing and he received a grant of 405 acres of land for his service. He named it "Oatry" after the Ottery River in his native England. This area of Maryland has now become Rockville, Maryland, a suburb of Washington, DC.

His wife, Grace, was born in Baltimore but lived in the Rockville area and probably admired the handsome dragoon in uniform. They were married in 1723 in the Rock Creek Parish Church and had nine children. After retiring from the military, he farmed his land, raising corn, cotton and tobacco.

His will left his estate to Grace and his daughters, which indicates his five sons had already left for other areas at that time. In addition to his estate consisting of his home and land it included six slaves.

8 Lt. John Richard Litton (1726–1804) m Sarah Ann Wilcoxen (1728–1808)

John Richard Litton was born and grew up at Oatry. His wife, Sarah, was born in the Rockville area. Some say her family was from Fincastle, Virginia, which is in Botetourt County just north of Roanoke. This might have been some of the draw for moving to Virginia. In any event, Richard Litton and some of his siblings apparently received some inheritance and left Maryland prior to their father's death. John and Sarah settled in Elk Garden, Russell County, Virginia, which is in the western tip of Virginia. This was around the time of the Revolutionary War and also the time of expansion to the west into Tennessee and Kentucky. John Litton served in the revolution and at least two of their sons did also.

On June 26, 1780, their son, Capt. Solomon Caleb Litton Sr., was serving at a frontier fort, Martin Station, in southeastern Kentucky, with his family on hand. The fort was attacked and overrun by Shawnee Indians commanded by a British Officer, Captain Harry Bird. Many of the inhabitants were massacred. Solomon, his wife, Martha Dunkin, and daughter were captured and then marched and transported by river, roughly four hundred miles, to Fort Detroit where they were held captive. He was sold to labor as a slave to a Shawnee Indian named Big Fish at a nearby Shawnee village. Solomon and Martha had two sons born during their incarceration at Fort Detroit. They were held until after the Treaty of Paris was signed and then released by the British on July 18, 1783. The family then walked together the long way back home to Virginia.

In Elk Garden, Virginia, there is a Solomon Litton Hollow Cemetery with 30 graves. Lt. John Richard Litton and Sarah Ann Wilcoxen are buried there as are several family members including Capt. Solomon and his wife, Martha.

7 James Edward Litton (1750–1840) m Mary Ann Castle (1752–1784)

James Edward Litton was born in Fincastle, Botetourt County, Virginia, which is about halfway from the Rockville area to Elk Garden, Virginia. Was he born during a progressive migration to Elk Garden? I wish we had more information as to how and why the families migrated.

James was of age to serve in the Revolutionary War but I haven't found any record of his service although his father and two brothers served. James was around Elk Garden when his brother Solomon got his letter out from his captivity in Detroit to the father and James to secure Solomon's land claims.

James married Mary Ann Castle who was born in Castlewood in Russell County,

Chapter 35: Litton — Early Virginians

Virginia–near Elk Garden. James was 18 and Mary Ann 16. They married in Fincastle, where James was born, and probably lived there until Mary Ann died 15 years later in 1784. If we are to believe the several ancestry family trees claiming their daughter, Sophronia, they moved for at least a short time to Berkeley Springs, Maryland, or Charles City County, Virginia, where Sophronia was born.

The following is what I have discerned from several Ancestery trees, which also seem to be discredited by rigid genealogists. Let the reader beware:

Mary Ann's parents were a very interesting couple. Her father, Jacob Castle (1717–1803), was called "the Hunter," "White Tassel" and also "Long Tassel" because of long light blond hair. Jacob was a frontiersman, a woodsman, a long-range hunter, an explorer and an adventurer. He made friends with the Indians, both the Shawnee and the Cherokee. He was thought highly of by the Indians, married one, hunted with them and bought land from them. In one land transaction it is reported he traded a hound dog, a knife and a shot of whiskey for the land. It is said he showed or led Daniel Boone to the Cumberland Gap for a way into Kentucky. One land transaction he made in the western tip of Virginia was called Castle's Woods, which became present day Castlewood, Virginia, the county seat of Russell County. During the French and Indian War, he was hired by the British to spy on the French and also accused of spying for the French–a charge he was acquitted of.

Jacob's father, Peter Cassell, had emigrated from Germany to Pennsylvania in the 1600s as part of the Dutch Mennonite groups coming into the Lancaster area of Pennsylvania. The name was changed from Cassell to the Anglicized spelling of Castle.

Mary Ann's mother, Sowege Gliding Swan (1710–1752), was a full-blooded Pekowi Shawnee Indian from Somerset County, Pennsylvania. Sowege and Jacob married in Pennsylvania and lived there and in mid Virginia before moving to Castlewood. They had several children. Sowege died in 1752, the year Mary Ann was born.

Jacob may have had several other wives. Some say he had as many as eight wives and twenty children. The "Blue Blanket" custom of the Native Americans allowed a quick marriage by association and, just as easily, a quick divorce by the wife placing the man's belongings outside her home.

James remarried in 1786 to Elizabeth Polly Mack (1764–1843). They lived in Russell County, Virginia, and also Burke, North Carolina. James died in Williamsburg, Whitley County, Kentucky, which is just west of Cumberland Gap.

So we come to Sophronia. Who were her real Litton parents? There is much more work to do here to get the true facts on the Castles and the Littons.

6 Sophronia Sena Litton (1780–1849) m Benjamin Sheets (1773–1842)

Sophronia is reported to have been born in Berkeley, James, Virginia. There is no town of

Chapter 35: Litton — Early Virginians

Berkeley or James County in Virginia. Berkeley is a former plantation on the James River in Charles City County. And Berkeley Springs is a town in Berkeley County, Maryland, near Martinburg where Sophronia and Benjamin married. I speculate that Sophronia was born in Berkeley Springs, Maryland. For more on Sophronia Litton and Benjamin Sheets see Chapter 34.

Chapter 36

Tracy — Early Maryland and then Moving West

Most probably, the Tracys originally came to America from Devon, England, where they descended from Normans from Tracy-sur-mer, Normandy, France. But, like many American families, they moved and spread after arriving on the shores of this country.

Tracys Landing in Anne Arundel County, Maryland, is 20 miles south of Annapolis. As far as we now know, this is where this branch of the Tracy family first settled in America. It is very near the shore of the Chesapeake Bay. There is very little left of the town and not much is known about it. There is a historic tobacco barn there called "tobacco house No. 2," built about 1805 and not much else of note. Tracys Landing is the earliest record of this Tracy branch in America. The family then expanded to the south and west.

Rutherford County, North Carolina, is in the southwestern area of the state on the South Carolina line and on the southern side of the Great Smoky Mountains which are the southern end of the Appalachian Mountain chain. The area is elevated and has rugged terrain with pleasant fertile valley areas which attracted pioneer families.

Kentucky and Indiana had the lure of the bluegrass area and the fertile midwestern open lands for adventurous pioneer families looking for new opportunities. The Louisiana Purchase in 1804 increased the flow of families heading west down the Ohio River and into the area. Westport, Kentucky, was such an area. It was established originally as the town of Liberty, back when Kentucky was considered part of Virginia. Kentucky became a state in 1792. The name of Liberty was changed to Westport in 1797. Located just up the Ohio River from Louisville, it now is in Oldham County, an eastern suburb of Louisville and the wealthiest county in Kentucky. Back in the late 1700s it was the wild frontier.

Chapter 36: Tracy — Early Maryland and then Moving West

Westport was located in Shelby County until 1798 when the area's name was changed to Henry County after Patrick Henry. Then, in 1823, they carved the area around Westport into a new county named Oldham County. This certainly complicated my tracing and following these ancestors. Someone could apparently be born in Shelby County, marry and live in Henry County and die in Oldham Country all while living in the same house.

As Westport grew it became a shipping point for hemp, tobacco, flour, and pork to areas down river and on to New Orleans. Westport became the county seat of the new Oldham County and there must have been some price gouging going on in the new and fast-growing area because some of the first business of the new county was to stabilize some prices. They set the tavern rates and ferry fees as follows:

Dinner: 37 ½ cents

Lodging: 12 ½ cents–about the same price as a half pint of whiskey

Ferry Fee: 25 cents–for a man and his horse

The county seat became a political football between Westport and LaGrange as Westport's fortunes eventually faded and it was bypassed by the railroad. The voters chose LaGrange. The Tracys moved on also.

10 William Tracey (c1665–??) m Anna Dunn (1661–1723)
They lived in England.

9 Patrick Tracy (c1689–??) m Rebecca Sarah Freeman (c1694–c1757)
These possible parents are believed to have lived in England and may have come to America.

They are not the Patrick Tracy and Rebecca Freeman of Massachusetts who are claimed by several Ancestry trees. The Rebecca Freeman of Massachusetts is a *Mayflower* descendant whom I have not connected with documentation to our Rebecca of England or Maryland. Something is amiss.

8 William James (Willie) Tracy (1713–1790) m Nancy Spaul (1720–1790)
William was born and died at Tracys Landing, Anne Arundel County, Maryland. Nancy was born and died in Maryland.

7 Pvt. Nathaniel Pradian Tracy (1743–1818) m Mary Ann Tidwell (1744–1810)
Nathaniel was born in Tracys Landing, Anne Arundel County, Maryland. As a young man he moved to the French Broad River or Rutherford County area of western North Carolina–the two areas are close but not the same.

Mary Ann was born in Rutherford County, North Carolina. Her parents, Abraham Tidwell (1731–1755) and Sarah Boshears (1733–1755), were approximately 13 and 12 years of age, respectively, when Mary Ann was born–if the dates are correct. Abraham and Sarah were both born in Knox County, Tennessee, married or eloped and traveled 150 miles south over the Smoky Mountains to Rutherford County, North Carolina, where Mary Ann was born. Abraham and Sarah both died in Rutherford County when Mary Ann was only 11 years old. At about age 23 Mary Ann married a Clifford Hill who died shortly thereafter in 1767.

Nathaniel and Mary Ann met and married in 1771 presumably in Rutherford County, North Carolina. He served as a private in the Revolutionary War with troops from North Carolina. He received bounty lands in Washington County, Tennessee (near Johnson City in the eastern part of the state), for his service from North Carolina. Their son, William, was born in Rutherford County in 1781.

According to a tax bill/census in 1795 they had moved to Shelby County (now Oldham County), Kentucky. According to another tax bill/census in 1810 they were in Henry County (now Oldham County). Mary Ann died there in Henry County (now Oldham County). Nathaniel died there later, when it was Westport, Oldham County, Kentucky.

6 William Tracy (1781–1846) m Elizabeth Tanner (1780–1848)
William was born in Rutherford, North Carolina, and presumably moved to Westport, Henry County (now Oldham County), Kentucky, with his parents in about 1800. Elizabeth was born in Shelby County (probably in the area that is now Oldham County), Kentucky. They married in 1802 and had 13 children. In the 1820 census they still lived in Westport, Henry County (now Oldham County).

Around this time steamboats were moving up and down the river. Perhaps it was getting too crowded for the Tracys. They had moved from Kentucky to Franklin in Johnson County, Indiana (just south of Indianapolis), by the time of the 1830 census. William died in Franklin, Indiana.

Elizabeth moved on and died in Golconda, Pope County, Illinois. Golconda is on the Ohio River in the very southeast tip of Illinois and Pope County is currently mostly made up by the large Shawnee National Forest. Why did she move several hundred miles west after her husband died? Two of her brothers had moved there earlier and brother John Tanner was still alive there. There was family there to care for her in her last two years. It is so interesting that families tended to stick together and kept moving west. Also, see Chapter 37: Tanner.

5 George Tracy (1803–1860) m Susan Puckett (1812–1897)
George was born in Franklin County, Kentucky. Susan was born in Virginia. I found no records of Susan's parents or where she was born in Virginia. They lived in Shelby County,

Chapter 36: Tracy — Early Maryland and then Moving West

Kentucky, where their son John was born, and later in Franklin County since their daughter Emily Francis was born there. The 1850 census lists him as a farmer in Franklin County.

Some Ancestry trees list George as dying in Belmont County, Ohio, which I think is a different George Tracy and incorrect. Susan died in Lexington, Kentucky. I presume she was living with or near her daughter Emily Francis who also lived in Lexington.

4 Emily Francis Tracy, "Fanny" (1845–1886) m Pvt. Charles William Sheets, CSA (1841–1903)
See Chapter 34: Sheets.

Chapter 37

Tanner — Switzerland, Virginia, North Carolina & on to Kentucky

As far back as we know, the Tanner family originated in Einsiedeln, Schwyz, Switzerland, with at least two generations of Tanners before Josia Tanner arrived in Virginia in 1625. He is first found in Bermuda Hundred, Henrico (now Chesterfield) County, Virginia, in the mid-17th century. Bermuda Hundred was the name given to the first administrative town authorized to be established after Jamestown. It was founded in 1613 about 50 miles up the James River from Jamestown at the point where the Appomattox River joins the James River and is now part of Hopewell, Virginia. The name was derived from the Island of Bermuda and was used due to the experiences of the *Sea Venture* shipwreck survivors. Hundred was a term used to define a new town or development that would support one hundred families.

Recall that we described the experience of Capt. Christopher Newport in Chapter 10 and Stephen Hopkins in Chapter 11. They both were on the *Sea Venture* that shipwrecked on Bermuda. Because of that shipwreck, Virginia claimed Bermuda and made it part of their colony. Years later Britain took it from Virginia and made it a separate colony and part of the British Commonwealth.

During the last half of the 17th century, Bermuda Hundred flourished as a frontier village, resisting Indian attacks and functioning as a shipping port for sugar and tobacco. Later, as the land became weaker from these demanding crops and more immigrants came to "crowd" the area, many began moving west. This included the Tanner family.

12 Josias Tanner (1603–1630) m Mary Ann Rachel Floyd (1610–1688)
Josias's parents and grandparents lived in Einsiedeln, Schwyz, Switzerland. They were

Chapter 37: Tanner — Switzerland, Virginia, North Carolina & on to Kentucky

Lutheran. Josias, we think, was born in Bavaria, Germany–not too far away. We don't know where he grew up, but in 1625, immigrated to Virginia, where he quickly married Mary Ann the same year. Mary Ann's parents were married in London in 1610, and immigrated to Virginia where Mary Ann was born the same year. They lived in the Bermuda Hundred settlement.

11 Joseph Edward Tanner Sr. (1629–1673) m Mary Browne Shippey (1632–1700)

We know very little about them. They were born in England, married and immigrated to America where they probably settled in the area of the Bermuda Hundred settlement but definitely Henrico (now Chesterfield) County where their son was born.

10 Joseph Gilbert Tanner II (1662–1698) m 2 Sarah Hatcher (Platt) (1665–after1706)

Joseph and Sarah were born, lived and died in Henrico (now Chesterfield) County, Virginia. Joseph was born in Varina Parish and died in Bermuda Hundred. Varina Parish and Bermuda Hundred were across the river from each other. This union was a 2nd marriage for both Joseph and Sarah. She died in Henrico County, probably in Bermuda Hundred also. Both Joseph and Sarah died relatively young–life was hard. See Sarah Hatcher's ancestors back in Chapter 10: Newport.

9 Lewis Tanner (1690–after1773) m 2 Margaret Haskins (1700–1765)

Lewis and Margaret were born and married in Henrico (now Chesterfield) County, Virginia. This was a 2nd marriage for both of them. Their son was born in the neighboring county as noted below. We do not know where Margaret died, but at least Lewis left and moved to the south-central area of Virginia, perhaps with his son and family. Lewis died in Mecklenburg County.

8 Matthew Tanner (1730–1806) m Lucy Creed (1735–1809)

Matthew was born in Prince George County, Virginia, but moved to south-central Virginia with his family. He married Lucy Creed who was born in Lunenburg County, Virginia. The 1782 Virginia census shows them living in Pittsylvania County, Virginia, which is just two counties west of Mecklenburg County. They both died in Pittsylvania County, Virginia, over 20 years later.

7 Lt. Josiah Tanner (1754–1807) m Martha Wooten (1756–1851)

Josiah and Martha were both born in Mecklenburg County, Virginia. They were married in about 1771 in Mecklenburg County, Virginia, by a Col. Robert Munford, without a

Chapter 37: Tanner — Switzerland, Virginia, North Carolina & on to Kentucky

license but by publishing three times in the church. The significance of this seems to coincide with a mention that Josiah enlisted in the military for the third time in 1770. I think Josiah was primarily a soldier and maybe secondarily a farmer or tradesman.

They had 13 children together and it is from these children's birth dates and event locations I have pieced together a reasonable idea of Josiah and Martha's lives and relocations:

- Sally
  - b 1773 Mecklenburg County, Virginia
  - m 1789 Spartanburg, South Carolina, to Pvt. Richard Crittenden
  - d 1852 Columbus, Bartholomew, Indiana
- Lucy
  - b 1775 Mecklenburg County, Virginia (or near Kings Mountain, York, South Carolina–which I think is inaccurate)
  - m ?
  - d 1860 Spartanburg, South Carolina
- Martha
  - b 1777 Mecklenburg County, Virginia
  - m 1793 South Carolina
  - d 1851 Greensburg, Decatur, Indiana
- Matthew
  - b 1779 South Carolina
  - m 1823 Indiana, to Margaret Stillwell
  - d 1834 Brownstown, Jackson, Indiana
- Samuel
  - b 1780 Kings, Pickens, South Carolina (There isn't a Kings in South Carolina)
  - m 1802 Henry (Oldham) County, Kentucky, to Mary Ann or Alexandra Pryor
  - d 1830 Golconda, Pope, Illinois
- Ann
  - b 1783 South Carolina
  - m 1802 Henry (Oldham) County, Kentucky, to John Alexander Pryor
  - d 1803
- Elizabeth
  - b 1786 Shelby (Oldham) County, Kentucky
  - m 1802 Shelby (Oldham) County, Kentucky, to William Tracy
  - d 1848 Golconda, Pope, Illinois
- Creed
  - b 1788 Shelby (Oldham) County, or Greensburg, Green County,?? Kentucky
  - m 1809 Henry (Oldham) County, Kentucky
  - d after 1830 Henry (Oldham) County, Kentucky
- Mary
  - b 1789 Shelby (Oldham) County, Kentucky
  - m 1803 Henry (Oldham) County, Kentucky, to James Tracy
  - d 1848 Greenwood Cemetery, Johnson, Gibson, Indiana (Originally buried on farm)

Chapter 37: Tanner — Switzerland, Virginia, North Carolina & on to Kentucky

    Kezia   b 1792 Shelby (Oldham) County, Kentucky
                  d 1793 1yr old
    John   b 1794 Shelby (Oldham) County, Kentucky
                  m 1829 Pope County, Illinois, to Lucinda
                  d 1865 Golconda, Pope County, Illinois
    Eleanor b 1797 Shelby (Oldham) County, Kentucky
                  m 1813 Henry (Oldham) County, Kentucky, to Thomas McGannon
                  d 1856 North Vernon, Jennings, Indiana
    Thomas b 1802 Henry (Oldham) County, Kentucky
                  m 1822 Madison, Jefferson County, Kentucky, to
                  Elizabeth Christian Glass
                  d 1843 Trimble County, Kentucky (at brother-in-law's house)

While living in Mecklenburg County, Virginia, they had their first three children Sally, Lucy and Martha. They then moved to the northwestern area of South Carolina around Spartanburg in about 1778 where children Mathew, Samuel and Ann were born. After the end of the war in 1783 they moved to Westport, Shelby County (now Oldham County), Kentucky, where the rest of their children, Elizabeth, Creed, Mary, Kezia, John, Eleanor and Thomas were born in Shelby or Henry (all now Oldham) County. And the 1800 Henry County (now Oldham County) tax list census confirms Josiah lived there.

Why the move to Kentucky? We don't know, but the Tracy family moved about the same time from an adjacent county in North Carolina to the same location in Kentucky. Two of the daughters marrying Tracy sons certainly indicates a close tie between the two families. Some of the family stayed in Kentucky, some moved to Indiana and some moved farther on to Golconda, Pope County, Illinois.

We learned much of the following from depositions Martha and their daughter Sally Tanner (Crittenden) made in 1843, when Martha applied for a widow's pension at age 87. During the Revolutionary War, Josiah served for 18 months as a second lieutenant of cavalry with South Carolina troops. These apparently were state militia troops. He served under Capt. Mcbee, his company commander of light horse troops, and Col. Roebucks, his regimental commander. These forces were under Col. James Williams and General David Morgan at the Battle of Kings Mountain in October 1780. Col. Williams was killed in the battle.

Josiah was wounded by a musket ball in the right elbow during the Battle of Kings Mountain. He returned home to recover from his wound and then returned to service. He was assigned to carry a letter from General Morgan to General Washington in Charlottesville, requesting he come to meet at Cowpens. Apparently, Washington responded since continental soldiers were part of the Patriot forces at the Battle of Cowpens in January 1781. Those battles were major victories for the Patriots and many feel they were a turning point in the War. In the fall of 1781, Josiah left the service and returned to his home in that same area around Spartanburg, South Carolina. Josiah was crippled by his war injury for the rest of his life. He later received a pension for 13 years for his service during the war.

Josiah died in 1807 in Henry County (now Oldham County), Kentucky. Almost twenty years later Martha remarried to an Abraham Lemaster in 1826 in Oldham County and later moved with her family to Indiana. After Abraham's death in 1837, Martha applied to the state of Indiana in 1843 for a widow's pension for Josiah's Revolutionary War service. It was approved and she received $131.64 per year for about 8 years until her death in 1851. She died in Vernon, Jennings, Indiana, at age 95. See Wooten in Chapter 38.

6 Elizabeth Tanner (1780–1848) m William Tracy (1781–1846)
See Tracy in Chapter 36.

Chapter 38

Wooten —
The Line that Connects Us

12 Thomas Wooten, 2nd Baron of Marley, (1585–1630) m Lady Mary Throckmorton (1588–1658)
See Chapter 9 for Thomas Wooten and Mary Throckmorton.

11 Thomas Wooten (1612–1669) m Sarah Jennings (c1620–1699)
Thomas was born in Castor, Northamptonshire, England, and immigrated to Virginia. Sarah's parents, Matthew Jennings and Sarah Wood, married and emigrated from England to Isle of Wight County, Virginia, where Sarah was born. Thomas and Sarah married, lived and died in Isle of Wight County.

10 Richard Wooten Sr. (1647–1687) m Frances Joyce Albrighton (1654–1688)
Richard and Frances were born, lived and died in Isle of Wight County, Virginia. Frances's parents, Joseph Albrighton and Pollyanna/Joyce, had immigrated to Virginia from England and met and married in Virginia.

9 Richard Wooten Jr. (1678–1738) m Lucy Hardy Council (1676–1738)
Richard Jr. and Lucy also were born, lived and died in Isle of Wight County, Virginia. They were married in the town of Isle of Wight. Lucy's parents, Hodges Council and Lucy Hardy, were both born in Isle of Wight County after their parents emigrated from England to Virginia earlier.

Chapter 38: Wooten — The Line that Connects Us

8 Pvt. Samuel Wooten Sr. (1726–1814) m Sarah Elizabeth Callaway (1729–1761)
Samuel was born in Mecklenburg County, Virginia. Sarah was born in Stepney County, Maryland, where her parents, John Callaway and Sarah Windsor, were from. They married in Mecklenburg County. Samuel served as a private with Virginia troops during the Revolutionary War under Captains Fleming and Young as well as Colonels McClenachan, Heth and Russell. Samuel and Sarah lived in Mecklenburg County, where their daughter, Martha, was born. They died there also.

7 Martha Wooten (1756–1851) m Lt. Josiah Tanner (1754–1807)
See Chapter 37 for Martha Wooten and Josiah Tanner.

Part 5

My Story

Watson Christen Smith (1936–) m Linda Knoop (1939–)
My intention in writing this book was not to dwell upon myself or even write about myself, but I'm told it is very much in order to include a biography. So, here goes.

The Beginning
Being born to a middle-class family in the middle of the Depression of the 1930s does cast a certain attitude and conservative bent on some of us due to family situations, core values and economics of the time. I'm sure those factors did affect me and still linger in many ways today.

I was born on August 9, 1936, at the Griffin Hospital in Derby, Connecticut, delivered by Dr. Rentch, our family doctor. At that time, we lived in Fairfield, then Devon, then Washington DC, then Orange, Connecticut, then San Diego, California, then back to Orange, Connecticut, then Anchorage, Kentucky, then Erie, Pennsylvania, then Shaker Heights, Ohio–all before I graduated from college. Our family moved principally due to our father's work and I didn't find it at all objectionable. I enjoyed the new homes, schools and neighborhoods, and I made new friends quickly and easily.

We had a dog named Mike, a Chesapeake Bay retriever, who was in our family principally because our father liked to go duck hunting. My first memories are of Mike having a fit around the cabinet radio. Cabinet radios in those days were very prominent pieces of furniture that

Part 5: My Story

Watson Christen Smith

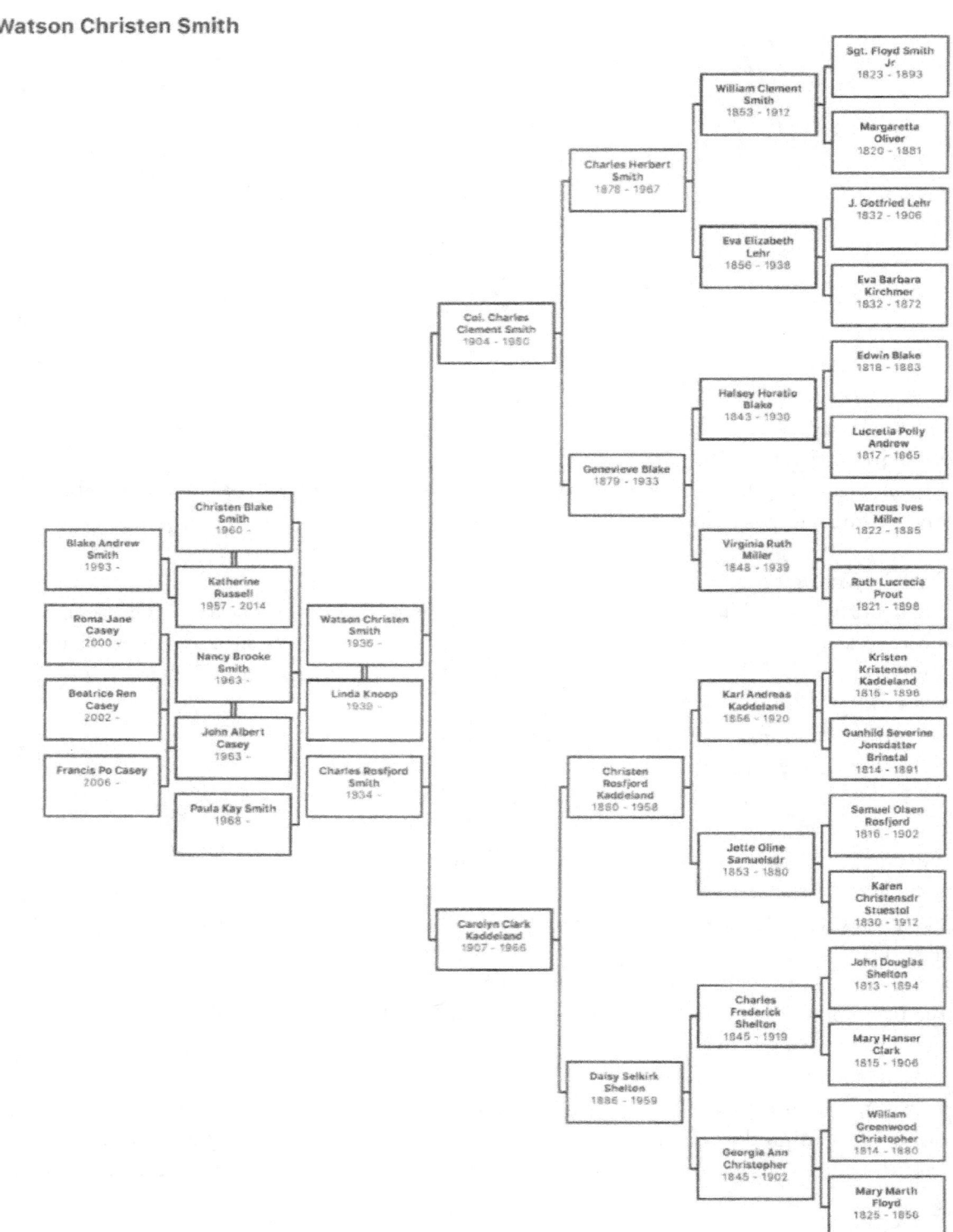

stood in the living room and the family gathered in the evening to hear the day's news and various programs. Mike became ill and was put down as I recall. This seems to be a sad first memory, but maybe it's only because of the ruckus of the event that I remember it so strongly.

My second oldest memory is on a visit to our Grandfather Smith's farm in Orange, Connecticut, for a week end stay. My older brother and I went to bed in an upstairs bedroom with the windows open. The crickets were chirping away and it seemed so strange and noisy. I didn't know what to make of it and was somewhat afraid. It kept me awake for a while, but not for long because I was in bed with my big older brother.

After that I remember Chevy Chase, Maryland, where we lived from 1939 to 1943. Our father had been called to active duty in the U.S. Army, and worked at the Pentagon until he went overseas to England in 1943. I remember our house at 201 Raymond Street, which we rented since we were only there temporarily due to the war. It was a small, comfortable, two-story home and I recall my bedroom area was a small cot in a small corner room, while my brother had a larger room and a real bed. I was only 4 or 5 years old and jealous.

School and Growing up

We entered school at the Chevy Chase Elementary School which was a short walk and across Connecticut Avenue. Usually, my older brother was there to lead me. But I remember occasionally walking home from school, by myself, at about age seven and in the second grade. Our parents let us grow up doing things and learning how to take care of ourselves. Times are very different now and I don't believe parents would even think of allowing that today. Children are overprotected to their detriment. But Connecticut Avenue is quite a bit busier.

Our mother always pushed us into things. One thing I remember, in Chevy Chase, was my brother getting a paper route to deliver the *Washington Star* newspaper in the afternoon. He was so good he got a wooden wagon with steel rimmed wooden-spoke wheels. It would hold three stacks of newspapers and had "Washington Star" painted on both sides. I was proud of him and helped when allowed to do so.

My most memorable time growing up was when we lived with my grandfather Smith from age 7 to 14 at Great Oak Farm in Orange, Connecticut. We moved there when my father shipped overseas in 1943. Those were formative years for me. We attended Orange Center School, joined Cub Scouts and Boy Scouts and also the 4-H club. The Orange Center School is now the Mary L. Tracy School. Mary Tracy was the school principal and also taught our 8th grade. She was a great teacher: stern, fair, kind, calm and dedicated to the school and the students' education. Orange was a great place to grow up. It was a rural, agricultural town just beginning to develop with housing subdivisions and with lots of room for a boy to roam and learn and do things. We had many friends, but responsibilities also. Our neighborhood and school friends created plenty of opportunity for ballgames of all kinds. Hide and seek was played on a grand scale over several acres of yards, fields and woodland where I think some remained hidden until dark put an end to the game. Ice hockey was played every winter when the local ponds froze. Sometimes we tried to play when they weren't so frozen and learned a wet lesson. Johnny Masick, one of my neighborhood playmates and classmates, went on to become a semi-pro or pro hockey goalie I'm told.

During the war years only used bicycles were available, and we learned how to fix and repair them ourselves. After the war I received a shiny new red bicycle for Christmas. I was so happy and proud because I usually got "hand me downs" from my older brother. I soon had a very minor accident, which scratched my new bike and upset me terribly. I went home bawling my eyes out. My mother had no sympathy for me, as I recall, and probably just rolled her eyes.

Although we walked and rode our bikes almost everywhere, we rode a school bus to school. If we were late catching the school bus, Mr. Hines would wait only a minute or two. If it was our fault that we were late, and the bus left without us, our mother would make us walk or ride our bikes the two miles to school. I preferred to walk, because then at the end of school, I rode the bus home and got out playing quicker.

While visiting Walter Clark, a friend down the road from us, a small Piper Cub airplane landed in their field. The pilot turned out to be a boyfriend of Walter's older sister who had literally dropped in to visit her. We naturally inspected the airplane, and he invited us to go for a ride. Of course, we accepted immediately without even thinking of asking our parents. We took off from that field and had about a 15-minute plane ride which included a view of my grandfather's house and farm. I was totally thrilled. When I got home later and described the trip to my mother, she took it in stride and didn't scold me at all. I wonder what she was really thinking.

Part 5: My Story

Young Entrepreneurship
Our grandfather taught us how to plant and raise a large garden, and how to hunt rabbits and squirrels to keep them away from the crops. He would clean and cook the rabbits for dinner. We raised vegetables for sale and had regular customers for them. I remember selling bushels of green beans to the local grocery store and we sold produce on the road out front. We grew apples and potatoes and stored them in the cellar of the garage, which had a dirt floor, to keep them cool and good through winter and into the spring. At times we picked apples to be sold at Howard Treat's roadside farm store. Sometimes our grandfather would take some apples to the local cider mill so we could enjoy apple cider for quite a while.

In Orange, our mother, again, lined us up with newspaper routes, first my brother and then me. We delivered, by bicycle, two daily evening papers, the *New Haven Register* and the *Ansonia Sentinel*. On Sunday we also delivered the *New York Times* and the *Herald Tribune*. As I recall we earned 1.5 cents per daily paper but 50 cents each for the big Sunday New York papers. This gave us about $5 a week of spending money. We received no allowances from our parents.

In the summer, when the days were long and we were out of school, we were occupied by garden chores, swimming lessons at Camp Wepawaugh, and the newspaper delivery. But, afterwards was our neighborhood softball game which we played until dark. In the winter when it got dark early, we played hockey first and then delivered our papers ending in the darkness and with unhappy customers who didn't like their paper getting there so late. My mother let me have it when the customers called her thinking we were irresponsible and had forgotten to deliver their paper. But, how could you play hockey in the dark?

A Boy's Best Friend
My dog "Streaky," an English Springer Spaniel, was my buddy on my paper route. He trotted along with me the whole 3 or 4 miles as I rode my bike. We had a few nasty dogs along the way which I always tried to avoid. Occasionally we had scraps with them which we ran away from or had to break up. One family had a Doberman, which was usually tied up, but barked and strained at his chain every time we came by. Unfortunately, one day he was loose and came running toward us. My dog did not see him coming and I was hurrying along, hoping to get away but fearful of what was about to occur. I knew my dog was no match for that Doberman. Just as the Doberman was crossing the road, running full speed at my dog, a car came and hit it solidly, killing it instantly. I was so relieved. A miracle had happened. The driver stopped and asked who it belonged to. I told him, and agreed that he could not have prevented hitting that dog. As he proceeded up to the house to tell the owners, Streaky and I proceeded on our way delivering newspapers with a big smile on my face.

Streaky was like most dogs, he would eat anything he was fed or could get into. He died from eating chicken bones he got out of the garbage. The vet came, diagnosed it and he was put down. I remember being very sad as I was digging a hole to bury him in the backyard. Our next-door neighbor lady saw me and asked what was wrong. I explained to her that I was burying our dog and that it also was my birthday. And with that I remember bursting out crying and then suddenly remembering that I was now 15 and shouldn't be crying. Our neighbor was very understanding and consoling as I recall, which was nice and helpful of course. But it was a bummer and still brings tears to my eyes as I think about it.

Wheels
When my brother turned sixteen and got his driver's license, we expanded our paper routes. We purchased a 1929 Model A Ford 2-door coupe for $40 and took on two additional routes. He would drive and I sat in the passenger seat to fold and shove the papers in the mailboxes or threw them closer as some customers wished. I was still too young to drive on the road, even though I had learned to drive by then around the farm. It was a good arrangement until he left for college and I had to revert to bicycle delivery and cut back to two paper routes.

Using the Model A every day, delivering newspapers, began to cause wear and tear on the twenty-year-old vehicle and we had to start maintaining it. This started a whole new interest for me: cars. In order to afford parts for our Model A, we bought a second Model A for $20. We took parts from the second one and exchanged them with those on the one that we used every day to keep it in good running condition. Then we sold the second Model A which gave the buyer a usable car, but with several latent repairs for them to make at some point.

While the Model A was our workhorse, we purchased a 1937 Ford Coupe with a disassembled engine for $35. We worked evenings to put it back together. I say we, but it was mainly my brother and his friend, Peter Allison, who did the work as I was still a freshman. I helped, but it was a learning experience for me inside that engine. The '37 Ford became our newspaper delivery vehicle until my brother left for college. Then the car sat waiting for me to become of age to drive it.

Early Mentoring and Employment
Our grandfather operated a small manufacturing company in his barn, fabricating steel tote boxes, which were used in factories to hold parts. With my parents' permission he hired me to help him when I was about 12 or 13. I hauled out the scrap steel and learned how to run various machines. Occasionally I got to load a truck shipping out the products, which I thought was a big deal since I had to put the shipping tags on the boxes and be sure

the trucker signed the paperwork. To me that was a very important position.

My grandfather left a large impression on me. He was a superb mechanic and skilled metalworker. I learned much about machinery and metalworking from him. He also trained us around the farm, which included a large garden and 350 apple trees. The apple trees were mostly unkempt but still bore lots of fruit. He was limited financially as to how much he could afford in equipment and had only so much time to work on the farm and his shop. The shop was his livelihood and took his primary attention. So, we helped some on the farm and worked a bit in his shop and in turn he mentored us. I'm very grateful for my time with him and all the experiences.

Louisville, Kentucky
Around 1951 our father took a position with General Electric in Louisville, Kentucky, which moved us to Dorsey Lane, Anchorage, Kentucky. They bought a nice 1-1/2 story Cape Cod-style home on 5 acres. The house and garage were surrounded by a white board fence so very typical throughout Kentucky. My father wanted the fence painted and wanted me to paint it. He bought the paint and contracted with me for my price to provide the painting labor. About halfway through the paint job I realized I had grossly underpriced the job and asked for an increase in the price. He would have none of it and I finished the painting for the originally agreed to amount. Lessons learned the hard way.

Until I was old enough to drive legally, I worked on farms. Some of it was day work where a farmer drove up to a line of workers, including me but mostly seasoned older men, and picked who he wanted for the day. One day, everyone declined to work for this one farmer, except one other black fellow and myself. We climbed onto his truck and he drove us to his potato field where we picked up potatoes, put them in bushel baskets and loaded them on his truck for 5 cents a bushel. I worked all day to earn $5, which was about the going rate at the time for farm workers, but on the low end. The interesting part of this is that summer I saved a very high percentage of my earnings because I came home dirty and tired, ate, took a shower and went to bed–never spending a nickel.

My parents wanted to have a vegetable garden and wanted me to tend it and also tend the peach trees adjacent to the garden. I did this until I was 16, had my license and my wheels. One day my mother was pressing me to tend the garden and I rebelled. I said I was leaving home and went to get in my car to leave, whereupon she came out, climbed in the car and said if I was leaving, she was going with me. This completely caught me off guard and I did not know what to do or say. So I just got out of the car and went for a walk, after which we made a compromise. After that year I did no more garden work–until I had a home of my own. All that experience taught me something, however, and now I love to putter in the yard and garden and even enjoy raising a few vegetables.

Eastern High School

I attended Eastern High School in Middletown, Kentucky. I was a B student, paid attention in class and did my homework, but nothing more. Apparently, I was well-liked since they elected me treasurer of the Senior Class which was an honorary do-nothing job. My interest at that time was cars.

In high school and college, I played amateur ice hockey with Randy Weber on the Louisville amateur team. We practiced and played in the old Armory building in downtown Louisville where Louisville's professional hockey team played. We also traveled to Cincinnati, Indianapolis and Memphis to play their amateur teams.

Cars

In high school I had many close friends including Barlow Brooks and Jack Petty. We were very much into "hot rods" and customizing our cars. It was a real fad with us and made us feel distinguished and accomplished. I rebuilt the 1937 Ford Coupe by installing dual exhausts, hydraulic brakes, a modified mercury engine, and a column-shift transmission with overdrive. Then I customized the car's body by removing all chrome, repairing rusted areas and repainting it an off white and turquoise color combination that was popular at the time on new cars.

My friends and I had drag-racing events on country roads to determine whose car could accelerate more quickly. Zero to sixty miles per hour was the challenge. I was doing well competitively until the new General Motors 1955 models came out with improved V8 overhead valve engines. We were no match for anyone who had access to their father's new car. We didn't have the wherewithal to beat Detroit. Also, by then I was moving on to college and my interest in cars had faded to a fond memory.

University of Louisville–Speed School and Delta Upsilon

After high school I migrated to the University of Louisville's Speed Scientific School, which is their engineering school. Their program was a five-year plan with co-op work jobs for half of the junior and pre-senior years. It was a great engineering education and well received by industry. I enjoyed the engineering courses and did well. My co-op jobs with GE and DuPont were excellent, paid well, and gave very good real engineering experience.

Part 5: My Story

At U of L, I pledged Delta Upsilon fraternity and gradually held several positions including president of the chapter twice. One spring, my parents and Grandfather Kaddeland were visiting on Engineer's Day, an open house, which Speed School held annually to show off their facility. After visiting the school, I invited them to visit our fraternity house. I had prepared for this by having the pledges clean and wax everything. The old house had not looked that good for some time. After showing my folks and grandfather around, I proudly asked my grandfather what he thought of our fraternity house. He quickly said that a good match (meaning a fire) would take care of it. Completely crestfallen at the time, I now must admit he was totally correct. Not many years after I graduated, the University bought the house and tore it down to build the new Faculty or Alumni Building.

I had very little connection with my fraternity brothers during my years after college and throughout my working years. But after that I connected with some of them and enjoy the time together. I went down to Louisville for my fiftieth reunion but few showed up. On another occasion, I met for a luncheon with Doug Abrams, Joe Parrish, Chuck Nabors, Charlie Frank and Walt Hamilton.

On a train trip returning from LA we stopped in Albuquerque, New Mexico, and spent a day with Mike Chynoweth and his wife, Ellen, which we really enjoyed. Mike and I were good friends in college. We were in mechanical engineering classes and Air Force ROTC together, as well as being DU fraternity brothers. Mike served 30 years in the Air Force as a pilot and also in nuclear weapons development management. They built a beautiful log home in a mountainside community just east of Albuquerque. He retired as a lieutenant colonel. We stayed in communication until he passed away a couple of years ago.

When we go to LA to visit with our daughter, Paula, I try to meet up with a fraternity brother, John Addleman. That is always a fun get-together, with many good recollections. After college and his tour in the Navy, John was in banking as a career. He also had a side job as Mayor for many years of his town of Rolling Hills, California, on the Palos Verdes Peninsula. And, I have talked with another fraternity brother, Harry Johnson, who was an Air Force pilot and retired as a lieutenant colonel. He was shot down over Vietnam and spent about 3 years in a POW camp before being released and brought home. He lives in his hometown in Iowa. There is a book written about the "Stryker" Air Force action in Vietnam, which specifically mentions Harry Johnson.

Many great memories of college life remain with me. Pledging. Friendships. Parties. Homecoming decorations. Intramural sports. Freiberger sings. ROTC parades. CO-OP jobs. Meeting and dating my future wife, Linda Knoop. And finally graduation. I graduated in June 1959 with a Bachelor of Mechanical Engineering degree and a U.S. Air Force Reserve Officer Commission as a 2nd Lieutenant. Again, I was elected Treasurer of my Senior Class (for the Speed School Mechanical Engineering Department) and also, again, it was an honor, but a do-nothing position.

Linda

In the fall of 1958, I had seen Linda in the Cardinal Inn, a small restaurant across from our fraternity house and asked Mac DeHart, a fraternity brother, who she was. Mac knew all the girls and introduced us. We began dating and over the next eight months became close. At graduation she helped my mother pin on my 2nd Lieutenant Bars. After graduation I took Linda up to Cleveland to spend a little more time with my parents. I asked my mother what she thought of Linda. Her reply was that "she certainly had a mind of her own." I took that as a compliment and definitely agreed with her. It's one of the remarkable traits that she still has. It was a nice visit, we returned to Louisville and I left from there to go west into the service. No commitments were made but we both certainly cared very much for each other and knew it was a serious relationship. After a few months, while on a phone call with her, I asked if she would like to marry. Her answer was yes.

U.S. Air Force

Upon graduation, Air Force ROTC Graduates had a responsibility to serve three years. Up until my senior year in college I had been scheduled to enter flight training to be a pilot. I was looking forward to it. Then my grandfather Kaddeland came to visit and encouraged me not to "waste my engineering education." I'm sure my mother put him up to it. Upon considering the thought, I changed from flying into Base Engineering. A contributing factor in my decision was that a high school friend, Richard Hudson, had become a pilot in the Air National Guard and had recently been killed in an airplane crash due to lack of oxygen tank maintenance. That changed my direction and redirected my life into engineering, construction and related business fields with which I have been most pleased.

Oregon

I received orders to report to Kingsley Field in Klamath Falls, Oregon, which was an Air Defense Command base, reactivated from being an abandoned WWII Naval pilot training base. Even though I had applied to be in the Base Engineers, I was assigned there as an Aircraft Maintenance Officer. I packed my few personal belongings in my 1957 Austin-Healy and drove west across the country to Oregon. Upon arrival the personnel officer told me they didn't need any more Aircraft Maintenance Officers and that since I had played some amateur ice hockey, I would become a  personnel services officer. In that assignment I looked after the movie theatre, gymnasium, hobby shop, ball team leagues and recreational equipment. Much of this I knew nothing about, but you learn fast, and I did a good job. Once I began to meet some other young officers, I became good friends with another Lieutenant, John Gentile. John was from New York City where he had studied architecture at Pratt Institute for a couple of years. He then went to the Naval Academy at Annapolis and, after graduation, switched to the Air Force. This was permissible since there was no Air Force Academy at the time. John worked in the Base Engineers and informed me that they had open slots. We petitioned Major Holloway, the personnel officer, and after about five months I was reassigned to the Base Engineer Design Section.

Marriage

In December 1959 I returned to Louisville, Kentucky, on leave, to marry Linda Knoop. We were married the day after Christmas at Concordia Lutheran Church in Louisville. My best man was my brother and the groomsmen were fraternity brothers Mac DeHart and Fred Stout and hockey player friend Randy Weber. All other close friends were off in the military service. After a short honeymoon in San Francisco, we returned over snow-covered mountain roads to Kingsley Field in Klamath Falls, Oregon. We tried unsuccessfully to get over the Green Springs Mountain and had to spend the night in

Ashland, Oregon, about 20 miles from our new home. I was broke at that moment, and had to write a bad check for tire chains. Fortunately, my meager Air Force paycheck was waiting for me back at the base, so I could cover the check before it got to my bank.

Our home initially consisted of one end of a rented duplex house with two small bedrooms. For furniture we had only a bed, footlocker and card table with two folding chairs. After a few weeks, things arrived from Linda's parents. We had ordered a few living-room pieces in San Francisco and locally we purchased a nice white rug, so it was beginning to look like a home. John Gentile insisted that we throw a party to introduce Linda to the other officers and their wives. He invited the group and they all came and drank to the extent that several (including a dog that was brought and fed vodka) were sick on our brand-new rug. The next morning, we rolled up the new white rug and hauled it out to the trash. My opinion of fighter pilots was completely changed. Linda was well accepted and later on got elected Vice President of the Officers' Wives Club.

After four months on a waiting list, we were able to get living quarters in the military base family housing which was quite nice for newlyweds with no furniture to speak of. We had a three-bedroom, two-bath home with living and dining room, fireplace, garage and all the military housing furniture we needed. In spite of our nice housing, we lived on a very tight budget which bothered me much more than Linda. She was thrifty and super about our humble beginnings and never complained. Linda made good friends with the neighborhood women–Rosemary Blanch, Joan Collins and Darlene Maxwell.

Base Engineers
I loved the work and applied myself well. Kingsley Field was a former WWII Naval Air Training Base. The base buildings had been hastily built of wood-frame construction during the war, and we had many challenges in maintaining and updating the facilities. The military gives young officers a lot of responsibility and the system and authority to get things done within limits. My experience in the U.S. Air Force and particularly the Base Engineers was a great training for later running my own businesses. I had many interesting experiences, a few of which are worth retelling.

Oregon is known for its snow in the mountains in winter, but one storm dropped 24 inches of snow in 24 hours. Along with it we had a power outage of about a 3- to 4-hour duration. All critical military facilities had backup generators which worked fine, but our 270 military housing units used electric heat. When the power came back on all of the units demanded heat which overloaded the transformers tripping their circuit breakers. Our emergency crews could not keep them engaged without reducing the load. The Air Police were called to go through the neighborhood with loudspeakers asking everyone to turn their thermostats lower, but not many did. So, we directed our crews to go with the

Air Police door-to-door and physically shut off half of the heat in every house. By the time we got that done and the power fully on, the houses had been without heat so long that pipes were frozen. Our crews only had two sets of equipment to thaw pipes and it was an impossible task which would take days to complete. We resolved the problem by sending teams of troops throughout the neighborhood shoveling snow up against the kitchen and bathroom exterior walls to insulate those walls against the -24 degree temperature. The crews worked all night and took breaks at our house and a few others where Linda and other families kept coffee and hot soup available.

During the storm our operational readiness for air defense was never compromised, partly because our snowplows continuously plowed the runways. The drivers of those big plow trucks worked over 24 hours straight. After the housing problem was under control, I rode with one of the drivers for a two hour stretch to help keep him awake. Quite an experience.

Another interesting experience was when a contractor was working on an aircraft missile storage facility (a Bunker). The operations people needed the use of the facility badly, so even though the contractor was not finished we arranged beneficial occupancy for the operations activity. They promptly took it over to store nuclear missiles, secured the area with armed guards and would not let the contractor in to finish his work so he could get paid. It was a mess and I think it went all the way up to the Sector Commander to finally get an ok for this poor contractor to get in to finish his work. The mission was always of primary importance and why we were all there.

After a bid opening on a project, the Base Contracting Officer and I went to lunch. At the restaurant we saw the winning contractor there so we sat with him for lunch, discussed the project and each paid our own lunch tab. Unknown to us, one of the unsuccessful bidders was having lunch there also. He called his congressman and filed a formal complaint thinking that we were getting lunch paid by the winning contractor. We had to all sign statements that we paid for our own lunches. That solved the complaint, but it made me doubly cautious to avoid improprieties during all my working years.

Gentile and Smith
John Gentile and I started a partnership, Gentile and Smith, to build a house to sell in the speculative Klamath Falls housing market. The housing market was good and we saw opportunity to use our spare time in the Air Force to make a nickel. We found a lot in an established subdivision with a beautiful view of Mt. Shasta 120 miles to the south. We designed the house and had construction fairly well complete when the U.S. Air Force had other plans for us. John received orders to go to Canada and I received orders to attend a 3-month Base Engineer training school at Wright Patterson Air Force Base in Dayton,

Ohio. We had always thought that even if one of us got transferred the other would be able to complete the project in a timely fashion, but both of us left and the house sat unfinished. Well, after I returned from Ohio it was winter and all I could do was wrap up the inside work. In the spring I got the exterior completed and the lot landscaped so that the house was ready for sale. By then the housing demand had dropped and we longed for a buyer. Finally, a young couple came by and offered us an amount less than we owed for materials and subcontractors. I went hat in hand to our lender, Cap Collier, Owner of Swan Lake Moulding Company, and explained our situation. I told him I thought we should accept the low offer and that I would pay the difference out of my meager Air Force pay over several months. He agreed and then he did something I have not experienced in all my business dealing of a lifetime. He forgave the balance I was going to have to pay saying, "You built a good house and we will just call it even." Needless to say, I was humbled and thanked him. Thirty-five years later, Linda and I drove by the house on a trip west. We stopped and introduced ourselves to the then current owner and talked about the house. They had owned the house for several years and liked it very much. We of course lost all our labor and effort, but I'm still proud of trying and glad for the experience it gave me.

Base Engineering Course and Blake
At the time I was assigned to attend the Base Engineering course, Linda was expecting our first child. We worked it out that she could fly east to Ohio, we could be together and she could deliver the child there. That arrangement worked well. We were together during the 3-month class time period and our son, Christen Blake Smith, was born at the Wright Patterson Air Force Base Hospital. Linda's mother came up to help. We enjoyed our time that fall in Southwestern Ohio and explored the area. Little did we know at that time that we would spend 50 years of our life just a few miles south in the Cincinnati area.

The Base Engineers School was completed in mid-December, so we were able to spend Christmas with Linda's family in Louisville before heading back west.

We returned to Kingsley Field in Oregon by driving across the country on a southern route to avoid winter weather. A memorable stop was with Linda's Uncle Paul Hund in Phoenix, Arizona. Paul was a realtor in Phoenix and a walking, talking chamber of commerce for the area. He wanted us to come there after the service and work with him. I was very tempted, but engineering was on my mind right then. The way Phoenix has expanded since that time, I'm sure we would have been successful. We visited Paul in later years and always enjoyed our time with him and Crystal. I think Linda was one of his favorite nieces.

Upon leaving the service, I applied for engineering positions all over the country. I put out over 50 resumes to Hawaii, Alaska, Oregon, California, and most states east. Two responses came back. Bechtel Corp. in San Francisco and A.M. Kinney Inc., consulting engineers, in Cincinnati, Ohio. Interviewing at Bechtel in San Francisco, I found that it was unaffordable to live in the city. I was facing at least an hour commute each way. Realizing that my father had done that from Orange, Connecticut, to New York City for several years, I was not going to subject my family to that, even with the great opportunity that Bechtel presented in their offer.

A.M. Kinney and Cincinnati

So, I accepted the job with Kinney in Cincinnati, and we returned to the Midwest. Cincinnati appeared to be a good location in that Linda's family was in Louisville and my parents were in Cleveland. After renting a short time in the suburb of Madeira, we purchased a ranch-style home at 804 Park Avenue in Terrace Park, a small village 18 miles east of downtown Cincinnati. We settled down and began civilian life in the corporate world. Linda was the homemaker and made good friends with our next-door neighbors, Bob and Ruann Terwillegar. That close family friendship still continues and includes our children. Blake was growing and keeping Linda busy. Our daughter Nancy Brooke Smith arrived in August of 1963. Linda's mother, Ruth, came up again for a few weeks to help us manage. Our family was growing.

804 Park Ave.

Linda, Blake and my mother, Carolyn Kaddeland (Smith)

Bob and Ruann Terwillegar Next-door neighbors and lifelong friends

After 3 years at Kinney's, during which I passed the Ohio PE exam and obtained my Ohio Professional Engineer License, I began exploring options to get in business for myself. I discussed this with a fellow engineer named Al Wu who was planning to start his own engineering firm with another fellow. While on vacation and visiting my parents in

Cleveland, I discussed it with my father. He indicated that if I found something worthwhile, we could get into it as a family business. So, while talking further with Al Wu, I also began searching for available businesses. My insurance agent, Al Rebstein, introduced me to Rolf Brooks, Senior Vice President of First National Bank of Cincinnati, who had a customer wanting to sell the Harvey P. Bertram Company.

A Family Business
I always had an interest in being an independent business person. That is, being in business for myself and running my own business. I'm a fairly cautious, reserved individual and not the swashbuckling entrepreneurial type. But I'm sure I developed this interest from my grandfather and my parents, as they always wanted to be in business for themselves even if their situation didn't always favor or present the opportunity. My grandfather started his Smith Manufacturing Company in his barn in the depth of the Depression after being laid off from his factory superintendent's position when the Derby Silver Company folded in 1933. He succeeded in providing a good living for as long as his years allowed. Our father had always wanted his own business and intended to start a copper wire business after the war but was prevented by copper strikes, affecting its viability. Our mother always pressed us to be productive and supported our entrepreneurial endeavors.

Bertram Company
Harvey Bertram was a sales representative in Cincinnati for an industrial fan manufacturer. He began a small shop to modify the products in order to service his customers' special needs. By 1965, this little shop had developed, through a succession of owners, into a small company with a specific industrial fan product line that was marketed nationally. We purchased the company and my father moved down from Cleveland to run it as President. I started working nights and weekends doing engineering design and testing work for the company. After about 4 months of this dual job, I gave Kinney notice and moved full time into the Harvey P. Bertram Company as Chief Engineer.

The company at that time consisted of 4 office and 10 shop employees. Our equipment comprised a few arc welders, and a small machine shop where aluminum castings were machined into axial fan wheels and propellers. The company was housed in 5,000 square feet of rented space, just a small section of a massive brick national guard armory from the Civil War era.

Leo Wortman, the General Manager, was a strong key employee for the company. He had grown up in the shop, knew the products and handled all the estimating, quoting and sales through the network of independent sales representatives. He and I worked well together and the company began to progress.

I liked the business. But very quickly I realized that I was trained as an engineer and not as a business person. So I started taking night classes at the University of Cincinnati. I took accounting, finance, business law and marketing. These courses gave me a basic foundation from which I could grow my business knowledge through actual experience.

Plant #2 Fire
The business was growing, so we added more employees and rented another factory building about a block away. Things were going well until a burglar arson fire gutted the additional factory building. This was the late sixties when there was much disruption nationally and our business was right in the middle of a distressed neighborhood. People would riot and set fires to buildings in protest against how they were being treated racially and for their lack of equal opportunity. When the fire department responded they were sometimes greeted by rioters with rocks and even weapons. The National Guard was activated and rode with the firemen. I recall seeing a fire engine going down the street with the windshield open and a guardsman sitting in the passenger seat. He had a BAR (Browning Automatic Rifle) sticking out the open window with the gun's tripod resting on the hood of the vehicle.

We had adequate insurance, and we recovered from the fire by renting another building and purchasing new equipment. The stress and disruption from an event such as this takes a toll on you. At that time my brother had joined the business and was in charge of the financial side—including the fire insurance claim. The stress of the situation often leads to incomplete insurance claims, because people simply fail to remember everything they lost. In order to file a complete claim, he had almost every employee walk through the ruins and recall what tools, equipment, materials and work-in-process inventory had been there. It was a tedious process and he did a very thorough job to get us proper restitution from the insurance company.

A New Plant
As a result of all this we purchased 5 acres of land and built a 40,000-square-foot plant in a new industrial park being developed on the east side of Cincinnati on Bach-Buxton Road in Clermont County. We had several employees that drove in from that area and they were quite happy with the choice of location. Others that lived in downtown Cincinnati were not so happy, but everyone looked forward to a new modern facility. I hired Al Wu's engineering firm to help with the plans and specifications for the new plant. The plant construction was completed and a grand opening was planned, complete with a cornerstone laying. In that cornerstone that will be opened someday is a list of all the employees, a product brochure and a schedule of events and speakers for that day's event. We were the

first plant to be built in the industrial park and it was a big deal for the county as well as us. Some county commissioners and the state representative attended, along with many others. Most all employees and their families attended.

One person who was not there was Leo Wortman, who died suddenly of a cerebral hemorrhage a week before the opening. We all felt the loss in several ways. He was really well-liked and a key person in the company. His widow, Rita, helped us honor Leo by cutting the ribbon at the opening.

This experience was quite sobering to us all and made me decide to quit smoking. I had smoked occasionally in college, but became a serious smoker when in the service, where you could buy a carton of cigarettes in the Base Exchange for $1. Trying to quit later I took up cigars which only led me back to cigarettes. After finally quitting in 1968, I never touched any form of tobacco again. I didn't need the government to tell me they were bad for my health.

Industrial Air Inc.
Along with the move to the new plant was a name change for the company to "Industrial Air Inc." which had actually been on our company logo for many years. It was more appropriate for what our products were about. We manufactured industrial fans and blowers from 12 inches to 12 feet in diameter to move air and exhaust contaminants in industrial applications. Our products were used for industrial ventilation and for exhausting fumes from mines, power plants and industrial plants. Most customers were in the U.S., but some products were shipped all over the world. It is interesting that they were also applied to some very small projects such as inflating hot air balloons.

Over the course of 23 years at Industrial Air we made products for many interesting projects and applications. Most were just explained to us, but we did get out to see some of the projects and how our fan products were installed and applied. For example, we supplied a 12-foot diameter fan for a cooling condenser on pad 39A at Cape Canaveral, Florida, which was where the first manned rocket was launched to the moon. Our fans were installed on pumping stations along the Alaskan pipeline and also a Russian pipeline supplying Europe. We supplied tens of truckloads of roof ventilators to tire plants around the world. On one project we shipped several fans to Japan that were installed on a floating paper mill being built on a barge that was then taken back across the Pacific Ocean, through the Panama Canal, down to Brazil and up the Amazon River for operation there. We built an 84-four-inch vertical wind tunnel for the U.S. Air Force to test parachute flares. In order to produce fans for nuclear power plants, we set up and implemented an aircraft quality assurance program to ensure product integrity. At one nuclear plant in Minnesota, they needed a fifty-four-inch fan to be moved in through a thirty-six-inch

Part 5: My Story

A large industrial fan

A mine ventilation fan shipped to a West Virginia coal mine

A *Cincinnati Enquirer* newspaper article with picture of a 10' diameter ventilation fan. I am standing in the fan.

The entire fan is shown as one of a group of these fans on the roof of the Miami Fort Power Station, North Bend, Ohio. Each fan unit measures about 20' x 20' and stands about 9' tall. They ventilate the boiler room building.

doorway for which we fabricated a product in pieces to be field assembled. The industrial applications were the fun and exciting aspect of the business.

I can't count how many suits and shoes I ruined trying to appear businesslike while on a job site with a rather nasty environment. I remember a few very distinctly. While at the Ford foundry at the old River Rouge Plant, we were up in the clear story of the roof structure, where a large group of fans were located in exhaust stacks. The foundry dust was literally 12 inches deep like heavy snow only black and dirty. At a copper mine ore-processing plant in Arizona, we walked through the plant and the next day my shoes came apart and my suit was full of small holes from the acid mist. In a Saginaw Steering Gear Plant in Michigan, most surfaces were covered with a light coat of oil from the use of cutting oil mist in their machining operations. I never tired of visiting the field applications of our products, but I got smarter as to how I dressed at the job sites by wearing protective boots and coveralls or less expensive casual clothing.

Societal and Marketplace Changes
The industrial workplace was where things happened in bringing products to the American consumer, and similarly all over the world. But things were changing. Industrial processes brought good things, good wages and a growing economy, but also waste and pollution. New environmental laws and the Occupational Safety and Health Administration caused major changes in American industry, the economy and in our business. "Factory" became a dirty word and became an unpopular place to work or operate. The new rules caused economic disaster for several industries and businesses.

Foundries became uneconomical with pollution-control equipment required to operate with clean exhaust stacks and therefore moved offshore. Some products were redesigned to eliminate the part or replace it with another material or design. Exhaust system designs were revised to capture pollutants or contain them at the source — and with good effect. I attended a one-week short course at North Carolina State University in Raleigh while working at Kinney's on this topic of industrial ventilation. After that I became one of the instructors for the course for the next 15 years. One week each spring I would head for Raleigh and many years it coincided with school spring break so Linda and the kids could join me for a nice week down where the azaleas and rhododendrons were in bloom. Most years I gave the lecture with a slide presentation on fans and their applications.

Our products were good and our manufacturing facility was also good, but we could foresee a downturn in the industrial fan and blower market. We added additional fan products and makeup-air equipment. We even started a plastics division to make corrosion-proof fans and air pollution equipment, but we lacked volume to really support production efficiency. We struggled to be profitable. Chuck wanted to leave and go into the real estate business. We discussed it all and agreed he would run the Smith Real Estate Company and I would continue at running Industrial Air.

We had a lady who was our controller named Catherine Miltz. She had been with the company since before we bought it and she was a wonderful, honest, dedicated, and hard-working lady who ran the accounting department and would not let anyone help her or let go of anything. She was a widow and was our father's age but had no intention of retiring. She and my brother worked well together, but without Chuck I had a severe problem. She finally agreed to allow us to get her an assistant, her daughter, and begin a gradual transition to retirement. Her daughter, Jean, assisted until Catherine retired and I hired a new controller. We had a grand retirement luncheon for Catherine which included a new car for her and gifts from many employees. Several weeks later Catherine called and came to our house as she had previously said she was going to do. She had some things to discuss. She had kept the vending machine coins separate from the business accounting and always paid the vendors in cash from the kitty she kept. She felt these were the employees' funds and didn't trust the new controller to keep them separate and safe and so she was giving them directly to me to do so. I most always did what Catherine told me to do because she was most always right–an honest, loyal employee and a kind, wonderful person.

We had a licensee in Canada, Dundas Foundry, who was in the fan business and agricultural equipment business also. They paid us a few dollars a year for a license to build and sell our products in Canada but never sold much of anything, despite my annual trips to encourage them. We explored other opportunities, dissolved our license with Dundas and purchased Canada Fans. It was a good little company with promise for growth and we had the products to help them grow their business in Canada.

Catherine Miltz receiving a retirement chair from the employees.

I wanted to make a long-term business plan to grow the company and knew I needed help to do so. We had a friend who was a business consultant with Ernst and Young. I talked with him and brought him in first to consult and then hired him as a vice president to help plan the company's growth. At first things went well and we hired more talent to lead the company. In the early eighties business was good but we were still struggling with our profit margin and you cannot grow without profits to support the growth. He and I differed on that.

In 1983 I could see the recession signs beginning. Our sales were dropping and I could not see the team we had put together properly dealing with it. In addition, my friend was running the operations side of the business and was keeping things from me. At a Friday staff meeting it came to a head when he confronted me over minor things and in ways that were clearly meant to show dominance in front of the team of managers. It was completely unnecessary, but I let him have his way and let it go. We were trying to build a team to work together, but this was not working. My secretary, Willie Rower, told me the scuttle-butt was my friend trying to force a takeover of the company by securing the loyalty of the managers. I was burned, but cooled off and reviewed the situation over the weekend. Monday morning, I terminated him, which brought a real surprise to him. In the next few weeks I terminated two other managers. The recession of 1983–1984 was on its way and the last thing I needed was people who were counterproductive to our survival.

Linda, the kids and Terrace Park
After about 5 years living on Park Avenue, in 1967 we bought a slightly larger house a few blocks away–still in Terrace Park. It was a very colonial Cape Cod-style home supposedly designed by Royal Barry Wills, located at 611 Floral Avenue. We lived there, with several additions and various remodeling, very comfortably for about 40 years.

611 Floral Ave.

Part 5: My Story

Our third child Paula Kay Smith arrived December 16, 1968. Paula had a slightly different upbringing than our first two children who were now moving right along in public school. Linda decided she did not want to just be a stay-at-home mom and wanted to complete her college degree, which I completely supported and agreed with. She enrolled in the University of Cincinnati and took night as well as day classes. Paula got the attention of a babysitter during the day classes and the attention of her siblings and father during the night classes. Linda graduated with a B.A. and honors as well as congratulations from the kids and myself. I was very glad for her. She is a smart lady and certainly put her education on hold to marry and follow me around in the Air Force, etc. She obtained her teaching degree and a job at Seven Hills Schools in Cincinnati where she taught for 15 years and received an honorary chair upon retirement. Paula got the benefit of being able to attend Seven Hills Schools at first with free tuition and later with reduced tuition due to Linda being on the faculty. So they went to school together.

Linda at Seven Hills

It's often small things that bring startling memories back to us. When we first moved into this newer house, our son Blake, who was 8 years old, started wandering quite far away from home. We decided that we best do something to keep him more interested around home. So, he and I built a tree fort around a large elm tree in the back yard, complete with rope ladder making it hard for girls to climb up. This worked well for its purpose and it became the site of many mock battles for Blake and his friends. The tornado of 1969 that tore through Terrace Park decimated the top of the tree, but the tree fort was unscathed. Not to be slighted, our daughters Nancy and Paula began a campaign for a girls playhouse. We therefore enclosed the lower level into a playhouse complete with windows and a door. Later when the kids were in high school it was all removed in order to build a new two-car garage.

Nancy, Tiger and Blake Terrace Park Labor Day Parade

As our three children grew up in Terrace Park, we spent considerable time with them, but nothing compared to parents of today. Terrace Park, Ohio, is an independent village with its own police and fire departments. It was relatively safe as neighborhoods go, and a great place for kids to grow up. With about 600 families, plenty of room, contained borders and good local government by the residents it served our family well. I served as Village Engineer for several years and also Chairman of the Board of Zoning Appeals.

Blake
As Blake grew up, I was coach of his Little League baseball team for two years, when he was in the first and second grades. The first year we lost every game. The second year we won every game because we had a star pitcher. After that I stepped down and retired. By then the kids knew more about baseball than I did.

When we sold the home in 2007, the new owners asked us why there was a blanket hung on the far end wall of a crawl space under a bedroom. It took a few moments to recall that our son, Blake, had a BB gun range under the house and the blanket was the backstop. It kept the BBs from rebounding back at the young marksmen who competed there.

Blake's Boy Scout troop had a great scoutmaster in Jim Allison. I was on the Scout Committee and helped as assistant scoutmaster. When Jim Allison stepped down, I became the scoutmaster for a while, but could not do much because I was working very long hours at Industrial Air. We did get some good camping trips in, and the boys got some good experiences from it. I wish I could have had more time to devote to it. Blake was a good Scout and probably one of the best campers in the troop, but I could not interest him in moving along with the merit badges to achieve a higher rank than Star.

Blake joined an outdoor adventure group at Linda's school and became a counselor. They traveled to many places including the Canadian Rockies and then biked to the west coast. On another trip they went to Alaska hiking and kayaking. He called one day and asked me to get his application to Xavier University, which he had completed, delivered for him. I did as he asked, thinking he finally is beginning to think of a future — or maybe he's getting tired of herding kids around the world. He attended Xavier and graduated with a degree in History–a family passion.

At Xavier, Blake met Katherine Russell, a girl from Indianapolis, Indiana. A few years later they married and gave us a wonderful grandson, Andrew.

Nancy
Our daughter Nancy grew up as a happy child. She graduated from Mariemont High

School where she was an excellent student, even taking advanced placement courses for college credit. Nancy was a worker and went out and got jobs at Burger King and other restaurants. A friend of hers got her a job working with her at the Cincinnati Country Club. She was carrying a tray of condiments when someone bumped her and she tipped the red ketchup all over a person in a pretty white dress. The person, it seems, was a club board member and Nancy thought she would be immediately fired. But the lady was very good natured and exclaimed that she always looked good in red. Life is full of experiences and the earlier we learn things the better we can cope with life's hardships and setbacks. Nancy was not a joiner but had some very close high school friends, Sylvia Stickley and Patty O'Donnell, who she still gets together with every year.

Nancy went on to Carnegie Mellon University where she studied Graphic Design which was her passion. While in high school she had done a catalog for us at Industrial Air which I was quite pleased with, and proud of her. It also calmed my anxiety about the expensive tuition I was about to shell out. She had a career in mind. She did very well at CMU, graduating with honors, and they asked her to stay there teaching for an additional year. After that, they helped her obtain a terrific design job at the *Washington Post* which launched her career.

She also met her future husband, John Casey, at CMU and although they went separate ways after college, they later met again in Cincinnati, married, and are raising three great grandkids.

Paula

Our daughter Paula, grew up as the youngest child and had the guidance of her older brother and sister, but she also had greater independence. From kindergarten through high school, she attended Seven Hills School where Linda taught, but care was given that she was not in Linda's class. It was a great academic school and prepared Paula for moving on to New York University where she graduated with honors in 1991 from the NYU film school. She had wanted to work in the film industry since she was a junior in high school.

Paula on Stonehenge during our 1976 England trip

Upon graduation from NYU, Paula went to Chicago seeking to use her film training, but only found work on TV commercials and tending bar to make ends meet. Hearing that films were being made in Seattle, she moved there, but found little real film work. Finally, she made a move to Los Angeles where she has found her career as an Assistant Director for Film and TV. When she had served her "apprentice time" I was only too happy to gift her the $5,000 she needed to join the Directors Guild. She works hard and earns her good salary.

Paula on the porch of the Grand Hotel, Mackinac Island

Hollywood is a very liberal place, but it doesn't treat its workers very well. They hire non-guild (non-union) personnel for lower-level jobs and pay them menial wages until they accumulate enough hours to become guild members. Then the fee to join is $5,000 which is very hard to accumulate while working on their films at their low wages. Quite a different attitude than that expounded by wealthy guild-member actors with their liberal political contributions. They seem to have a caste system with barriers to entry in order to protect their own high-paid status.

St. Thomas

St. Thomas Episcopal Church in Terrace Park is part of the community and one of the attractions to living there. Linda and I taught Sunday School when the kids were there. I served on several committees, was elected Junior Warden twice and then Senior Warden, each for three-year terms. During the church's major expansion, I was on the building committee and oversaw construction progress along with Pierson Davis. The rector, Bob Gerhard, and his wife, Ernestine, were very good friends. We took three trips to Europe and one to Canada with them. Ernestine and Linda were close friends, and with other ladies they regularly went to the Cincinnati Symphony together. Bob was a good friend and got me into golf which I'll explain below. We enjoyed traveling with

Church photo

Bob and Ernestine as well as their friendship.

St. Thomas was an active church under Bob Gerhard's leadership. They got involved in social issues and community events. They held open forums on the local teacher strike and worked with local charities taking in flood victims to our homes. We were involved where needed and continuously active to better people's lives in the surrounding area.

A Helping Hand

At the end of the Vietnam War, refugees were coming to the U.S. A call went out for sponsors and, of course, St. Thomas formed a committee, on which I was asked to serve. We discussed how we might be of assistance in areas of concern such as helping with English, housing, medical, food, employment, etc. Various offers were made. The church owned a small house in the community that had been a clothing exchange, which could be used. I pledged a blue-collar job at Industrial Air. St. Thomas Church offered to sponsor a refugee family and bring them into the community.

Several months later, a Cambodian family arrived during a snowstorm — they had never seen snow before. The family consisted of a husband and wife, a baby boy, a mother-in-law and a niece, with the proverbial "clothes on their backs" and a suitcase or two. After about a week of introductions and orientation for them and for us, I arranged to take the husband, Kan Oum, to start his employment. I found he had a rudimentary ability to speak English. We drove to the Industrial Air plant and I introduced him to the shop management and left him in their care. He was given an assembly job and worked well. After a few weeks of driving him back and forth to work, I found out more about Kan. He had been trained by the French in Cambodia in mining engineering and had technical skills. I transferred him to the Engineering Section where he quickly fit in and worked well.

After becoming an American citizen Kan kept working to help other refugees, by sponsoring them. During his lunch breaks, he would type letters on a manual Cambodian language special-character typewriter. One weekend he drove to New York City to petition the United Nations regarding various refugee issues. A few years later, they got word that his father-in-law was alive and held in Vietnam. He flew to Cambodia, somehow entered Communist Vietnam, got his father-in-law's release and brought him to the United States. I remember him telling me that to get across the border exiting Communist Vietnam into Cambodia, he had to give the guards his watch for permission to leave Vietnam.

Kan began taking engineering courses, in the evening, at the University of Cincinnati and obtained a degree in Mechanical Engineering. With that degree and experience gained at our company, he moved on to better positions at General Electric's aircraft engine division and other related companies. We still have a friendship and correspond at Christmastime.

St. Thomas Housing Corp.
St. Thomas Episcopal Church in Terrace Park, Ohio, had always been a strong Christian community with charitable outreach to the surrounding region, which led the congregation to get involved in housing for the less fortunate. The St. Thomas Housing Corp. committee evaluated different approaches and efforts. I was asked to be part of the effort and served as vice president. We had groups going to needy people's homes to make repairs. Another group assisted Habitat for Humanity for many years. I helped on a few Habitat houses. Those projects were good and people were involved, but the need was greater and the talent pool we were drawing from were professional white-collar parishioners. The group was led by a very active and capable former Proctor and Gamble executive named Jud Gale. We had developers, architects, engineers, builders, realtors, lawyers, accountants and business people and decided we would undertake an Affordable Housing tax credit project.

Under this Federal program, developers can obtain and sell federal tax credits in order to finance housing for the working poor. Beginning with a $10,000 donation, we obtained and sold tax credits, obtained a State of Ohio housing grant and obtained bank loans to build and operate a one-hundred-unit low-income housing project in Amelia, Ohio, called Thomaston Woods. It was a model that many followed. As of this date, that project has been serving the area for over 30 years.

In order to make the project more helpful to the residents we hired a Social Services Director to assist families with many programs. We had a Community Building with Head Start, Child Care, After School Programs, Homework Room, Swimming Lessons, Neighborhood Watch and Job Training. It was very rewarding to see families grow and prosper. One goal was to enable families to move on to own their own home.

Linda started the Homework Room, which was particularly successful. Many of the children were "latchkey kids," who needed afternoon care and supervision while their parents were at work. What better way to help than having a room staffed by former teachers who would help them get their homework done before they went out to play. The former teachers were Linda and other St. Thomas volunteers.

Several years later we constructed a 13-unit elderly housing facility, called Thomaston Meadows, on a vacant area of the same property. Again, we used federal housing programs and State of Ohio financing. They planted a redbud tree with an adjacent small plaque for my work on this.

The Royal and Ancient Golfers of St. Thomas
About 1991, our rector at St. Thomas, the Reverend Robert Gerhard, had just received a new set of golf clubs as a gift from the parishioners for 25 years of service. Bob had played golf on his day off for years. He offered his old set of clubs to me if I would join him on a regular basis. Previously, I had hit the ball a little, on occasion, when I needed to for business association. But I had little fondness for the game, since I could not really afford the time to play. I worked so many hours that I felt I could not take time from my family for a game that took so much time to play. Time was always a limiting factor in my life, but now I had more time. I accepted and found I really could enjoy the game, the scenic beauty of

The Royal and Ancient Golfers of St. Thomas

the courses and the friendships with the players.

Most of the fellows who played were retired and members of St. Thomas or their friends who gathered weekly on Fridays. Usually there were around 8–12 players and it became a close group. We called the group the Royal and Ancient Golfers of St. Thomas. In December we usually had a Christmas party with spouses at Stump's Boat Club, thanks to Ken Bassett's sponsorship.

We established an annual golf tournament to raise money for a Thomaston Woods Scholarship Fund and raised roughly $10,000 annually for several years. The Scholarship Fund provided educational funding for the low-income residents of Thomaston Woods. The purpose was to help the residents fund additional education to improve their occupational opportunities. We funded college courses at the University of Cincinnati as well as simple short workshops to help people get ahead.

Farming

In about 1972, Chuck and I purchased a farm just north of Owensville, Ohio, about 10 miles east in Clermont County, which we used for weekend retreats. It had a pond for fishing and Chuck bought a big surplus army tent for overnight camping. We had good times there.

Around 1978, we sold that farm and each bought farms much farther to the east in South Central Ohio. The Appalachian Highway, Ohio Route 32 had just opened for good access to this part of Appalachia and the property values were very reasonable. His farm was in Adams County at the end of Hackleshin Road where he recruited a rent-free caretaker, planted corn one year and after that 50,000 Christmas trees, which he marketed under the name Mr. C's Christmas Trees.

I purchased a farm of mostly wooded acreage five miles farther east on Beaver Ridge Road in Pike County, where we intended to build a cabin for weekend retreats. After hiking around and locating a wooded site for a hidden cabin we set up our campsite and had great expectations. This came to a halt when we visited the site a week later and found everything gone. Picnic table, lawn chairs, tools, tarps, lanterns, pots, pans, etc. had all been taken. We then realized that the poverty of our new neighbors was not going to allow our plans to develop in that location or even in that region.

Our good friend Bob Terwillegar had a farm 10 miles south in Adams County, where he had built a pond and cabin. He had experienced some minor theft but nothing compared to our loss. I realized that Bob, who was an excellent schoolteacher, had engaged and interacted with his neighbors and built a rapport of respect. Bob ran summer camps at his farm and got to know his neighbors. Our scout troop spent weekend campouts there. I had no time to do what I knew was Bob's successful approach to the Appalachian culture.

We used our farm for hiking and weekend day trips which we enjoyed and sold it about 5 years later, in 1983.

Travel

As a family we traveled quite a bit and enjoyed seeing the country and many parts of the world. I'll let Linda expand on our travels. Here are a few pictures.

Canadian Rockies

Picton, Ontario, Canada

Malibu, California 2004

Haddeland cousin Norway 2015

Utah 2015

Canada fishing with Don Brown

Part 5: My Story

McCoys and Michigan

Industrial Air had a sales representative, Alan McCoy, in Detroit, Michigan, with whom we became very good friends. They had vacation property up north in Michigan and invited us to visit with them or use the place by ourselves. They owned an old one-room schoolhouse, which always was in varying states of repair, just northeast of Grayling, Michigan. We got permission to use their schoolhouse for the first time, on a trip north in the winter to test out the skiing. We arrived in the evening during a snowstorm, parked on the road and dragged our bags and kids in. The one big room was quite what we expected, but did have some interesting features. One side was lined with beds and we quickly remembered that the McCoys had six children. The rest of the room was occupied by a large, round table surrounded by eight chairs and a large potbellied stove and a crib. The entry area by the front door had been turned into a small one-person kitchen. The bathroom was an outside outhouse and, of course, unheated. We turned on the electric blankets on the beds we picked to use and fired up the potbellied stove to glowing red. It was still cold in there. This was around 1971 or 1972 when Paula, our youngest, was about two. She was put in the crib, just far enough from the stove that she could not touch it. We crawled into bed and slept.

The next morning, we awoke to see that the perimeter of the room was about an inch deep in snow that had sifted in through the walls during the night. But all was well. When we got outside that morning we saw our car buried by a passing snowplow, which took quite a while to dig out, after we dug a path to it through the two feet of snow. We ventured into Grayling for some provisions and discovered a church rummage sale where we outfitted the family with skis, boots and poles, all for under $100. Back to the schoolhouse we went to try our skill at the sport of skiing on the hill beside the schoolhouse. We carried the skis up the hill, put them on and slid down the hill with varying degrees of success, but it was great learning experience and we really enjoyed ourselves. After that experience we were quite smitten with enjoying Michigan in winter.

Later, Al McCoy inherited another cabin from his father who previously would not let Al and his tribe of six kids use the place for fear of damage from rug rats rummaging through his home. They invited us to join them after Christmas for several years, during which our families became close with many memorable experiences. Their cabin is a two-story log structure with a wonderful fireplace which everyone gathered around in friendly conversation and community. Al's father was part of a group of 35 families that bought 10,000 acres of clear-cut timbered land just west of Otsego Lake back in the 1930s. They created two lakes and each family got a homesite around one of the lakes. They later sold about half the property and still retain half. It is a wonderful property and Al and Ruth now live there year-round. In the years we visited with them, we would usually arrive in the dark and it was difficult to find the correct snow-covered gravel drive. Several times we had to park and hike the last mile through the snow in the dark. One time I was ready to break into another cabin for shelter for my family when I saw off through the woods the light from the McCoy's cabin. It was always a sense of accomplishment and relief when we arrived. Our visits included skiing, skating, and hunting and talking about the fan business. We certainly enjoyed our visits to the McCoy's cabin — and still do.

The Cabin–(the Twig House)
After visiting with the McCoys several times in Michigan, we became interested in a vacation home there of our own and began exploring various areas for a possible location. We liked Charlevoix for the lake and proximity to ski areas. We rented in Charlevoix during vacations for three years, enjoyed the area, and began looking at property. We finally settled on our log cabin on Oyster Bay of Lake Charlevoix. It is a little ironic that one of the properties we first looked at and thought was a dump ended up our final choice. The roof leaked, the bathroom was a mess, the wiring was just plain dangerous. The place needed work, but in the end we liked the location, it was affordable, priced right and fixable.

We closed the purchase by mail in November 1984 and came up for the first time in the middle of a snowstorm after Christmas. The snow was beautiful, we had a great time and I think back to that first visit in our own cabin with every winter snowstorm we experience here.

Our fun time changed drastically one year later when the water rose to flood the cabin. The water had been rising in the lakes and was cause for concern, but we were told it just goes up and down all the

time. I came up with some friends to fish and enjoy a long weekend, but arrived to see three inches of water in the cabin. My friends went fishing while I started calling contractors to build a dike. The dike with pumps removed the water, but we needed to find a real solution or abandon the place. We had a house mover raise the log structure 5-½ feet and filled the lot to the level of the dyke. During the raising, all the interior walls were removed and the contractor, Milan Pylsek, called to see how we wanted to rearrange the interior. Linda and I came up to meet with him on a zero-degree day and we could not agree on where to put the interior walls. After probably 20 minutes of heated discussion, Milan got frustrated with us and told us he was going for coffee and would meet us there when we finally got it together. Well, we did finally agree and went for coffee with Milan at the restaurant, where we drew our floor plan on a paper napkin for him to follow. He did a wonderful job. Managing property and remodeling from a distance of 508 miles away is challenging.

Many more changes have been made over the years to the cabin as we called it. Our granddaughter, Frances, at about age four, labeled it the "Twig House." For such a little girl to label a 12-inch log a twig surprised us but nobody had a better name. It still is the Twig House!

Change
The economic recession of 1984 through 1986 hit our business hard. Our industrial customers did not do much capital spending during recessions when they didn't know what the future would bring. So our sales fell dramatically. We had to lay people off to survive. At that time, we had about 200 employees and we cut back to 70. People who had worked for us for over 10 years lost their jobs. I had to let go all of the key employees whom we had recruited over the recent few years to grow the business. We cut both salaried and hourly employees and yet we were still losing money. I was under severe stress and could not see much more that could be done until the economy recovered. I remember thinking then of how my grandfather Smith must have felt during the Depression when the Derby Silver Company closed its doors.

On top of all this, due to the stress, I developed a pinched nerve in my neck which was very painful and created numbness in my left arm and hand. My doctor sent me for spinal tests and they recommended surgery. The operation was successful and I had immediate relief. After a short recovery, I went back to work as much as I could. But I quickly realized I could not continue to work and also have a healing recovery. I took a medical leave and my brother Charles (Chuck as we called him) returned to run the business.

After about six months I had decompressed, healed and was ready to get working again. Chuck asked that I wrap up the two subdivisions, which he had started under our Smith Real Estate Co. We had felt that the manufacturing business should be responsible for the assets that they utilized and therefore we had made Industrial Air pay rent for their use of the factory building and property to Smith Real Estate Co. Smith Real Estate Co. in turn invested in two farm properties which we intended to develop into residential subdivisions. Chuck had begun roadbuilding but had put it on hold to return to run Industrial Air. So, I commenced where Chuck had stopped. I was the bulldozer and backhoe operator, moving dirt and spreading gravel. I dug in the underground electrical and the telephone lines. For the next year and a half, I worked at Hickory Hill just east of Newtown, Ohio, and at Williamsburg Estates near Williamsburg, Ohio, grading the roadbeds and drainage ditches and then contracting the paving work to complete the two projects. And then I worked with realtors to sell the parcels to residential customers.

Chuck saved Industrial Air. How exactly he did it I still don't know, but his legal, business and accounting skills and ability to see a bigger picture certainly were in effect. I had done most of the personnel reduction which tore me up, but he did the real hard cost cutting and saw it through. After his running the business for two years, we both agreed that we had had enough of the industrial manufacturing field and decided to sell the company. I knew I could not stand the stress anymore, even though I loved the product and the industrial marketplace. And he wanted to invest in other, more profitable, ventures. It is probably a good thing also, since he suffered a heart attack during the sale negotiation process. Fortunately, I was able to step in for a short few meetings to keep the sale moving. Chuck recovered and returned. We completed the sale in December 1984, and Industrial Air became a mixed memory for us. I still missed it but knew I could not return to it.

Energizer
One division of the company that the buyer did not purchase was Energizer. No, not the battery company, but the name is the same. Energizer was an air-to-air heat exchanger product we had acquired which was for residential furnaces and industrial applications. I took the pieces of the division and moved them to a small rented facility and organized the business to operate it until it could be sold. Our son, Blake, joined me and ran the manufacturing shop. He did a great job operating the shop, but the product sales were very erratic. Within about a year we sold the business. I took a small deposit and a note for the business but the buyer went bankrupt in his other main business and never paid us for the assets he purchased.

A Different Work Setting
After selling Industrial Air and Energizer, I invested with varying degrees of success in the stock market and in small buildings wherever I found a bargain. After 23 years in the manufacturing business, I wanted to do something different. I did not want to deal with

the stress of managing employees and the variable industrial equipment market. My plan was to find distressed buildings which I could rehabilitate and lease out to develop a rental income stream.

Old Milford Building
My first acquisition was a 130-year-old hand-hewn log frame building at 233–235 Main Street in Milford, Ohio, an adjacent village to Terrace Park. I rehabbed the building and rented it out, hiring our son, Blake, to replace the old siding. It was quite a change from running a manufacturing company with 200 employees and 150 independent sales representatives to repairing plaster, woodwork and electrical wiring. I found I really enjoyed it and I had time to enjoy life a bit.

Royal Pines Apartments
With all that experience on Thomaston Woods, a few of us, including Jud Gale, Rick Hosea, Brynn Walden and Vernon Frierson, decided to do our own affordable housing tax credit project. We purchased an existing apartment complex of 94 units and remodeled the two buildings, obtained and sold the tax credits for the financing. The result was good. The apartments were affordable for low-income tenants and we made a nickel for all our work.

Rose Hill Apartments
Brynn Walden and I became partners on another apartment project which Brynn had been managing for the owner who wanted to sell. Rose Hill is in an older section of Cincinnati that at one time was a very wealthy upscale neighborhood. The 26 apartments were very large with solariums, fireplaces, beautiful Rookwood tile work, and even butler's pantries. The basement had storage rooms and laundry rooms. The 4th floor attic had bedrooms where the servants had lived. We remodeled the apartments, turned the entire complex into condominiums, with an owners' association, and sold the units. It was a fun project.

New Zealand
Since Brynn was a partner in some of these real estate projects, I got to know him fairly well. Brynn was a native New Zealander who came to America and was active in developing rental apartment projects. He had a team of construction workers who were quite good at rehabbing old buildings and as above noted we worked together on a few projects. I basically was an investing partner but did get involved from a design and engineering perspective without pay. Brynn had a brother, Chris Walden, who lived in Middletown, Ohio, was a wildlife artist and active in wildlife conservation. As such, he promoted and led a team of wildlife artists on naturalist tours to the north island of New Zealand. In about 1990, Linda

and I joined one of his two-week trips and then extended the trip on our own for two more weeks on the southern island of New Zealand. The part of the trip with Chris was wonderful and included offshore fishing, Maori cultural events and of course visits to several very unique wildlife preserves. The two-week excursion, on our own to the South Island, centered on Christchurch and ventured out in all directions from there. The whole experience reminded us of the United States back when life was simpler and small towns were viable. I was so taken by the fishing that I recruited a friend, Don Brown, and his nephew, Mason, to take another trip there two years later, just for the fishing. We fished and fished, mostly releasing, but keeping enough for dinner. Fabulous trips to a great country.

Ingalls Bldg. Co.
My financial goal at this time was to develop a group of commercial rental properties that would provide income and long-term growth in value. Blake was working with me to find properties and the plan was that he wanted to get into the management side of it as I got more into a retirement mode and was only an investor. We looked at many buildings all over Cincinnati and northern Kentucky. We settled on the historic Ingalls Building, a 100-year-old, 16-story office building at 4th and Vine Streets in downtown Cincinnati. It was the first highrise concrete building in the United States. It was a great building, solid concrete and in a great location. The problem was we paid too much, it was almost vacant and the downtown office rental market was terrible. We listened to the realtors brag about how easily they could find us tenants and did not know the market ourselves. I broke a cardinal rule my father had taught me—"Never invest in anything you don't understand." Linda advised me not to get into it. The engineer in me got enamored with the historic architecture and possible potential of the building and I purchased the building. We did not understand the downtown office market. We struggled with it for about 5 years and I finally gave it up to the company that held the mortgage. The Ingalls building was the most grievous and costly business mistake of my life. It was equally devastating for

**Ingalls Building
Cincinnati, Ohio**

Blake who worked tirelessly trying to make a go of it. The building has since been sold a few times and is now becoming a Marriott Hotel.

Antrim Bldg. Co.

When in Charlevoix I became acquainted with Bob Kern, a local real estate agent, who had originally lived in Dayton, Ohio. Bob was my age and a former Air Force officer, so we had some things in common. He knew his way in the commercial real estate business and led me to several good investments which of course gave him commissions. We purchased the Judy's Restaurant property at Antrim and State Streets. Remodeling the building there and leasing it worked out well. I labeled my new company Antrim Building Company after this property. Then he led me to an old house on South Bridge Street which we remodeled and leased for office use. He later advised me well on the timing to sell those two buildings.

Bob and Joyce Kern joining us out to dinner.

Bob's Real Estate One office operated out of Charlevoix and he wanted another office in East Jordan, about 10 miles away on the South Arm of Lake Charlevoix. He offered me a deal where if I bought this building, he would lease it from me. Well, how could any investor in real estate pass up a deal like that. I bought the building and he leased it. Several years later he decided to close the office and he sold the

East Jordan Bldg., Real Estate One Office, Now a BC Pizza Restaurant

building for me. Bob was a good friend with good instincts in real estate.

In the mid-1990s, Bob brought a deal on a large vacant building on the north side of Charlevoix that had formerly been a manufacturing facility for Weather-shield where they previously manufactured multiple products including gun cases and automotive seat covers. I bought the building on a land contract and began dividing it up to rent to smaller tenants. Bob was my rental agent and was very successful at bringing in tenants. The front offices were rented as offices and the rear area was divided into self-storage spaces. I was trained mainly as an engineer, but had been a small business person all my life. This venture I labeled as the Charlevoix Commercial Center and I consider it the best business investment I was ever in. It was my last business and the last property sold when I finally decided to retire at age 75.

Retirement and SCORE
I always enjoyed working and applied myself to whatever the job was. It was expected by my employer or by my family and I felt obligated and happy to comply. Beginning at around age 12 with selling garden produce and newspaper routes, to running a manufacturing company with 200 employees, to being a sole proprietor investor in rental real estate and all the other ventures along the way, I feel blessed with the opportunities. Except for my time on college co-op jobs with large corporations and my time in the Air Force I always worked for or owned a small business. Small business is not for the weak. Either working for or being the owner requires a certain mindset and dedication if the business is to be successful and benefit all involved. It takes a team, and after you move on you miss the many fine people with whom you've crossed paths. And after officially retiring I still miss the challenge and the activity. I missed not being in business and wanted to be involved in some way.

In a conversation with Bill Hicklen at Christ Episcopal Church he talked about being involved in SCORE. SCORE is organized under the Small Business Administration and originally stood for Service Corp of Retired Executives. I joined up and became part of a wonderful, quite talented group of individuals from all types of businesses who counseled small business owners on how to start and operate their companies. I learned a lot that I didn't know, even though I had been a small business person for most all of my working years, and I worked quite hard with SCORE for about 5 years–learning and giving. The counseling and seminars we provided guided many entrepreneurs in their endeavors to be successful and earn a nickel. The activity was good for me, helped others and satisfied my withdrawal pains from no longer being in business,

Cabin Addition
In 2000 we did a major addition to the cabin. It only had one bedroom after the raising in 1986 and that remodeling project. Any visitors slept on roll-out beds and cots in the main open area. So, we added a real bedroom wing with two bedrooms and an additional bath and a much nicer entry hall with a grand front porch. To accomplish this, we had the garage picked up and relocated, which was an interesting part of the project. The result was just what we needed to more adequately house ourselves and guests. In subsequent years when our grandkids spent much of the summer with us it worked out well.

After we added on to the cabin in 2000, we had room to invite guests to visit. Great golf courses are abundant in Northern Michigan and so for several years I invited a group of four to eight players to come up to stay four days and play golf, usually in September. We called it the Northwest Michigan Invitational Tournament. Leaving at around 5 or 6 a.m. we could play a course on the way up from Cincinnati, play three more days and then drive back. Needless to say, these were avid golfers and we were exhausted by the last day. We played all the great courses in the area and it was a challenging task to check out the various courses and schedule the tee times, gather the food, etc.

We even had golf-driving contests afterward. These contests were associated with a few drinks and bragging as to who could drive a golf ball across Oyster Bay. Nobody won, as the distance was too great, but there are many golf balls for someone to retrieve from the bottom of Oyster Bay on Lake Charlevoix. Of course, there were prizes, side wagers, and a few arguments as well, but I think it was a memorable outing for all who attended. I certainly enjoyed every minute of the event.

From left: R & A golfers in Michigan
Chuck Smith, Don Brown, Bob Cunningham, Mike Getz, Ed Haushalter, Lee Cole, myself, Bob Lowery

Downtown

In 2007, after 10 years of downsizing, we sold our home of 40 years in Terrace Park and moved to downtown Cincinnati — to try city living and a simpler lifestyle. Rather than commit to purchasing a condominium, we decided to rent for a few years and see how we enjoyed the city. We rented a double-sized unit in the Phelps Building on East Fourth Street with 3 bedrooms, and a tenth-floor view of Lytle Park and the Ohio River. We were within walking distance of shopping, restaurants, banks, library, museums and ball parks. We enjoyed our time there. After two years, the Phelps announced that they were converting the building into a Marriott Hotel and everyone must vacate.

The Phelps Apts.
Our 10th floor apartment was in upper left corner of the picture

We found another apartment building next door, at the 550 Building, for considerably higher rent and only a second-floor location, but, we enjoyed our time there for the next year.

Charlevoix

After that year, we did some evaluation and realized we were spending more time in Michigan at our cabin than we were in the expensive apartment. So, we made the big decision to move to the cabin full time and

550 Apts.
We had a 2nd floor unit on the right corner of the picture

make visits back to Cincinnati and other places as we wished. The tax savings alone would pay for considerable travel. Downsizing again, we sold our second car and reduced our remaining stuff to that which fit into a large U-Haul trailer. We hauled it to Charlevoix, Michigan, on New Year's Eve 2010, arriving on an unusually warm, snowless evening, which was perfect for driving. The next day, New Year's, a snowstorm hit in full force, but we were snuggly settled and resting before the fireplace.

Little did we think when we bought the cabin in 1984, that we would ever retire here. And even when we added on in 2000, little did we envision living here full time. But here we were. It was a transition that we've enjoyed but had many surprises. I'm a projects type of person, always looking for things to do to improve a situation, and I found many things to do. Previously when we came up in the winter it was for a very short visit to ski and enjoy the snow. The baseboard electric heating system was adequate, but it was expensive to operate over a longer period of habitation. Our first month's electric bill was $880. So, we installed a new high-efficiency heat pump system. Our car was a front-wheel-drive minivan which proved touchy in getting up the hill in the snow, so an all-wheel-drive vehicle was purchased. And so it went on with many such projects. People who grow up here in northern climates know all these things and I thought I did too, but there is always more to learn.

Our time at our home here on Lake Charlevoix has been most pleasant. People make many different choices for vacation and retirement locations and many shake their head when they hear we came here to retire. Why up in the cold north? Why not where your friends and family are? Life takes many twists and turns. One factor is that we love our spot on the water and the different seasons that bring us very different views. Winter is very bleak with no one around, but the views of the frozen lake and the snow on the evergreens are magnificent, especially on a sunny day after a snowstorm. Spring is late coming but as in all areas the new plant life springing up brings cheers, and we additionally have the ducks, loons, geese and swans returning to make life interesting. And then, the spring is a needed time of preparation for when all those friends and relatives who questioned our sanity for being here, suddenly decide that Charlevoix is a nice place to visit in the summer. Charlevoix population triples in the summer months, the restaurants get crowded, the boat traffic is heavy and Oyster Bay is frolicking with boat rafting parties—all of which we love to watch from our front deck. The fall is the very best with peace and quiet again as the leaves change to so much more brilliant colors than ever seen in Cincinnati. Also, fall shows us the large flocks of geese passing through on their way south along with the "Snowbirds."

Part 5: My Story

Visitors and Roma and Bea
Living in a resort area brings you many visitors over the years and we invite and enjoy them whenever they come. Two regular visitors for years were Roma and Bea Casey, our granddaughters from New York City. They came every summer for about 10 years and attended a day camp, and we enjoyed their company for several weeks. They made some

friends, but I think we and they became very close from their visits. In their first visit and experience here, Linda walked Bea and Roma up our drive which meanders through a large evergreen woods. We live three miles from town. Bea kept asking if they were in the woods yet, and Roma remarked that she hadn't seen a taxi since they got there. Relaxing, nature walks, swimming, boating and skiing are big up here and I think they learned quite a bit about all of that during their time here. They know the water and the woods now and enjoy their visits.

Our grandson, Andrew, visited most summers with his parents and ended up going to Central Michigan University to finish his degree in history. He now lives in Petoskey, Michigan, and has become as much a Michigander as we are. Needless to say, we are delighted to see him periodically. He helps with chores and he likes a free meal along with use of our coin-free laundry machines.

My Big Brother
My brother, Charles R. Smith, or "Chuck," or "Chas R" as we called him, and I have always had a good relationship together. He is two years older, taller, smarter and was always very focused in what he was doing. Even as children, he was the one with ideas (good or bad) and new interesting ventures.

I usually seemed to follow and got into the mechanics of making things work. At times I got to lead, as with Industrial Air. But we worked together and accomplished many successful ventures with paper routes, farming, manufacturing and property development. We both had our successes and our failures. Some of these I have described, but it would take another book to discuss them all in detail. See more about Chuck in Appendix A.

Christ Church Charlevoix
Previously, when in Charlevoix we occasionally would attend Christ Episcopal Church, but now that we are here year-round, we have become more active and involved. Linda got into women's groups and activities. I served as an usher, a term on the Vestry and a few committees. Later on, I was co-chair of a committee to build a columbarium which turned out very nice. The church is active with serious outreach programs and various people work very hard to make and keep it so. The dedication of many at Christ Church provides a very welcoming atmosphere to the many summer residents as well as newcomers, such as ourselves. We feel blessed to have found such a faith-filled, caring Christian community for our new church home.

Last Thoughts
I could ramble on here for several pages, but meaningful thoughts must be more concise.

Part 5: My Story

We all are formed by our God, family, environment and peers. Some of this we have a say or a choice in.

We all have a God of some kind to give us morals, orientation and direction, or we think we are self-made and infallible — and eventually flounder. God has given me an understanding that something much larger than ourselves has created the universe and all in it. My Christian faith has given me a moral compass with ten commandments to guide my behavior, and an understanding of forgiveness, when I recognize how I fall short. My faith in God is like an ocean tide coming and going depending upon how diverted and preoccupied I become with secular events and things. But my belief in God and faith in Jesus are always there to some degree. I believe God created us as individuals to make choices and decisions on how to live our lives and to live with the rewards and the consequences. The growing lack of understanding for the need of religion and spiritual guidance in our country disturbs me greatly.

Our families have a major influence in our lives. I was fortunate to have been brought up in a wholesome, caring family who gave me direction and support, but with expectations of behavior and performance. This I feel is a major factor in my outcome. The sum of my young experiences created building blocks for the future, just as we gain more knowledge each year in school built upon what we learned in previous classes. Our home and neighborhood environment has a great deal to do to with who we are as adults. I feel very blessed to have grown up in 20th century middle-class America. But the country is changing. The growing number of dysfunctional families in our country is allowing more children to grow up without parental care and direction. This disturbs me greatly.

The United States, as a country, is said to be capitalistic. Having been a small business person for many years I am ingrained to that fact. It has built the country and provided an economy which the world has envied. In my experience, I have seen many businesses succeed and others fail for which there are many reasons. Ingenuity, planning, hard work and dedication are required for success and many do not understand or appreciate that need. I wish the schools and colleges would recognize and support the need for hands-on small-business education, so more Americans can be self-employed and masters of their own future.

There has probably always been an influence by business and union persons in the affairs of government, with expected paybacks of favors from government. This is wrong, anti-capitalistic and destroys the fabric of the free-enterprise system. Small businesses are the backbone of the system by their creation of new, growing ventures and the resulting jobs added. Small businesses usually do not engage in the practice of milking the government, and are more often the victim of government regulation. Government sponsored or favored business activity, other than in emergencies, is not capitalism and usually ends up

Part 5: My Story

hurting the average citizen.

    Relationships between people are strange phenomena. Sometimes nice, friendly and peaceful, while other times ugly, hateful and warlike. As I have researched our family for this book, I find we fit right in the mold of human activity. Probably not any better nor worse. And, of course, that is to be expected since we all are one large family in this world. My parting words are—Love your neighbors as yourselves for we are all family. I'll leave The Last Word for Linda.

Part 6

The Last Word

Linda really isn't into writing about herself, so this is a collaborative effort between us.

Linda Knoop (1939–) m Watson Christen Smith (1936–)

Linda Knoop was born on November 25, 1939, at the Kentucky Baptist Hospital in Louisville, Kentucky. At the time my parents lived on Cornell Place in the Crescent Hill section of Louisville near where my mother had grown up.

During WWII, my father worked at Bowman Field as a civilian employee for the military, which qualified us to live in a government housing project called Fincastle Heights. While there, at age 3 or 4 years, I remember, as one of my first memories, walking outside on a sidewalk by myself as being a wonderful experience.

Another early memory is of my mother holding an old earthenware bowl in the crook of her arm and stirring up cake batter for a birthday cake. Cake mixes were not used much at that time and things were made from scratch. I still have the bowl, which dates back to the 1800s. It originally belonged to a neighbor that my mother referred to as "Miz Hershey." All the women in my family, Mother, my aunts and my

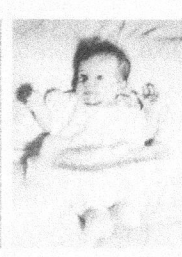

older cousins, were very good cooks. But, I do remember my cousin Peggy made their first cake from a store-bought cake mix and my aunts enjoying their first taste of a box cake and saying — "mmm, pretty good."

When I was 3 to 6, my mother was very sick with subacute bacterial endocarditis, a very rare disease which was incurable at that time. She was in the hospital for long stays. My father had to work. My brother, Paul, went to school. I had to go live with my Aunt Susie Redman and I wasn't happy. Susie wasn't mean, but just not nice as I recall. But who could blame her? She had already raised two children who were adults by then. During some of mother's hospital stays I lived with my Aunt Christine and Uncle Jake whom I liked better.

My mother's illness was so severe at this time that they had to hire a woman to do ironing for us. Her name was Olla, she was the only black person I had ever met. Once, when Olla was there, my brother and I were being punished for something or other and confined to our upstairs bedrooms. Dickie Bennett, a friend of my brother, Paul, came into our backyard and called up to us. We decided that we could trade comic books with him. We tied all of my hair ribbons together to make a rope and used it to lower all our comic books down to Dickie. But, before Dickie could get his comics up to us, Olla started laughing so hard my mother caught on to our activity and put an end to it, leaving us with no comic books.

We never got spanked for anything, only sent to our room for punishment. The worst thing I remember happening was when my brother got a BB gun that he had wanted forever. The first day he had it he shot me in the leg and I ran home crying. The BB gun went into the rubbish. To this day I feel badly about being such a crybaby and telling on him. It couldn't have hurt that much, and he took it so hard.

Fortunately, penicillin helped my mother and then when I was about 10, she was cured by a new streptomycin drug, developed during the war. She returned home and lived to be 98. I got to come home also.

I have an early memory of walking on a downtown sidewalk with my parents when I was about 12 years old, and my father leaving us to go across the street to talk with a man. Our mother said nothing about it and my father returned back across the

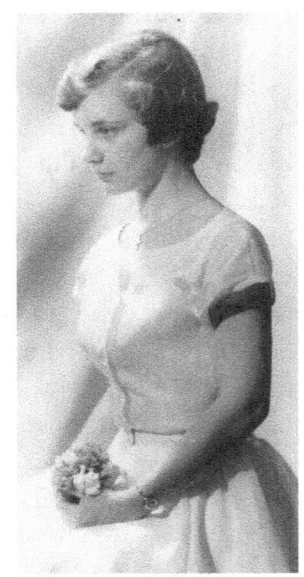

Linda's church confirmation picture

street and said nothing. Later on, mother told us it was our grandfather, William James Knoop, whom my father had thrown out of the house years before for philandering and bringing home a disease to my grandmother which caused her death. My grandfather William Knoop was estranged from the family, and my other grandparents had died before I was born, so I never got to meet, know and enjoy any of my grandparents.

Just about our favorite relatives were our Uncle Paul Hund and his wife, Peenie. She was a nurse and they always used last names. Hers was Penick which got shortened to "Peenie." They had no children of their own and were especially good to us. My brother was named for Uncle Paul and we named our daughter Paula after my brother. So now Paul(a) is the third generation of that name in the family.

My parents were very strong Missouri Synod Lutherans and we went to Concordia Lutheran Church at the upper end of Broadway every Sunday. We attended the church's Concordia Lutheran Day School from first through eighth grade. My first-grade teacher was a young man named Mr. Like and all I remember of that year was spending an inordinate amount of time playing house under the teacher's desk with my friend Sue Hurst. After Mr. Like, and probably in the second grade, my father's young cousin, Loretta Knoop, taught us, and if I cried I was excused from almost anything. From third grade up through eighth grade I had men for my teachers, and gone were the tears and house play. Pastor Eberhard and Mr. Rice took a much more serious view of education and I became a good student.

Concordia provided a very good, solid education. However, we had to leave early in the morning and take two city buses to get to the school at the church in downtown Louisville by 8 a.m. Some of our neighbor's children, Sue and Larry Hurst, also went to Concordia because it was such a good school. My brother, Paul, was two years older than I was, and so in charge of all of us and we had to mind him. We did and he did a good job, especially on the buses which were full of city school kids. The city school kids teased us and would have frightened us had it not been for Paul, who stood up for us. One of our transfers was at Eighth and Broadway where we stood under the awning of a drugstore and ate candy we bought there while we waited. Sometimes we would slip into the store to read the comic books without buying them — until we got caught.

At school we had pageants and programs but not plays. For a pageant we dressed in costumes (usually we were draped in dyed lengths of material and held a shepherd's crook or something that symbolized what we represented). We just stood very still, tableaux fashion, while a narrator read the script that corresponded with our scene, from the Bible, of course. For programs, we memorized sections of the text (the Bible, of course), stood in a line with our class and stepped forward when it was our turn to recite. The first graders had one line each, and by the time we were in the eighth grade we were expected to recite whole stanzas. For this I always got a new dress and had my hair curled in rag curlers the night before. I hated the curlers — they hurt. I don't remember anyone ever forgetting their lines. Someone must have, once or twice at least, but I don't recall it.

At the end of the school year, in June, we went on an all-school picnic to Cherokee Park, to a place called "Big Rock." Our mothers fixed the food, we went in cars, stayed all day, and always had our picture taken. My mother saved all these pictures and all my report cards in a box in her closet. I remember what I wore, what we ate, who my boyfriends were at given times, but I do not remember any grades on those report cards. But I did get good grades.

The closest friends I remember from childhood in Fincastle were the Hurst children, Larry and Sue. My brother made a friend named Dickie Bennett. They all grew up in Fincastle.

We spent a good bit of time at my Aunt Christine's, almost every Sunday evening. She was not the oldest of my mother's eleven adult siblings, but she seemed to occupy the position of grandparent. Whenever anyone came from out of town, they stayed at Aunt Christine and Uncle Jake Ossman's. They did not have a large house by any means, but she, Jake and their daughter Evelyn always made room for whomever needed a place to stay. The rest of the family visited them at Christine's so she always had lots of cooking to do. Everyone did pitch in to help, but Christine still had the brunt of the work. I never heard her complain a bit.

After church on Sunday or in the evening, and after we got a car, we would go over to Uncle Jake and Aunt Christine's for dinner. After dinner and maybe watching *One Man's Family*, the women met in the kitchen to talk and the men were in the living room talking. Our cousin, Evelyn, was older and got to talk with the women. My brother and I had to sit on the couch quietly and do nothing. We could not go outside because they had a mean dog named Brownie. I felt so mistreated and was so bored.

My father's closest friend was also his cousin, Herman Stauss. We spent nearly every Friday evening at Herman and Emma Stauss's house in the Highlands of Louisville. I remember Emma as one of the nicest women I've ever known. They had two sons, Stuart and Gerald. My brother, Paul, and the two Stauss boys would go up to their attic bedroom and play all evening. I don't ever remember even seeing the upstairs. Again, I was left to sit on the couch and "read a book."

In addition to the Stausses, my parents saw Stan and Johnnie Pflum every week or so. Mother and Dad always had friends, entertained and went out often. The Pflums were another close cousin of Dad's. They had no children, so once again Paul and I were to sit on the couch and read a book whenever Mom and Dad visited them. We never had a babysitter that I can recall.

Part 6: The Last Word

Saturdays my dad worked a second job at a printing shop and we spent the day getting ready for church the next day. My mother braided my hair so tight that it literally pulled the corners of my eyes. Even my father told her not to pull it so hard. But it would never do for me to look anything but perfect for Sunday School and church the next day. Since we left so early for church there was not time to braid my hair before we left on Sunday morning.

My mother made all my clothes and most of hers. She was such a good seamstress that several of their friend's wives asked her to sew their clothes. This enabled her to make a little money until she was able to get out to work. She also made my wedding dress, which was so beautiful that our daughter Nancy wore it for her wedding also.

Concordia Sunday School had a Christmas pageant every year and the kids all sang Christmas hymns as an appropriate scene was displayed on the stage. The last year I was in school there I was chosen to be Mary. I was so proud even though it meant that, in that part, I couldn't sing the carols with the choir.

My father had a sister, Olivia Knoop, whom we only saw regularly at Concordia Church on Sundays. When church was over, everyone gathered on the walk out front and Olivia stood in one corner and my mother stood in the farthest corner from her. My dad would say, "I'm going over and talk with Pill" (his name for his sister). He would spend five or ten minutes talking with her before we left for home. Dad would take Paul and me to see Olivia at her house several times a year. It was the small house where their family had grown up. My father had given his share of the house to Olivia when their parents died. Olivia was the quintessential old maid; lived in the same house she'd always lived in; worked at the same bank job for forty years; saw the same family members periodically; etc. The only time Olivia was ever in our house was when my brother, Paul, returned from service in the Army in Germany and my parents had a big open house for him. Then suddenly to our surprise, Olivia, late in life, married a man named Joe Kaelin. My mother could not stand Joe, so we saw even less of them after that.

I started high school at Southern High School, but when I was a sophomore I transferred to Eastern High School because my parents built a new house on Primrose Drive in St. Matthews, which was a different section of Louisville. The new house was my parents' dream and my father did a considerable amount of the work himself. He worked very hard on it. It was a modest three-bedroom home with a carport on a nice lot on a quiet street. The family lived there until after I married in 1959.

I knew no one at Eastern High School when I enrolled there and I invited the first girl I met home one day. My parents weren't home and I was to clean up the kitchen. So, I turned the frying pan from breakfast on and we went into my bedroom. The pan caught fire and set the wall by the stove on fire. My new friend left immediately and I never saw her again. I put the fire out, called my father and he came right home from work. I don't recall my father fussing at me at all. The first thing he said was, "Are you alright?" The wall had to be repaired, and ever since then I have been afraid of fires.

I started working at Schiller Hardware, downtown on Market Street, when I was 14 years old. I realized later in life that Mr. Schiller hired me at such a young age in order to help me earn the money for college. My parents didn't have the money to send me to college then. I spent a good bit of time at the Schillers' home because their daughter, Carolyn, was a good friend of mine.

My other close friends in high school were Judy Pullen and Donna Pardo at Eastern High School. I dated some nice boys and went to all the proms and dances. I had a wonderful teacher named Ms. Sarah Moss Phillips, who recognized that I was smart and encouraged me to go on to college. Chris also went to Eastern, but graduated the year before I started there, so we never crossed paths in high school.

During these high school years, I worked at a Kroger store in St. Matthews and at a ladies clothing store, which was much more fun than Kroger's. I also worked later at Maud Hundley's shop. She made clothes and accessories for wealthy and famous people. I got that job because my mother sewed for Maud.

Paul
My brother, Paul, skipped third grade in school and went on to Southern High School, where he graduated at age 15. He then went to Western Kentucky University in Bowling Green, Kentucky, on an Army ROTC scholarship. There he met and married Nettye Jean Brown who was also a chemistry major. They had their first child, Karla Jean Knoop, while they were in college at Western. Paul graduated, received a commission as a 2nd Lieutenant and entered the Army for a 29-year career as an officer. He retired as a full colonel. They had various postings around the United States where we visited them on vacations. They had three more children, Bob, Julie and Lisa.

A happy gathering of the Knoop and Smith kids - from left Lisa Knoop, Karla Knoop, Paula Smith, Julie Knoop (Scott), Bobby Knoop, Nancy Smith and Blake Smith

Part 6: The Last Word

Karla Knoop never married, but has a daughter Kira McKnight, who is planning to marry this year. Bob Knoop and his wife, Karol, have her son and grandson. Julie Knoop married Karl Scott but they have no children. Lisa Knoop and Jason do not have children either, so Paul has only one grandchild and one step-grandson. Paul and Nettye always visited family whenever they had time off.

Nettye died in 2010 after receiving diligent care from Paul through a long illness. Paul remarried in 2014 to Carmen Orr (Merritt). They lived in a retirement community called Patriot's Landing in DuPont, Washington, near Fort Lewis-McCord Joint Military Base, Paul's last posting. Carmen had two daughters and one son from a previous marriage. Carmen died in 2020. See Paul's autobiography in Appendix A.

School

After graduating from Eastern High School in 1957, I went on to Murray State College in Murray, Kentucky. My parents had not been to college and my mother had not graduated from high school, so I don't feel they placed any importance on my going to college as a girl. They had other priorities which they did work very hard on. I only had saved enough for one year and even though I had a job on campus I could not afford a second year. So I transferred to the University of Louisville where I could live at home, work in the university library and take classes, majoring in art and history.

Chris

I also had made friends with a young man named Mac DeHart, who became a fraternity brother of Chris's and introduced me to Chris at a fraternity football game. Chris and I started dating after that introduction and were pinned and later engaged. We went to Cleveland to visit his folks at the end of his senior year. The Smiths lived in a large Tudor-style house in Shaker Heights. Chris's mother, Carolyn, was rather shy, but they became good friends with their next-door neighbors, the Hodoskys. Mrs. Hodosky got Carolyn into the local garden club and introduced the

Smiths to other neighbors, so they had a nice social life while in Shaker Heights.

Chris went out west to Oregon to begin his military service and I stayed in Louisville to plan our wedding. By fall Chris had enough leave time accumulated that he could return to Louisville and we were married on December 26, 1959, at Concordia Lutheran Church in Louisville, Kentucky.

Our reception was at my parents' home, and we flew west to honeymoon a few days in San Francisco before driving up north to the snow country of Klamath Falls, Oregon. San Francisco still is a great place for us to visit. We especially enjoy the tourist things such as the cable cars, Fisherman's Wharf and Chinatown.

Oregon
Kingsley Field was the base where Chris was stationed in Klamath Falls, Oregon. It was a new base and all the officers' quarters were good size. We had a three-bedroom house with government furniture for the two and half years we were there. It was a nice house for us because many of our family came to visit us. Also, once we had a terrible storm and lost our electricity and heat. We had a fireplace and logs so we had many of the non-commissioned officers' wives in to stay warm by the fire until the Base Engineers were able to restore the heat in all the housing units.

In the fall of 1960, Chris was sent to a school for training at Wright Patterson Air Force Base near Dayton, Ohio, for a couple of months. I went with him, and Blake was born at the Air Force Base Hospital in Fairborn, Ohio. We spent Christmas with my parents in Louisville and then drove west across the country back to Oregon with Blake in a portable baby bed in the back seat.

We lived next door to Rosemary and Claude Blanch. Rosemary and I became good friends. They were the first Mormons I had ever met. They had their sixth child shortly after we moved in. They had all boys. Claude was a pilot and was gone quite a bit. And even when he was home, he never did anything to help with the kids or around the house. Claude was a hunter and whenever he shot a deer, he'd bring it home and hang it in the garage for Rosemary to dress, butcher and skin–the whole nine yards. She was treated like the women in the 19th century might have been treated, but she didn't complain and somehow developed into a strong, self-reliant person with a strong faith and capacity to enjoy her life.

Later it was found that, unbeknownst to anyone, Claude had been having an affair for years. When he was transferred overseas, he took the woman with him and left Rosemary with now seven children (they finally had a daughter) in Utah where they were then living. At the divorce hearing the judge made a special restitution for Rosemary by making Claude buy from Rosemary all of his prize premium firearms, hunting and fishing equipment.

Rosemary still had to go to work to support her children, including each of the boys' year-long mission trips for the Mormon Church. How she managed to do all this I don't know. She was a strong woman. Rosemary finally remarried to an older man and all the kids made it through college ok. Claude came back occasionally to visit the kids and Rosemary accepted this as if nothing had happened. Rosemary and I stayed in contact for many years.

After we married and were in Oregon, my parents built a new two-bedroom brick home next to Aunt Christine and Uncle Jake at 212 Fenley Avenue in Crescent Hill. These were very happy years for them. They also saw Christine and Jake almost daily.

Kingsley Field where we were stationed in the Air Force was a small base, but the family housing area where we lived was a few miles away with no shopping or anything but farms and views of the mountains in the distance. I naturally got to know several of the neighbor wives: Rosemary Blanch, Joan Collins, Marilyn Johnson, Marge Oliver and Darlene Maxwell. Darlene was president of the Officer Wives Club and somehow got me elected as Vice President. I don't remember much of what we did except organize occasional parties at the Officer's Club.

When Chris got out of the Air Force, he received an engineering job offer in Cincinnati. We returned east and settled in a small house on Park Avenue in Terrace Park, a small village in the eastern suburbs of Cincinnati. Nancy was born while we lived there.

Chris's Parents
Chris's parents lived in the Shaker Heights section of Cleveland when we married, but they moved to Cincinnati after the purchase of the Industrial Air business in 1963. They bought a large one-floor brick home in 1964 on Tupelo Lane in the village of Indian Hill which

was the next suburb to where we lived in Terrace Park.

Chris's mother developed cancer and died in 1966 after a year of illness. Chris's mother had a sister, Marcia Kaddeland (Dreisbach) who worked in Washington on the staff of Congressman Herlong from Florida. Her personality and lifestyle were as different from Carolyn's as they ever could be. Marcia visited us for Thanksgiving for a number of years. She was great fun and always knew the latest scoop from Washington since she worked for the Congressman. Marcia had two sons, Bill and Jim, and we usually visit with Bill and his wife, Susan, when in New York City.

A year later, Chris's father, Charles, got in touch with a woman he had dated in college, Eleanor Richmond. She still lived at the same address and had the same phone number and car license plate number. They married within a year and began traveling together with several trips to Europe.

About 1968 we moved to 611 Floral Avenue in Terrace Park. This was a little larger home and served us well for many years with various add-ons and remodeling. Paula was born while we lived there.

University of Cincinnati
After Blake and Nancy were in school, I found time on my hands and decided to take classes at the University of Cincinnati and possibly finish my college degree. If I could not get a babysitter, I took Paula to class with me. I soon developed a friend and classmate, Trina. They lived near the University and Trina's mom would babysit Paula for me. I took day and night classes to get the classes and credits I needed. I graduated from the University of Cincinnati in 1974 with a degree in history and education, which included one year of student teaching. Chris and the children came to my graduation and were supportive. I was disappointed that my parents did not come to my graduation. They were supportive in many things, but I was hurt by their lack of understanding that I needed and desired an education. Looking back, I think my degree moved me away from my parents in some way. At least it felt that way.

Seven Hills Schools
We enrolled Paula in a preschool program at Seven Hills School to get her started, but also so I would be able to do my student teaching while all the kids were in school. It was through this that I found a teaching job there. I taught 6th grade at their Lotspeich School with a teaching partner, John Demoe, for several years. Then I moved over to the High School for a few years before going back to Lotspeich for a few more years with Judy Flanagan as my teaching partner. I worked very hard to be a good teacher and feel I succeeded at serving my students well. Before leaving school each day, I would have the next

day's lesson plan completed and setting on my desk, in case for some reason I was not there the next day. I worked evenings and was up at 5 a.m. most days to work on school plans and projects. All totaled I taught at Seven Hills about 15 years, from 1975 through 1991 and received a commemorative chair upon retiring. I thoroughly enjoyed teaching and after retiring I volunteered as a classroom assistant in the Cincinnati Public Schools for several years. I had several reasons for retiring after only 15 years. The stress of the hard work took a toll on me and we wanted to spend more time up north at the cabin. Plus, our children were then out of college and our expenses were less demanding. Mainly, I needed a break and wanted to do other things.

Teacher Linda's Seven Hills school picture

One special memory about Seven Hills was their annual 6th grade trip to Camp Innisfree in Michigan at Pyramid Point within the Sleeping Bear Dunes National Lakeshore. Gus and Paula Leinbach, owners and operators of Camp Innisfree, ran the camp for environmental education. They did a wonderful job of handling the children and educating them in how to understand, respect and enjoy nature, the outdoors and the environment.

Another special memory is a "Time Line" Project I had the children work up. Part of my share of the teaching was history, which was my college major and always an interest. For the time line project, groups of kids in the class would be assigned to create long time lines of events from specific periods of history. We then would assemble these various time lines end-to-end around the classroom and up and down the hallway to the amazement of the other classes. We even talked of continuing it on to the headmaster's office which startled him until he understood what we were doing. The project was a great success. The high school French teacher, whose daughter was in my class, told me that every time she and her daughter talked about history the daughter would look up at the wall to remember where in the time line was the period they were talking about.

Paula went to Seven Hills School tuition-free or with reduced tuition because I taught there. She went with part of her class to Russia in the 8th grade in 1983. Most private schools sent their students to France. But Seven Hills had a connection to Russia through a teacher whose father was a U.S. diplomat there. They flew to Paris, stayed a day or two, then flew on to Moscow for their visit and returned back through Paris to the USA. It was very educational for her.

Rosetta

My mother's sister, Rosetta, was married to a Presbyterian minister and career Army Chaplain, John Rhea. They had a daughter, Judie, who was a year or so older than I. The Rheas didn't live in Louisville much except when Uncle John was stationed overseas Aunt Rosetta and Judie would come and live in Louisville. This was also so Judie could finish high school where she had started. Uncle John retired from the Army and took a Presbyterian Church position in Louisville. They bought a large home in Hurstborne Estates near St. Mathews. After that, anyone visiting the family in Louisville stayed with John and Rosetta.

About 1980 my parents moved to SEM Laurels in Milford, Ohio, to be near us as they aged. After my father died, mother moved to St. Paul's Village in Madisonville which was connected to her church and with friends there she stayed busy. After she began to have health issues, she moved back to SEM in their SEM Haven Section of assisted living.

Traveling

Traveling has been a main form of recreation for us. Chris enjoys going places and seeing various areas and places. I enjoy seeing more cities, museums and artistic places, so we combine our interests and ventures. This way we have had many very wonderful trips around the United States and the world.

The Schoolhouse

One of our early travels and our first trip north was a winter visit to McCoy's Schoolhouse in 1970. As we were leaving Terrace Park on a balmy winter day for Cincinnati, we passed the LaCrone's house, where we stopped and chatted. Fred and Peggy LaCrone grew up and had lived in Michigan quite a while before moving to Terrace Park where he was Assistant Rector of St. Thomas Episcopal Church. They could not believe we were going north to "enjoy" some winter activities. Well, we were and we did.

We drove north to Grayling, Michigan, and arrived at the McCoy's schoolhouse on a snowy evening. The one-room schoolhouse was old and Al McCoy was working to restore it as a vacation spot for his family. We parked on the roadside and dragged our gear through the snow and began to get settled for the night. The place was stone cold and was mostly filled with a potbellied stove, a table with chairs and beds with electric blankets for

8 people. Al and Ruth McCoy have six children and this was their place, complete with an outhouse. Chris fired up the stove, everyone selected a bed. We placed Paula, then about age 2, in a crib near the stove but far enough away that she could not reach to touch it, and we all went to bed.

The next morning, we awoke to a sunny day with the night's new snow covering everything outside. Inside we had snow also as it had infiltrated through the walls to accumulate about two feet into the room. The wood-burning potbellied stove soon warmed us up. Venturing outside, it was beautiful. We dug out the car which was buried due to the recent snowfall and the snowplow's contribution, and went to town. At a church rummage sale, we bought ski gear to outfit four of us for about $100. With our skis we climbed a hill beside the school house to begin skiing. Or let us say learn how to enjoy falling in the snow. After a few days, Blake, Chris and even Nancy were able to advance to a real ski hill with lifts, while I got to watch and take care of Paula. This was to become a pattern, but it did introduce us to northern Michigan which we all have come to thoroughly enjoy.

We made many, many more weekend and longer vacation trips to northern Michigan. Several were after-Christmas trips to ski and visit the McCoys. Others were to take Paula to Camp Merameg and then to explore various areas on our own. Finally settling on Lake Charlevoix and finding a place of our own there to purchase; and then, twenty-five years later, moving there to live full time. It all started with a short initial trip to the schoolhouse.

Business Trips
The kids and I got to tag along on several trips that Chris was taking mainly for business. In fact, he always had some business interest whenever we went on a trip. That was his passion. Through that, we had some memorable trips that we probably would not have taken otherwise. Five people can ride in a car for the same cost as one. When he was teaching a course at North Carolina State University we joined him if it fit with spring break for the children. The kids and I enjoyed the hotel pool while he had classes. Wives were invited to some sales meetings in Florida and New Orleans, so I got to enjoy some sunshine and music. A trade association meeting in Bermuda included wives when we probably would not have chosen that location to visit on our own. But it was a delightful trip. Chris made trips to Canada to promote the business, and we tagged along, getting to see and enjoy areas we would otherwise have missed.

Alaska
When my brother, Paul, got a new assignment we would visit them if it was feasible with location, cost and school schedules of myself and the children. We visited them in Alabama, North Carolina, Utah, Washington state and Alaska. When we learned in 1973 of their

move to Fort Richardson, near Anchorage, Alaska, we told them we were coming to visit. We began planning the visit and my parents immediately said they wanted to go also, so we included them. In order to help with cost of the trip, I decided to make and sell hand-painted wooden Christmas tree ornaments. I had my Dad and Chris cut thin plywood ornaments from figures and patterns which I drew up. Chris put eyelets in them and I hand painted and put strings on them. We gave lots away as gifts to family and friends, but we also sold about $600 worth — which in spite of being a small part of the total trip cost, ensured our commitment to going.

Our trip plans called for flying to Winnipeg, Canada, then riding the train to the West Coast where we planned to take the Alaskan ferry up to Juneau. We had always wanted to take the Canadian train through the Rockies. Upon arriving in Winnipeg, we found the trains on strike which negated our train trip and we flew to the West Coast to meet the ferry. Upon reaching Juneau, my parents, myself and the girls flew on to Anchorage, while Chris and Blake continued on the Ferry to Skagway to hike the gold rush Chilcoot Trail and then come on to Anchorage. They enjoyed the hike and experience while we spent time with Paul, Nettye and kids, catching up on things.

When Chris and Blake arrived in Anchorage, we rented a car for Paul and Nettye in exchange for us using their station wagon and camper and taking three of their kids with us to tour Alaska. This allowed us an easy and economical way to explore and for our kids and cousins to spend time together. Then we took the train up to Mt. McKinley, where we saw the mountain in the clouds and happened to see the bears eating a caribou which was featured in *National Geographic* magazine. This was a wonderful trip and great experience — to an amazing area.

Forty years later, in 2013, Chris and I finally got to see the Canadian Rockies with a car trip to Glacier National Park, Banff, Lake Louise and on to the West Coast for another visit with Paul.

Green Valley
Chris's father, Charles, and his wife, Eleanor, had begun wintering in Green Valley, Arizona, which is a retirement community just south of Tucson. They encouraged us to visit, so we did. At Christmastime, in 1974, we went by train to Flagstaff and rented a car to drive down to Green Valley. They had built a small two-bedroom adobe-style home on a hillside, with a beautiful view across the valley to the mountains on the horizon. They toured us around to Tubac, a quaint old town, Old Tucson, a movie set, pecan orchards and down across the border for lunch in Nogales, Mexico. Chris and his brother visited several times on business matters and Chris drove their car back twice so Charles and Eleanor could fly. On one car trip, in 1983, I flew to Oklahoma City where he met me and we visited with

Ron and Marylyn Johnson, whom we knew in Oregon while Chris was in the Air Force. They were neighbors and Chris worked with him in Base Engineers. Ron was dying of Lou Gehrig's disease, but we were able to have a very nice visit. Marylyn has since remarried.

England and Scotland
In 1976, while America was enjoying a bicentennial, we drove to New York and flew to visit England and Scotland. I did research and wrote letters to get bed and breakfast reservations, which really worked out well. It was very reasonable for the five of us to travel there for four weeks. We explored London and all the sites there and even had tea at the Ritz. The children enjoyed it and learned much.

Nancy remembers it well. Paula particularly enjoyed feeding the pigeons in the parks. Blake was 14 at the time and able to navigate well in the city and on the Underground. He asked if he could go to the British Museum on his own, which we allowed after much worried thought. He went and returned without any problem. Would parents allow that today? I doubt it, but for him it was a good experience.

After London, we traveled by train to Canterbury and a day trip to the Cliffs of Dover where we all got sunburned during a day at the beach. Chris still has a piece of the chalk cliff he hauled back. In Canterbury, we visited the Cathedral and the Roman Ruins, as well as the ancient town walls and gates. We then traveled by train west to Salisbury, where we took a day trip out to Stonehenge, where 8-year-old Paula immediately started climbing the Henge. Moving on, we went to Bath and then Shakespeare's hometown of Stratford-upon-Avon to explore and see *Romeo and Juliet*.

Of course, Chris could not miss an opportunity to explore some business possibilities by having a meeting with a British man. The gentleman was kind enough to loan us a car for the weekend, which enabled us to explore the midlands for a few days, including Coventry, York, Flamborough and all the sites. We met him Monday morning in Manchester to return the car and move on by train to Inverness, Scotland.

In Inverness, we stayed at a B&B in the home of Mrs. McBean, who was about 80 years of age. We arrived late in the evening because our train had broken down. She took us in and fed us homemade scones and cookies–delightful. The next day for breakfast we had fresh raspberries which she and her daughter had picked that morning. That fortified us to go on an excursion boat to search for the Loch Ness Monster. We didn't find Nessie, but still had an enjoyable boat ride. Returning from Inverness, we next visited Edinburgh where we toured the city and walked the Royal Mile several times, exploring everything. After separating to see different things, we arrived at the Robert Burns monument where we had agreed to meet Chris. Waiting for him to show up and getting more frustrated, we looked around and found each other waiting on opposite sides of the monument.

After Scotland, we then visited another businessman, Nigel Moyer, and his family in Teaside. They were so gracious and spent two days with us. His wife, Estelle, was a local judge, and they were a very interesting family. While Chris and Nigel did their business, Estelle and their children took me and our children on a delightful picnic and showed us the countryside. Later, we had an enjoyable dinner at their house. Our daughter Nancy and their daughter Philipa became pen pals for several years.

Returning to London, we all had last things to see in our final day, before returning to the U. S. This was a memorable trip for our family. Chris and I returned to London for a few days in 2000 and then took the Chunnel to Paris where we spent a week. Wonderful memories.

Europe with the Gerhards

Bob and Ernestine Gerhard were good friends of ours. Bob was our Rector at St. Thomas Church and played golf with Chris. Ernestine and I were part of a small group of women who had dinner and attended the Cincinnati Symphony every month. We took three European trips with them and also a trip to Stratford, Ontario, Canada, to see some plays.

In 1986, the Gerhards invited us to go with them on a trip to Rome, Italy. On the morning we were to leave, of course, Chris had an important meeting. I told him I was going with or without him. It was close, but he made it. We flew to Paris where we spent a few days, took the night train to Rome, where we stayed for two weeks, and then went on to Istanbul for a week before returning home.

Bob and Ernestine Gerhard

In Rome, we were with a church group that had a morning program and then toured every afternoon, taking us to all of the normal places, but also into nondescript churches to see special works of art not normally open to the public. In the Forum one day, someone called out our name, we turned and saw Becky Shundich, a neighbor from Terrace Park — it's such a small world. Our group got to attend an audience with the Pope, and Bob arranged a special visit to the catacombs under St. Peter's Cathedral. There is so much to see in Rome. We also took a side trip to Florence for a few days.

We flew on to Istanbul, where I had insisted we stay in the Para Palace Hotel, an old British hotel where Agatha Christie had stayed. At that time, Istanbul was a very polluted city, with heavy smog that descended upon us in our non-air-conditioned rooms. Ernestine announced at breakfast the first morning that her bag was packed and she was leaving to go home. Well, the day was nice and Bob encouraged her to stay. She did and we had a great week there despite the nauseous nightly smog.

In 1989 we took a three-week trip to Portugal and Spain with Bob and Ernestine. We landed in Lisbon, where we stayed a few days and then drove to Salamanca, Spain, to join a church group similar to what we did in Rome. On the drive across Spain, we stayed in Paradors in Toledo and within the Alhambra in Granada. These were government-operated facilities at historic sites which made you feel like you were living back in time. Our last few days were spent in Madrid, where I enjoyed the Prado Museum and evening strolls.

Russia is a big country and was still a very controlled society when we visited there with the Gerhards in 1997. We flew to Paris for a day and then on to Moscow where we boarded an English-speaking river cruise ship which was our home for the Russian visit. Moscow was getting ready for their 850th anniversary. We were bussed from the ship daily to visit Moscow, including a day in the Kremlin, before traveling the river, lake and canal waterway to St. Petersburg. The Kremlin is like a Government City within the massive brick and stone walls. Inside we were allowed into certain buildings but not others. Ernestine had researched some artifact she wanted to see and it was in a forbidden-entry, former church building. Somehow, she got in, saw what she wanted to see, and didn't get arrested. We were all relieved when she rejoined us.

Along the waterway we had various stops where we were always met by quiet elderly ladies selling handicraft lace and fresh wildflowers. We bought their flowers, feeling their sales were their livelihood. At one city, we were told we had an hour to browse through their department store where they now had many shades of lipstick instead of only the one standard color. Bob and Ernestine played cards every evening, so we bought them a deck of Russian cards, which we gave them at dinner. The next day they informed us that some of the cards were missing.

St. Petersburg is a big city with lots of history. We saw Peterhof, some beautiful icons at a monastery, the Summer (Pushkin) Palace, the Hermitage Museum, the Kirov Opera, Church of our Savior and generally enjoyed the city. We returned from Russia through Helsinki, Finland, which was interesting.

Other Traveling
When we started looking back at all our travels, it seemed to overwhelm us. Looking back through the albums brought out so many memories of pleasant times and wonderful experiences. In addition to the trips I have written about above, we traveled to New Zealand, Belgium, Norway, Nova Scotia and so many trips within the U.S. to see family and friends. There is not a book big enough to hold it all.

Part 6: The Last Word

Downsizing
After many years in Terrace Park, we realized we were spending much time and effort maintaining two homes. I wanted to simplify our life and also to enjoy the many events available in downtown Cincinnati. So, we began getting rid of the cherished possessions we had spent a lifetime accumulating, sold our house in 2007 and moved to a 10th floor apartment overlooking the river in downtown Cincinnati. We enjoyed the proximity to the Library, the University Club for an occasional dinner, handy shopping, my monthly symphony, the proximity of Christ Church Cathedral and the diversity of the people. After three years we decided that we were enjoying our home in Michigan more and we were spending over half the year there. It was not practical to keep the apartment, so we moved to Michigan full time in 2010.

This is the last word.

Oyster Bay, Charlevoix, Michigan 2021

Appendix A

Charles Rosfjord Smith

Charles Rosfjord Smith was born on April 16, 1934, at the Griffin Hospital in Derby, Connecticut. His formative years were during WWII, with our Grandfather Smith at Great Oak Farm in Orange, Connecticut. He attended Orange Center School and then Hillhouse High School in New Haven.

Charles was a good student and was admitted to Massachusetts Institute of Technology. In preparation, our parents arranged for him to attend a summer school session at Phillips Andover Academy just prior to entering his freshman year at MIT. Always an adventurer, he decided to ride his bicycle from Orange, Connecticut, to Andover, Massachusetts, which he did. It was only a balloon-tire bicycle, not one of the thin-tire models of today with many gearing levels to make peddling easier. He carried everything to camp along the way and reported his whereabouts to our mother every day or so. He arrived as planned and we drove up with the rest of his belongings to meet him at the school. I was proud of him.

He was at MIT for two years before deciding engineering was not for him, which disappointed his parents. The Korean War was active at that time so he joined the Army for a two-year enlistment. Fortunately, the war ended before he was shipped overseas. He returned to Louisville, where we lived then, and entered the University of Louisville to graduate with a business degree in accounting. He then went on to obtain a law degree by going to night school while working a day job in accounting. The GI Bill paid for his schooling. He passed the CPA exam and the Kentucky Bar to practice law in Kentucky.

While at U of L, Charles married Barbara Schilb. Barbara was a registered nurse and worked at a Louisville hospital. She gave Charles the nickname "Chuck." After law school, they moved to Indianapolis, Indiana, where he had a good job as Assistant Treasurer of Buehler Corp. They had three boys, Charles Theodore Smith, William Francis Smith and Matthew Kaddeland Smith.

Appendix A: Charles Rosfjord Smith

About 1967, Chuck joined us at Industrial Air, as treasurer, and moved his family to the Cincinnati area where they built a new home on Mildred Lane in Milford, Ohio. Since Milford is right next to Terrace Park, our families got to see quite a bit of each other. Our children were close in age so they got to know each other well. Barbara was active raising their children, got on the Miami Township Life Squad, and was elected as a Miami Township Trustee. She and Chuck also bought the Milcroft Inn with a bar. All these activities got in the way of their marriage and they divorced.

Marilyn Neuhaus, his second wife, had two children, Todd and Linda Bermudez, by her first marriage. They built a new home in the Hickory Hill subdivision which was a project he started and I completed while he was running Industrial Air. After all of their children were raised, Chuck and Marilyn spent half the year in Fort Myers, Florida. While there he perfected his golf game and also built the largest fish farm in Florida, where he grew tilapia fish for market.

Chuck had a prospective buyer for his fish farm — from Columbia. He was not sure the buyer was real or fake. He wanted to meet, evaluate and negotiate, but he was leery of going to Columbia alone. He asked me to go with him. I certainly am no bodyguard and had never been to South America, but I said yes, I would go with him. It seemed like an adventure and it was. We flew to Bogota, Colombia, and were met by Ricardo, a serious businessman, engineer and entrepreneur. He had many businesses and many farms, including a tilapia farm. Over the next few days, we were driven around by his armed bodyguard in an armored SUV to tour his operations, We were very impressed with his innovative farming methods and the efficiency of his operations in a country where rebel activities were an active threat and where poverty abounds. I could write a book about this trip. Negotiations were successful. Ricardo bought the farm.

Chuck and Marilyn enjoyed their time in Florida. They owned two different homes on Ft. Myers Beach before moving to Gulf Harbor, a gated community on the south side of Ft. Myers. Marilyn died of cancer in 2016. Chuck then sold the Florida property and returned to Cincinnati full time. He most recently has moved to the New England Club retirement community and is selling his home of many years in Hickory Hill.

Linda and I have tried to maintain good family relationships with all of his family and we feel reasonably successful there. I sincerely trust all the children will continue that effort.

Appendix A: Charles Rosfjord Smith

A family gathering upon our return from Alaska in 1973.
From the left rear: W.C. Smith, Charles T. Smith, Charles C. Smith, Blake Smith, Charles R. Smith, Matthew Smith, Barbara Schilb (Smith), Linda Knoop (Smith), William Smith, Paula Smith, Nancy Smith

Marilyn and Chuck visited many times along with their dog Bridget. Marilyn loved the shopping.

Leslie Sheimer and Chuck visited us in 2018 and 2019. We have enjoyed Leslie's company and consider her part of the family when we are all together.

We have always enjoyed a little family competition. A "short" game of Chinese checkers fits the bill.

Appendix B

Col. Paul Robert Knoop

I greatly appreciate Paul's autobiographical contribution, which follows:

Paul R. Knoop, Colonel (Ret) U.S. Army (1937–)

Early Life
Many people, quite unlike me, can remember astonishing details of their early life. My earliest memories are after we moved to the Fincastle neighborhood in Louisville, Kentucky, when I was about four or so (even that is with a caveat). As has been mentioned elsewhere, Fincastle was constructed as a housing area for government employees and families. With Dad's employment at Bowman Field as the supervisor of a supply section supporting the Army, we were authorized housing there. It was so new that the yards were still mud and had no grass, which was great, I am sure, for Mom.

Across the court from us was a Navy Petty Officer and his wife. He was a builder of the old stick-model airplanes, covered in tissue paper and "doped" for strength. Of course, I was fascinated by them, and when he received orders for overseas, he gave me one of his recently completed models, a rather large one. Mom and Dad wanted to hang it in my room, but no, I was determined to play with it.

**Happy kids
Paul with sister Linda**

Appendix B: Col. Paul Robert Knoop

Picture me, at about 6 years of age, on the floor in our small living room, pushing the plane around on the carpet, and Linda, in the hallway toward the front door, says, "Watch me how I can walk backwards." You can guess, of course — she sat down on the plane, I believe the first or second day I had it! Lots of crying by both of us.

I do remember the end of the War in Europe, and all the kids in the neighborhood running up and down the street banging on pots and pans, blowing whistles, etc., to celebrate "something important."

Some years later, I was given a used and repaired BB gun by a friend who had gotten a new one for Christmas. While out with the guys, Linda started bugging us about something. I pointed the gun at the ground in front of her and promptly shot her in the leg! So much for my experience with guns. It disappeared into the trash that evening when Dad got home, and I was treated to some "physical disciplining."

**Paul Knoop
About age 6**

One other memory resulting in a valuable lesson was that when riding on the handlebars of a bicycle, if you stick your foot into the spokes, the abrupt stop throws you and the bike owner over the front wheel. I only did that once.

I began schooling at Camp Taylor Elementary and every day for two years walked each way. At the time that was no challenge. I was sure it was several miles till I measured it; turns out, it was only about 1-¼ mile, following the creek, through the woods to "civilization." In the winter, the snow presented a challenge, especially the day I walked on the frozen creek. It was not completely frozen! Soaked to the knees, I was quite cold for most of the day. Another memorable event involved a book satchel that I had received as a Christmas gift from Olivia, Dad's sister. One day, after a wonderful snow when I had to walk the road rather than through the woods, I spent about an hour using the book satchel as a sled on a nice hill in Fincastle. This made me late getting home and by the way, ruined the book satchel which was embossed paper covering cardboard. Yet one more physical disciplining when Dad got home from work.

After the 2nd grade, when Linda started school, Dad enrolled us in school at Concordia Lutheran Church, which was our family church. The school was a two-room arrangement, with the church organist teaching grades 1–4 and Pastor Eberhardt grades 5–8. As I was supposed to be in the 3rd grade and it was over-full, I was elected to skip that and go into the 4th grade. (This later proved to me a disadvantage, as I was only 16 when I started college—too young, I realized later...) Linda and I had to walk to the city bus stop at a grocery store some distance from home; turns out now, it was only about a third of a mile, but lots uphill, either through the woods or a longer way by sidewalk.

After finishing 8th grade at Concordia, I started high school at Okalona High, which closed after my freshman year and was replaced by the newly built Southern High School. A somewhat normal education there, except for working on the yearbook staff my senior year. One of my assignments was to take photos of a school play for the yearbook. The photos did not come out, earning me the nickname of "Kiss of Death" by the advisor who was also the Drivers Training instructor. We probably had a bad experience or two in that class, which I do not remember.

During the latter part of high school, Dad purchased a lot on Primrose Drive in St. Matthews on which to build a home. Over the summer we did a lot of work together on this, both after he came home from work and on weekends/holidays. I learned a lot from this adventure, and one thing I remember is that during one of these work sessions I heard him utter the one and only obscenity he ever used in my presence: he referred to someone as a "Horse's Ass!" Mild, but nevertheless, it was memorable.

This was the summer before I left for Western Kentucky State College, and my eventual career was plotted at a pool hall in St. Matthews, within walking distance from home. There I met Tom Ballard across the pool table, and he had just finished his freshman year at Western. In talking, he mentioned ROTC, and told me some things about it. I was very much intrigued, and followed up when I registered, signing up for Army ROTC (they had an Air Force program also, but wearing glasses, that was really a show-stopper for me).

Academically at Western, I was mediocre at best, repeating several classes and spending a fifth year (making up for skipping the 3rd grade), but partly because you could not take ROTC, and major in Chemistry, without at least one session of summer school or other make-up work. ROTC was really the only subject in which I did well. I was a member of the Pershing Rifles, an honorary military organization. I was in charge of their color guard, presenting the National Colors at sporting events, part of their Exhibition Drill Team, and the leader of their Drill Platoon which participated in national competitions. Also, I was chosen to become a member of the Scabbard and Blade, the advanced ROTC society. With their help, I did manage to receive a Regular Army (RA) Commission as a 2nd lieutenant.

Appendix B: Col. Paul Robert Knoop

From left:
Nettye's Parents — Arantz Carl (Buster) Brown and Maxie Lavonne Smith (Brown)

Newly weds — Nettye Jean Brown (Knoop) and Paul Robert Knoop

It was here that I met, dated, and married Nettye Jean Brown, also a Chemistry major, who was much smarter and more dedicated to studying than I. She assisted immeasurably in my graduation, since even with an extra year, I had to take a correspondence course in German for enough credits to graduate. She did most of the coursework and I took the exam, following her tutelage; the course was scientific German, the exam was translating material from a German chemical textbook. I could recognize enough of the chemical terms to allow a reasonable and passable translation of the text.

In the summer of 1958, when Karla was born, I was at ROTC summer camp at Ft. Knox, Kentucky. I was granted a three-day pass to come home to see mother and daughter; what an experience, and what a blessing!

Military Career
Following graduation in June of 1959, I was commissioned in the Chemical Corps. At that time, all RA Officers had to spend two years detailed to one of the Combat Arms branches; I was detailed to Field Artillery, and thus we went to Ft. Sill, Oklahoma, for my Officers Basic Course as a "cannon cocker." We rented an apartment close to the post, and bought a clunker 1954 Chevy, our first car. It barely lasted through the 6-month course, and I had to have it towed away as salvage, then beg or borrow rides for the final days of out-processing and preparing to move.

The course was not too difficult except being away from home so much of the time, with Nettye Jean being pregnant with Bob, and his birth about halfway through the course.

Appendix B: Col. Paul Robert Knoop

During this time, and for the next 29 years, Nettye Jean bore the brunt of our life together; to this day, I am amazed at how she held our family together, and what she managed to personally accomplish while doing that!

Orders to Germany arrived, assigning me to the 3rd Gun Battalion, 82nd Artillery. Little did I know it was a 280mm Atomic Cannon unit, but during the basic course I did get to see one on a drive-by during a demonstration. So much for being prepared on arrival at Giessen, Germany, in the fall of 1959. Before leaving the U.S., I did have time to help move Nettye Jean, Karla, and Bob to her parents' home in Tuscumbia, Alabama, to wait for her orders to Germany after I had a place to live and permission to bring them over.

I arrived in Giessen in time to join my Battalion in Grafenwoehr, where I spent much time away from home. Recently while reviewing letters to our parents during that time, I was amazed at how much time I was away from home for field duty and other training.

Nettye Jean, Karla, and Bob arrived in March of 1960, and we were settled "on the economy" in Giessen in an apartment above a downtown Gasthaus/Metzgerei, for several months before receiving on-post housing in May of that year. One note on their trip to Germany was the flight from McGuire AFB, New Jersey. They and several other families were on a charter flight accompanying lots of GIs being reassigned to Germany. The NCO in charge of the soldiers assigned each family on the plane at least one soldier to be responsible for helping them board, get settled on the plane, during the flight, and deplaning at Rhein-Main Terminal, to link up with their sponsor. Nettye Jean had a super young GI who really looked after them, brought them meals, changed diapers, etc. It would have been a miserable flight without his help and support. I never did find out who he was to thank him. He was one of many young soldiers who helped make my career successful.

The Gasthaus owner and her friends were amazed at "Boobie" and would continually relieve Nettye Jean of him when we would go down to the restaurant to have a beer or meal. There was another young lady living in the other apartment on our floor. She was a great help in caring for Bob and Karla, and assisted with shopping, etc. Karla picked up quite a bit of German from her during the few months we lived there. We did receive housing on post, living in a second-floor apartment close to the Kaserne where I worked. Several of our neighbors were officers I worked with, so that was helpful to Nettye Jean, especially when we were in the field, as she did not drive. I had purchased a 1951 (I believe) Buick that was a real challenge to maneuver in some of the narrow streets and alleyways. It served us well for most of our tour there.

Duty with the 82nd Artillery Battalion was training, exercises, training, broken up by two- to three-week stints in the field near our designated war-time position. During the cold-war period, the U.S. had nuclear-capable units in the field 24–7 on a rotating basis. During this short period, we did not train, but remained ready to execute our war-time

Appendix B: Col. Paul Robert Knoop

mission. BORING. Several times a year we would go to Grafenwoehr for live firing exercises and Army Training Tests to evaluate our proficiency, and there was always a big winter exercise, Winter Shield, with forces deploying from the U.S. I recall participating in two of those. During my assignment, I was first a Gun Platoon Leader, responsible for employment of a 280mm gun section (there were two sections in each Battery) and then after special schooling, the Special Weapons Officer for the Battery. The section, consisting of myself and four enlisted personnel, was responsible for the assembly of our nuclear weapons when directed to be fired. Of course, our training was done with dummy rounds, and meticulously checked and rechecked. The school for this training is the only course in which I excelled, finishing as the Honor Graduate.

In July of 1961, I completed my two years as an Artillery Officer and became a Chemical Officer. In August I moved into the BOQ at Mannheim, Germany, until family quarters became available. Nettye Jean, the kids, and I moved into temporary housing on the economy (again) in October until on-post housing was available. I was assigned to the 15th Chemical Group, first to the 59th Maintenance Company and later to the 9th Depot Company in May of 1962. There was no duty travel during this period, and our parents had an opportunity to visit and travel with us. The work was a real learning experience for me, not knowing anything about repairing gas masks or flame throwers and whatever, or about moving Chemical supplies around Germany. It is of note here that all these units were disbanded later (see a later paragraph on this), but the 9th Chemical Company has been reactivated and is now a part of the Chemical Battalion stationed at Joint Base Lewis-McChord in Washington. "What goes around comes around." Julie was born in the Army hospital in Heidelberg in January of 1962, just before we left Mannheim for reassignment to Ft. McClellan, Alabama, and so we began preparations to return to "the land of the round doorknob" as the U.S. was known.

Government quarters were provided at Ft. McClellan since I was there for the long Career Course at the Chemical School. Nothing much of note during this period from January to November of 1963 except for my promotion to Captain in July and the birth of Lisa in October, a short time before I graduated and was reassigned to the 2nd Infantry Division at Ft. Benning, Georgia. I spent three years there on the Division Staff and as the Commander of the 26th Chemical

Appendix B: Col. Paul Robert Knoop

Detachment, a five-man team in support of the Division. Lots of field training and exercises to take me away from the home we purchased in Columbus near the post, since there was no hope of getting into government quarters for a young captain.

June of 1965 found us returning to Ft. McClellan for my duty as an instructor in the Chemical School. However, while I was in the hospital for a back issue, an officer from the school visited and informed me that I had been transferred to the 100th Chemical Group to take command of the 18th Chemical Detachment which, as it turned out, was alerted for deployment to Vietnam as part of the initial massive buildup. The detachment left by ship from Oakland Army Terminal in August of 1965. The boredom of the month-long sea voyage was broken up by a brief stop in Hawaii and a later stop at sea to repair a leak in the hull, just below my cabin, which was sustained when we caught the effects of a typhoon. We arrived at Cam Ranh Bay and then my unit, along with the other Technical Intelligence units aboard the ship, moved to Nha Trang, just up the coast, to what was then Field Force 2 Headquarters. We remained there until February of 1966, when all the detachments were moved to Saigon for duty with the Combined Intelligence Center, Vietnam, in the Military Assistance Command headquarters. This was not a rewarding assignment for me or many, many others. Fortunately, my family could remain in the family housing at Ft. McClellan but had to move into different quarters.

I was assigned back to the Chemical School, arriving in September 1966 for duty (finally) as an instructor. During this assignment I was promoted to Major. In May of 1969 I became the Deputy Director of Instruction for the school, remaining in that position until January 1970 when I was transferred to the 701st Air Defense Group at Ft. Fisher AFS, located at Kure Beach, North Carolina.

That unit was a Radar Site and Air Defense BUIC (back up interceptor control) site responsible for monitoring and warnings for the East Coast generally from New Jersey to Florida and south. Ft. Fisher was a small base with only three Army Officers and two NCOs along with the Air Force personnel, and housing was available only for key personnel, so we had to live in Wilmington, about 25 miles north of the site. An interesting assignment, as after getting established in my primary job as Director of the Battle Staff Support Center, I really had nothing to do except during a monthly exercise. I approached the Air Force Colonel who was commanding and asked to be his Executive Officer, since he was not authorized that position, but had to fill it anyway. I learned a lot from that assignment, especially that an Air Force executive officer is an administrator, not an assistant commander. I made numerous trips to Colorado Springs, our higher headquarters there to deal with administrative and personnel matters for the base, and to NORAD (North American Air Defense Command) for my primary job at Ft. Fisher. Family life was good, with beach activities and travel opportunities, etc. Wilmington was a reasonable distance from our parents, and we could see them frequently during our time there.

We enjoyed going to oyster roasts put on by the local volunteer fire department as fundraisers. Julie had hot dogs, while the rest of us emptied the buckets of roasted oysters on stacks of newspaper on plywood sheets atop sawhorses. We would go through several buckets during the evening; I would like to try that again now! On visits to our families, we would usually take a cooler of oysters fresh from the boat. One day Karla came home from school and described her lunch; after some questioning and discussion, Nettye Jean finally figured out they had tacos for lunch! This was also my first exposure to tacos which became an occasional meal in the future.

We left Wilmington in August of 1972 when I was transferred to Alaska, with duty station at Ft. Richardson near Anchorage. My assignment was to the Operations Center as the Plans Officer for USARAL (U.S. Army Alaska Headquarters.) We moved into temporary housing on post (sound familiar?) awaiting our permanent house. This was probably the best assignment for us; the job was interesting and challenging, lots of opportunities for travel and adventures, quite an experience with the weather, and good for the kids, especially skiing for Bob and Karla. Karla became a good skier and was an instructor at the Arctic Valley ski slope, and Bob was a member of their Ski Patrol.

I worked in the USARAL Command Center, and also served as the briefing officer for all official visitors to the Command until February of 1973. I was reassigned to the Alaskan Command Operations Center (ALCOM) at Elmendorf AFB, adjacent to Ft. Richardson, as a Watch Officer/Emergency Actions Officer. There I worked shifts with four other officers and five senior NCOs until ALCOM was disestablished in October of 1974 and I moved back to the 172nd Infantry Brigade, which replaced USARAL as the senior Army element in Alaska. Promoted to Lieutenant Colonel in June of 1975, I was the Chief of Plans and Operations Division until we returned to "the lower 48" in June of 1976, where I was the 9th Infantry Division Chemical Officer at Ft. Lewis, Washington.

This was another great job and great place to be stationed for the next three or so years. It was here that we decided that we would probably retire in the area when that time came. Karla had graduated from high school before we left Ft. Richardson, and entered college at Utah State University in Logan, Utah, where Bob followed upon his graduation in 1977. There was, however, a good bit of travel for me, with exercises and training, including returning to Germany on several occasions. What followed a high point was somewhat a low point from an assignment viewpoint, the Military Personnel Center in Alexandria, Virginia, as the Chief of the Chemical Officer Assignments Branch. We purchased a house in Upper Marlboro, Maryland, near Andrews AFB. Being in the Washington, DC, metro area, with its many free educational opportunities, somewhat made up for the lack of satisfaction with my job and the long commute, despite the high cost of living. This turned

Appendix B: Col. Paul Robert Knoop

out to be a short assignment, as I was selected for promotion to Colonel and assigned to Dugway Proving Ground, Utah, as the Director of Materiel Test. Here I was working for my seat-mate during the Advanced Class in 1963! I attempted to supervise several hundred civilian employees, including about a dozen PhD scientists and engineers, a skill I had not been taught or exposed to before. I learned quickly to be careful just what I said or how I said it, after being the subject of several union complaints. I became adept at apologizing for unintended slights or criticisms. It was here that Julie started college at Utah State, and Lisa decreed that "no way was she going to college in Utah." As an aside, Utah granted in-state tuition rates for military personnel, and while at Ft. Lewis earlier, we had established residence in Washington, thus Lisa "chose" the University of Washington for college. This was great, as at that time we had three children in college at the same time for several years. Their part-time and summer jobs, combined with my salary as a Colonel, made that possible without any of us going into debt.

Dugway was an interesting assignment, but I was glad that we could return to Ft. Lewis for my final assignment in 1984. I was the First Corps Chemical Officer and was an integral part of the Corps' staff. Lots of travel, many trips to Korea, several to Alaska, Hawaii, and other installations in the U.S. for supervision and training of subordinate units of the Corps. All in all, a great final assignment. Knowing we would retire here, we purchased a house in Fircrest in 1986, not far from the post, and began making it a home.

My early retirement in 1988 was forced by being asked in 1987 to move to Washington, DC, into a position I knew was to be eliminated soon after I got there. Argue as I did about just having bought a house, the job offered going away, and being two years from retirement in this area, the assignment officer gave me the choice of taking the assignment or putting in my retirement papers; I chose the latter, allowing me to retire in July of 1988. Having been an assignment officer, I knew he had a job to fill, but still, he had to find someone else to fill that job and then to fill mine a short time later.

All the children were at the ceremony as was Mom, and while sitting on the back deck of our house, I noted with some degree of pride that we had put four children through college, all of whom were now employed and healthy, we had a house that was paid for, two vehicles, and no debt. Not bad at all!

I need to digress here for just a moment on my assignment history of 29-plus years to remark that every unit to which I had been assigned, except Dugway Proving Ground, was deactivated; everything from the five-man detachment through a Division, two major commands, a branch of the Army, a school, and an overseas Theater of Operations. Several were later reactivated, but this was still in keeping with my high school nickname which you may recall, "Kiss of Death."

Appendix B: Col. Paul Robert Knoop

Life After Retirement

It was quickly apparent that life was quite different when I could not, rather than did not, have to put on a uniform and go to work. Yard work, home maintenance and repairs consumed several months during which Nettye Jean and I took lessons in the McChord AFB craft center, learning to frame pictures. We had many things that needed to be either framed or re-framed to fit in our home, and the cost of framing became an extravagance. Do-it-yourself became a necessity, and we quickly learned how do an acceptable job at a reasonable cost.

This became a very enjoyable hobby for me, and as I learned more and my skills became more than acceptable, the frame shop asked me to join them part time, which I did. Soon I was teaching their basic framing classes, and then doing some of the difficult jobs. More training and study led me to move to the Ft. Lewis shop until the first payday after that move. The regulations at that time required retired RA officers to forfeit a portion of their retirement pay when working for the federal government, and my pay was being reduced by about $1,000 because I was earning around $500 at this part-time job. I ended that phase of my career quickly, and soon after that Nettye Jean told me to get out of the house and find something to do!

I found an art gallery and frame shop close to our home and in 1990 was hired as a framer and designer. The arrangement was that I would work only when the shop needed help and when I wanted to work, a good arrangement for both of us as it reduced his overhead and allowed Nettye Jean and me time to travel. With continued study, attending professional classes, seminars, etc., I eventually became certified by the Professional Picture Framers Association and was awarded the CPF designation in 1991. I became involved in the local chapter of PPFA and beginning about 1995 served several terms, first as treasurer, then president and newsletter editor over the next 10 years.

In 2005, Nettye Jean's health began to deteriorate, and I became her full-time caregiver, which helped me feel a little better about all the time she had spent taking care of our family while I was away doing Uncle Sam's business. Cancer was quickly taking its toll, and in August of 2010 she passed away peacefully at home in Fircrest. She had been in Hospice care for several months, so although she was not in any pain, it was a blessing for her, as she had been continually active throughout her life and was now bedridden.

In December of that year, I moved into Patriots Landing, a retirement community in DuPont, Washington, which is principally for former military and spouses. I became quite active in our church there and served on the Resident's Council as president for two terms.

A year later I met Carmen Merritt (née Orr), whose husband, Ed, had recently passed away, and we married on the 4th of July in 2012. Carmen has three children, Dee Dee Linderer, living in California; Scott Lundberg, living in Olympia; and Christine Hall, who

Appendix B: Col. Paul Robert Knoop

lives in Missoula, Montana, and 12 grandchildren and step-grandchildren.

Our wedding was a very private ceremony but followed a month later by a reception for our families, friends, residents, and the staff of Patriots Landing. Several cruises and other travels as well as Patriots Landing activities kept us busy until Carmen's health made that impossible. She died peacefully while hospitalized in October of 2020.

To wrap up this narrative, my family remains "healthy, wealthy, and wise," scattered from Washington to Florida. Karla lives in Salt Lake City, Utah, and has retired from her job as a hydrologist with an environmental engineering firm. She has a daughter, Kira, living in New York City working as a managing director and executive producer for One Thousand Birds, a sound studio. Bob and his wife, Karol, are living in Harvest, Alabama, where he is the proverbial "rocket scientist," working for Aerojet Rocketdyne as a Chief Project Engineer based in Huntsville, Alabama. Julie and husband, Karl, live in Safety Harbor, Florida, and she works as a certified care manager and patient advocate. Lisa and her partner, Jason, live in Georgetown, a neighborhood of Seattle, Washington. She is employed as a content strategist and communications professional by the University of Washington in their Student Housing Division.

My plan now is to stay busy and remain at Patriots Landing until I leave feet first. Hopefully, the current COVID pandemic will ease soon, allowing me to travel again to visit family and friends before that happens.

A Knoop Family gathering
Back Row - Jason, Paul, Julie, Karl
Middle Row - Nettye, Ruth, Bob, Karol
Front Row - Kira, Lisa, Karla

Carmen and Paul

Appendix C

Spahr

Genevieve Blake (1879–1933) and Charles Herbert Smith (1878–1967) had a daughter, Susie Virginia Smith (our Aunt Virginia). She was born in New Haven, grew up in Shelton and on Great Oak Farm in Orange, Connecticut. She attended the Gateway School for Girls in New Haven and then Wellesley College in Wellesley, Massachusetts, where she graduated.

About 1939 she married Edward Carl Spahr Jr. (our uncle Edward) and they had one child, Virginia Miller Spahr. Edward was a very personable, good-looking man who had a good job as a salesman for a company in Shelton. I remember him as a well-dressed man who drove a big, shiny Buick automobile.

Edward's father, Edward Carl Spahr Sr., was a well-respected master builder of large homes in Derby and Shelton. As noted in Chapter 15, he built our grandparent Kaddeland's home. While still working in his seventies, he fell from a high scaffolding and died from his injuries.

Aunt Virginia and Uncle Edward owned a large two-story home on High Street in Milford and lived well until the war years caused his sales to drop. He took up drinking and lost his job. This resulted in marital problems and Virginia divorced him. He died from a fall in a bank office where he struck his head. After the divorce from Edward about 1948, Virginia took additional college courses to obtain teacher credentials and taught school until retirement.

Aunt Virginia and her daughter Virginia lived with us at Great Oak Farm and stayed there after we moved to the Midwest. She cared for her father (our grandfather) until his death in 1967. She then moved to a condo in Hamden to be nearer to her daughter Virginia, who lived nearby in North Haven.

During her retirement years she was very active in the New Haven Women's Club, serving as the club president and involved in many good civic projects. During a visit, I remember her taking me with her to East Park in New Haven for the dedication of a grove of dogwood trees, which the Women's Club had donated. She was a leader. I remember her as a very fair and kind person, but a dedicated, hard-working lady, who usually accomplished what she set out to do. She also had a good sense of humor when she allowed herself to relax.

Susie Virginia Smith (Spahr) as a child and her engagement picture

Aunt Virginia's daughter, Virginia Miller Spahr, our cousin Ginnie, spent several years growing up with us at Great Oak Farm, so we got to know her well before we moved to the Midwest. Ginnie went to Orange Center School, Hillhouse High School in New Haven and then a few years in college. She married Bradford John (Jack) Ferns, and they had two daughters, Suzanne Virginia Ferns and Sarah Elizabeth Ferns. Ginnie had a good job at Yale University in their Endowment Department where she oversaw their patents among other things. Ginnie retired from Yale and now lives in Hamden, Connecticut, in the very nice condo that previously was her mother's.

 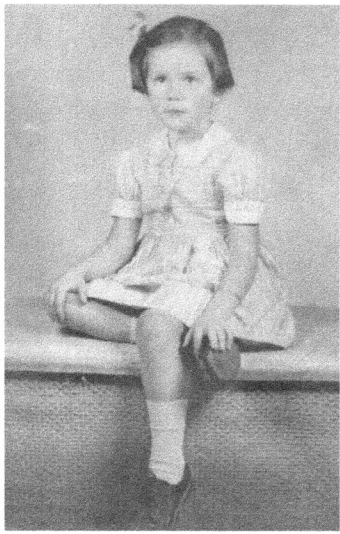 

Virginia Miller Spahr as baby, as a child and her engagement picture

Photos from more recent visits where we enjoyed her always happy spirit.

Appendix D

Dreisbach

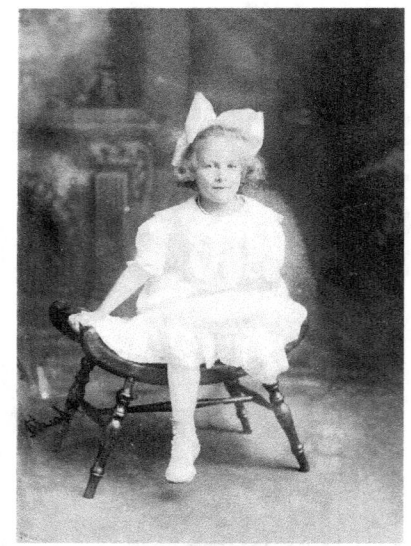

Our mother, Carolyn Clark Kaddeland, had a younger sister, Marcia Jane Kaddeland (1917–2013) — younger by ten years. Marcia grew up in the Kaddeland house at 21 Spring Street in Shelton, Connecticut. She graduated from Shelton High School and attended Vassar College. In 1942, during the war, Marcia married William Garrish Dreisbach (1916–1960) at St. Paul's Episcopal Church in Huntington, Connecticut. I don't remember anything about the wedding ceremony, but I distinctly recall that as they left the church, William Dreisbach was in uniform and I was part of a group throwing confetti. And, I remember our new Uncle Bill later telling us that it took him a week to clean the confetti out of his car. I guess we did a good job. I was five years old.

Aunt Marcia worked in Washington during the war. After the war, Uncle Bill went to Yale Law School on the GI Bill and then they moved to Winter Park, Florida, where Uncle Bill practiced law. They had two children, William

Appendix D: Dreisbach

Shelton Dreisbach and James Dreisbach. Uncle Bill became an Assistant District Attorney in Fort Lauderdale, Florida, but died of an overdose of sleeping pills. Marcia moved to Washington D.C. where she worked for Congressman Herlong, their Florida representative, until she retired. While in the USAF I had a trip to Washington, DC, to review our base's family housing proposals. While there I visited Marcia at the Capitol. She gave me the grand tour.

Marcia owned a home in Georgetown and did volunteer work with the DAR. For a period of time, she was the National Secretary for the organization. Since her father was an immigrant, she had compassion for new citizens, and participated at naturalization ceremonies by giving small American flags from the DAR to all of the new citizens.

Our Aunt Marcia came to visit us several times and it was always a nice time. She visited our mother and it was interesting that they got along so well even though they were ten years apart. After our mother died, Marcia came several times to visit with us at Thanksgiving time. Linda and Marcia were kindred spirits and it was always interesting to hear family stories and some of the Washington scuttlebutt.

As Marcia got older, she didn't travel so far as to visit us in Cincinnati. Her son Bill was in New York City and she visited him there. So, after our daughter Nancy located in New York City, we occasionally met up with Marcia there. It was always a pleasant gathering.

From the left:
Susan Knox (Dreisbach), Bill Dreisbach, W.C. Smith, Katherine Dreisbach, Beatrice Casey, Frances Casey, Will Dreisbach, Linda Knoop (Smith)

From the left:
W.C. Smith, Aunt Marcia Kaddeland (Dreisbach), Aunt Virginia Smith (Spahr), Marilyn Neuhaus (Smith), Eleanor Richmond (Smith), Linda Knoop (Smith), Charles R. Smith

Appendix D: Dreisbach

We have met with their son Bill and his wife, Susan Elsie Knox, most times when we visit New York City. Bill retired from a long career with ABC as a sound engineer. Susan recently retired from a long career in accounting at Lincoln Center. Our gatherings always include discussions about family genealogy with their daughter, Katherine, and an update from their son, William "Will." Will is an Army Reserve Captain and had active-duty tours in both Iraq and Afghanistan. His normal job is with the NYC Public Housing Administration.

Linda always enjoyed Marcia's visits

General References

Various sources have brought to me information from many directions, and I have endeavored to recognize and footnote information from these many sources. In spite of good intentions, finally used information tends to be blended into a story that includes many sources and much that is implied and therefore defies any single or main source. That being said, these general references have been major sources throughout this book.

In Part 1: Those Europeans, I acknowledge *The Anglo-Saxon Chronicles* as a vital source without which our early ancestry would be unknown. Those early monastery scribe original authors preserved a history that would otherwise have been lost.[99]

Also in Part 1, an invaluable source was the *Plantagenet Ancestry of Seventeenth-Century Colonists*, which provided a flow of connection from early times on to those early families in America in the subsequent parts of the book. The wealth of genealogical data that the book provided was extremely important in my research.[100]

Throughout the research for this book, I continuously relied on Wikipedia for information on locations, historical events and personal histories, as well as background information. The site's contributors' narratives, references and original sources provided much detail to be correlated with other sources.

In the course of building a family tree I have relied upon my World Explorer Membership with Ancestry.com for referenced genealogical facts, connections to other trees, links to other websites and connections to other sources. While data continuously needs multiple sources to verify accuracy, many times we only need to get a direction to start looking and Ancestry has provided that.

Family Search was a frequently referenced website used both as an alternative source and a verifying source when conflicting information arose. I'm very indebted to the availability of information and the ease of access.

---

[99] Savage, Anne, *The Anglo-Saxon Chronicles* translation, William Heinemann Ltd., London, 1983
[100] Faris, David, *Plantagenet Ancestry of Seventeenth-Century Colonists*, Genealogy Publishing Co., Inc., Philadelphia, 1996

Find a Grave website provided much information for verifying the whereabouts of several relatives at the end of their lives, supplying needed facts and connections to others. Many thanks to the many volunteers who make that website a great resource for us lay genealogists.

And, of course, I need to acknowledge all the historians, writers and genealogists who over the centuries have recorded and documented so much factual information and memories that have become common public knowledge. As a neophyte in this field of endeavor I recognize their efforts, acknowledge their authorship and continue to be amazed at what is generally known of what happened in our past.

Acknowledgements

No document is ever complete without acknowledging the many sources and much assistance obtained and used in bringing it together.

First, I must thank my father, Charles Clement Smith, for his interest and work on the family's heritage. This rubbed off on me and spurred me to pick up where he left off. Eleanor Richmond, my father's second wife, encouraged him during his later years to continue his efforts during his retirement. Her interest and dedication helped us wrap up and publish his book, *Autobiography of a Connecticut Yankee*.

Katie Dreisbach, my niece, who through her genealogical interest and efforts connected me to many people who had valuable connections and input.

Tracy Shelton who connected us to the Sheltons we did not know and also connected the top and bottom of the Shelton branch of the tree through Selah Shelton.

Jan Lanner of Portland, Oregon, who made the email introduction to the Norwegian cousins, Svein and Synnove Haddeland. This introduction proved to develop into such an enjoyable welcoming visit with them and their daughter Anna. They helpfully enlightened us on the Norwegian Kaddeland branch of the tree.

Bill Dreisbach who discussed the Greenwoods with me at some point, which led to an interesting chapter.

Nettye Jean Knoop, my sister-law, for her work on the Knoop side. There is so much more to do with the Knoop family ancestry in Louisville, Kentucky.

Our son, Christen Blake Smith, for his collaboration on the life of Pvt. Charles W. Sheets, CSA, which is such an interesting story.

Our grandson Blake Andrew Smith for his introducing me to Thomas King's book entitled *The Truth About Stories*.[101] This gave me considerable insight into how to think about

---

[101] King, Thomas, *The Truth About Stories*, House of Anansi Press, Inc., Toronto, 2003

people's lives. Also, as a historian, he enabled us to do research and have much discussion about the historical happenings surrounding various lives. He also accomplished much valued further research and drafting of the narrative on Major General Daniel Gookin.

Without my father's interest in the family's history, I would not have been able to gather and present what is assembled here. His interest at an early age preserved much of the records and pictures, and his later return to the task of gathering added data provided me with a good starting place. I am grateful for his efforts.

Many thanks to our daughter Nancy for her review of the manuscript and cover design. She and her husband, John Casey, offered many constructive corrections and ideas for clarifying revisions.

My wife, Linda, is an avid reader and also a good writer, so I naturally endeavored to have her participate in this venture. As a former English teacher, she was invaluable in proofreading my writing and then she got very interested in writing her own story in Part 6: The Last Word.

I am indebted to Linda's cousin Mary Judith Rhae (Wiley) for a short family visit in October of 2020 where we conferred and exchanged information about the Hund family. Her now-published book *Obstacles and Gratitudes,* covers the Hund family in Part 1 of the Appendix. We have shared several memories, facts and pictures, many of which are included in chapter 29.

I appreciate the efforts of the team at Mission Point Press — Doug Weaver, Ed Hoogterp, Sarah Meiers and Darlene Short, who professionally, skillfully and diligently worked to make this book a reality for me. Thank you.

Index

Adams, Henry Sr. (1583–1646) 201, 202
Adams, John (1687–1729) 201
Adams, John Jr., President (1735–1826) 202
Adams, John Sr. (1691–1736) 202
Adams, John Quincy, President (1767–1848) 202
Adams, Capt. John (1661–1702) 201
Adams, Joseph (1625–1694) 202
Adams, Joseph (1654–1736) 202
Adams, Prudence (1765–1842) 201, 202
Adams, Samuel (1740–1773) 201, 202
Adams, Capt. Samuel Henry (1612–1688) 201, 202
Adams, William (1714–1793) 201
Adela of France, Saint (1009–1079) 39
Adelaide, of Normandy, of Aumale (c1030–before 1090) 31, 32
Adele of Vermandois (915–960) 38
Aelfgar III, Earl of Mercia (c1002–c1062) 17
Aelfgifu of Mercia (c997–c1097) 10, 17
Aelfgifu of Northumbria (997–1042) 10, 15
Aelfgifu of Shaftsbury 14
Aelfgifu (968–1002), wife of Aethelred II, King of England 15
Aelfthryth, wife of King Edgar, the Peaceful, King of England 14
Aelfthryth of Wessex (877–929) 10, 14, 38
Aethelbald 12, 13, 38
Aethelred I, King of Wessex (c837–871) 13
Aethelred II, the Unready, King of England (968–1016) 15
Aethelwulf, King of Wessex (c795–c858) 12, 38
Albrighton, Frances Joyce (1654–1688) 245

Alden, John, of the *Mayflower* 67, 202
Aldridge, Sarah B. (c1700–c1740) 226
Alfred, the Great, King of England (849–899) 13, 14, 38
Alice/Alix, wife of Ranulph de St. Liz 33
Alpaida, wife of Pepin II of Herstal 36
Allinor II, de Holland (1387–1405) 62, 63
Alwara/Awara (c955–c1055) 16
Andrew, John (c1759–1789) 127
Andrew, Jonathan (1701–1739) 127
Andrew, Jonathan (1715–1797) 127
Andrew, Jonathan (1786–1848) 127
Andrew, Lucrecia Polly (1817–1865) 127, 128
Andrew, Samuel (1620–1701) 127
Andrew, Rev. Samuel, Yale College (1656–1738) 127, 128
Andrews, John (1575–1663) 127
Andrews, John Hotolf, Sheriff of London (1410–1456) 51
Andrews, Lady Margaret Elizabeth Anne (1445–1485) 51
Andrews, Thomas (1539–1593) 127
Andrews, William (1595–1659) 127
Ansegisel of Metz (602/12–662/79) 35, 36
Anthony, Mary (1622–1691) 153-155
Arnulf of Metz, Saint (582–640) 35
Arnulf I, Count of Flanders (890–965) 38
Arnulf II, Count of Flanders (960/1–987) 39
Aslaksdatter, Gunlaug (1683–1775) 115
Astley, Elizabeth (1526–1600) 20
Audley, Hugh de (c1289–1347) 60
Audley, Margaret de (c1325–1348) 60
Aurebekk, Targjer Torelsdatter (1788–1858) 115

335

Index

Awara/Alwara (c955–c1055) 16
Bacon, Elizabeth (1738–1831) 156, 164
Bacon, Jeremiah (1717–1746)155, 156, 164
Bacon, Lt. Nathaniel Jr. (1674–1758) 156
Bacon, Nathaniel Sr. (1630–1705) 152, 153
Bailey, Lydia (1658–1728) 52, 186
Baldington, Lady Agnes (1403–1428) 194
Baldwin, Eunice (1738–1764) 127
Baldwin I, Margrave of Flanders (c830–879) 37, 38
Baldwin II, Margrave of Flanders (c865–918) 10, 14, 38
Baldwin III, Count of Flanders (940–962) 39
Baldwin IV, Count of Flanders (980–1035) 39
Baldwin V, Count of Flanders (1012–1067) 39, 40
Bandt, Margaret (1736–1805) 172
Banyster, Gennett (1527–561) 194
Barents, Tryntje (1636–1705) 165, 166
Barre, Lady Elizabeth de la (1402–1468) 161
Bass, Hannah 202
Bassett, Kenneth 153
Bassett, Mercy (1676–1756) 154
Bathurst, Mary Jane (1630–1682) 134
Be Arce/Bearse, Augustine/Austin 163
Beardsley, Charity (1731–1780) 143
Beardsley, Ruth (1789–1854) 145, 146
Beauchamp, Anne 56
Beauchamp. Margaret 59
Beauchamp, Phillippa de (??–c1386) 60
Beaufort, Joan (1374–1440) 55, 56, 57
Beaufort, John (1371–1410) 59
Beaufort, John (1404–1444) 59
Beaufort, Margaret (1443–1509) 59
Beaumont, Katherine (??–1435) 51
Beavis, Sarah (1057–1105) 132
Beckett, Thomas 43

Beers, Sarah Ann (1760–1818) 127
Begga, wife of Ansegisel of Metz 35, 36
Belchum, Anne (1475–1528) 52
Bennett, Elizabeth Lydia (1586–1654) 189, 190
Berenger, Count of Rennes 28
Bertrada of Laon 36
Blake, Betsey (c1610–??) 128
Blake, Capt. (1604–??) 125
Blake, Edwin (1818–1875) 127
Blake, Freelove (1745–1825) 126
Blake, Genevieve (1879–1933) 98-101, 104, 130, 131
Blake, Halsey Horatio (1843–1930) 128-131
Blake, John Sr. (1652–1690) 125
Blake, Richard (1780–1857) 127
Blake, Sarah (1675–1737) 189
Blake, Stephen (1687–1755) 126
Bledja, Heluna (784–814) 24
Bloecker, Mary Agnes (1833–1869) 207, 208
Bohun, Humphrey de (c1276–1322) 49, 50
Bohun, Margaret, Countess of Devon (1311–1391) 50
Boleyn, Lady Anne Boetler, Aunt of Queen Anne Boleyn (1475–1555) 132
Bond, Ann (1563–1628) 203
Boyington, Lady Ann(1495–1515) 203
Bradford, William 75
Bradock, Capt. John 167
Braybrooke, Gerald de Sr. (1264–1325) 19
Braybrooke, Sir Gerald II (1307–1359) 19
Braybrooke, Sir Gerald III (c1332–1403) 19, 51
(Braybrooke), Henrietta (1172–1210) 18
Braybrooke, Sir Henry de (1188–1234) 18
Braybrooke, Ingabald (1146–1167) 18
Braybrooke, Ingabaldus (1118–1167) 18
Braybrooke, John de (1220–1293) 19
Braybrooke, Nicole (c1386–1411) 19

Index

Braybrooke, Sir Reynold/Reginald de (1356–1426) 51
Braybrooke, Robert de (1168–1210) 18
Brewster, Fear 76
Brewster, Galfridus (1350–1410) 74
Brewster, Humphrey (1410–1443) 74
Brewster, Sir James, Knight (1380–1441) 74
Brewster, Sir John (1325–1379) 74
Brewster, Jonathan 76
Brewster, Love 75
(Brewster), Margaret (1381–??) 74
Brewster, Patience (1600–1634) 76
Brewster, Sir Robert, Knight (1440–1505) 74
Brewster, Sir William, Knight, Oxford Univ. (1470–1510) 74
Brewster, Elder William, of *Mayflower* Compact, Chief of the Pilgrims (c1566/8–1644) 74–76
Brewster, William (1536–1590) 75
Brewster, William II, Archbishop of York (c1505/10–1558) 75
Brewster, Wrestling 75
Brewes, Lady Margaret De (1412–1479) 133
Brindsal, Gunhild S. J. (1814–1891) 115
Brome, Isabel (1435/45–1513) 194
Bronson, Hannah (1738–1783) 198, 199
Bronson, Sgt. Issac (1645–1719) 198
Bronson, Issac (1670–1751) 198, 199
Bronson, Issac (1707–1799) 198, 199
Bronson, John (1602–1680) 198, 199
Bronson, Susanna (1718–1812) 201
Browme, Anna (1470–1560) 198
Brown, Nettye Jean (Knoop) (1936–2010) 298, 299, Appendix B
Brownson, Cornelius (1470–1560) 198
Brownson, Cornelius (1490–1550) 198
Brownson, Cornelius (1525–1560) 198
(Brownson), Joan (c1552–1617) 198
Brownson, John (1548–1623) 198
Brownson, Roger (1576–1635) 198
Bruce, Robert 50
Bryce, Elizabeth "Elspie" (1686–1734) 86
Bunce, Katherine (1610–1683) 186
Burton, Grace Hartley (1703–1791) 232, 233
Bush, James Edward (1880–1944) 210
Cady, Esther (1686–1734) 201
Caewlin (c535–c592) 11
Calloway, Sara Elizabeth (1729–1761) 246
Carew, Mary (1530–1568) 20
Carrington, John (1640–1690) 199
Carrington, Noadiah (1706–1738) 199
Carrington, Dr. Peter (1669–1727) 199
Carrington, Samuel (1732–1815) 199
Carrington, Sarah (1765–1844) 199
Carloman 36
Carloman I 36
Carter, Joan (1556–1632) 190
Cassell, Peter 234
Castle, Jacob, the Hunter, White Tassel (1717–1803) 234
Castle, Mary Ann (1752–1784) 233, 234
Cenred/Coenred (640–??) 11
Ceowald 11
Cerdic (??–534) 10
Charde, Elizabeth Abigail (1589–1643) 204
Charlemagne, Charles the Great, Charles I, King of the Franks, Holy Roman Emperor (742–814) 36, 37
Charles VII, King of France 57
Charles, the Bald, King of West Fancia (823–877) 12, 13, 37
Charles III, the Simple, King of France 28
Chavez, Hannah (1670–1760) 166
Chaworth, Elizabeth (1391–1467) 19
Chaworth, Sir Thomas (1385–1459) 19

Index

Cherington, Esther (1575–1616) 127
Christopher, Clement (1709–1769) 166
Christopher, Georgia Ann (1847–1902) 146, 147, 167
Christopher, Johannes Hans (1626–1688) 165, 166
Christopher, John Sr. (1650–1720) 166
Christopher, John Jr. (1699–1750) 166
Christopher, John Bluet (1730–1800) 166
Christopher, Peter (1590–1620) 165
Christopher, Spicer Samuel (1759–1811) 166, 167
Christopher, William Bluet (1785–1815) 167
Christopher, William Greenwood (1814–1880) 167
Clare, Gilbert de (1243–1295) 60, 62
Clare, Margaret de (1292–1342) 60
Clark, Abigail (1715–1771) 52, 186
Clark, Asahel 2 (1789–1861) 200, 202
Clark, Daniel (1683–1732) 186
Clark, Elizabeth (1653–1690) 199
Clark, John (1541–1598) 186
Clark, Sir John Richard (1503–1559) 186
Clark, Joseph (1652–1716) 186
Clark, Mary Hanser (1815–1906) 146, 200
Clark, Thomas (1570–1627) 186
Clark, Thomas (1690–1765) 198
Clark, Capt. Timothy (1732–1824) 146, 198, 199
Clark, William (1610–1681) 186
Clark, William (1763–1814) 199
Clarke, James (c1580–c1650) 196
(Clarke), Joane (c1580–c1645) 196
(Clarke), Sarah (1613–1675) 196, 197
Clarke, Lt. William (1609–1690) 196, 197
Clarke, Capt. William Jr. (1656–1725) 197, 198
Clere, Margaret (1433–1498) 133

Cobham, Joan (1340–1388) 50, 51
Cobham, John (1320–1408) 50
Coenred/Cenred (640–??) 11
Collins, Martha (1666–1750) 190
Cooke, Katherine Carew (1541–1601) 186
Cooke, Maude Manda (1526–1588) 192
Corbet, Anne Juliana (1470–1548) 161
Corbet, Joanna "Anna" (1495–1538) 68
Cornwall, Edmund (1422–1498) 160, 161
Cornwall, Sir Edmund de (1382–1443) 160, 161
Cornwall, George (1532–1594) 160, 161
Cornwall, Richard de (1360–1443) 160, 161
Cornwall, Sir Thomas de (1407–1472) 160, 161
Cornwall, Lord Thomas (1467–1537) 160, 161
Cornwall, William (1562–1625) 160, 161
Cornwell, Elizabeth (1716–1787) 155, 156, 164
Cornwell, Sgt. John (1640–1707) 164
Cornwell, Capt. Joseph (1679–1742) 164
Cornwell, Sgt. William (1609–1678) 153, 154, 160–164
Council, Lucy Hardy (1676–1738) 245
Courtenay, Elizabeth (??–1395) 51
Courtenay, Sir Hugh de (1303–1377) 50
Courtenay, Margaret (1328–1395) 50
Creed, Lucy (1735–1809) 241
Cummings, Robert E. Lee (1868–1915) 209
Cuthwine (c565–592) 11
Cuthwolf, Citha (592–??) 11
Cynric (495–560) 11
Dakeney, Elizabeth (1311–1388) 19
Darcy, Sir Arthur (1505–1561) 20
Darcy, Sir Edward (1543–1612) 20
Darcy, Isabella (c1600–c1669) 21, 169
Darcy, Richard, Lord of Knayth (1424–1458) 19, 20
Darcy, Sir Thomas (1467–1537) 20
Darcy, Sir William (1443–1488) 20

Index

Dauncy, Alison (1429–1453) 194
David, the Saint, King of Scots (??–1053) 33
De Shelodonne, Isabel (1035–??) 132
De Shelodonne, Robert (1033–1070) 132
De Shelodonne, Robert (1055–1107) 132
De Shelton, John I (c1080–c1150) 132
De Shelton, John II (c1100–c1145) 132
De Shelton, John III (c1140–c1190) 132
De Shelton, John IV (c1160–c1225) 133
De Shelton, Ralph (1180/1200–1244/5) 133
De Shelton, Ralph (1229–??) 133
Deane, Eleanor (1586–1654) 202, 204
Deane, Margery (1610–c1630) 198, 204
Denton, Abraham (1675–1729) 48, 194
Denton, James, 14th Dean of Litchfield (1470–1532) 194
Denton, James (1492–1532) 184, 194
Denton, John (c1345–??) 194
Denton, John (1375–after 1401) 194
Denton, Martha (1710–1763) 48, 194, 195
Denton, Richard (1504–1548) 194
Denton, Richard (1557–1619) 194
Denton, Rev. Richard (1603–1662) 47, 48, 194
Denton, Sir Robert John (1445–1497) 194
Denton, Samuel (1631–1713) 48, 194
Denton, Thomas (1332–??) 194
Denton, Thomas (1401–1427) 194
Denton, Sir Thomas (1427–1453) 194
DePlais (1326–1405) 133
Derby Silver Co. 138, 157, 158
Despencer, Galfridus Geofrey (c1190/1200–1242) 184
Despencer, John (1235–1274) 184
Deverell, Alice (1305–1386) 185
Doda wife of St. Arnulf of Metz 35
Dolling, Mary 81, 82
Dorothy, Lady, of Warde (1528–1587) 189

Dreisbach, James (1950–) Appendix D
Dreisbach, Katherine (1980–) 135, 136, Appendix D
Dreisbach, William Garrish (1916–1960) Appendix D
Dreisbach, William Shelton (1946–) 135, 136, Appendix D
Dreisbach, Capt. William (1983–) Appendix D
Dubbin, Elizabeth (1631–1696) 153–155
Dunkle, Mary (1745–1782) 227
Dunn, Anna (1661–1723) 237
Dunster, Henry (1592–1646) 185, 186
Dunster, Henry, 1st President of Harvard College (1609–1658/9) 185, 186
Dunster, Rose (1603–1650) 185, 186
Dymoke, Sir Edward, Kings Champion (1508–1566) 46
Dymoke, Frances (1539–c1610) 47
Dymoke, Lt. Col. John 47
Dymoke, Robert, Kings Champion 46
Eadgifu, wife of King Edward, the Elder 14
Eafa of Wessex (c732–772) 11
Ealdgyth of Mercia (c1034–c1086) 15, 17
Ealhmund of Kent (c750–784) 11
Ealhswith (??–c888) 13
Eathelflaed, mother of King Edward, the Elder
Ecgberht/Ecgbryth/Egbert, King of West Saxons (c775–839) 12
Ecgfrida, 1st wife of Uchtred 15
Edgar, the Peaceful (943/4–975), King of England 14
Edmund, the magnificent (921–946), King of England 14
Edward, the Confessor, King of England 15, 31
Edward, the Elder (c871–924), King of England 14
Edward I Plantagenet (1239–1307), Longshanks,

Index

King of England 44, 46, 49, 55, 60–62
Edward II Plantagenet (1284–1327), King of England 44
Edward III Plantagenet (1312–1377), King of England 45, 55, 59
Edward IV, of March (1442–1483), King of England 58, 59
Edward V 58
Edwards, Elizabeth (1791–1845) 167
Eleanor of Aquitaine (1122–1204) 43
Eleanor of Castile (1244–1290) 44, 49, 60, 61
Eleanor of Normandy, 2nd wife of Baldwin IV 15
Eleanor of Provence (1217–1291) 44
Elgiva/Elgira of England, (870–964) 13, 24
Elizabeth, de Burgh (1332–1386) 45
Elizabeth of Rhuddlan (1282–1316) 49
Elizabeth of York 59
Elizabeth I (1533–1603), Queen of England 46, 59
Elizabeth II (1926–), Queen of England 46
Elleigh, Lady Catherine De (1204/5–1260) 133
Elton, John (1648–1686) 155
Elton, Mary (1710–1739) 153–156
Elton, Richard (1679–1765) 155
Emma, 1st wife of Richard I, 1st Duke of Normandy 28, 30
Emma de Saint Liz/Elizabeth (1110–1146) 18, 23
Emma of Normandy, wife of Edward, the Confessor 15
Enguerrand II, Count of Ponthieu 31
Eoppa (706–??) 11
Erburon, Jone (c1540–c1640) 190
Ermendgarde, wife of Louis, the Pious 37
Ermentrude (823–869) 37
Eystrinsson, Rognvald (825–894) 27

Fairchild, Rachel (1749–1815) 126
Faust, Katherine "Katie" (1879–1947) 210
Fauth, Catherine (?? –1717) 172
Ferrers, Mary de (1394–1457) 60
Ferns, Bradford John "Jack" Appendix C
Ferns, Sarah Elizabeth Appendix C
Ferns, Suzanne Virginia Appendix C
Fielding, Alice 179
Fisher, Elizabeth (1596–1639) 71–73
Fitzgilbert, Richard De St. Valery (1002–after 1053) 29
Fitzhugh, Henry (1429–1472) 63
Fitzhugh, Lady Elizabeth (1460–1513) 63
Fletcher, Hope (1624–1704) 153, 154, 190
Floyd, Mary Ann Rachel (1610–1688) 240, 241
Floyd, Mary Martha (1825–1868) 167
Ford, Abigail (1619–1688) 197, 198, 204, 205
Ford, Thomas (1587–1676) 204
Fox, Maria Elizabeth (1705–??) 172
Francis, Maud (??–1424) 62
Fraser, Thomas 87
Frazier/Fraser, Elizabeth (1710–??) 87
Freeman, Maj. John (1622–1719) 76, 77
Freeman, Rebecca — Maryland 237
Freeman, Rebecca Sarah (1694–1757) — Massachusetts 77
Freeman, Deacon Thomas (1653–1716) 77
French, Joseph (1730–1781) 143
French, Phoebe (1768–1831) 143–145
Frionnlaith, King of Ireland 24
Frotho, Gorm Enske, King of Sjaelland in Denmark (830–c875) 24
Frothoson, Harold, Parcus, King of Sjaelland in Denmark (858–899) 24
Gabbard (Shelton), Tracy 135
Gael, Thomas (1506–1546) 192
Gael, Thomas (1522–1588) 192

Index

Gael, Thomas (1552–1606) 193
Gale, Abel (1635–1721) 194
Gale, Edmund (1602–1642) 193
Gale, John (1571–1650) 193
Gale, John (1670–1750) 194
Gale, Hannah (1731–1817) 48, 86–88, 195
Gale, Hezekiah (1710–1784) 48, 194
Gammel, Gorm Haraldsson (890–c958), King of Denmark & East Anglia 24
Gandolfsdotter, Althilda (??) 24
Gascoigne, Dorothy (1476–1526) 185
Gascoigne, Elizabeth (1471–c1559) 46
Gascoigne, Sir William (1428–1463) 60
Gascoigne, Sir William V (1445–c1486) 46, 60, 185

Gaunt, John (1340–1399) 55, 59
Geoffrey I of Brittany 29
Getting, Agatha (c1284–??) 133
Gilbert, de St. Valery (c977–c1077) 29
Gilbert, Chloe (1787–1872) 127
Gilbert, John (1683–1727) 189, 190
Gilbert, Jonathan Sr. (1617–1682) 189
Gilbert, Jonathan (1648–1698) 189
Gilbert, Mary (1713–1757) 189
Gilbert, Richard A. (before 1550–1626) 189
Gilbert, Thomas Sr. (c1559–before 1659) 189, 190
Glandfield, Elizabeth (1565–1616) 69
Glyndwr, Owain 56
Godgifu, Lady Godiva (c1010–c1086) 16
Godwinson, Harold II, King of England 17, 30
Gookin, Major General Daniel (1612–1687) 78–82
Gookin, John 79
Gookin, Capt. Samuel (1652–1730) 81, 82
Gorm Haraldsson Gammel (890–c959), King of Denmark & East Anglia 24
Gormson, Harald Blaatland, Bluetooth, King of Denmark (910–986) 25, 28
Govan, Jonet (??–after 1665) 86
Graves, Rebecca (1630–1664) 201
Green, Grace (1586–1686) 164
Greenwood, Mary (1763–1806) 166, 167
Greenwood, William Clyde 167
Gregg, Anne (1716–1794) 182
Gregg, Hugh 182
Gregg, Joseph 179
Gregorie, Margaret (c1682–1746) 181
Griffith, Arden Evans (1802–1870) 209
Griffith, Olive (1838–1907) 209
Grifo 36
Gruffydd Ap Llewelyn, King of Wales (c1011–1063) 17
Gruffydd, Nest Verch (1059–1152) 17
Gunnora of Denmark/Gonnor De Crepon, Dutchess of Normandy (936–1031) 25, 28, 29
Haddeland, Anna 114
Haddeland, Frank 115
(Haddeland), Snnove 114, 115
Haddeland, Svein 114, 115
Hale, Martha Hannah (1618–1695) 164
Hall, Jane (1653–1724) 155
Hall, Capt. John Sr. (1584–1673) 153–155
Hall, Capt. Richard Sr. (1620–1691) 153–155
Hall, Sarah (1622–1664) 153–155
Hall, Sarah (1654–1726) 125
Harald, Bluetooth, Blattland, Gormson, King of Denmark 25, 28
Harcourt, Emma De (c1200–1265) 184
Hardecanute Sigurdsson, King of Denmark (814–c850/884) 24
Harold II Godwinson, King of England 17, 30
Harold, Parcus, King of Sjaelland in Denmark

Index

(c846–899) 13, 24
Harris, Abigail (1656–1723) 164
Harris, Capt. Daniel (1615–1701) 153, 154
Harris, John (c1540–c1650) 190
Harris, Mary (1692–1742) 189, 190
Harris, Rachel (1707–1799) 169, 170
Harris, Thomas (1580–c1634) 190
Harris, Walter (1556–1618) 190
Harris, Capt. William (1665–1751) 190
Harrod, Riley Wilson (1888–1957) 211
Harry, Thosamine (1581–1641) 188
Harvey, Ann Mary (1440–1504) 74
Harvey, Carrie F. (1870–1960) 209
Harvey, Lady Mary (1470–1510) 74
Haskins, Margaret (1700–1765) 241
Hatcher, Edward (1633–1711) 70
Hatcher, Sarah (1665–after 1706) 70, 241
Hatcher, William (1614–1680) 70
Hatton, Dorothy Jane (1536–1591) 68
Hawisia de Ridel (c1083–??) 33
Hawise, sister of Richard II, Duke of Normandy 29
Haywarde, Margery (1561–1616) 161
Hedges, Levy (1791–1874) 179
Henrietta (Braybrooke) (1172–1210) 18
Henry I, King of England (c1068–1135) 33, 42
Henry II Plantagenet, King of England (1133–1189) 43
Henry III, Holy Roman Emperor 39
Henry III Plantagenet, King of England (1207–1272) 44
Henry IV Bolingbroke, King of England (1367–1413) 45, 55, 56
Henry V, King of England (1386–1422) 45, 56, 57, 63
Henry VI, King of England (1421–1471) 57, 58
Henry VII Tudor, King of England (1457–1509) 20, 59
Henry VIII, King of England 133
Herbert, Ann (1588–c1639) 134
Heritage, Lady Agnes (1478–c1557) 185
Herleva of Falaise, mother of William, the Conqueror 30
Hildegard of the Vinzgau (757/8–783) 36, 37
Hills, Dorothy (1370–1408)185
Hills, Elizabeth Cutter (1601–1670) 190
Hills, Francis (1605–1680) 198, 199
Hills, Hannah Joanis (1618–1692) 184–186
Hills, John (1602–1688) 185
Hinman, Sarah (1608–??) 188
Holand, Allinor II de (1387–1405) 62, 63
Hollister, Lt. John 141
Hollister, Mary (1704–1782) 141
Hoorde, Maria (1425–1498) 161
Hopkins, Caleb 73
Hopkins, Constance 72, 73
Hopkins, Damarius 72
Hopkins, Giles 72, 73
Hopkins, Irene (1742–1792) 201
Hopkins, Oceanus (1620–1627) 72
Hopkins, Stephen (1581–1644) 71–73
Horton, Rachel (1650–1714) 205
Hovel, Elizabeth (1526–1616) 198
Hoye, Ase Jansdatter (1752–1817) 115
Huffman, Maude Mae (1888–1952) 211
Hugh de Saint Liz (c1079–c1110) 33
Hughleville, Ada (1005–1039) 29
Hughleville, Ada (1039–1114) 18, 29
Hund, Charles D. (1822–1897) 216, 217
Hund, Charles William (1895–1972) 217–219
Hund, Christine Mae (1905–1993) 217–219
Hund, Emily Francis (1896–1989) 217–219
Hund, George Washington (1893–1980) 217–219

Index

Hund, George Washington Sr. (1861–1935) 217–220, 231
Hund, Gladys Julia (1913–2004) 217–219
Hund, Harry Seabolt (1902–1990) 217–219
Hund, Joseph Henry (1906–1979) 217–219
Hund, Jurgen Andres (c1800–1871) 216
Hund, Paul Emmit (1907–1991) 217–219
Hund, Roger Otis (1901–1980) 217–219
Hund, Rosetta (1912–2009) 217–219, 221
Hund, Ruth (1909–2008) 213–223
Hund, Susie Elizabeth (1894–1974) 217–219
Huntington, Samuel, Lt. Governor 136
Hyanno, John, Sachem (1595–1680) 162, 163
Hyanno, Mary "Little Dove" (c1618–1695) 153, 154, 160–164
Ine (670–??) 11
Ingild of Wessex (632–718) 11
Ireland, Constance (1602–1665) 193
Isabella of France (1292–1358) 44
Isabelle d'Anglolene (1188–1246) 43
Itta, wife of Pepin I 35
Ives, Mary Hall (1792–1863) 156
Ivo de Newmarche, of Braybrooke (1096–1146) 18, 33
Jackson, Abigail (1505–1616) 198
Jennings, Sarah (c1620–1699) 63, 245
Joan of England Plantagenet, of Acre (1272–1307) 55, 60, 61
John, of Gaunt (1340–1399) 55, 59
John Plantagenet, of Magna Carta, King of England (1167–1216) 19
Johnson, Mary (1674–1709) 154, 155
Johnson, Mary (1741–1774) 199
Judith of Bavaria (797–843) 37
Judith of Brittany, Lady (982–1017) 29, 30
Judith of Flanders (c843–870) 12, 37, 38
Judith of Lens (c1054–c1086) 32, 33

Kaddeland, Carolyn Clark (1907–1966) 105–107, 110, 111, 121–124
Kaddeland, Christen Christensen (1815–1896) 115
Kaddeland, Christen Rosjford (1880–1958) 117–121, 147–149
Kaddeland, Karl Andreas (1856–c1920) 114–117
Kaddeland, Marcia Jane (1917–2013) 148, Appendix D
Kaelin, Joseph Frank (1899–1984) 213
Kaye, Isabel (1595–1638) 185
Kaye, John of Woodsome (1528–1594) 185
Kaye, Richard (1564–1597) 185
Keil, Anna Elizabeth 216
Kent, Mary 71
Kerrick, Rose (1572–1627) 186
Kidder Motor Vehicle Co. 98, 99
Kilgour, Christiane (c1630–??) 201
Klacksdatter/Dannesbod, Thyra (844–935) 24
Knoop, Albert John (1863–1932) 208
Knoop, Anne (1865–1927) 208
Knoop, Frank (c1826–1898) 207
Knoop, Frank Albert (1874–1951) 210
Knoop, Frank Clemens (1853–1936) 208, 209
Knoop, George Washington (1887–1970) 211
Knoop, Henry F. (1854–1937) 208
Knoop, Herman Edward (1880–1965) 210
Knoop, John Henry (1877–1960) 210
Knoop, John William (1868–1955) 208
Knoop, Julie Lynn (1962–) Appendix B
Knoop, Karla Dianne (1958–) Appendix B
Knoop, Linda (Smith) (1939–) Part 6
Knoop, Lisa Ann (1963–) Appendix B
Knoop, Luella (1864–??) 208
Knoop, Mary Agnes (1857–1928) 208
Knoop, Minnie Lee (1889–1946) 211

Index

Knoop, Oliva M. (1903–1974) 212,213
Knoop, Olivia Marie (1884–1968) 210
Knoop, Col. Paul Robert (1937–) 207, 214, 220–222, Appendix B
Knoop, Robert Elmer (1893–1971) 211
Knoop, Robert Erskin (1959–) Appendix B
Knoop, Robert Fridolin (1908–1983) 212–215
Knoop, Rosa (1859–??) 208
Knoop, Rosa A. (1855–1856) 208
Knoop, William James (1881–1951) 210, 211
Knoop-Schorch, Louis (1895–1962) 211
Knox, Susan Elsie (1950–) Appendix D
Knud 115
Knudsen, Christen, of Mjaland (1790–1816) 115
Knudsen, Morten 115
La Launde, Johanne De (1345–??) 194
La Launde, Johanne De (1378–after 1401) 194
La Pole, Joan de (1372–1434) 51
La Pole, John de (1335–1380) 50, 51
Lambert, Susan (1590–1637) 168
Lambert II, Count of Lens (??–1054) 31
Langton, Eupherne/Euphemia (1443–1471) 20
Larkin, Mary (1652–1707) 82
Launce, John (1597–1639) 21, 169
Launce, Mary (1625–1710) 21, 169
Ledet, Christina (1190–1271) 18
Ledet, Wischard 18
Leete, Catherine (1642–1693) 188, 189
Leete, John (1570–1648) 189
Leete, Thomas (1520–1582) 189
Leete, Thomas II (1554–1616) 189
Leete, Gov. William (1612–1683) 189
Lehr, Eva Elizabeth (1856–1938) 94, 96, 97, 101, 102, 104
Lehr, Gottfried (1832–1906) 96, 104
Lental, Elizabeth (1424–1489) 161

Leofwine, Ealdorman of the Hwicce (c950–1023) 16
Leofric, Earl of Mercia (968–1057) 16
Limer, Elizabeth Agnes (1540–1599) 52
Lincoln, Isabelle (1394–1462) 185
Litten, Caleb Polleckfield, the Elder (1678–1763) 232, 233
Litten, James Edward (1750–1840) 233, 234
Litten, Lt. John Richard (1726–1804) 233
Litten, Michael (1647–1720) 232
Litten, Saphronia Lena (1780–1849) 227, 228, 234, 235
Llewelyn Ap Seisyll 17
Lord, Mary (1506–1546) 192
Lou, Anne de (1240–1275) 184
Louis, the Pious (778–840) 37
Louis IV, King of France 28
Lowery, Mary 87
Lucas, Annah (1712–1752) 126
Lucas, Lady Anne (1561–1629) 63
Lucas, Joane (1512–1610) 168
Lucas, Maria Mary (1620–1659) 152
Luttrell, Sir Andrew (before 1330–1378) 51
Luttrell, Elizabeth (??–??) 51
Luttrell, Hugh (before 1364–1428) 51
Lutz, Elizabeth Henrietta (1880–1962) 210
Lyker, Elizabeth (1632–1691) 125
Mack, Elizabeth Polly (1764–1843) 234
Malcolm II of Scotland 15
Malcolm III, King of Scotland 42
Mallory, Judith (1689–1760) 201
Manhattan Gas Light Co. 90–92
Mann, Lady Maud (c1500/15–c1558/88) 75
Margaret of Anjou 57, 58
Margaret of Holland 59
Markenfield, Alice (1506–1563) 185
Markenfield, Ninian (1474–1528) 185

Index

Martel, Charles (688–741) 36
Martyn, Joanna (1537–1567) 161
Mathilde of Saxony (939–1008) 39
Matilda of Flanders (1031–1083) 30, 31, 40, 42
Matilda of Scotland (1080–1118), "Queen Maud of England", Court of Argon 42
Matilda/Maud of England, the Empress (1102–1167) 42, 43
Maud/Matilda, Countess of Huntington (c1074–c1130) 32, 33
Mauleverer, Dorothy (1528–1590) 185
Mauleverer, Robert (1495–1541) 185
Maynell, Isabel (after 1337–1393) 19
McCaughry, Jane 178
McGhee, Velma Ruth (1414–1481) 74
McGinnis, Mary (1773–1860) 228
McLean (Bassett), Polly 153
Meffert, Emma Louise (1876–1941) 210
Melchior, Anna Marie (1650–1709) 166
Menn, Barbara (1597–1644) 165
Merbury, Alice/Celillia (1364–1417) 161
Merkel, Anna Susanne (1824–1915) 216, 217
Merkel, Johann Tobias 216
Merrill, Ann Agnes (1509–1560) 52
Merrill, Sir John, the Elder (1470–1529) 52
Merrill, Thomas Windsor de (1440–1485) 51
Miller, Ann (1633–1680) 151–156
Miller, "Gov." Benjamin (1672–1747) 154, 155
Miller, Capt. Ichabod Jr. (1739–1824) 156, 164
Miller, Deacon Ichabod Sr. (1709–1788) 155, 156
(Miller) Isabel (1613–1666) 150–156
Miller, Jeremiah (1780–1848) 156
Miller, John/Martin (c1560–1633) 150
Miller, Thomas (1609–1680) 150–156, 190
Miller, Virginia Ruth (1848–1939) 128–131, 158, 159
Miller, Watrous Ives (1822–1885) 156–158
Miller, Watson John (1849–1911) 138, 157, 158
Moffat, David, Established Moffat Library, Washingtonville, NY 182, 183
Moffat, Elizabeth "Betsey" (1739–c1788) 176–178, 182
Moffat, Samuel (before 1679–after 1710) 181
Moffat, Samuel (1704–1787) 182
Moffat, Samuel III (1744–1807) 182, 183
Moffat, William (1675–1748) 181, 182
Montagu, Alice (1398–1462) 63
Montagu, John, 3rd Earl of Salisbury (1350–1400) 62
Montagu, John de, 1st Baron Montecute (c1330–c1390) 62
Montagu, Sir Thomas, 4th Earl of Salisbury (1388–1428) 62
Montagu, William, 1st Earl of Salisbury 62
Montgomery, Gen. Richard 88, 177
Monthermer, Margaret (1329–1394) 62
Monthermer, Ralph (1262–1325) 61, 62
Monthermer, Thomas (1301–1340) 62, 63
Moore, Benjamin, Bishop of New York 94
Moore, Clement Clarke 91
Morgan, Gen. John Hunt 229–231
Morgan, Mary (1678–1749) 198, 199
Morken/Morton, Margery (1553–1637) 189
Mortensen, Knud, of Mjaland (1752–1823) 115
Mortimer, Edmund de (1351/2–1381), 3rd Earl of March 45
Mortimer, Lady Elizabeth de (1370/1–1417) 45
Mortimer, Roger 44, 45
Moulthrop, Hannah (1709–1748) 199
Mowbray, Mary Cave Melton (1564–1603) 164
Mullens, Priscilla, of the *Mayflower* 67, 202
Neeb, Anna R. (1856–1931) 208
Neill, Janet (1647–??) 201

Index

Nettleton, Sarah (1642–1728) 152–154
Nettleton, Samuel (1620–1659) 152
Neville, Alice (1431–1503) 63
Neville, Anne (??–1480) 58
Neville, Cicely (1415–1495) 57
Neville, Eleanor (1398–1472) 45
Neville, Joan (1443–1486), (daughter of John Neville (1416–1482) 60
Neville, John (1416–1482), 3rd Lord Raby, son of Ralph Neville (1364–1425) 60
Neville, Ralph (1364–1425), 4th Lord of Raby, 1st Earl of Westmoreland 55–57
Neville, Ralph (1392–1457) 60
Neville, Richard, 5th Earl of Salisbury (1400–1460) 56, 63
Neville, Richard, the Kingmaker, 16th Earl of Warwick (1428–1471) 56–58
New Haven Fire Dept. 94–96
Newmarche, Albreda de (1146–1168) 18
Newmarche, Awbreria (1120–1146) 18
Newmarche, Bernard de (1075–1133) 18, 29
Newmarche, Geoffrey (c1025–c1100) 18, 29
Newmarche, Ivo de (1096–1146) 18, 33
Newmarch, Elizabeth, (wife of John Neville (1416–1482) 60
Newport, Capt./Adm. Christopher (1561–1617) 68–70
Newport, Capt. John Christopher (1536–1691) 68
Newport, Marian (1611–1646) 70
Newport, Thomas (1491–1551) 68
Nicholson, Ann (c1768–??) 88
Nicholson, John/Daniel (1717–1788), father of Col. John 176
Nicholson, Col. John (1743–1811) 88, 176–179, 182
Nicholson, John C. 176

Nicholson, Margaret (1669–1834) 176
(Nicholson), Mary (1720–??), mother of Col. John 176
Nicholson, Samuel 176
Neope, Princess Mary (1600–1624) 163
Ogive of Luxembourg (995–1035) 39
Olafsdotr, Gyrthe (905–??), Queen of Denmark 25
Oliver, John (c1800–??) 91
Oliver, Margaretta (1820–1881) 91, 93, 94
Olsen, Jette Samuelsdtr (1853–1880) 116
Osbern Fitz Richard (1055–c1100) 17, 18
Osbern, Nest Verch (1082–1163) 18, 29
Osburg/Osburth of Wessex (810–876) 12
Ossman, Jacob 215
Papia I de Crepon (c936–c1031) 29
Papia II, Moriton, de Normandy, (c980–c1075) 29
Parcus, Harold (c846–899), King of Sjaelland in Denmark 13, 24
Parker, Lady Margaret (1509–1558) 133
Passon, Margery (1532–1570) 164
Patience (Miller) (1789/90–1856) 127
Payne, Anna (1621–1668) 189
Peck, Edward William (1582–1686) 164
Peck, John III (1530–1619) 164
Peck, Martha (1641–1708) 164
Peck, Deacon Paul (1608–1695) 164
Peck, Stephen William (1562–1619) 164
Pepin I, the Elder, the Old, of Landen (c580–640) 35
Pepin II of Herstal (c635–714) 36
Pepin, the Short, King of France (714–768) 36
Percy, Sir Henry, Hotspur, 1st Earl of Northumberland (1364–1403) 45, 56
Percy, Sir Henry, 2nd Earl of Northumberland (1393–1455) 45, 46, 56, 57

Index

Percy, Sir Henry, 3rd Earl of Northumberland (1421–1461) 46, 58, 59
Percy, Sir Henry, 4th Earl of Northumberland (1449–1489) 59
Percy, Margaret (1437–1486) 46, 60, 185
Phesy, Agnes (1540–1610) 168
Philippe, de Hainault (1311–1369) 45, 55, 59
Piccott, Lora, (c1273–??) 19
Piggot, Elizabeth (1536–1590) 188
Plais, Joan De (1326–1405) 133
Plantagenet, Edward I, Longshanks, King of England (1239–1307) 44, 46, 49, 55, 60–62
Plantagenet, Edward II, King of England (1284–1327) 44
Plantagenet, Edward III, King of England (1312–1377) 45, 55, 59
Plantagenet, Elizabeth, of Rhuddlan/England (1282–1316) 49, 50
Plantagenet, Geoffrey (1113–1151) 42, 43
Plantagenet, Henry II, King of England (1132/3–1189) 43
Plantagenet, Henry III, King of England (1207–1272) 44
Plantagenet, Joan of England (1272–1307) 61
Plantagenet, John, King of England (1167–1216) 43
Plantagenet, Lionel, Duke of Clarence (1338–1368) 45
Plantagenet, Phillipa, of Clarence (1355–1378/9) 45
Pollard, Joan (1344–c1362) 185
Polleckfield, Johanna (1655–1720) 232
Poppa of Envermere, 2nd wife of Richard II, Duke of Normandy 30
Poppa De Renness (872 –??) 27
Post, Catherine Ann (1766–1828) 90, 172–175
Post, John (1740–1817) 172–175

Potter, Delila (1804–1860) 209
Poynings, Eleanor (c1422–c1484) 46
Prence, Gov. Thomas (1600–1673) 76
Prence, Mercy (1631–1711) 76, 77
Prince, Daniel 145
Prince, Joseph 144, 145
Prout, Dr. Ebenezer (1656–1735) 21, 169
Prout, Harris (1732–1822) 170
Prout, Hugh (1556–1619) 168
(Prout), Margaret (1623–1685) 168
Prout, Ruth Lucrecia (1821–1898) 156, 158, 170
Prout, Thomas (1528–1561) 168
Prout, Capt. Timothy (1620–1702) 168
Prout, William (1588–1654) 168
Prout, William (1699–1789) 169
Prout, William (1779–1822) 170
Puckett, Susan (1812–1897) 238, 239
Pylston, Mary/Priscilla (c1589–??) 150, 151
Ragnarsson, King of Denmark (782–803) 24
Ragnhild, wife of Rognvald Eysteinsson 27
Ranulph de Saint Liz (c1030–1047) 33
Record, Lady Beatrice De (c1150–c1200) 133
Redburga 12
Reukauf, Adolf (1879–1968) 224, 225
Reukauf, Ernestine A. (1878–1933) 210, 212, 213, 224, 225
Reukauf, Frederick Fridolin (1849–1934) 224, 225
Reukauf, Louise "Lulu" (1890–1953) 224
Rhae, Mary Judith (Wiley) 304
Richard, Fitz Scrob 17
Richard I, the Fearless, First Duke of Normandy (933–996) 25, 28
Richard I, the Lionheart, King of England 43
Richard II, the Good Duke, Duke of Normandy (963–1027) 18, 29, 30, 33

347

Richard II, King of England (1367–1400) 55
Richard III, Duke of Normandy (1001–1027) 30, 33, 39, 40
Richard, 3rd Duke of York (1411–1460) 57
Richard III, King of England 58, 59
Richards, Eunice (1716–1749) 198, 199
Richmond, Eleanor (1904–2000) 111–113
Risen, A. B. (1820–1859) 209
Risen, Mary Elizabeth (1853–1935) 208–210
Ritter, Catherine (1796–1869) 89, 90, 171, 175
Ritter, Johan Petrus (??–1717) 172
Ritter, John Michael (1734–1799) 172
Ritter, John Peter (1698–1747) 172
Ritter, Peter (1758–1811) 90, 172–175
Robert, Archbishop of Rouen 30
Robert, Duke of Normandy, son of William and Matilda 31
Robert I, the Magnificent, Duke of Normandy (1000–1035) 30, 31
Robert II, King of France 39
Roberts, John (1668–1721) 189
Roberts, Sir John Roberts of Burway (1510–1610) 187
Roberts, Jonathan (1707–1788) 189, 190
Roberts, Priscilla (1736–1810) 170, 191
Roberts, Samuel (1638–1726) 187–189
Roberts, Samuel William (1608–1690) 187
Roberts, Lord William (1576–1675) 187
Roberts, Sir William Thomas (c1548–c1548) 187
Robinson, Gresell (1665–after 1687) 86
Robinson, Pastor John 75
Rogers, Rev. Ezekial 150–153, 190
Rognvald Eysteinsson (825–894) 27
Rognvaldsson, Rollo/Rolf, the Viking King (845–931) 27, 28
Rohrbach, Therese/Josephine (1798–1874) 216

Rollo/Rolf Rognvaldsson (845–931) 27, 28
Roone, Charles 91
Roote, Mary (1650–1701) 198, 199
Rosfjord 121
Rotrude of Trier 36
Rozala of Italy (950/60–1003) 39
Rowland, C. N. S. 93
Rupe, Malinda (c1811–1850) 228
Rupe, Nicholas (1767–1835) 228
Saint Arnulph, of Metz (582–640) 35
Saint Liz/Elizabeth, Emma de (1110–1146) 18, 23
Saint Liz, Hugh de (c1079–c1110) 33
Saint Liz, Ranulph de (c1030–1047) 33
Saint Liz, Simon I de (??–c1111) 32, 33
Saint Valery, Gilbert de (c997–c1077) 29
Saint Valery, Richard Fitzgilbert de (1002–after 1053) 29
Sandrenham, Constance (1543–1593) 127
Sandys, Edith 20
Sanford, Gen. Henry Shelton 146, 147
Savage, John (1627–1684) 153–155
Savage, Mary (1663–1732) 155
Savage, Mary Abigail (1602–1639/40) 127
Scrope, Eleanor (1424–1471) 19
Scrope, John (c1388–1455) 19
Seabury, Bishop Samuel (1729–1796) 91, 173, 174
Selcraig, Alexander (c1651–1721) 201
Selcraig, Johne (1625–1650) 201
Selkregg, Osee (1768–1825) 201, 202
Selkregg, Ruth Adams (1791–1885) 200, 202
Selkrigg, John (1734–1790) 201
Selkrigg, William (1671–??) 201
Selkrigg, William (1710–1756) 201
Sexton, Abigail (c1750–after 1828) 186
Shatswell, Elizabeth 190

Index

Sheets, Benjamin (c1773–1842) 227, 234, 235
Sheets, Charles Sr. (c1811–1876) 228
Sheets, Pvt. Charles William, CSA (Robert) (1841–1903) 217, 228–231, 239
Sheets, Henry Harrison (1740–1810) 227
Sheets, Martin (c1700–1782) 227
Sheets, Mary Frances (1876–1931) 217–220, 231
Sheets, Peter (c1680–after 1840) 226
Shelton, Alfred (1792–1857) 137, 145, 146
Shelton, Abbie B. (1868–1944) 135
Shelton, Abigail "Abby" (1800–1823) 144
Shelton (Davis), Becky 135
Shelton, Charles Frederick (1845–1919) 134, 146, 147
Shelton, Daisy Selkirk (1886–1959) 134, 147–149, 199
Shelton, Dalta De (1128–??) 133
Shelton, Lt. Daniel (1668–1728) 134–141
Shelton, Edward de Forest 147, 148
Shelton, Edward Nelson (1812–1894) 135–137
Shelton, James (1629–1716) 134
Shelton, James, Gentleman (c1585–c1668), to Virginia in 1610 134
Shelton, Jane de Forest (1843–1914) 132–135
Shelton, John Douglas (1813–1894) 134, 135, 146, 200
Shelton, John Frederick (1879–1967) 135
Shelton, Joseph (1696–1782) 141, 142
Shelton, Sir John (c1249/53–c1333), 13th Lord of Shelton 133
Shelton, Sir John (c1380–1431), 17th Lord of Shelton 133
Shelton, Sir John (1451–before c1500), 20th Lord of Shelton 133
Shelton, Sir John William (c1472–1539), 21st Lord of Shelton, High Sheriff of Norfolk 133

Shelton, Sir John (1504–1558), 22nd Lord of Shelton 133
Shelton, Sir John De (c1080–c1150) 132
Shelton, Sir John II De (c1100–c1145) 132
Shelton, Sir John III De, (c1140–c1190) Lord Mayor of Stradbrooke, 1st Lord of Shelton 132, 133
Shelton, Sir John IV De (c1160–c1225), 2nd Lord of Shelton 133
Shelton, Polly (1806–1841) 144, 145
Shelton (Bixler), Nancy Louis 135
Shelton, Nathan 135
Shelton, Nolan 135
Shelton, Sir Ralph (1315–1358), 14th Lord of Shelton Manor, Built Old Shelton Hall and St. Mary's Church in Norfolk 133
Shelton, Sir Ralph (c1330/4–c1385), 15th Lord of Shelton Manor 133
Shelton, Sir Ralph (c1361–1429), 16th Lord of Shelton Manor 133
Shelton, Sir Ralph (1430–1497), 19th Lord of Shelton Manor 133
Shelton, Sir Ralph (c1530/5–1580), 23rd Baron of Shelton, High Sheriff of Norfolk 134
Shelton, Sir Ralph (1560–1628), 26th Baron of Shelton 134
Shelton, Sir Ralph De (c1180–1245), 4th Lord of Shelton 133
Shelton, Sir Ralph De (1229–??), 6th Lord of Shelton 133
Shelton, Maj. Roland Huntington (1919–2001) 136
Shelton, Roland Frederick (1954–) 135, 136
Shelton, Selah (1770–1831) 143–145
Shelton, Thomas (1606–1683) 134
(Shelton), Tracy Gabbard 135, 136
Shelton, William (1739–1812) 136, 142, 143

Index

Sheldonne, Isabel De (1035–??) 132
Sheldonne, Robert De (1033–1070) 132
Sheldonne, Robert De (1055–1107) 132
Sherman, Grace (1659–1712) 21, 169
Sherman, Rev. John (1613–1685) 21, 169
Shippey, Mary Browne (1632–1700) 241
Shockley, Sarah (c1718–1761) 166
Shute, Anne (1557–1650) 189
Sibella, Susan (1563–1555) 194
Sida, Queen of Denmark (830–860) 24
Sige, 2nd wife of Uchtred 15
Sigurdsson, Hardacanute, King of Denmark (814–850/84) 24
Simon I de Saint Liz, the Crusader (c1070–c1111) 32, 33
Skinner, Joan (1510–1580) 192
Slade, Maria (1553–1610) 189
Smith, Anna (1740–1812) 142, 143
Smith, Blake Andrew (1993–) Part 5
Smith, Col. Charles Clement (1904–1980) 98, 104–113
Smith, Charles Harold (1858–1919) 209
Smith, Charles Herbert (1878–1967) 98–103
Smith, Charles Rosfjord (1934–) 102, 290, Appendix A
Smith, Charles Theodore (1962–) Appendix A
Smith, Christen Blake (1960–) Part 5
Smith, Daniel (1710–1786) 86, 87
Smith, Daniel 2 (1763–1810) 85, 88, 179
Smith, Deborah (1742–1834) 173, 174
Smith, Derrick (1730–1790) 85–88
Smith, Dinah (1635–1730) 194
Smith, Duncan (1635–after 1665) 86
Smith, Elizabeth (1702–1740) 127
Smith, Elmira 89, 179
Smith, Floyd Jr. (1823–1893) 91–94
Smith, Floyd Sr. (1791–1874) 85, 89, 175, 179

Smith, John (1665–after 1687) 86
Smith, John Nicholson 89, 179
Smith, John Rock 48
Smith, Juliet 89 179
Smith, Margaret Matilda (1450–1487) 185
Smith, Mary Rock (1640–1713) 48, 194
Smith, Matthew Kaddeland (1966–) Appendix A
Smith, Nancy Brooke (1963–) Part 5
Smith, Paula Kay (1968–) Part 5
Smith, Samuel William 97, 103
Smith, Susie Virginia (1907–2007) 98, 101–103, 105, 112, Appendix C
Smith, Watson Christen (1936–) Part 5
Smith, William Clement (1853–1912) 94–97
Smith, William Francis (1964–) Appendix A
Smyth, Mary (1535–1627) 75
Sowega, Gliding Swan (1710–1752) 234
Spahr, Edward Carl Sr. (1875–1940) 118, Appendix C
Spahr, Edward Carl Jr. (1909–1947) Appendix C
Spahr, Virginia Miller (1941–) Appendix C
Sparrow, Rebecca (1655–1740) 77
Spaul, Nancy (1720–1790) 237
Speght, Anne (1568–1598) 185
Spencer, Daniel (1694–1769) 52, 186
Spencer, Elias (1750–1828) 186, 187
Spencer, Galfridus Geoffrey De (c1190/1200–1242) 184
Spencer, Gerard I (1576–1646) 52
Spencer, Ens. Gerard II, "Jared" (1614–1685) 52, 184
Spencer, Sir Henry Badby (1392–1476) 185
Spencer, John (1300–1386) 185
Spencer, John II (1505–1558) 52
Spencer, John Hodnell (1418–1479) 185
Spencer, John Le De (1235–1274) 184

Index

Spencer, Lady Margaret (1445–1524) 184, 185, 194
Spencer, Michael (1531–1599) 52
Spencer, Sgt. Nathaniel William Jr. (1658–1722) 52, 186
Spencer, Nicholas (1340–1395) 185
Spencer, Ruth (1654–1744) 186
Spencer, Sally (1783–1852) 170, 187
Spencer, Thomas (c1366–1435) 185
Spencer, Thomas (1441–1475) 185
Spencer, William (1264–1328) 185
Spencer, Sir William III (1470–1532) 185
Sprota, De Bretagne (911–940) 28
Squire, Edith Rosamund (1587–1672) 201, 202
Stacey, Miriam (1683–1746) 194
Stafford, Hugh de (1342–1386) 60
Stafford, Margaret (before 1364–1396) 55, 60
Stafford, Ralph de (1301–1372) 60
Steven, King of England 43
Stevens, Eulah/Julia (1896–1967) 211
Stow, Dorothy (1662–1710) 189, 190
Stow, Rev. Samuel (1623–1704) 153, 154, 190
Stratton, Lady Elizabeth (c1410–1485) 51
Stratton, John (c1390–c1439) 51
Strong, George (1556–1636) 203
Strong, Hannah (1659–1694) 197, 198
Strong, John (1515–1534) 203
Strong, Elder John (1605/6–1699) 142, 197, 198, 202–205
Strong, John III (1626–1698) 198
Strong, John IV (1665–1749)198
Strong, Richard John (1585–1613) 204
Strong, Robert Lestraunge (1440–1519) 203
Strong, Sarah (c1696–1749) 198
Strong, Selah Sr. (1680–1732) 142, 205
Strong, Selah III (1737–1815) 142, 143
Strong, Susannah (1743–1816) 142, 143, 205

Strong, Thomas (1638–1689) 205
Strong, Thomas II (1708–1760) 205
Sweyn Forkenbeard, King of Denmark (??–1014) 30
Sweet, Lady Margaret Walker (1513–1567) 186
Swynford, Katherine 55, 59
Tailboys, Sir George (c1467–1538) 46
Tailboys, Anne (1520–1566) 46
Tanner, Elizabeth (1780–1848) 238, 244
Tanner, Joseph Edward Sr. (1629–1673) 241
Tanner, Joseph Gilbert Jr./II (1662–1698) 70, 241
Tanner, Lt. Josiah (1754–1807) 241–244, 246
Tanner, Josias (1603–1630) 240, 241
Tanner, Lewis (1690–1773) 241
Tanner, Matthew (1730–1806) 241
Tapp, Jane 128
Tempest, Dousabella (c1475–c1500) 20
Terry, Abigail (1680–1706) 205
Teyes, Margaret (??–1349) 62
Thomson, Helen (1678 –??) 201
Thompson, Susanna (1707–1783) 205
Thorne, Martha (1679–1730) 48, 194
Throckmorton, Sir Arthur (1557–1626) 63
Throckmorton, Sir George (1480–1552) 63
Throckmorton, Lady Mary (1588–1658) 63, 245
Throckmorton, Sir Nicholas (1515–1571) 63
Tidwell, Mary Ann (1744–1810) 237, 238
Tomine, 2nd wife of Karl Kaddeland 116, 117
Tompkins, Mary (1748–1769) 201
Tracy, Emily Francis "Fanny" (1845–1886) 228, 230, 239
Tracy, George (1803–1860) 238, 239
Tracy, Pvt. Nathaniel Pradian (1743–1818) 237, 238
Tracy, Patrick (c1689–??) Maryland 237
Tracy, Patrick (1689–??) Massachusetts 77

Index

Tracy, William (c1665–??) England 237
Tracy, William (1781–1846) Maryland 238
Tracy, William James "Willie" (1713–1790) Maryland 237
Treat, Abigail (1660–1727) 127, 128
Treat, Gov. Robert 127, 128
Trumble, Hannah (1673–1747) 198
Tudor, Edmund 59
Tudor, Henry VII (1457–1509), King of England 20, 59
Tully, Mary (1681–1738) 186
Tunstall, Grace (1540/50–1617) 193
Uchtred/Uhtred, the Bold, of Northumbria (??–1016) 15
Underwood, Mary Sudbury (1575–1623) 198
Uvedale, Alice (1351–??) 133
Vaux, Anna Catherine (1488–1571) 63
Vaux, Sir Nicholas (1460–1523) 63
Vierling, Wilhelmia (1850–1899) 224, 225
Wadam, Margery (1575–1608) 193
Waltheof, Earl of Huntington and Northumbria (c1054–1076) 32
Ward, Mary (1640–1711) 70
Warringer, Elizabeth (1640–1684) 198
Warsted, Lady Elizabeth Joan (de Varsteed) (1422–1445) 185
Watson, Martha (1739–??) 166
Webb, Hannah (1665–1694) 201
Webb, Sarah Jane (1468–1560) 194
Weis, Viola T. (1897–1986) 211
Weld, Capt. Joseph 62, 190
Weld, Mary (1627–1711) 62, 153, 154, 190
Weldebof, Joan De (1227–1302) 19
Welles, Elizabeth (1670–1747) 134
Welles, Samuel 139
Welles, Gov. Thomas 139, 140
Wentworth, Mary Love (c1569–1627) 75

West, Lady Jane De (c1558–c1606) 134
Wetmore, Elizabeth (1687–1743) 155
Wetmore, Hannah (1681–1722) 156
Wetmore, John (1646–1690) 155
Wetmore, Thomas (1615–1681) 153, 154, 189
Wettin, Margaretha Saxony (c1433–c1500) 133
White, Elizabeth Ann (1631–1687) 127
White, Elder John 190
White, Mary (1626–1650) 189, 190
Whitebread, Alice (1583–1628) 52
Whitman, Agnes (1519–1556) 203
Whitton, Lady Elizabeth (1555–1621) 188
Whorlwood, Mary Margaret (1535–1626) 63
Wilcoxen, Sarah Ann (1728–1808) 233
William I, Long Sword, Duke of Normandy (893–942) 28, 38
William I, the Conqueror, Duke of Normandy (1027/8–1087) 17, 30–32, 40–42
William II Rufus, King of England 31
Willicke, Esther (1590–1673) 153, 154
Wilmot, Anna (1669–1728) 199
Windebank, Helen 1596–c1656) 47, 48, 194
Windebank, Sir Thomas (1548–1607) 47
Wodehouse, Mary Amy (1534–c1565) 134
Wood, Hannah (1606–1684) 134
Wooten, Martha (1756–1851) 63, 241–244, 246
Wooten, Richard Sr. (1647–1687) 63, 245
Wooten, Richard Jr. (1678–1738) 63 245
Wooten, Pvt. Samuel (1726–1814) 63, 246
Wooten, Thomas (1612–1669) 63, 245
Wotton, Thomas, 2nd Baron of Marley (1585–1630) 63, 245
Wulfthyrth of Wessex (825–870) 13
Ziegler, Annie Belle (1862–1954) 208

www.ingramcontent.com/pod-product-compliance
Lightning Source LLC
Chambersburg PA
CBHW081305070526
44578CB00006B/805